Comprehensive C

Comprehensive C

David Spuler

PRENTICE HALL

New York London Toronto Sydney Tokyo Singapore

© 1992 by Prentice Hall of Australia Pty Ltd

All rights reserved. No part of this publication may be reproduced, stored in a retrieval system, or transmitted in any form or by any means, electronic, mechanical, photocopying, recording, or otherwise, without written permission of the publisher.

Acquisitions Editor: Andrew Binnie
Production Editor: Fiona Marcar
Cover design: John Windus

Printed in Australia by Impact Printing, Brunswick, Victoria.

1 2 3 4 5 96 95 94 93 92

ISBN 0-13-156514-1

**National Library of Australia
Cataloguing-in-Publication Data**

Spuler, David, 1969 —
    Comprehensive C.

    Bibliography.
    Includes index.
    ISBN 0-13-156514-1.

    1. C (Computer program language). I. Title.

005.133

Library of Congress Cataloging-in-Publication
Data are available from the publisher.

Prentice Hall, Inc., *Englewood Cliffs, New Jersey*
Prentice Hall Canada, Inc., *Toronto*
Prentice Hall Hispanoamericana, SA, *Mexico*
Prentice Hall of India Private Ltd, *New Delhi*
Prentice Hall International, Inc., *London*
Prentice Hall of Japan, Inc., *Tokyo*
Prentice Hall of Southeast Asia Pty Ltd, *Singapore*
Editora Prentice Hall do Brasil Ltda, *Rio de Janeiro*

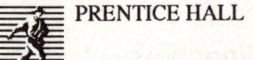

PRENTICE HALL
A division of Simon & Schuster

Contents

Preface — xiii

Part I: The C Language

Chapter 1 Introduction to C — 3
- 1.1 A first C program — 3
- 1.2 Adding two numbers — 5
- 1.3 Basic types — 8
- 1.4 The if statement — 9
- 1.5 The for loop — 10
- 1.6 The while loop — 12
- 1.7 Logical operators — 12
- 1.8 Symbolic constants: #define — 13
- 1.9 Functions — 14
- 1.10 A larger program: guess my number — 16
- 1.11 Exercises — 17

Chapter 2 Variable declarations and types — 19
- 2.1 Basic types — 19
- 2.2 Declaring variables — 20
- 2.3 Numeric constants — 21
- 2.4 Character constants and escapes — 22
- 2.5 Variable initialization — 23
- 2.6 Arrays — 24
- 2.7 User defined type names: typedef — 25
- 2.8 Type qualifiers — 26
- 2.9 Implicit type conversions — 28
- 2.10 Exercises — 30

Chapter 3 Operators — 31
- 3.1 Arithmetic operators — 31
- 3.2 The assignment operator — 33
- 3.3 L-values and r-values — 34
- 3.4 Relational operators — 34
- 3.5 Logical operators — 35
- 3.6 Increment and decrement operators — 36
- 3.7 Extended assignment operators — 38
- 3.8 Bitwise operators — 39
- 3.9 Structure operators — 43
- 3.10 Pointer operators — 43

3.11	Type conversions: the type cast operator	44
3.12	The sizeof operator	45
3.13	The ternary operator	46
3.14	The comma operator	47
3.15	The array reference operator	47
3.16	The function call operator	48
3.17	Operator precedence	48
3.18	Associativity	49
3.19	Order of evaluation problems	50
3.20	Exercises	54

Chapter 4 Control statements 56

4.1	Statements and blocks	56
4.2	The if statement	57
4.3	The while loop	58
4.4	The for loop	59
4.5	The do loop	60
4.6	Local variables inside loop blocks	61
4.7	The break statement	62
4.8	The continue statement	62
4.9	Infinite loops	62
4.10	Empty statements and empty loops	63
4.11	The switch statement	63
4.12	Immediate program termination: exit, abort	65
4.13	The goto statement and labels	66
4.14	Long branching: <setjmp.h>	67
4.15	Exercises	68

Chapter 5 Structured types 70

5.1	Accessing members	71
5.2	Operations on whole structures	71
5.3	Name spaces	72
5.4	Arrays of structures	72
5.5	Unions	74
5.6	Bit-fields	75
5.7	Enumerated types	76
5.8	More types with typedef	77
5.9	Self-referential structures	78
5.10	Exercises	79

Chapter 6 Strings 80

6.1	Simple strings: arrays of char	80
6.2	String library functions: <string.h>	82
6.3	Strings revisited: pointers to char	86
6.4	Functions with string arguments	89

6.5	String constants	89
6.6	Omitting the null terminator	90
6.7	Exercises	91

Chapter 7   Functions   93

7.1	Defining functions	93
7.2	Functions returning no value: void functions	95
7.3	Functions with no parameters	95
7.4	Non-prototyping (non-ANSI functions)	95
7.5	The return statement	97
7.6	Local variable declarations	97
7.7	Global variables	98
7.8	Call-by-value parameter passing	99
7.9	Storage classes for variables	101
7.10	Variable initialization	103
7.11	Exercises	106

Chapter 8   Pointers   108

8.1	Declaring pointer variables	108
8.2	Pointer operators	109
8.3	NULL pointers	109
8.4	Call-by-reference using pointers	110
8.5	Generic pointers: pointers to void	111
8.6	Dynamic memory allocation	111
8.7	Incrementing pointers and address arithmetic	113
8.8	Pointers and arrays: the relationship	114
8.9	Exercises	115

Chapter 9   Input and output   117

9.1	Formatted output: printf	117
9.2	Formatted input: scanf	122
9.3	Line input/output: gets, puts	126
9.4	Character input/output: getchar, putchar	127
9.5	Exercises	128

Chapter 10   File operations   129

10.1	Text files	130
10.2	Error handling: ferror, perror	134
10.3	Binary files: fread, fwrite	135
10.4	Direct access: fseek, rewind, ftell	136
10.5	Temporary files: tmpnam, tmpfile	141
10.6	Removing and renaming files: remove, rename	141
10.7	Character pushback: ungetc	141
10.8	Buffering: fflush, setbuf, setvbuf	142

10.9	Redirecting input/output: freopen	143
10.10	Exercises	144

Chapter 11 The preprocessor 145

11.1	Preprocessor directives	146
11.2	Including files: #include	146
11.3	Macros and symbolic constants: #define	148
11.4	Conditional compilation	154
11.5	Other directives: #error, #line, #pragma	159
11.6	Predefined names: __LINE__, __FILE__	159
11.7	Exercises	160

Chapter 12 Standard library functions 162

12.1	Examining characters: <ctype.h>	163
12.2	Memory block functions: <string.h>	164
12.3	Mathematical programming: <math.h>	165
12.4	Utility functions: <stdlib.h>	168
12.5	Times and dates: <time.h>	176
12.6	Signal handling: <signal.h>	179
12.7	Standard definitions: <stddef.h>	180
12.8	System constants: <limits.h> and <float.h>	180
12.9	International programs: <locale.h>	181
12.10	Further reading	183
12.11	Exercises	183

Part II: Advanced Issues

Chapter 13 Large programs 187

13.1	Independent compilation	187
13.2	External variables	188
13.3	Function prototype declarations	189
13.4	Definition versus declaration	190
13.5	Single file scope: static	190
13.6	Header files	191
13.7	Header file of extern variables	192
13.8	Header file of function prototypes	195
13.9	Automatic generation of header files	196
13.10	Header file organization	199
13.11	The make utility	201
13.12	Creating your own libraries	206
13.13	Exercises	209

Chapter 14 Functions and pointers revisited — 211

- 14.1 The main function — 212
- 14.2 Command line arguments — 212
- 14.3 Exit status: return value of main — 220
- 14.4 Accessing environment variables — 220
- 14.5 Recursion — 221
- 14.6 Variable length argument lists: <stdarg.h> — 225
- 14.7 Pointers to functions — 229
- 14.8 Passing sub-arrays to a function — 231
- 14.9 Removing the 0..n−1 array index restriction — 232
- 14.10 Dynamic arrays — 233
- 14.11 Exercises — 239

Chapter 15 Efficiency — 242

- 15.1 When to optimize — 242
- 15.2 The C optimizer — 243
- 15.3 Profilers for C — 243
- 15.4 Timing C code — 244
- 15.5 Algorithm improvements — 245
- 15.6 Code transformations — 250
- 15.7 Efficiency in C — 255
- 15.8 Space efficiency — 266
- 15.9 Further reading — 271
- 15.10 Exercises — 272

Chapter 16 Debugging techniques — 275

- 16.1 Symbolic debuggers — 275
- 16.2 The lint source code checker — 276
- 16.3 Debugging output — 277
- 16.4 Assertions: <assert.h> — 282
- 16.5 Self-testing code — 284
- 16.6 Robust code — 284
- 16.7 Encapsulating dynamic memory allocation — 285
- 16.8 Using signals for debugging — 291
- 16.9 Further reading — 294
- 16.10 Exercises — 294

Chapter 17 Program style — 296

- 17.1 Comments — 296
- 17.2 Indentation — 297
- 17.3 Braces — 298
- 17.4 Blank lines — 299
- 17.5 Spaces — 299

17.6	Variable names	301
17.7	Multiple else-if statements	301
17.8	Efficiency and compactness versus readability	302
17.9	The goto controversy	303
17.10	Retaining unnecessary else clauses	303
17.11	Boolean types	304
17.12	Global variables	304
17.13	The preprocessor	305
17.14	Further reading	306
17.15	Exercises	306

Chapter 18   Portability   307

18.1	Compilation problems	308
18.2	Run-time problems	311
18.3	Data file portability	314
18.4	Further reading	315
18.5	Exercises	315

Chapter 19   UNIX systems programming   317

19.1	UNIX software tools	317
19.2	Executing UNIX commands: system	318
19.3	Errors: <errno.h>	318
19.4	Low-level file operations	319
19.5	Accessing the environment: getenv, setenv	323
19.6	File protections and access times	324
19.7	Process control	324
19.8	Signals: <signal.h>	333
19.9	Further reading	337
19.10	Exercises	338

Appendix A.   C for Pascal programmers   339

A.1	Overall program structure	339
A.2	Statements and blocks	340
A.3	The if statement	340
A.4	Loops	341
A.5	The switch statement (replacing case)	342
A.6	Operators	343
A.7	Data types and variable declarations	344
A.8	Arrays	345
A.9	Records	345
A.10	Pointers to records	346
A.11	Other types	346
A.12	User defined types using typedef	347
A.13	Functions and procedures	347
A.14	Symbolic constants	348

A.15	Extra features of C	348
A.16	Pitfalls for Pascal programmers	349

Appendix B. Common errors in C   350

B.1	Off-by-one errors	350
B.2	Expression errors	351
B.3	Type errors	355
B.4	Flow of control errors	357
B.5	Array index out of bounds	359
B.6	Unclosed comments	359
B.7	Passing structs by value, arrays by reference	360
B.8	Multi-byte characters	360
B.9	Backslash in DOS filenames	360
B.10	Pointer errors	360
B.11	Macro errors	363

Appendix C. Complicated declarations   370

C.1	Declarators and abstract declarators	371
C.2	List of declarations	372

Appendix D. Answers to short exercises   373

Bibliography   386

Index   390

Preface

C was originally designed by Dennis Ritchie as a low-level systems programming language for an early version of the UNIX operating system. C was the successor to two other languages: BCPL by Martin Richards and B by Ken Thompson. C was intended to retain the efficiency of assembler, while providing more of the advanced control flow of a higher level language. Most of the UNIX operating system is written in C.

From its small beginnings, C has spread to many different systems. It is still the basis of all UNIX environments, but has also been moved to many other systems. In particular, personal computers now boast dozens of different C compiler packages.

C is now the language of choice for many programmers, because of its great flexibility and wide applicability. C's best features are, in my opinion, its powerful operator set, its terseness (less typing) and its large standard library. It is also *the* language for UNIX operating systems which provide a large variety of supporting software utilities.

Assumed audience background

The reader is expected to be familiar with the basic ideas of computer programming, such as statements, variables and loops. I give no explanation of programming in terms of step-by-step methods for boiling eggs. I assume that the reader will have already learned at least some of another computer programming language (ideally Pascal).

Although hopefully catering for the not-so-experienced programmer, there is also much in this book for the experienced C programmer in the way of hints, tips and traps. Experienced C programmers may also benefit by learning the new aspects of C (since the ANSI standard), especially the new way of defining functions by prototyping.

Organization of the book

The book is divided into two major sections: The C Language and Advanced Issues. The first section introduces the C language and provides basic coverage of all the main features of the language. The second section covers a number of issues that are useful when the basic ideas are understood.

The first chapter provides a tutorial-like discussion of how to get started programming in C. Using the material in the first chapter as a basis, Chapters 2 to 12 cover all the various aspects of the C language. All of the syntactic possibilities of the language are examined, as well as most aspects of the standard library. Various chapters cover all the different variable types, the operators, the control structures, function declarations and the preprocessor. These sections are not intended to be read in order of appearance. Instead, the reader should flip to the sections of particular interest.

Chapters 13 to 19 discuss a number of advanced issues and the reader is assumed to be reasonably proficient with the use of C. The issues in writing large programs are examined, as are techniques for debugging programs, methods of speeding up programs, and style and portability issues. The UNIX operating system is examined separately from the point of view of the programmer in Chapter 19. Again, sections of interest should be read at will and there is no particular continuity between these chapters.

A number of appendices are provided to cover various topics. Appendix A introduces C for the Pascal programmer learning C. A large number of well-known errors that may occur in C programs are examined in detail in Appendix B. Appendix C explains how to define complicated types using `typedef` declarations. The answers to some of the exercises are presented in Appendix D. Appendix D lists a number of books used by the author while writing this book.

Introductory and advanced C courses

Comprehensive C can be used as a text for both introductory and advanced C courses. The book contains examples of working code with which the student can experiment, and the end of each chapter presents a number of short-answer questions as well as longer programming exercises.

A course on Introductory C would make use of the hands-on tutorial introduction in Chapter 1 (and also Appendix A if students already know Pascal). The instructor can then pick topics from any of Chapters 2 to 12, in his/her preferred order.

An Advanced C course will make use of Chapters 13 through 19. In addition, some of the more advanced material on file operations, the preprocessor and lesser used library functions may also be included. Again, the particular order of topics is largely at the discretion of the instructor.

UNIX, DOS and other systems

In the past I wrote C programs only under the UNIX operating system. However, during the writing of this book I have done much work in a DOS environment. Hence, the book is biased towards these two particular environments, although favoring UNIX in some areas. I have noted differences between the UNIX and DOS environments, and the book should be useful to programmers using either system. Although users in other environments may be slightly disadvantaged, C is a very portable language and there are not too many differences.

The ANSI standard

At the time of writing, the ANSI standard for C has been finalized for some time now. This standard defines exactly what features compilers should support, and what action they should take under most circumstances. Only obscure details are left undefined. The

ANSI standard defines not only the language, but also the form of the standard library header files and functions. Details of how to obtain a copy are given in the Bibliography.

This book is intended to cover ANSI C, and all programs in the book are written using the (relatively new) prototyping notation. Where applicable, I have mentioned differences between ANSI C and old style non-ANSI C. Although covering most features of ANSI C, I have mostly shied away from a discussion of whether obscure language features are "standard" or not. I do not feel that such discussions serve much purpose (except for compiler implementers). A good programmer should be able to follow well-trodden paths and avoid use of obscure features that are not clearly standard.

The standard library

In many ways, C is divided into two main sections: the compiler and the standard library. The standard library is a suite of ready-written commonly used functions, that can be used by any C program. To make use of them it is only necessary to `#include` the appropriate header file. The header files declare the library functions, and any symbolic constants required. The linker should automatically link in the required functions at compile-time.

All C programs make use of functions from the standard library. For example, all input and output operations must be performed using standard library functions. Because they are so prevalent, discussion of the C language invariably involves discussion of the use of these functions. The standard library functions are discussed in Chapter 12 and in many other sections.

The future with C++

There is a successor to the C language, the C++ language. C++ maintains a high level of upward compatibility and almost all C programs will also compile on a C++ compiler. Some of the enhancements to C made in C++ are small additions (e.g. call-by-reference is added), but the major enhancement is the addition of constructs for the object-oriented programming paradigm. This paradigm aims to help the programmer define "objects" to which "methods" are applied. These objects are all encapsulated, and design of programs in C++ becomes a matter of defining a number of objects and the interfaces to these objects via methods. The advantages to the programmer are that encapsulation aids debugging and maintenance, and that code can be reused easily.

The C++ language is still evolving and there is as yet no standard for C++. I have only written a few C++ programs (although one was a B-tree) and am probably not the best person to comment on the future of C++. Nevertheless, I do not believe that C++ will supersede C in all areas. C is a superbly powerful low-level language. However, while C has the advantage in systems programming, I believe that C++ will become better for applications programming. Perhaps the best indicator of the future of C++ is that I plan to learn C++ more completely.

Source code offer

A floppy disk containing C source code for most of the program examples in the book, as well as some of the larger programming exercises (this includes some useful software tools!), is available from the author for $20.00, including shipping and handling charges. Simply photocopy this page, fill in your address and the type of disk required, and send it to the address given below.

Mail $20.00 to:
Source Code Offer
Spuler & Associates
P.O. Box 1262
Aitkenvale 4814.
AUSTRALIA
Name: _____
Address: _____
_____
_____
Computer: Macintosh _____   IBM _____
Diskette: 3.5"   800K _____   1.4M _____
5.25"   360K _____   720K _____   1.2M _____

Bugs and typos

Though most of the code in this book has been tested to a greater or lesser extent, there will always be bugs. There will also be typos and other minor formatting errors. There may also be mistakes due to major misconceptions on my part. I am curious to hear about all such mistakes, and also eager to hear suggestions for improvements, extra hints and tips, and ideas for other sections. At the discretion of the author, bug reports and suggestions of sufficient merit may be rewarded with a free copy of the source code. Please send all correspondence to the address given for the source code offer, but marked as "Bug Reports".

Acknowledgments

Many of the ideas for this book have come from the experiences of C programmers other than myself. There are a number of people whom I have to thank for sharing their knowledge with me. Thanks to Cameron "The Yak" Gregory for sharing every little tip or trap he came across. Thanks to Dave Bonnell for allowing me to draw upon his superb programming ability, not to mention putting spaces in all the right places. Thanks to Stuart Kemp for granting me reprieve from hassling me about my book often enough to answer the odd question. Thanks to Robert Goodwill for discussions on various aspects of C programming. Thanks to Chris Jones for letting me look over her shoulder, and for telling me I used too many commas. Thanks to Jim Bell for solving in five minutes a problem that had been puzzling me all morning. Thanks to Professor Gopal Gupta for introducing me to `troff`, and to trees that grow upside-down!

In addition to the people above, a large number of local people have provided comments on various drafts of this manuscript. Thanks in this respect to Gavin Walker, Colin Adams, Olivier de Vel, Angie Markovic, and Jeroen van dem Muyzenberg (what a name, Dutchy!). Thanks also to my anonymous reviewers and especially to Peter Jones who did an amazingly detailed technical review that sorted me out on a number of issues.

In addition to the above-mentioned people, some ideas have come from reading the international electronic mail groups, `comp.std.c` and `comp.lang.c`. Thanks in particular to Steve Clamage, Doug Gwyn and Rex Jaeschke, and also to all other contributors there.

The staff at Prentice Hall have been of immense help in getting this book off the ground. In particular, thanks to Andrew Binnie for listening to a scruffy unshaven conference delegate about this book he'd been writing.... Thanks to Ian MacArthur for patiently listening to many queries about layout details. Thanks to Chris Richardson for courteously answering a number of my questions. Thanks to Fiona Marcar without whom the final layout would have been far more stressing.

A number of people have provided me with personal encouragement. In particular, thanks to Paul whose friendly mocking tone made me indignant enough to just do it! Thanks also to our notorious secretaries, Bev and Kim. Very special thanks to my sweet Anita for always being there. Special thanks to Michelle for the pleasant reassurance of her faraway presence. Finally, thanks to my parents, whose continual faith in me has always been a solid base on which to build.

David Spuler

Part I
The C Language

Chapter 1
Introduction to C

This chapter aims to introduce the reader quickly to the most important aspects of C programming. Emphasis is placed on writing working programs using the basic elements of the language, rather than on full understanding of all the finer points of C. Subsequent chapters will expand on the material that is covered here.

It is assumed that C is not the reader's very first exposure to computer programming. For example, it is assumed that the reader knows what variables and operators are used for. The idea of assigning values to variables should be familiar, as should the idea of specifying *if this, do that* using `if` statements.

1.1 A first C program

A very simple C program to print the words `"Hello World"` on to the screen looks like:

```
#include <stdio.h>
main()
{
    printf("Hello World\n");
}
```

There are a number of steps in getting this program to run. These steps are standard for the execution of all programs written in C:

Type the program in (using a text editor),
Compile the program into an executable, and
Run the executable version.

It is important to type the program in *exactly* as it is shown. Notably, letters should be typed in the right case. For example, `main` must be in lower case — `MAIN` would be incorrect. C is a case-sensitive language and upper case letters cannot replace lower case letters (except inside the string constant `"Hello World"` where any letters are valid).

The other important features to watch when typing the program in are the *semicolon* at the end of the line starting with the word `printf`, and the *backslash* in the two-character sequence \n. Although all blank lines are ignored by C compilers, the blank line after the first program line should be included to improve the readability of the program.

1.1.1 Compiling the program

The method of compiling a C program is standard for all UNIX systems and is discussed below. There is no standard method for compiling C on other systems and the method will depend on which machine you are using and even on what C compiler is being used. It is not possible to cover all the various methods and you should consult your local compiler documentation.

The program can be typed in using any UNIX text editor. All C programs must be given filenames with the suffix ".c". Assuming you have named the C program "prog.c", the program is compiled using the command:

```
cc prog.c
```

One of two things can happen: either the program will compile correctly, or there may be some error messages. If there are any errors in the program, the `cc` compiler will tell you about them by producing an error message. You must then find the mistake and correct it using the text editor, and then attempt to compile the program again.

If control is returned to you with no error messages after typing "cc prog.c", the program has compiled correctly. The compiler has created a file named "a.out". This is the *executable* version of the program that you can run by typing:

```
a.out
```

The program should output the words `Hello World` to the screen.

1.1.2 Explanation of the program

All of the lines in the program presented above have a specific purpose. Let us look in detail at each line of the program. The first line of the program:

```
#include <stdio.h>
```

includes a file named "stdio.h" from the system area. This file is a special C file, called a *header file*. Including header files allows the use of the standard library functions. In this case, the inclusion of <stdio.h> allows the `printf` function to be used to produce the output. Almost every program you ever write should include <stdio.h> at the top of the program.

The second line of the program (ignoring the blank line) is:

```
main()
```

This specifies the start of the main block of code. As we'll see later, the line actually defines `main` as a *function*, but for now, think of the line as showing where the program statements begin. Execution of a program always starts at the top of the `main` function.

The program statements must be inside a pair of left and right braces:

```
main()
{
    program statements
}
```

The program shown above has only one statement and it is this statement which produces the output. The program line:

```
printf("Hello World\n");
```

calls the `printf` standard library function which is declared in `<stdio.h>`. The `printf` function is the most common method of producing output in C programs.

Notice that there is a *semicolon* at the end of the `printf` statement. Semicolons are very important as they serve to terminate a statement. Leaving out the semicolon will cause an error message during compilation of the program.

The first argument to the `printf` function is called the *format string*. The format string is usually a *string constant*, such as `"Hello World\n"`. String constants are sequences of characters between pairs of double quotes that do not extend over more than one line.

The two-character sequence `\n` in the format string is an *escape* that is used to go to the next line (i.e. `\n` stands for newline). The `printf` function does not automatically move to the next line when it is finished doing its output, and the programmer must explicitly place a `\n` escape in the string to `printf`. This may seem inconvenient, but it does permit a sequence of calls to the `printf` function to slowly build an output line (e.g. one word at a time).

1.2 Adding two numbers

This section presents and discusses another small C program. The new program asks the user to input two numbers, adds the two numbers together and prints out the result. This program introduces a number of new concepts: comments, keyboard input and variable declarations. The C code for the program is:

```
/*------------------------------------------------------------*/
/* ADDTWO.C:  Add two numbers and output the sum             */
/*------------------------------------------------------------*/

#include <stdio.h>

main()
{
    int x, y, sum;

    printf("Enter two integers: ");    /* Prompt */
    scanf("%d%d", &x, &y);             /* Get input */
    sum = x + y;                       /* Add them */
    printf("The sum is %d\n", sum);    /* Print the sum */
}
```

The first thing you notice about this program is the box of dashes at the top of the program. These lines are actually all instances of *comments*, as are the explanations after each program statement. A comment is started by the two-character token /* and finished by the two-character token */. Comments can span multiple lines of a program but do not nest — it is not possible to put one comment inside another comment. The box of comments at the top is a nice way of making comments stand out, by placing lines of dashes between the tokens /* and */, and ensuring that the comments line up. This is just a matter of style — an equivalent way of putting the comment in the program would be:

```
/*
ADDTWO.C:   Add two numbers and output the sum
*/
```

which declares a multi-line comment.

Comments are completely ignored by the compiler, and are only used to record information useful for humans. For the purpose of running the program shown above, there is no need to type in the comments. However, every program you write should have regular comments explaining what the program is doing and how it is doing it. In particular, a good program should have a comment at the top identifying its purpose. You should place comments in a program even if you are the only one to use it — in a month you'll forget how the program worked!

The next noticeable difference between this program and the first program is the use of *variables*. This program declares the variables x, y and sum in the program line:

```
int x, y, sum;
```

These variables are declared as integer variables by using the type name `int`. This restricts the variables to containing integer values only (e.g. 1, 10, −5), and prevents them containing fractions such as 0.5 or 3.14.

All the variables are declared in one line here. Also possible is the use of three separate declarations. The three program lines given below would be equivalent:

```
int x;
int y;
int sum;
```

Variable names are usually called *identifiers*. Identifiers can be very long — most compilers permit identifiers up to 31 characters long. Identifiers should start with a letter and may contain letters (upper and lower case), digits and underscores. Strictly speaking, identifiers can also start with an underscore, but this class of identifiers is reserved for system use and should not be used by most programs. Some examples of legal identifiers are:

```
x    y    high_score    value2    MAX    MenuEntry
```

Note that the case of the letters is important and the identifiers `temp` and `Temp` would identify totally different variables.

All variable declarations must appear before the program statements. Hence, the general form of the active part of a program is:

```
main()
{
    variable declarations
    program statements
}
```

Now let us examine the statements in the program. The first statement:

```
printf("Enter two integers: ");
```

is in the same form as the `printf` statement in the first program, except that there is a comment added to the end of the line. Notice that this statement uses the feature of `printf` that it does not automatically go to the next line, thus allowing the user to type the input just after the colon in the prompt.

The second statement is not so familiar. The line:

```
scanf("%d%d", &x, &y);
```

uses the `scanf` library function to perform input. Note that the `scanf` function will ignore spaces and carriage returns in the input, and the two numbers can be typed in with spaces between them, or each on a different line.

Like `printf`, the `scanf` function is declared in <stdio.h>. The `scanf` function uses a *format string* to specify what input is required. The two-character sequence %d specifies that an integer is required, and thus %d%d specifies that two integers are required. The next arguments to `scanf` are &x and &y, which tell `scanf` to store the two integers in the variables x and y. The need for the & characters is quite an advanced area and is discussed in Chapter 9. For the present merely ensure that the &'s are always present, as leaving them out will cause the program to crash when it is run (even though it will compile correctly).

The next program statement:

```
sum = x + y;
```

is an *assignment statement*. This statement uses the + addition operator to add x and y together, and then assigns the result to the variable sum. The = character is called the *assignment operator* in this context.

The + operator is not the only operator available for arithmetic computation. The arithmetic operators are shown in Table 1.1.

The next statement is a slightly different use of the `printf` function. The statement:

```
printf("The sum is %d\n", sum);
```

will print out the characters:

```
The sum is
```

followed by the value of the sum variable. This is an example where the `printf` function uses a *format string*, as `scanf` does. The %d sequence in the format string specifies where the value of sum is to be placed. These format specifiers can be placed

Table 1.1. Arithmetic operators

Operator	Meaning
+	Addition
−	Subtraction
*	Multiplication
/	Division
%	Remainder

anywhere in the format string, and it is possible to write a statement such as:

```
printf("The sum of %d and %d is %d\n", x, y, sum);
```

to give output similar to:

```
The sum of 2 and 3 is 5
```

Note also that *expressions* are allowed as arguments to `printf`. Thus it would be possible to avoid using the variable `sum` and pass the expression `x + y` directly to the `printf` function:

```
printf("The sum of %d and %d is %d\n", x, y, x + y);
```

1.3 Basic types

In the example above the variables were declared of type `int`. The `int` type is one of many, and most variables in C programs are declared as one of the basic types shown in Table 1.2.

Table 1.2. Basic data types

Data type	Meaning
int	Integer
char	Character
float	Floating point (real number)
double	Double precision (real number)

Using this knowledge, let us create another version of the program to add two numbers, this time using real numbers. With the new program, the user can type in numbers such as 3.14 and 2.718, in addition to ordinary integers. The variables are declared to be of type `float` and this means that the `%d` format specifications for `printf` and `scanf` must be changed to `%f`.

```
/*--------------------------------------------------------------*/
/* ADDTWO.C:   Add two REAL numbers and output the sum          */
/*--------------------------------------------------------------*/

#include <stdio.h>

main()
{
    float x, y, sum;

    printf("Enter two numbers: ");   /* Prompt */
    scanf("%f%f", &x, &y);           /* Get input */
    sum = x + y;                     /* Add them */
    printf("The sum is %f\n", sum);  /* Print the sum */
}
```

1.4 The if statement

C has the usual form of conditional statement: the `if` statement. It is used to choose whether or not to do something based upon a condition. The `if-else` construct can be used to choose between two actions based upon a condition. The meaning of the statement becomes: *if* the condition is true, execute the first block *else* execute the second block. Thus, a program to print out the maximum of two numbers is:

```
/*--------------------------------------------------------------*/
/* PRINT_MAX.C:   Print the maximum of two input integers       */
/*--------------------------------------------------------------*/

#include <stdio.h>

main()
{
    int x, y, max;

    printf("Enter two integers: ");   /* Prompt the user */
    scanf("%d%d", &x, &y);            /* Read in x and y */
    if (x > y) {
        max = x;
    }
    else {
        max = y;
    }
    printf("The maximum is %d\n", max);   /* Print maximum */
}
```

This example has braces round the statements to be executed. In cases where there is only one statement, the braces are not necessary. For example, it would be possible to have:

```
if (x > y)
    max = x;
else
    max = y;
```

However, the use of braces promotes good style, especially when just beginning to learn the language.

The `if` statement above uses the > operator to test if one variable is greater than another. There are a number of other similar operators to test simple conditions about variables, called *relational operators*. The full list of relational operators is shown in Table 1.3.

Table 1.3. **Relational operators**

Operator	Meaning
==	Equal
!=	Not equal
>	Greater than
<	Less than
>=	Greater than or equal
<=	Less than or equal

It is unfortunate that the assignment operator (=) and the relational equals operator (==) are so similar. It is a common (and particularly hard to find) bug for new C programmers to write:

```
if (x = 3)         /* INCORRECT */
```

instead of:

```
if (x == 3)        /* CORRECT */
```

in an `if` statement. The first statement assigns 3 to x and then tests whether x is non-zero (true). This is a bad error that causes the `if` statement to perform incorrectly and overwrites the old value of x. Unfortunately, many compilers do not issue a warning when this occurs.

1.5 The for loop

Only a limited amount can be achieved with only `if` statements, and the use of *loops* gives a great deal more expressive power. C has three types of loops: `for` loops, `while` loops and `do` loops. The first loop we will examine is the most flexible — the `for` loop. Although it can be used for many purposes, we will look at using the `for` loop to count from 1 to 10. A program to print out the numbers from 1 to 10 is:

```
/*-----------------------------------------------------------*/
/* COUNT_TO_10.C:  Print the numbers from 1 to 10            */
/*-----------------------------------------------------------*/

#include <stdio.h>

main()
{
    int i;          /* Variable used by the for loop */

    for (i = 1; i <= 10; i++) {     /* Count i from 1 to 10 */
        printf("%d\n", i);          /* Print out i */
    }
}
```

There are two parts to the `for` loop: the loop *header* "`for(...)`" contains all the information specifying how the looping is to be performed, and the loop *body* is the block of statements (in this case there is only one) between the left and right braces. The statement or statements inside the loop body are executed on each iteration of the loop.

Notice that the loop body is *indented* by a number of spaces. These spaces are ignored by the compiler and are included in the program only to make the program more readable. The use of indentation to indicate the body of a loop is very good style and the programmer should ensure that there are spaces or tabs before every statement inside a loop.

The `for` loop header is quite complicated and introduces a number of new features of C. The loop header:

```
for (i = 1; i <= 10; i++)        /* Count i from 1 to 10 */
```

has three sections, all separated by semicolons. The first section is used to initialize `i` using the assignment operator (=). The second section shows the condition for the loop to continue and uses the relational operator <= to ensure that `i` is less than or equal to 10. The loop body is executed only if this condition is true. The third section of the loop header is executed *after* the loop body has been executed and is executed *every* time the loop body is executed. In the example above, the ++ increment operator is used to increment `i` by 1. C has two special purpose unary operators for incrementing and decrementing a variable, as shown in Table 1.4.

Table 1.4. Increment/decrement operators

Operator	Meaning
++	Increment
--	Decrement

These operators can be used anywhere and not just in `for` loops. They can be used as statements to increment or decrement a variable, as below:

```
i++;            /* Add 1 to i */
i--;            /* Subtract 1 from i */
```

Both operators can be used as either prefix or postfix operators (i.e. before or after the variable). The difference in the meaning of placing the operators before and after variables is discussed in Section 3.6 and when just incrementing or decrementing a variable there is no difference between the two — the choice is a matter of style.

Now let us write a program to count down from 10 to 1. All three sections of the `for` loop header must be changed. The first section is changed to `i = 10` to start at 10, the third section uses the decrement operator in `i--`, and the second section is changed to `i >= 1` which continues execution until `i` is less than 1.

```
/*---------------------------------------------------------------*/
/* COUNT_DOWN.C:  Print the numbers from 10 down to 1            */
/*---------------------------------------------------------------*/
#include <stdio.h>

main()
{
    int i;          /* Variable used by the for loop */

    for (i = 10; i >= 1; i--) {     /* Count i from 10 to 1 */
        printf("%d\n", i);          /* Print out i */
    }
}
```

1.6 The while loop

Another common type of loop is the `while` loop. The `while` loop specifies a condition under which execution of a loop body is to continue. The loop body continues executing *while* the condition is true.

The `while` loop does not have the first and last sections that the `for` loop had (i.e. the initialization and increment sections). However, anything possible with a `for` loop can be achieved using a `while` loop. For example, the `for` loop:

```
for (i = 1; i <= 10; i++) {
    printf("%d\n", i);
}
```

has a `while` loop equivalent:

```
i = 1;
while (i <= 10) {
    printf("%d\n", i);
    i++;
}
```

The main reason for use of the `for` loop for counting is that it conveniently places the initialization and increment together and is more readable. However, there are situations when there is no need for the first and last expressions, and a `while` loop should be used. The choice between `for` loops and `while` loops is merely one of style.

1.7 Logical operators

We have already seen how to test a single condition in an `if` statement or a loop condition. However, there are many situations where it is necessary to test more than one condition. The logical operators provide a means of testing any number of conditions. The full list of logical operators is given in Table 1.5.

The logical operators are commonly used to test conditions of the form: if this is true *and* that is true, do this. For example, the condition:

```
if (x % 2 == 1 && x < 100)    /* odd AND less than 100 */
```

Table 1.5. Logical operators

Operator	Meaning
&&	Logical and
||	Logical or
!	Logical not

tests if x is odd and less than 100. The first condition "x % 2 == 1" uses the remainder operator (%) to test if the remainder is 1 when x is divided by 2, and the second condition is "x < 100". The && operator states that the if condition is true if the first condition is true *and* the second condition is true. In a similar manner, the condition:

```
if (x % 2 == 1 || x < 100)    /* odd OR less than 100 */
```

would test if x was odd *or* less than 100 (i.e. any odd number or an even number less than 100 would cause the condition to evaluate to true).

1.8 Symbolic constants: #define

When a program needs to use a particular number it is bad style to use this number in the main program code. A symbolic constant should be defined to associate a meaningful name with the number. This name is then used in place of the number in the program code. For example, the use of the constant 10 in the counting examples above is bad style, and a better version would use a symbolic constant:

```
/*--------------------------------------------------------------*/
/* COUNT_TO_10.C:   Print the numbers from 1 to 10              */
/*--------------------------------------------------------------*/

#include <stdio.h>

#define MAX 10          /* Define MAX as a Symbolic Constant */

main()
{
    int i;         /* Variable used by the for loop */

    for (i = 1; i <= MAX; i++) {   /* Count i from 1 to MAX */
        printf("%d\n", i);          /* Print out i */
    }
}
```

The hash sign (#) must be the first non-whitespace character on the line (i.e. only spaces or tabs are allowed before the hash sign). Whitespace is also permitted in many other places on the directive line: immediately after the hash sign, before the symbolic name and between the symbolic constant name and its value. As seen in the example, comments are also permitted on preprocessor directive lines. There should be *no semicolon* after the number. A semicolon at the end of the line is an error, and will usually cause a compilation warning later in the program (where the symbol is used).

The value of a symbolic constant is not restricted to a numeric constant and can be any expression, even one involving another symbolic constant. In fact, symbolic constants are just a special case of a general macro expansion facility which is discussed in Chapter 11. Some other examples of symbolic constant definitions are:

```
#define MAX        10
#define LENGTH     (2 * MAX)
#define FALSE      0
#define one        1
```

It is common style for symbolic constant names to be in upper case, but as seen in the examples, it is not illegal to use lower case letters.

1.9 Functions

Functions are used to break up a large program into smaller units. Although the advantages of using functions are not easily seen in small examples, functions do make programs easier to design and easier to read. If your program has a large number of statements, perhaps it is time to use one or more functions. Similarly, when a function gets large, it should be broken up into smaller functions. Most C programs consist of a number of functions calling each other.

Functions should be defined before the `main` function. A new function must be placed above the `main` function in the file. More generally, functions should be defined before they are used. It isn't absolutely necessary, but the methods of removing this limitation will be ignored for the present.

The modified program to print the first 10 numbers using a function called `print_number` to print each number is:

```
/*--------------------------------------------------------------*/
/* COUNT_TO_10.C:  Print out 1 to 10 using a FUNCTION!          */
/*--------------------------------------------------------------*/

#include <stdio.h>

#define MAX 10          /* Define MAX as a Symbolic Constant */

/*--------------------------------------------------------------*/
/* Define function 'print_number' to print its argument         */
/*--------------------------------------------------------------*/
void print_number(int n)
{
    printf("%d\n", n);              /* Print out the number */
}

/*--------------------------------------------------------------*/
/* Start of program execution                                   */
/*--------------------------------------------------------------*/

main()
{
    int i;

    for (i = 1; i <= MAX; i++) {    /* Count i from 1..MAX */
        print_number(i);            /* Print out i */
    }
}
```

The `print_number` function is called a "void function" because it does not return a value. The `void` keyword is used to start the definition of the function, and specifies that the function returns a `void` value (i.e. returns no value). This type of function corresponds to the notion of procedures in other languages, such as Pascal.

Now let us modify our program to print out the *squares* of the first 10 numbers. The square of each number must be calculated. Although this is trivial to do in one line, let us look at using another function called `square` to calculate it.

```
/*-----------------------------------------------------*/
/* PRINT_SQUARES.C:  Print the SQUARES of 1 to 10      */
/*-----------------------------------------------------*/

#include <stdio.h>

#define MAX 10     /* Define MAX as a Symbolic Constant */

/*-----------------------------------------------------*/
/* Define function 'square' to calculate the square    */
/*-----------------------------------------------------*/

int square(int x)
{
    return x * x;          /* Return square of the number */
}

/*-----------------------------------------------------*/
/* Define function 'print_number' to print the number  */
/*-----------------------------------------------------*/

void print_number(int n)
{
    printf("%d\n", n);     /* Print out the number */
}

/*-----------------------------------------------------*/
/* Start of program execution                          */
/*-----------------------------------------------------*/

main()
{
    int i;
    int sq;

    for (i = 1; i <= MAX; i++) {  /* for i = 1 to MAX */
        sq = square(i);           /* Calculate square */
        print_number(sq);         /* Print out square */
    }
}
```

The main difference between the `square` function and the `print_number` function is that the `square` function uses the `return` statement to return its value. This difference occurs because `print_number` is a `void` function that does not return a value and hence does not need to use the `return` statement. The `return` statement exits a function immediately, returning the result.

The other difference appears in the *usage* of the `square` function and the `print_number` function. The `square` function has its returned value assigned to a variable, whereas the `print_number` function is simply called. This is because `print_number` is a `void` function and does not return a value.

Functions can take any number of parameters, but can only return one value (using the `return` statement). Functions cannot change the value of variables passed as arguments to them. It is wrong to try to calculate the square of a number using a call such as:

```
square(x, sq);              /* INCORRECT */
```

The `square` function cannot change the value of `sq`, no matter how cleverly it is defined. Any change to the variable inside the function is not passed on to the outside call. The value of the variable passed as the argument to the function call is not changed. This is called call-by-value parameter passing and is covered in Section 7.8.

1.10 A larger program: guess my number

We will now consider the task of writing a program that generates a random number and asks the user to guess the number. At every guess the computer produces messages indicating whether the guess was too low or too high. A sample execution of the program is:

```
Enter your first guess: 50
Too low.
Enter your next guess: 75
Too high.
Enter your next guess: 67
Too high.
Enter your next guess: 60
Too low.
Enter your next guess: 63
You got it right!
```

This program uses a `while` loop to continue asking for further guesses if the guess is incorrect. The program source code is:

```c
/*--------------------------------------------------------------*/
/* GUESS.C:   guess my number program                           */
/*--------------------------------------------------------------*/

#include <stdio.h>
#include <stdlib.h>         /* Define the rand() and srand() */
#include <time.h>           /* Define the time() function */

#define MAX_NUMBER 100      /* Numbers in the range 1..100 */

/*--------------------------------------------------------------*/
/* Generate secret number using C's random number library functions */
/*--------------------------------------------------------------*/

int generate_secret(void)
{
    /* Generate a random number in the range 1..MAX_NUMBER */

    srand(time(NULL));                  /* Seed number generator */
    return rand() % MAX_NUMBER + 1;     /* Generate the number */
}

/*--------------------------------------------------------------*/
/* Start of program execution                                   */
/*--------------------------------------------------------------*/

main()
{
    int guess;
    int secret_number;                  /* The number to be guessed */
```

```
            secret_number = generate_secret();    /* Generate secret number */
            printf("Enter your first guess: ");   /* Get the first guess */
            scanf("%d", &guess);
            while (guess != secret_number) {      /* While guess is wrong */
                if (guess < secret_number) {      /* Guess too low? */
                    printf("Too low.\n");
                }

                if (guess > secret_number) {      /* Guess too high? */
                    printf("Too high.\n");
                }

                printf("Enter your next guess: ");  /* Get the next guess */
                scanf("%d", &guess);
            }
            printf("You got it right!\n");
        }
```

The program uses the `rand` standard library function (declared in `<stdlib.h>`) to generate a large random number. The `%` remainder operator is used to truncate this large number to the range 0..99 and 1 is added to bring the number into the range 1..100. The `srand` function is used to seed the random number generator and the `time` function (declared in `<time.h>`) is used to provide a new seed (based on real time) every execution. Without the use of the `srand` and `time` functions, the same random number would be generated by `rand` every time the program is executed. More discussion of the generation of random numbers is given in Chapter 12.

1.11 Exercises

1. Which of the following are valid identifiers?

    a) `i`
    b) `run_2`
    c) `for`
    d) `2i`
    e) `Temp`
    f) `TEMP`

2. What is wrong with the following code fragment?

    ```
    sum = x + y
    printf("%d\n", sum)
    ```

3. Is the following use of nested comments legal in C?

    ```
    /* large comment
        /* small comment */
    */
    ```

4. Write a program to ask the user for a number and then output that many stars on a single line. *Hint:* Use `printf` with no `\n` in the format string to produce a single star. Use a `for` loop to count out the correct number of stars.

5. Modify the program in the previous exercise to ask the user for the number of *lines* of stars to be output and then produce output similar to:

    ```
    *
    **
    ***
    etc
    ```

    Hint: Place the for loop in the previous exercise inside another second for loop to count the lines.

6. Write a program to ask the user for a positive integer, n, and print out the sum of the integers from 1 up to n. If the user enters a negative number, display an error message and ask again for a positive integer.

7. The sq variable can be left out of the main function in the program printing squares of numbers, given in Section 1.9. Modify the program so that it doesn't need the variable. *Hint:* Combine two statements into one by passing a function result directly to the argument of another function.

8. The guessing game program asks the user for a guess in two different places. There are two sequences of printf and scanf function calls that are almost identical. Modify the program so that a function is called to get the guess from the user. The function should have no parameters; it should prompt for the guess, receive the guess as input from the user and then return the guess as the function result.

9. Modify the guessing game program to count the number of guesses taken and finish the game with an appropriate message when the user makes 10 incorrect guesses.

Chapter 2
Variable declarations and types

This chapter examines how to declare and use variables. Variables are always declared and used as a particular *type*. A variable may have only one type. There are different rules for the usage of each type, and a variable must always be used in a manner that is consistent with its type. The types available in C include fundamental types (such as integers) and types derived from these basic types (such as arrays of integers). The full list is:

- Basic types
- Enumerated types
- Arrays of a type
- Pointers to a type
- Structures and unions

This chapter covers basic types and arrays. Structures, unions and enumerated types are covered in Chapter 5. Pointers are very special and are covered in Chapter 8.

2.1 Basic types

C supports a number of integral and floating point data types. The basic data types in C are given in Table 2.1.

Table 2.1. **Basic types**

Data type	Meaning
int	Integer
char	Character
float	Floating point (real)
double	Double precision (real)

These basic types are intended to closely match the implementation's byte and word size. A `char` is intended to be a single byte, and an `int` to correspond to the normal word size on a machine. See Table 2.2 for variants on the basic types.

Table 2.2. Qualified basic types

Data type	Meaning
short	Short integer
long	Long integer

`short` and `long` integers are integers with a (possibly) different number of bytes, so as to reduce memory usage (`short`) or to enhance the range of integers that can be represented (`long`). For example, on a machine where an `int` is 4 bytes, a `short` may be 2 bytes and a `long` consist of 8 bytes. The range of values for particular numbers of bytes are shown in Table 2.3.

Table 2.3. Range of values

Number of bytes	Range
1 byte	−128 ... 127
2 bytes	−32768 ... 32767
4 bytes	−2147483648 ... 2147483647

Hence, a `short` variable could be used if values are in the range −32768..32767 and space saving was important. A `long` variable is used when integer values with a large magnitude must be stored (i.e. large positive or negative integers). Note that it depends on the implementation whether `short` and `long` are actually different from `int` — they may be identical sizes in some implementations. For example, on my system a `short` is 2 bytes, an `int` is 4 bytes, but a `long` is the same as an `int` (4 bytes). The fundamental type, `int`, is adequate for most programs and is most commonly used because mixing `int` with other types can possibly reduce the speed of the program.

Both `float` and `double` types are used to hold real numbers. The only difference is that a `double` variable has a greater level of precision. For even greater precision, the type "`long double`" can be used.

2.2 Declaring variables

Variables are defined in C by the following syntax:

```
type name_list;
```

where `name_list` is either a single variable name, or a list of comma-separated names. Some examples of variable declarations are shown below:

```
int i;              /* Declare i as an integer */
char ch, ch2;       /* Declare ch and ch2 as char */
```

Variable declarations and types

Declarations can appear in two places. Global variables can be declared at the top of the program, before the `main` function. Local variables can be declared after the left brace at the top of `main`.

```
#include <stdio.h>

int x;          /* Global variables */
int y;

main()
{
    int i;      /* Local variables */
    int j;
    ...         /* executable statements */
}
```

The difference between local and global variables only becomes apparent when a program has more than one *function*. For the present, your programs should use only local variables, declared inside the braces. Global variables are examined further in Chapter 7.

2.3 Numeric constants

It is quite obvious that programs need to use numbers. C programs allow a few different forms of numerical constants. Decimal integers such as 1, 10 and 399 can be used directly in any expression and have type: `int`. Negative integers are permitted using a minus sign. Positive integers can have an optional + sign. Some examples of integer constants are shown below:

```
x = 20;
y = -1;
```

2.3.1 Octal and hexadecimal constants

C also permits the use of octal and hexadecimal integer constants. Any integer starting with 0 is assumed to be an octal constant. Hexadecimal constants are specified using the prefix `0x` or `0X`, and may use any of the letters `a-f` or `A-F` as digits. Some examples are:

```
z = 077;            /* Octal 77 == Decimal 63 */
x = 0x1F;           /* Hex 1F == Decimal 31 */
```

2.3.2 Floating point constants

Floating point constants can also be placed in programs. These can be specified using decimal point format or exponential notation. As expected, negative constants can be specified by a prefix minus sign. Some examples are:

```
pi = 3.14159;
x = 3.1E+3;         /* x = 3100 */
y = -2e-4;          /* y = -0.0002 */
```

The exponential notation is quite flexible. Both e and E are allowed (and are equivalent), and the + sign in 3.1E+3 is optional.

The type of floating point constants is double. The constants can also be used with float variables although efficiency may suffer because the compiler has to add conversion code. When using float variables it is better to define float constants using suffixes as discussed below.

Note that there is an important distinction between the constants 1.0 and 1. The type of 1.0 is double, whereas the type of 1 is int. It is important to use the correct type of constant because otherwise the compiler may need to add extra code to perform a type conversion.

2.3.3 Suffixes for constants

Integer and floating point constants can be qualified by suffixes. The type of an integer constant can be modified by the suffixes: u, U, l, or L. The suffix u or U specifies unsigned; l or L specifies long. Floating point constants can be modified by the suffixes: l or L for long double; f or F to specify a float constant (the default is a double constant). Some examples of the use of suffixes for constants are shown below:

```
y = 30UL;            /* 30 unsigned and long */
v = 2.0e-5F;         /* 0.00002 float type */
```

2.4 Character constants and escapes

When using character variables it is useful to be able to assign them the values of particular letters, or compare them with letters. For example, after reading a user's response to a menu choice, we may wish to determine what letter was chosen (e.g. A, B or C). Character constants can be used by placing a letter inside a pair of single quotes:

```
if (ch == 'a' || ch == 'A')    /* if ch is a or A */
```

In addition to the normal letters, we would also like to be able to use special characters. *Escapes* are codes for special characters indicated by a backslash followed by a single letter. For example, the tab character can be specified as '\t' and a newline can be specified using '\n'. The single quote character can be represented using the escape '\''. The complete list of escapes is given in Table 2.4.

The numeric value of a character can also be used to specify a character constant. The value can be represented in octal or hexadecimal, but not in decimal. A character sequence \x is used to start a hexadecimal escape (e.g. \xFF is character 255). Any digit after the backslash starts an octal escape and this makes decimal numbers unavailable. Only three octal digits or two hexadecimal digits are allowed since this is adequate to represent the entire range 0..255. Some examples of the use of escapes are shown below:

```
ch = '\0';           /* Null character (zero) */
ch = '\123';         /* Some strange character: 123 octal */
ch = '\x20';         /* Character 32 (ASCII space) */
```

Variable declarations and types   23

Table 2.4. Escape sequences

Escape	Meaning
\a	Bell (alert)
\b	Backspace
\f	Formfeed
\n	Newline
\r	Carriage return
\t	Tab
\v	Vertical tab
\\	Backslash
\?	Question mark
\'	Single quote
\"	Double quote
\ooo	Octal number
\xhh	Hexadecimal number

Note that there is an important difference between '0' and '\0'. The constant '0' represents the character 0 as typed at the keyboard which has ASCII value 48, whereas the escape constant '\0' represents ASCII value 0.

2.5 Variable initialization

C permits variables to be given initial values which is a very convenient feature. A variable is initialized by adding an extra part to its declaration — an = sign followed by an expression. This expression is often a single constant, but can be more complicated. Variables can be initialized to any constant expression (non-constant expressions are allowed in some cases — see Chapter 7). The example below declares two variables with initial values, and then prints out these values:

```
#include <stdio.h>

main()
{
    int x = 1;                    /* Initialize x to 1 */
    char ch = 'Z';                /* Initialize ch to letter Z */

    printf("x = %d\n", x);        /* Print out the values */
    printf("ch = %c\n", ch);
}
```

All types of variables can be initialized — arrays, strings and structures can all be initialized in C. However, discussion of initialization of these types is deferred to Chapter 7.

2.6 Arrays

Arrays are a convenient notation for storing a number of data values together. Let us first look at one-dimensional arrays. The syntax for the declaration of an array variable is:

```
element_type arr_name[SIZE];
```

where `element_type` is the type of the elements that are to be contained in the array, and `SIZE` is the size of the array. The expression specifying the `SIZE` must be a constant expression that can be evaluated at compile-time. Note that this constant expression is the *size* of the array, not the largest value. For example, the array declaration:

```
int arr[10];
```

declares 10 array locations from `arr[0]` to `arr[9]`. The array reference `arr[10]` is an illegal reference for this array.

There is no (easy) way to specify the range of the index for an array. For example, there is no way of specifying an array from `a[10]..a[20]`. The lower bound of the index range is always zero and the upper bound is $n-1$, where n is the size of the array. A complicated method to change array index ranges involves the use of pointers (see Section 14.9).

Arrays may contain any type of element: arrays of `int`, arrays of `float`, arrays of `char`, arrays of structures, arrays of pointers, etc. Arrays of `char` are used to represent strings and their special features are discussed fully in Chapter 6.

Array elements are set or accessed using the square brackets notation `arr[index]`. The index inside the square brackets can be any expression that evaluates to an integer. The program below stores the squares of each integer in an array and then computes the sum of the elements stored in the array (i.e. the sum of squares from 0 to 99):

```
#include <stdio.h>

#define ARR_SIZE   100

main()
{
    int arr[ARR_SIZE];
    int i, sum;

    for (i = 0; i < ARR_SIZE; i++)
        arr[i] = i * i;                 /* Store in array */

    sum = 0;
    for (i = 0; i < ARR_SIZE; i++)      /* Add up array */
        sum = sum + arr[i];
    printf("The sum is %d\n", sum);     /* Print the sum */
}
```

The first `for` loop in this program stores the square of `i` in array element `a[i]`. The second `for` loop adds each element to `sum`.

2.6.1 Multi-dimensional arrays

The array in the previous section was a one-dimensional array. There are situations where it can be useful to have arrays with more than one dimension. For example, it is useful to represent a chess board as an 8-by-8 two-dimensional array, indexed by integers representing row and column.

Arrays of any dimension can be declared in C. The dimension is always fixed at compile-time (as is the size). Multi-dimensional arrays are an extension of one-dimensional arrays. To declare multi-dimensional arrays, add another set of brackets containing another constant integer expression (the size of the second dimension). To reference elements of a multi-dimensional array, add another pair of square brackets containing another index (e.g. a[i][j]). Note that the Pascal-like notation, a[i,j], is wrong. Some examples of the use of multi-dimensional arrays are given below:

```
int a[10][20];                  /* a[10,20] is Wrong */
double values[MAXSIZE][2];

x = a[3][15];                   /* a[3,15] is Wrong */
temp = a[i + j][p];
```

2.7 User defined type names: typedef

The `typedef` keyword is used to specify new type names. Usually, `typedef` definitions appear before variable declarations. The `typedef` keyword is needed in each different declaration — there is no special section for `typedef` declarations.

Although `typedef` declarations are very strange at first, a simple rule helps explain them — the new type name is always the identifier on the right. Note that this identifier may be in the middle of some other non-alphabetic symbols. For example, array square brackets appear on the right when declaring an array type. Some example `typedef` declarations are:

```
typedef int data_type;          /* "data_type" is int type */
typedef int array_type[10];     /* "array_type" is array type */
```

These newly defined type names can be used in variable declarations, and also in further `typedef` definitions, as below:

```
data_type data;                 /* "data" is int variable */
typedef data_type arr[5];       /* "arr" is array of int type */
```

A good example of the use of `typedef` is the definition of a new type, `boolean`, as a synonym for `int`. This is particularly worthwhile in combination with symbolic constants for `TRUE` and `FALSE`:

```
#define TRUE   1
#define FALSE  0
typedef int boolean;      /* define new type "boolean" */
```

2.8 Type qualifiers

Variables can be qualified by a number of keywords to indicate special features of the variable. For example, we have already touched on the `short` and `long` qualifiers which affect the size of the integer representation of a variable. The possible qualifiers are:

```
short       long
unsigned    signed
const       volatile
```

All of these qualifiers are applied in variable declarations before the type of the variable name:

```
short int i;
unsigned char ch, next;
long double value;
const int x = 1;
```

Note that when the type of the variable is `int`, the `int` keyword can be omitted. Hence it is quite common to see variable declarations such as:

```
short i;             /* Equivalent to:  short int i;  */
```

2.8.1 The short and long qualifiers

The `short` and `long` qualifiers indicate to the compiler to use a smaller or larger data type, if possible. These keywords are more like requests than demands. The compiler is free to ignore the advice, so the actual size of these types is compiler-dependent. For example, there are machines where `short` and `long` are both implemented exactly as `int`. Though all sizes are implementation defined, it is realistic to assume:

```
sizeof(char) ≤ sizeof(short) ≤ sizeof(int) ≤ sizeof(long)
```

Not all combinations are legal — there is no such thing as a "`short char`". Usually, the compiler will silently ignore impossible requests. Some example variable declarations are:

```
short x;
long double big;
```

2.8.2 The signed and unsigned qualifiers

The `signed` and `unsigned` qualifiers apply to integral variables. They indicate whether to consider the leftmost bit of the internal representation of an integer value as a sign bit. When the `unsigned` qualifier is used, the leftmost bit is assumed to be part of an `unsigned` positive integer (i.e. not the sign bit). The `signed` qualifier states that the bit is the sign bit, allowing negative values. The compiler generates code that ensures that this bit is interpreted correctly. Variables qualified by `unsigned` cannot represent negative values but can represent larger positive integers than is possible with the equivalent `signed` type.

These qualifiers can be useful in special cases when it is important to ensure that a variable is treated as a non-negative. Some operators have undefined behavior on negative values (e.g. % >>) and it may be important to ensure their operands are treated as if they are positive. For example, overflow can make a large number become negative.

The most common use of unsigned or signed is with characters. It is not defined whether a char is signed or unsigned by default. This creates problems if the sign bit is set in a char value. Will a character greater than 127, such as 255, be converted to integer 255 or integer −1? If the char type is signed the conversion will give −1; if unsigned the result will be 255. When the char variable is explicitly signed or unsigned, the compiler should generate the correct code. Otherwise, the choice is arbitrary and implementation-defined.

When dealing with bytes it is usual to use "unsigned char" variables. This ensures that the bytes are never considered to be negative numbers. The conversion from unsigned char to int is guaranteed to yield a non-negative integer.

The unsigned qualifier has the effect of doubling the magnitude of positive values that can be represented by a type by disallowing negative values. When *n* is the number of *bits* in a type (usually 8 bits per byte), the ranges for both the signed and unsigned type are as shown in Table 2.5.

Table 2.5. Value ranges

Data type	Range
signed	$-2^{n-1} \ldots 2^{n-1}-1$
unsigned	$0 \ldots 2^{n}-1$

2.8.3 The const qualifier

The type qualifiers const and volatile are relatively new and some older compilers may not support their use. Both are *access modifiers* that change the method of access for a data object.

The const qualifier is used to indicate that the value of a variable does not change during program execution. The compiler is free to store such variables in read-only memory. const can be used to declare *symbolic constants* without using #define. This method has the advantage that the scope of the constant names is correct (within the enclosing block), rather than ranging over the entire program as is the case with #define. However, const declarations are not true "constants" and are not permitted in many constant expressions, such as the size in an array declaration, the constant for a case label in a switch statement or the initializer of a global variable. Hence, const variables are mostly used to represent constants in calculations (e.g. pi, e). Some examples of const declarations are:

```
const int time_delay = 100;
const char newline = '\n';
const float pi = 3.14159;
```

It is not legal to assign a value to a `const` variable and the compiler should produce a warning. Instead of using assignment, `const` variables must be initialized in their declaration. They must always be initialized — how else do they get a value?

The `const` qualifier may also be used in a special way to indicate that a function does not change the elements of an array. Arrays are passed by reference and could therefore be changed by a function. If the compiler knows that an array parameter is declared as `const`, it should warn about statements that may change that array. A good example is the proper definition of the `strcpy` standard library function:

```
char *strcpy(char dest[], const char source[])
{
      ...     /* dest[] changes;  source[] does not */
}
```

Using `const` with pointer variables gives rise to a special case. The declaration:

```
const char *ptr = "text";
```

declares a pointer to data that is not changing, but does not define the pointer variable as `const`. The pointer can be assigned to or incremented, but expressions dereferencing it cannot change the data it points to. It is also possible to define a pointer variable that does not change, whereas the data it points to does.

```
char *const ptr;          /* ptr cannot change, but data can */
const char *ptr;          /* ptr can change, but data cannot */
```

Note that the distinction does not arise with array variables, because they cannot be assigned values.

2.8.4 The volatile qualifier

The `volatile` qualifier is very rarely used. It is needed when accessing a very special type of memory location, such as a shared memory variable, or the location of a raw device. For example, some machines allow special memory locations to be used for input of data from raw devices. To read data from the device, the program must repeatedly examine that location. Unfortunately, the compiler does not know that it is a special location. It may see a series of references to the location that appears not to have changed. The optimization phase may remove the "redundant" references, thus wrecking the code. The `volatile` qualifier informs the compiler that the location is special, and prevents optimization.

2.9 Implicit type conversions

There are many situations in C where type conversions are carried out automatically by the compiler. In particular, when different types are used in arithmetic expressions, a number of conversions are performed automatically by the compiler, so that the programmer rarely needs to worry about combining different types. Because there are so many implicit conversions, the explicit type cast operator is used quite rarely. In fact, the type cast operator often appears in expressions so as to provide *documentation* about a conversion, rather than to force one!

The full list of situations where implicit type conversions occur is given below:

- Assignment operators
- Arithmetic operators
- Other operators
- Passing arguments to a function
- The `return` statement inside a function

When assigning a variable an expression of a different type, a type conversion is performed. All possible combinations of `int`s, `short`s, `long`s and `char`s can be used interchangeably, but there is never any warning if a value from a large type cannot be represented by the smaller type (this is a form of overflow or underflow), in which case the result of the conversion is undefined. The same problems can also arise when converting between `signed` and `unsigned` values of the same basic type (e.g. converting a negative `signed` value to an `unsigned` type is undefined). Conversion is also legal between the floating point types, `float`, `double` and `long double`, but the precision is lost when converting a large type to a smaller type. Automatic conversion between `float`s or `double`s and integer types is performed without any warning, and converting from a floating point type to an integral type causes truncation to the nearest integer.

There are many type promotions applied to operands of arithmetic operators. Arithmetic operators will convert operands if they have different types. The operand with the "smaller" type is promoted to the "larger" type, usually without any compilation warning. For example, if one operand is a `float` and the other is an `int`, the `int` is promoted to type `float`. Because these conversions are towards the "larger" type there is no problem of overflow or loss of precision. The hierarchy of types from largest to smallest is:

```
long double
double
float
unsigned long
long
unsigned int
int
short
char
```

There are a few exceptions to the rule of "convert to the larger type". If `long` cannot hold all values of an `unsigned int`, when this pairing of types appears, both are converted to `unsigned long`. Another special case is that when one type is `char` and the other is `short`, both are converted to `int` or `unsigned int` (whichever type is large enough).

The arithmetic operators are not the only operators that force type conversions. Most operators that require a particular type will carry out "reasonable" type conversions to get the correct type. The details are beyond the scope of this book (see Kernighan and Ritchie, 1988).

Type conversions are also carried out when passing arguments to a function. When using prototyping function declarations (i.e. the normal declarations with types in the parameter list) the type conversions are identical to those for assignment (converting the argument type in the function call to the parameter's type in the function definition). For non-prototyping function declarations, `short` or `char` arguments are converted to `int`, and `float` arguments are converted to `double`.

Type conversions are performed on the expression of a `return` statement. The conversions are identical to those for assignment, where the conversion is between the type of the expression being returned and the declared return type of the function.

2.10 Exercises

1. What is the default type of real constants such as 3.14? How can a constant be declared with a different type? What is the difference between the constants 1.0 and 1?

2. When using character escapes, what base numbers can be used? How can the single quote character be used in a program? What is the difference between `'0'` and `'\0'`?

3. Write a program to print out the values of `'A'..'Z'` in your local character set (in ASCII they should be consecutively 65..90). *Hint:* A character variable can be printed out as an integer using `%d` and as a character using `%c`.

4. Is the initialization in the variable declaration below legal? Does it matter if x is local or global?

    ```
    int x = 3 + 4;
    ```

5. What is the difference between the two declarations below?

    ```
    short x;
    short int x;
    ```

6. What is the smallest value an `unsigned` variable can hold? Is the number of distinct values representable by `signed int` and `unsigned int` different? Are the smallest and largest values different?

7. What is the purpose of the `volatile` specifier? Use `volatile` to write a time delay loop that cannot be optimized by the compiler.

8. What is the purpose of the `const` specifier? Can the `const` specifier completely replace the use of `#define`?

Chapter 3
Operators

C has many different operators, and all of the operators are examined in this chapter. Of these, the most important are the arithmetic, relational, logical and increment operators. Knowledge of these common operators is assumed in subsequent chapters. Other more advanced operators, such as the bitwise operators and pointer operators can be studied as required. In some cases, the operators are examined in more detail in a later chapter. For example, the structure operators are examined again in Chapter 5 and the pointer operators are examined again in Chapter 8.

3.1 Arithmetic operators

C has the usual arithmetic operators as shown in Table 3.1.

Table 3.1. Arithmetic operators

Operator	Meaning
+	Addition
−	Subtraction
*	Multiplication
/	Division
%	Integer remainder (modulus)

These operators can be combined in many ways to form quite complicated expressions. Some examples of arithmetic expressions are:

```
y = x + 1;
a = b * 2;
remainder = num % divisor;
quotient = num / divisor;
```

All the arithmetic operators (except %) apply to all of the basic types: `char`, `short`, `int`, `float`, `double`, etc. Integer arithmetic is performed if both operands are of integral type. Real arithmetic is performed if one or both operands are of `float` or `double` type. If only one operand is `float` or `double`, the other operand is promoted to that type. Generally, if the two operands are of different type, the lower type operand is promoted to the higher type. The result of this is that, in most instances, the programmer need not worry about the types of operands to arithmetic operators.

One instance where the types are important is the division operator, /. If either of the operands are floating point (`float` or `double`), the other operand is converted to floating point, and floating point division is carried out. When both operands are some integral type, integer division is performed. When division is applied to integers, the result is a truncated integer, not a `float`. For example:

```
7 / 4   == 1
7 / 4.0 == 1.75
```

The truncation direction (i.e. towards or away from zero) on negative integer operands is implementation-defined. Hence it is best to avoid using negative operands as much as possible.

Remainder (%) is only permitted on the integral types. It returns the remainder of an integer division. For example:

```
7 % 4 == 3
```

When both operands are positive, the result of n%p is guaranteed to be between 0 and p-1, inclusive. Results are implementation-defined if the second operand is zero, or either operand is negative. However, it is guaranteed that when n>0 and p<0, n%p is in the range:

```
p < n%p < -p
```

This is equivalent to:

```
abs(n%p) < abs(p).
```

Although the result of both / and % on negative operands is undefined, they are both dependent on each other because ANSI requires that the identity below always be true:

```
(x/y)*y + x%y == x
```

The + and − tokens are unary operators as well as binary operators for addition and subtraction. The compiler can determine which operation to perform by counting the number of operands to the operator. These unary operators are given in Table 3.2.

Unary minus returns the negation of its operand. Unary plus performs no operation, returning its operand unchanged. Unary plus is almost useless and was added by ANSI for symmetry with unary minus (it is not supported by many older compilers). Some examples of the usage of these operators are given below:

```
y = -x;
y = 3 * + x;      /* same as  y= 3 * x;  */
```

Table 3.2. Unary arithmetic operators

Operator	Meaning
−	Unary minus
+	Unary plus

3.2 The assignment operator

The assignment operator is a single equals sign. The left operand of the assignment operator must be a variable. The right operand can be any expression. Some examples of assignment statements are:

```
n = n + 1;
y = x * 2;
```

The assignment operator returns a result equal to the value placed in the variable (effectively the result of evaluating the right operand). It is of the same type as its left operand (i.e. the type of the variable). This property of returning a value is not found in some other languages (e.g. Pascal). It allows the assignment operator to be used in the middle of expressions, giving rise to advanced uses such as:

```
x = y = 0;
```

which sets both x and y to zero. Note that = is right associative, so the statement first sets y to zero, then propagates this value into x. In other words, the statement has the same effect as:

```
x = (y = 0);
```

The value returning property of the assignment operator is sometimes used for efficiency in statements such as:

```
if ((x = a + b) > 10)
```

which sets x=a+b, and then tests if x>10. However, whether this statement really is more efficient depends on the implementation.

The single equals sign is not the relational equality operator, as it is in some other programming languages. The relational operator equals is "=="; two equals signs. Do not use "=" to compare equality. It is a common error to write

```
if (x = y)
```

instead of

```
if (x == y)
```

The first is syntactically correct, but has a totally different meaning to that intended. It means assign y to x, and then check if the variable x is non-zero. In other words, if y is zero, the condition is always false; if y is non-zero, the condition is always true. The value of the variable x is also changed leading to obscure bugs.

3.3 L-values and r-values

This section examines two common terms used when discussing operators. The assignment operator requires that its left operand be an l-value, and its right operand be an r-value. The names l-value and r-value stand for left-hand-side-value and right-hand-side-value. One way to remember is that the assignment operator requires a variable on the left side, and a value on the right side, as below:

l-value → variable
r-value → value

An l-value is any expression that can be assigned a value; more generally, anything that has an address (i.e. a place to store a value). L-values can be a single variable name (e.g. x) or a composite variable (e.g. `x[3]`, `node.str[20]`).

An r-value is any value that can be stored. It can be a single constant, a variable, or any compound expression. Any l-value is also an r-value, because any variable used on the left can also be used on the right. However, not all r-values are l-values — a constant is an r-value, but not an l-value.

3.4 Relational operators

Relational operators are used to compare two values. They apply to all C's basic types, both integral and real. The relational operators are shown in Table 3.3.

Table 3.3. Relational operators

Operator	Meaning
==	Equal
!=	Not equal
>	Greater than
<	Less than
>=	Greater than or equal
<=	Less than or equal

Relational operators return 1 for true, 0 for false. The type of their result is `int`. There is no such thing as a separate boolean or logical type in C, and most programs use `int` to represent a boolean type. The relational operators are most commonly used in the conditional expressions of `if` statements and loops:

```
if (n < 10)            /* if n is less than 10 */
if (x == y)            /* if x equals y */
while (x > y + 1)
```

It is unfortunate that the assignment operator (=) and the equals operator (==) are so similar. It is a common and particularly elusive bug for new C programmers to write "=" instead of "==" in an `if` statement.

3.5 Logical operators

The logical operators in C are shown in Table 3.4. Logical operators return 1 for true, 0 for false and the return type is `int`. In evaluating their result, they consider 0 to be false, and any non-zero value to be true. This is consistent with the relational operators, which return 1 for true, and zero for false.

Table 3.4. Logical operators

Operator	Meaning
&&	And
||	Or
!	Not

Logical-and and logical-or are both binary operators. They both use two-character notation (two ampersands and two vertical bars). The single characters (& |) are operators for bitwise-and and bitwise-or (covered later). Be careful always to use && or || because it is an error to use & or | instead of && or ||.

The exclamation mark, logical-not, is a unary prefix operator which applies to a single operand. The logical-not operator returns 0 if the operand was non-zero, 1 if it was zero. Logical operators most commonly appear in the conditions of `if` statements and loops:

```
if (!x)                 /* if x is zero */
if (!(n < 10))          /* if not n less than 10 */
if (n < 10 && y == 2)   /* if n < 10 and y equals 2 */
```

All of these examples use the logical operators in an `if` statement. However, the use of these operators is not limited to conditional expressions. They can be used, for example, to set boolean flags.

```
int flag;         /* int used because no boolean type */
flag = x > y && a == 3;    /* Flag is true if x>y and a==3 */
```

3.5.1 Short-circuiting

Not all of a boolean expression involving the logical operators is always evaluated. In fact, only as much of the expression as is necessary to determine the result is actually evaluated. Parts of the expression having no effect on the result are ignored.

If the first operand of an && is false, or the first operand of an || is true, then the second operand is not evaluated at all. If either of these cases occur, the result is completely determined by the first operand. There is no need to evaluate the second operand to determine the result. The identities below show the justification for short-circuiting:

False AND anything ≡ False
True OR anything ≡ True

This process is called short-circuiting and is guaranteed by the ANSI standard. Short-circuiting improves the efficiency of evaluating a boolean expression by doing as little work as is necessary. This is important in complicated expressions where whole sub-expressions can be ignored.

The examples below show short-circuiting at work in boolean expressions of `if` statements. Short-circuiting does not only occur in the conditions of `if` statements and loops. It occurs everywhere the && or || operators are used. For example,

```
if (p != NULL && p->next != NULL)
    statement
```

is equivalent to:

```
if (p != NULL) {
    if (p->next != NULL)
        statement
}
```

Similarly, for the logical-or operator (||):

```
if (p == NULL || p->next == NULL)
    statement
```

is equivalent to:

```
if (p == NULL)
    statement
else if (p->next != NULL)
    statement                       /* the same statement */
```

Short-circuiting can be used to do things very efficiently but, if you are not aware of it, it can cause very subtle bugs. One problem appears in complicated conditional expressions such as:

```
if (x != y && fn(1, 2) )
    ...
```

If the first term is false (i.e. x equals y), the second term is not evaluated. The function is not even called! If the function call should produce some output, this output never appears.

Short-circuiting is only a problem if terms in the expressions involve side effects (e.g. increment, assignment, some types of function calls). When side effects occur in logical expressions, it is sometimes necessary to rearrange the code. For more discussion of the problems of short-circuiting in relation to side effects, refer to Section 3.19.1.

3.6 Increment and decrement operators

C has two special purpose unary operators for incrementing and decrementing a variable. These are shown in Table 3.5. Some examples of their usage are shown below:

```
i++;            /* increment i */
a[j]--;         /* decrement jth element of a[] */
```

Table 3.5. Increment/decrement operators

Operator	Meaning
++	Increment
--	Decrement

These operators offer a very convenient shorthand for x=x+1 and x=x-1 and are very common in C programs. They can be applied to any simple or compound variable (i.e. any l-value). The type of the variable must be an integral type or a pointer type.

The increment and decrement operators usually correspond exactly to low-level machine operations, and are very efficient. Incrementing a variable using x++ is usually more efficient than the equivalent expression x=x+1 because the computer usually performs the increment operation faster than addition. Although a smart compiler could notice that the effect of the statement is just an increment, the use of the ++ operator makes it easier for a compiler to generate fast code.

Both increment and decrement operators can be used as either prefix or postfix operators (i.e. they can be placed before or after a variable). The meanings of placing the operators before and after the variable are only different when the increment appears in the middle of an expression. There are four cases as shown in Table 3.6.

Table 3.6. Forms of increment/decrement

Expression	Meaning	Effect
x++	Post-increment	Increment x, return OLD value of x
++x	Pre-increment	Increment x, return NEW value of x
x--	Post-decrement	Decrement x, return OLD value of x
--x	Pre-decrement	Decrement x, return NEW value of x

The idea is that if the operator is placed after the variable, the increment operation is applied after the result to be returned is calculated. If the operator is left of the variable, the increment operation is carried out before the return result is calculated. The difference appears in statements where the result of the increment operator is used for something else (e.g. assigned to a variable):

```
y = x++;      /* increment x, y = old value of x */
y = ++x;      /* increment x, y = new value of x */
```

There is no difference when the operators are used solely for their effect. The two statements below are identical in effect and the choice between the two notations is one of style only.

```
x++;          /* increment x */
++x;          /* increment x */
```

The increment and decrement operators cannot be applied to expressions. For example, the expressions "3++" and "(x+y)++" are illegal and cannot replace "3+1" or "(x+y)+1". The operand to ++ or -- must be a variable (i.e. an l-value). However, the result of increment or decrement is not an l-value. Hence expressions such as (p++)++ attempting to replace p=p+2 are also illegal.

3.7 Extended assignment operators

As well as the common assignment operator (=), C has some special assignment operators. The extended arithmetic operators are given in Table 3.7. Note that there are four more extended assignment operators, the bitwise and shift assignment operators, and these are discussed later in this chapter.

Table 3.7. Extended assignment operators

Operator	Meaning
+=	Add to a variable
-=	Subtract from a variable
*=	Multiply a variable
/=	Divide a variable
%=	Remainder a variable

These operators require a variable on the left-hand side and an expression on the right-hand side. They are a shorthand way of applying binary operators to a variable. For example, instead of:

```
x = x + 10;
```

the extended arithmetic operator, +=, can be used to write the equivalent:

```
x += 10;
```

Generally, instead of:

```
x = x op value;
```

it is possible to write:

```
x op= value;
```

The extended assignment operators allow any variable on the left-hand side and any expression on the right-hand side. This means they can save a lot of typing and are very efficient, as the address of the variable is calculated only once. Some examples of the use of extended assignment operators are:

```
x *= 2;              /* Double x */
n -= 10;             /* Subtract 10 from n */
y[4] += x * 2;       /* Add x*2 to y[4]   */
```

There must be no spaces between the characters of the operator (i.e. not "+ ="). If there is a space, the compiler will think they are two separate operators (plus and assignment) and will produce a compilation error.

3.8 Bitwise operators

C provides a number of operators to access individual bits of the internal binary representation of integers. The bitwise operators are given in Table 3.8. The bitwise operators only apply to integral operands. They apply a logical operation to each bit of their operand.

Table 3.8. Bitwise operators

Operator	Meaning
&	Bitwise and
|	Bitwise or
^	Bitwise exclusive-or
~	One's complement

Bitwise-and (&), bitwise-or (|) and bitwise-exclusive-or (^) are binary operators. They take two operands, apply the bitwise operation on both and return the result. Bitwise-and will set a bit in the result if the corresponding bits in both operands are set; bitwise-or sets the bit if either bit is set; and bitwise-exclusive-or sets the bit if either is set, but not both. The notation & and | is similar to the logical operators && and ||, and it is important not to confuse them.

One's complement (~) is a unary prefix operator. It returns the value of its operand with all the bits complemented (i.e. 1's change to 0's and vice versa).

```
y = ~x;                 /* Get the complement of x */
bits = x & mask;        /* Get some of the bits */
```

Note that the ~ operator does not change the value of a variable when used in a statement such as:

```
~x;         /* INCORRECT */
```

and, in fact, this statement does nothing at all. The value of ~x must be assigned to some variable, as in the example above.

The three binary bitwise operators, &, | and ^, all have corresponding assignment operators. The extended bitwise assignment operators are given in Table 3.9. One of the main uses of these operators is in setting and clearing bits in variables, which is the topic of the next section.

Table 3.9. Extended bitwise operators

Operator	Meaning
&=	Extended bitwise and
|=	Extended bitwise or
^=	Extended bitwise exclusive-or

3.8.1 Setting and clearing bits

A common use of bitwise operators is to clear or set groups of bits of an integer. Individual bits can be set using bitwise-or. Individual bits can be cleared using bitwise-and with unary complement. To extract individual bit fields all the other bits can be zeroed using bitwise-and.

```
x |= mask;        /* Set bits set in mask */
x &= ~ mask;      /* Clear bits set in mask */
x &= mask;        /* Clear all bits not set in mask */
```

In these examples, mask contains all the bits that are to be set or cleared; that is, all the 1's in mask specify the positions of the bits affected. Other bits of x are unchanged.

The values of particular bits can be extracted using ordinary integers. The integers for each bit are shown in the Table 3.10. Remember that bit zero is the rightmost bit of an integer. Characters usually have 8 bits; ints have at least 16 bits. Integers for groups of bits can be calculated by adding the relevant integers.

Table 3.10. Values of binary bits

Bit	Decimal	Hex	Octal
0	1	0x01	01
1	2	0x02	02
2	4	0x04	04
3	8	0x08	010
4	16	0x10	020
5	32	0x20	040
6	64	0x40	0100
7	128	0x80	0200
8	256	0x100	0400
9	512	0x200	01000
10	1024	0x400	02000
11	2048	0x800	04000
12	4096	0x1000	010000
13	8192	0x2000	020000
14	16384	0x4000	040000
15	32768	0x8000	080000

Note that octal and hexadecimal integer constants are very commonly used for bitwise operations (octal integers have prefix 0 and hexadecimal integers have prefix 0x). In octal notation each digit represents three bits; in hexadecimal each digit represents four bits. The mapping from digits to bit patterns is shown in Table 3.11.

Table 3.11. Bit patterns

Digit	Octal bit pattern	Hex bit pattern
0	000	0000
1	001	0001
2	010	0010
3	011	0011
4	100	0100
5	101	0101
6	110	0110
7	111	0111
8	–	1000
9	–	1001
A	–	1010
B	–	1011
C	–	1100
D	–	1101
E	–	1110
F	–	1111

Some examples of the use of octal and hexadecimal constants as bit masks are shown below:

```
x &= 037;          /* Leave only lower 5 bits */
x |= 01;           /* Set the zeroth bit to 1 */
x &= ~07;          /* Clear the lower 3 bits */
bit0 = x & 01;     /* Extract zeroth bit */
```

3.8.2 Bit shift operators

In addition to bitwise logical operations, C provides two operators to shift bits left and right. Table 3.12 gives the shift operators.

Table 3.12. Shift operators

Operator	Meaning
>>	Shift right
<<	Shift left

The shift operators apply only to integral operands (char, int, short, long). They are both binary operators. The left operand is the value to be shifted. The right operand is the number of shifts to be performed. Some examples of the use of shift operators are:

```
y = x >> 1;            /* y = x shifted right by 1 */
bit = (x >> 3) & 01;   /* extract bit 3 from x */
```

The effect of these operators is to shift the bits left or right, and return the shifted value as the result. Shifting left is equivalent to multiplying by a power of 2. Shifting right is (usually) equivalent to division by a power of 2. The equivalence is:

shift by 1 bit ≡ divide/multiply by 2,
shift by 2 bits ≡ divide/multiply by 4,
shift by 3 bits ≡ divide/multiply by 8,
shift by n bits ≡ divide/multiply by 2^n

Shifting left will fill the rightmost bits with zero, and is equivalent to multiplication even if there is an overflow (i.e. because both operations would overflow in this case). Right-shifting positive numbers is always equivalent to division, but right-shifting negative numbers is not always equivalent to division. Right shifting will either fill the leftmost bits with zero or will sign-extend (i.e. leave the sign bit unchanged as well as shifting it). Sign extension on positive values also fills with zero. Sign extension on negative values fills the leftmost bits with one. Shifting with sign extension is equivalent to division but, unfortunately, sign extension is not guaranteed.

Right shift on variables designated as `unsigned` will fill with zeros, because the values cannot be negative, and is always equivalent to division. This is a good reason for using `unsigned` variables — to ensure that shifting pads with zeros. For example, `unsigned char` is commonly used for accessing bytes that are not known to be all positive. The use of `char` without the `unsigned` keyword may cause bytes 128..255 to be treated as negative integers.

Shifting is usually faster than multiplication. Hence, shifts can be used instead of multiplication or division, when the multiplication or division is by a power of 2. However, this conversion is not recommended because it is less readable and because of the dangers with negative numbers mentioned above.

Another danger is that the shift operators have the "wrong" precedence. Their precedence is lower than addition, whereas multiplication has precedence higher than addition. Hence, when replacing:

    x = a + b * 2;

by a shift, it is a common error to write:

    x = a + b << 1;   /* INCORRECT */

in which case, the compiler interprets the expression as:

    x = (a + b) << 1;

which is not equivalent to what was intended. The solution is to use brackets:

    x = a + (b << 1);   /* CORRECT */

The shift operators do not affect their left operand. For example, the statement:

    x << 1;   /* INCORRECT */

doesn't double x — in fact, it does nothing at all. Worse still, errors like this are not usually detected by the compiler. To change x, use the *extended shift operators* given in Table 3.13.

Table 3.13. Extended shift operators

Operator	Meaning
<<=	Shift left
>>=	Shift right

The correct way to multiply a variable by 2, using shifting, is:

```
x <<= 1;          /* CORRECT */
```

3.9 Structure operators

These operators are used to reference elements of a struct or union. The period applies to variables of a structured type (i.e. struct). The pointer dereference operator, ->, applies to pointers to a structured type (struct or union). The syntax is:

```
str.name
ptr->name
```

where str is a variable of struct type, ptr is a pointer to a struct type, and name is a field in the struct. Some examples of the use of these operators are:

```
data = node.value;
data = ptr->value;
ptr  = ptr->next;
```

Note that "p->name" is equivalent to "(*p).name". The -> operator is sometimes referred to as the "right arrow" operator. Further discussion of the structure operators is given in Chapter 5.

3.10 Pointer operators

The two main operators used with pointer variables are given in Table 3.14. The other operator that applies to pointers is the dereferencing, or right-arrow operator, ->, for referencing members of structs pointed to by a pointer variable. This operator was discussed in a previous section.

Table 3.14. Pointer operators

Operator	Meaning
&	Address operator
*	Indirection operator

The address operator (&) is a prefix unary operator that returns the address of its operand. Its operand must be a variable that has an address (i.e. an l-value). Note that bit-fields and register variables are l-values without addresses.

The indirection operator (*) is a prefix unary operator that applies to a pointer. It returns the object to which the pointer was pointing. This is called *dereferencing* a pointer (as is use of the -> operator). Some examples of the use of pointer operators are:

```
ptr = &x;       /* Assign address of x to ptr */
y = *ptr;       /* Use the value that ptr points to */
*ptr = 1;       /* Set the variable that ptr points to */
```

The address and indirection operators are almost the opposite of each other. They are related through the identities shown below. Assume that p is a pointer variable, and that x is not a pointer.

```
&(*p) == p
*(&x) == x
```

It is unfortunate that the symbols for the pointer operators are identical to those for bitwise-and and multiplication. This can be confusing to new programmers, but the compiler has no trouble — context allows them to be distinguished. For more discussion on how to use these operators, refer to Chapter 8.

3.11 Type conversions: the type cast operator

Type conversions are very easy to achieve in C. A type conversion, or type cast, is actually a unary prefix operator. This process of type conversion is called *type casting*. The syntax of a type cast is:

```
(type) expression
```

This will convert the value of the expression to the type in the brackets. Most conversions are possible, though some are not allowed. Conversion from float to int causes a truncation of the non-integer part. Conversion from double to float loses precision. Conversion from long to int, or from int to short, may cause loss of the higher order bits. Some examples of the use of type casting are:

```
y = (int) real_value / 10;      /* Cast to int and divide by 10 */
approx = (int) exact_value;     /* Truncate real to integer */
```

Because of all the automatic type conversions, the need for explicit type casting does not arise very often. In fact, the type cast in the second example above is not actually necessary because a real value is automatically truncated to an int. However, in this case the type cast is good documentation to indicate that the programmer is aware that a truncation is taking place.

Type casting is used with both float and int variables. For example, the code below forces integer division instead of real division by ensuring that both types to the / operator are integer:

```
float a, b;
int y;

y = (int) a / (int) b;         /* Force integer division */
```

Type casting to the null type, `void`, is used to throw away the returned value of a function or an expression. This prevents warnings from `lint` or a strict compiler.

```
(void) fn(x, y);
```

In addition, if the compiler does not support prototyping, type casts are often needed on function arguments to ensure that the correct type is passed. To some extent, the problem is solved by the automatic promotions applied in the absence of a function prototype definition. `char`s and `short`s are promoted to `int`s; `float`s are promoted to `double`s. Note that this explains why all `printf`s numeric options apply only to `int`s and `double`s.

It is important to be aware of the high precedence of type casts, especially when mixing `int`s with `float`s or `double`s. Make sure to place brackets around the expression you wish to be type cast. For example, if x is `int` and a is `double`:

```
x = (int) a / 2;
```

is interpreted as:

```
x = ( (int) (a) ) / 2;
```

which causes integer division to be performed, giving possibly incorrect results due to truncation. The use of brackets can ensure the correct interpretation:

```
x = (int) (a / 2);
```

where real division will be performed, and then the result converted to `int`.

3.12 The sizeof operator

The keyword `sizeof` is used as an operator to calculate the size of types and variables. Its syntax is:

```
sizeof expression
sizeof (type)
```

The `sizeof` operator returns the size of a variable, expression or type. The calculated size is in terms of bytes (characters). Hence, the expression below is always true:

```
sizeof(char) == 1
```

The `sizeof` operator is a prefix unary operator. It can be applied to both types and variables. More generally, the `sizeof` operator can be applied to any type-declarator or any expression. If applied to a type name, or a type-declarator, the type must be enclosed in brackets. When the operand is a variable or expression, brackets around its operand are not strictly necessary, but make it much more readable. For complex expressions, brackets are often necessary because the precedence of the `sizeof` operator is very high.

When applied to an expression, the `sizeof` operator does not evaluate the expression — only its type is used, which is determined at compile-time. Any side effects in the expression will have no effect at run-time.

The `sizeof` operator is quite clever. When applied to an array type, the result is the full size of the array — that is, (usually) the number of elements in the array multiplied by the size of each element. The `sizeof` operator is also aware of problems like structure alignment which make the size of a structure non-obvious (i.e. not necessarily the sum of the sizes of its fields).

Using `sizeof` makes code machine-independent. It is better to use `sizeof` than to assume the size of a type (e.g. assuming an `int` is 4 bytes). An example of the use of `sizeof` is:

```
printf("The size of int is %d bytes\n", sizeof(int));
```

3.13 The ternary operator

C has a special purpose ternary operator (also called the conditional operator or the ternary conditional operator), specified by a question mark and a colon. Unlike other operators, the two symbols are separated. The format of the ternary operator is:

```
condition ? exp1 : exp2
```

If the condition is true (non-zero), the first expression is returned; otherwise the second expression is returned. The "true" case comes first, then the "false" part. The ternary operator acts like an `if-else` statement. Its purpose is to efficiently execute statements such as:

```
if (condition)
    y = exp1;
else
    y = exp2;
```

using the compact notation:

```
y = (condition) ? exp1 : exp2;
```

As well as allowing a compact notation for such `if` statements, it allows them to be considered as a single expression. This is very useful because it allows conditional expressions in arguments to functions, in macros, in `for` loops — anywhere an expression is useful. The examples below show the ternary operator used in expressions:

```
max = (x > y) ? x : y;                      /* maximum */
abs = (x >= 0) ? x : -x;                    /* absolute value */
printf((sex == M) ? "male" : "female");     /* choose string */
```

The return type of the ternary operator depends on its last two operands (the two expressions). If they are the same type, the ternary operator returns that type. If the types of the two operands are different, the type of the result is the highest of these types. The type of the result is known at compile-time and does not depend on whether the first expression is true or false during execution.

3.14 The comma operator

The comma is a special operator in C. It specifies that two expressions be executed in sequence. This may seem useless, as programs always execute in sequence. However, there are some situations where the syntax only allows a single expression (`for` loops are the main example). To perform two actions in the one expression, it is necessary to combine the actions into a single expression using a comma.

The comma in function parameter lists (and other lists) is not an operator. There are two totally distinct uses of commas. The compiler uses context to determine whether the comma is a comma operator, or merely a separator in a list. The syntax for the comma operator is:

```
expression1 , expression2
```

The main example of its use appears in the headers of `for` loops. For example, the `for` loop header below increments `i` and decrements `j` at the same time:

```
for (i = 0, j = n; i < n; i++, j--)    /* Change both i and j */
```

Note that the above example does not use the return value of the comma operator and this is quite typical. Nevertheless, the comma operator does return a result — the value of the second operand. The type of the result is the same as the second operand. It is possible to place any number of expressions in sequence:

```
expression1 , expression2 , ..., expressionN
```

in which case the value and type of the result is that of the last operand.

3.15 The array reference operator

The special notation for using arrays is actually a strange kind of binary operator. The square brackets are a postfix operator denoting array reference. The form of the array reference operator is:

```
exp1[exp2]
```

In its most common usage, the `exp1` must be an array or pointer variable and `exp2` is an integral expression. However, because of the algebraic identity discussed in Section 8.8, `exp1[exp2]` is equivalent to `exp2[exp1]`. Hence, one of the operands must be an array or pointer type, and the other an integral type. Note that the more general form is rarely ever used.

For most situations in programming there is no need to consider the square brackets as an operator. However, there are some situations where the *precedence* of the square brackets is important. Consider the expression below:

```
++arr[i];
```

Does the ++ operator apply to the array variable or the array element? Operator precedence answers the question — the square brackets have higher precedence than ++, causing the square brackets to be evaluated first and the ++ operator applies to the array element.

3.16 The function call operator

The notation for function calls is also a postfix binary operator. Generally speaking, there is no need to think of function calls as an operator, but it is important when declaring variables of the type: pointer to function. This section is very advanced and should be skipped unless you need to declare pointers to functions.

Brackets can be a little confusing. Brackets can be used normally, around an expression to enforce operator precedence (i.e. to evaluate the correct sub-expressions). Brackets, with a type name inside them, in front of an expression, cause a type conversion. In addition to these two uses, brackets after an expression are a unary postfix operator indicating a function call. The distinction between the three can be made as follows:

Type conversions — brackets *before* the expression
Normal bracketing — brackets *around* the expression
Function calls — brackets *after* the expression.

The syntax for the function call operator is:

```
expression ( argument_list )
```

For ordinary function calls, the "expression" is simply the name of the function being called. For more complicated uses, expression can be a pointer to a function, or any expression that produces a pointer to a function.

Inside the brackets is a comma-separated list of expressions. These are the arguments sent to the function call. The comma here is a list separator, not the comma operator. Some examples of the function call operator are:

```
swap(x, y);
fp(a, b, c);    /* fp is a pointer to a function */
```

3.17 Operator precedence

Precedence is the mechanism specifying the order in which to evaluate parts of an expression when there are no brackets to ensure a particular order. As an example, does a+b*c mean (a+b)*c or a+(b*c)? The rule that determines this is that the operator with higher precedence is evaluated first. For this example, multiplication (*) has higher precedence than addition (+), so the meaning is: a+(b*c).

When deciding between pairs of operators on the same precedence level (e.g. the same operator) their *associativity* is used to determine which to evaluate first. For example, when performing two additions they are carried out left-to-right because the + operator has left-to-right associativity. Associativity is discussed in the next section.

There are many different precedence levels for C operators. Unary operators always have precedence over binary operators. A way to remember the precedence of the most common binary operators is:

logical < *relational* < *arithmetic*

This has the consequence that the most common type of condition does not require brackets. For example, the condition:

```
x > 1 && y < i + 1
```

tests if `x` is greater than 1 *and* `y` is less than `i+1`. Because of the operator precedence, the condition evaluates as if bracketed as follows:

```
(x > 1) && (y < (i + 1))
```

A more detailed version of the precedence hierarchy is:

assignment < logical < bitwise < relational < shift < arithmetic

The complete operator precedence list is given in Table 3.15.

Table 3.15. Operator precedence

Operator	Precedence
() [] -> .	highest precedence
! - + ++ -- ~ * & (type) sizeof	
* / %	
+ -	
<< >>	
< <= > >=	
== !=	
&	
^	
|	
&&	
||	
?:	
= += -= *= /= %= &= |= <<= >>=	
,	lowest precedence

3.18 Associativity

Associativity is used to determine the order to evaluate expressions when the rules of precedence cannot determine the order. This happens when two operators are the same, or the two operators are at the same precedence level. For example, what is the evaluation order in the following examples?

```
a + b + c
a + b - c
a * b / c
x = y = 0
&x++
*ptr++
```

For most binary operators, the evaluation is from left-to-right, as expected. The first three examples become:

```
(a + b) + c
(a + b) - c
(a * b) / c
```

For the assignment operators (normal assignment and extended assignment), the evaluation is from right-to-left. The above example becomes:

```
x = (y = 0)
```

which allows "x=y=0" to set two variables to zero.

For unary operators, the evaluation is from right-to-left. The examples become:

```
&(x++)
*(ptr++)
```

The first is illegal because & requires an l-value and ++ does not produce one. The second accesses where ptr is pointing to using the * dereferencing operator, and increments ptr after this dereference.

The array reference operator, [], and the function call operator, (), have left-to-right associativity. However, because of the form of the operators on the same precedence level, their associativity is mostly unimportant.

The ternary operator has right-to-left associativity. This is only relevant when it is nested inside itself.

The comma operator, logical operators and relational operators all have left-to-right associativity. Hence, a good general rule is: *all non-assignment binary operators have left-to-right associativity.*

Table 3.16 summarizes the associativity of C's operators.

Table 3.16. Associativity of operators

Operators	Associativity
Assignment operators	Right-to-left
Other binary operators	Left-to-right
Unary operators	Right-to-left
Ternary operator	Right-to-left

3.19 Order of evaluation problems

In C, the order of the evaluation of *operands* for most binary operators is not specified. This makes it possible for compilers to apply very good optimizing algorithms to the code. Unfortunately, it also leads to some problems that the programmer must be aware of.

Order of evaluation of *operands* is a different concept to order of evaluation of *operators*. The evaluation of operators is completely specified by brackets, operator precedence and associativity, but evaluation of operands is not. To see the effect of order of evaluation of operands, consider the expression:

(a + b) * (c + d)

Which is to be evaluated first: (a+b) or (c+d)? Neither bracketing, precedence nor associativity decide this order. Bracketing specifies that both additions must be evaluated before the multiplication, not which addition is evaluated first. Associativity does not apply, because the two + operators are not near one another (they are separated by a * operator). Precedence does not apply because the brackets override it.

The order of evaluation depends only upon how the compiler chooses to evaluate the operands of the * operator. Intuitively, we would assume that the evaluation would take place left-to-right. However, the order of evaluation of the operands to the multiplication operator, and most other binary operators, is not specified in C. Different compilers may choose different orderings.

Usually the order does not matter. In the example above, it does not matter which addition is done first. The two additions are independent, and can be executed in any order. However, if an expression involves side effects, the result is sometimes undefined. The result may be as intended, or it may be incorrect. Sometimes it will be correct when compiled without optimization, but incorrect after optimization. Results may differ on different machines and the code is not portable.

A *side effect* is an operation that affects a variable being used in the expression or affects some external variable used indirectly in the expression. The most common example of a side effect is the increment or decrement operator. Any assignment operation deep inside an expression is also a side effect to the variable it changes. A function call can also be a side effect if it modifies a variable used in the expression (either as a parameter, or globally), modifies some other external variable on which another sub-expression depends (i.e. a global or local `static` variable) or if it produces output or accepts input. The full list of side effects is given in Table 3.17.

Table 3.17. Side effects

Operation	*Meaning*
++	Decrement
--	Increment
=, +=, etc.	Assignment operators
fn()	Function call (some kinds)

To see the effect of side effects, consider the increment operator in the expression below. It is a dangerous side effect.

y = (x++) + (x * 2);

Because the order of evaluation of the addition operator is not specified, there are two orders in which the expression could actually be executed. The programmer's intended order is:

```
temp = x++;
y = (temp) + (x * 2);
```

and the incorrect order is:

```
temp = x * 2;
y = (x++) + (temp);
```

In the first case, the increment occurs before x*2 is evaluated. In the second, the increment occurs after x*2 has been evaluated. Obviously, the two interpretations give different results.

If there are two function calls in the one expression, the order of the function calls can be important. For example, in the code below:

```
f() + g()
```

if both functions produce output or both modify the same global variable, the result of the expression may depend on the order of evaluation of the + operator (which is undefined).

Most binary operators have unspecified order of evaluation — even the assignment operators. A simple assignment statement can be the cause of an error. Consider the example:

```
a[i] = i++;
```

This has two interpretations. Is the array subscript the old or new value of i? It isn't clear whether a[i] or a[i+1] will be assigned the value.

Another form of the order of evaluation problem occurs because the order of the evaluation of arguments to a function is not specified in C. It is not necessarily left-to-right. For example, consider the function call:

```
y = fn(a++, a)
```

Which argument is evaluated first? Is the second argument the new or old value of a?

3.19.1 Safe and unsafe operators

There is no order of evaluation problem with *unary operators* as they have only one operand to evaluate. The *structure operators* also give no problem as only one of the operands can be evaluated (the first). The second operand is a field name which needs no evaluation — it is not an expression. The *comma operator* is also a completely safe operator. Its specified order for evaluation of operands is left-to-right. Furthermore, it always evaluates both its operands.

The *logical operators*, && and ||, are almost safe. Their specified order of evaluation is left-to-right. However, it is possible to *not evaluate* some operands. Depending on the value of the first expression, any side effect in the second expression can occur once or not occur at all. This occurs due to the *short-circuiting* of logical operators.

Short-circuiting refers to the fact that when evaluating expressions involving the logical operators (&& and ||), the expression is only evaluated up to what is necessary to determine the result of the expression (i.e. true or false). If the first operand of the && is false or the first operand of the || is true, the second operand is not evaluated. Consider the example:

```
    if (x == 0 && y == z++)
        ...
```

If x equals zero, the second expression is evaluated and z is incremented. However, if x is non-zero, short-circuiting prevents the evaluation of the second operand and z is not incremented. Note that there is no problem if only the first expression contains side effects, as all the side effects will be executed exactly once, and will be executed before the second expression is evaluated.

The *ternary operator* (?:) has its order of evaluation fully specified: evaluate first operand, if true then evaluate second else evaluate third. Hence the order of evaluation is fixed, but, as with the binary logical operators, whether each operand is actually evaluated is not fixed. There is a problem when the second or third expression involves side effects. Depending on the value of the first expression, the side effect can occur once or not occur at all. As with the logical operators, side effects in the first expression pose no problem.

The *ordinary binary operators* are completely unsafe. This includes the arithmetic, relational, bitwise, shift, assignment and extended assignment operators. The order of evaluation of their operands is not specified at all.

3.19.2 Sequence points

UNIX programmers have a partial solution to order of evaluation problems: `lint`. The `lint` utility will find many order of evaluation ambiguities: it will find those involving increment, but will not find those involving function calls. A more complete solution is still required.

No amount of brackets can be a solution. Brackets do not affect the order of evaluation of operands. They only affect the order of evaluation of operators (i.e. they only change the precedence and associativity).

An extreme solution follows the motto: if there are no side effects, there is no problem. With this aim, the code is written so that increment and decrement operations are done in separate statements (i.e. different lines). Assignments are not placed in the middle of expressions. Function calls that may cause dangerous side effects are also separated out to separate lines.

A less extreme solution is to separate any *dangerous* side effects. Some side effects are no problem. For example, if a variable with a side effect appears only once in an expression, it is not a problem. Only dangerous side effects need be separated out, and side effects that are not dangerous are left alone. To separate side effects, temporary variables may be necessary to hold values of sub-expressions.

The concept of *sequence points* is useful in determining how to break up an expression into sub-expressions. Sequence points are points in the program where it is guaranteed that all side effects in the code so far have taken place. The main example of a sequence point is the semicolon terminating a statement. Once the whole expression has been evaluated, all side effects will have occurred. Other examples of sequence points are after the first operand of the comma operator, ternary operator or a binary logical operator, and also at the (only) operand of a unary plus operator. The sequence points are summarized in Table 3.18.

Table 3.18. Sequence points

Token	Meaning
;	End of a statement
||	Logical-or operator
&&	Logical-and operator
,	Comma operator
?:	Ternary operator

When writing code, try to satisfy the following condition: between successive sequence points, any variable with a side effect is referenced only once. Simply put, if a variable has a side effect in a statement, ensure that the variable occurs only once in that statement. If such a variable does occur twice, the sub-expression causing the side effect should be separated out. If a variable has no side effect in a statement, it may occur any number of times in the statement.

3.20 Exercises

1. Give an example of a binary operator from the relational, logical and arithmetic operators. Is there a unary relational operator? Which operators are unary and which are binary? What is the order of precedence of these three types of operators?

2. What type do the relational and logical operators return? What possible values can they return?

3. Write a program to read in an integer and output whether it is odd or even. *Hint:* Examine the remainder when divided by 2 using the % operator. Alternatively, examine the lowest bit using the bitwise-and operator, &.

4. A prime number is one which is divisible only by 1 and itself. Write a program to read in a number and output whether it is prime or not. *Hint:* An easy test for divisibility is to examine the remainder from the % operator.

5. How is it possible to abbreviate the assignment statement below? What advantage other than conciseness does this give?

    ```
    sum = sum + i;
    ```

6. What is wrong with the assignment statement below to calculate the average of two numbers?

    ```
    average = a + b / 2;
    ```

7. Write a program to print out the size, in bytes, of all of the basic types — int, char, short, long, float, double. Declare an array variable and print out its size.

8. What is the difference between the two uses of ++ below?

    ```
    i++;
    ++i;
    ```

    What is the output of the program fragment below? Incorporate these lines into a small program to check your answer.

    ```
    int x = 1, y = 0;

    y = x--;
    printf("x = %d, y = %d\n", x, y);
    ```

9. What is wrong with the `if` statement below? Under what circumstances will a problem occur?

    ```
    if (x < y && ++i < j)
    ```

10. Write a program to ask the user for his/her income in whole dollars and output the tax that should be paid. Assume that the first 5000 dollars are tax-free, the next 20000 dollars are taxed at 25% and any excess is taxed at 50%. Note that the amount of tax to be paid may not be whole dollars.

11. (advanced) Write a program to print out the binary representation of an integer input by the user. *Hint:* Each binary digit can be accessed using bitwise-and with a mask generated by shifting a 1 into the correct position using the left shift operator.

Chapter 4
Control statements

This chapter deals with the elements of the C language that allow the programmer to choose which statements are executed in what order. The most obvious idea is that statements placed one after the other are executed in sequence. There is the `if` statement to select between two sequences of statements, and the `switch` statement to select between a number of sequences of statements. There are three types of loops which allow repetition of statements: `for` loops, `while` loops and `do` loops.

In addition to these basic constructs, there is the `break` statement to skip prematurely out of a loop and the `continue` statement to skip part of an iteration of a loop. The `goto` statement can be used to jump anywhere within a function, and the standard library functions `longjmp` and `setjmp` can be used to jump between functions. There is also the `exit` library function call to exit the program prematurely. There is also the `return` statement to exit from a function, but this is discussed in Chapter 7.

4.1 Statements and blocks

In their simplest form, statements are merely single lines in a program *terminated by a semicolon*. Examples of simple statements include assignment statements and function calls. A statement can span multiple lines (e.g. if it gets too long). There can also be more than one statement per line. Some example statements are:

```
x = y + z;
printf("Hi There\n");
x = 2;   y = 3;              /* Two statements on one line */
```

Sequences of statements can be grouped as a single statement if they are placed inside braces (i.e. "curly brackets", { and }). Groups of statements inside braces are called *blocks* (or compound statements). Blocks are used everywhere in C (as with other structured languages). Loops operate on blocks. The body of a function is a block. An example of a block is shown below:

```
{                   /* A block containing two statements */
x = y + z;
printf("Hi There\n");
}
```

Although a block is like a single statement, there is no need for a semicolon after the closing right brace of a block. In fact, a semicolon after a right brace can be a syntax error (e.g. before an `else`).

4.2 The if statement

The usual form of selection statement, the `if` statement, is supported by C. Its syntax is:

```
if (condition)
    statement
```

The `if` condition (the expression inside the brackets) is considered true if it is non-zero, false if zero (this is true of all conditional expressions in C).

The statement of the `if` may be a single statement or a block. The first example shows a single statement:

```
if (x > y)
    max = x;
```

The second example shows a block used as the body of the `if` statement:

```
if (i >= 0) {
    printf(" i>=0 \n");
    i--;
}
```

The first form is correct, but not as common. If the statement to be executed is a single statement, as in the examples above, it is good practice to place it in braces anyway, until you are fluent in C. It is not necessary — just a safety net to prevent bugs.

4.2.1 The else clause

The use of the `else` keyword adds another clause to the `if` construct and specifies the statements to be executed if the condition is *false*. The syntax is:

```
if (condition)
    statement
else
    statement
```

The `else` clause is used to decide between two alternative statements or sequences of statements. For example, the `if-else` statement below calculates the maximum of a and b:

```
if (a > b)
    max = a;
else
    max = b;
```

Note that a semicolon is required after max=a before the else keyword, because a single statement is used. If the if-part of the statement is a block, there cannot be a semicolon before the else. There is either a semicolon or a right-brace before an else, but not both. The example below shows the correct placement of semicolons:

```
if (x == 0) {
    printf("Error: x is zero\n");
    y = 0;
}                       /* No semicolon here */
else {
    y = 1000 / x;
    printf("y= %d\n", y);
}
```

4.2.2 The if-if-else ambiguity

There is a well-known "problem" with the if-if-else construct that causes confusion to new programmers. The problem appears in statements where an if statement is nested inside another if statement, as below:

```
if (x == 0)
    if (y == 0)
        statement1;
    else
        statement2;
```

Which if does the else belong to? The indentation here shows the correct correspondence. However, the compiler does not examine indentation (it ignores whitespace). The compiler matches each else with the "closest" if (i.e. the first if before the else). In this example, the indentation (what the programmer wanted) and the compiler's interpretation are the same:

```
if (x == 0) {
    if (y == 0)
        statement1;             /* y == 0 */
    else
        statement2;             /* y != 0 */
}
```

Under most conditions, the closest-if rule is not too confusing. But, for safety it is often better to place braces around if statements. This is especially true if the first statement in the if statement is a major control flow statement such as another if statement or a loop.

4.3 The while loop

A while loop is used to execute a sequence of statements a number of times. The syntax is:

```
while (condition)
    statement
```

The brackets are necessary around the condition. The statement may be a single statement or a block.

The statement or block is repeatedly executed *while* the condition is true. The condition is tested the first time, and then re-tested at the start of each new iteration. The example below prints out the numbers from 1 to 10, by initializing `i` to 1 before the loop and incrementing `i` within the loop.

```
i = 1;
while (i <= 10) {
    printf("%d ", i);
    i++;
}
```

The body of a `while` loop is not necessarily executed at all. If the condition is false to start with, the loop is not executed — it is simply skipped over. A `while` loop is used when you wish a block to be executed zero or more times.

4.4 The for loop

In other languages, `for` loops are a particular type of loop. For example, in Pascal, `for` loops increment an integer variable through a fixed range. In C, a `for` loop is an extension of the `while` loop. Its syntax is:

```
for (expression1; expression2; expression3)
    statement
```

The above `for` loop is equivalent to the `while` loop:

```
expression1;
while (expression2) {
    statement
    expression3;
}
```

The first expression is usually used to initialize variables before the loop. The second is the condition that must be true for the loop to continue execution. The third is used to move onto the next iteration (often incrementing a counter).

Most commonly, `for` loops are used to count an integer over a fixed range. The method of using a `for` loop to count from 1 to n is shown below:

```
for (i = 1; i <= n; i++)         /* Count 1 to n */
    ...
```

This is equivalent to:

```
i = 1;
while (i <= n) {
    ...
    i++;
}
```

The equivalence with `while` loops is exact in all instances of `for` loops (except for a minor difference involving the `continue` statement). The choice between `for` loops and `while` loops is one of style. It is possible to use either in most cases. The purpose of the `for` loop was to group the actions of initialization and increment. Hence, `for` loops are used when there are simple actions at the end of each iteration (such as incrementing a variable).

One or more of the three expressions can be empty. If the first or third expression is empty, no initialization or increment is carried out. If the second expression is empty, an infinite loop is specified. In fact, having all three expressions empty is the usual form of an infinite loop. Some examples of `for` loop headers with missing fields are:

```
for (; n >= 0; n--)        /* No Initialization */
for (i = 0; i <= 100; )    /* No Increment */
for (;;)                   /* Infinite Loop */
```

4.4.1 The comma operator in for loops

The comma operator finds its main use in `for` loops. It is an operator that causes sequential evaluation of its arguments. In this way, it is almost like a semicolon (though the semicolon is not an operator). The comma combines its two operands into a single expression. Syntactically, the `for` loop can only have one expression in each of its three places. The comma operator makes it possible to do more than one thing at the start of the `for` loop, and after each iteration (i.e. the first and third expressions). Semicolons separate the three expressions and commas separate the actions in each expression. The example below increments i and decrements j:

```
for (i = 0, j = 1; i < n; i++, j++)    /* i=0..n-1; j=1..n */
    ...
```

Because the `for` loop is so flexible, it can be used for many things. It is not restricted to counting an integer, as the following `for` loops show:

```
                /* Traverse linked list */
for (ptr = head; ptr != NULL; ptr = ptr->next)
    ...
                /* Traverse linked list with trailing pointer */
for (prev = NULL, ptr = head; ptr != NULL;
            prev = ptr, ptr = ptr->next)
    ...
```

The comma operator makes it possible to write the most cryptic code, by allowing the user to do many things at once inside the `for` loop header. It should be used sparingly.

4.5 The do loop

C's form of post-tested loop is called the `do` loop (also called the `do-while` loop). The syntax of a `do` loop is:

```
do
    statement
while (expression);
```

However, it is rare that a loop has only one statement and the most common form is:

```
do {
    statements
} while (expression);
```

The do loop is slightly different to the while loop in that the condition is not tested before the first iteration. Because the condition is not tested initially, a do loop is always executed the first time. Thus a do loop is used when a block must be executed at least once. A good example of such a situation is waiting for user input:

```
do {
    scanf("%d", &x);        /* Get an integer from user */
    if (x < 0) {
        printf("\n Incorrect. Enter a positive integer:");
    }
} while (x < 0);            /* while input is invalid */
```

The do loop is not used as often as for or while loops. This is not because of any major flaw. Experience has shown that programmers tend to use loops with the condition tested at the top of the loop (i.e. while loops and for loops).

4.6 Local variables inside loop blocks

It is legal in C to declare variables after any left brace. This is useful in loops to declare variables closer to their use. As functions become larger, it becomes annoying to declare all variables at the top of a function. In the example below, j is declared as a variable local to the loop body of a for loop. The variable j can only be referenced within the loop body and will be undefined after the for loop.

```
for (i = 1; i <= 10; i++) {
    int x;                  /* Local variables */
    int j;

    x = 0;
    j = i * 2;
    ...
}
```

Note that variables can be declared inside any block at all, not just loop blocks.

The C language permits these local variables to be initialized. The syntax for initializations inside blocks is identical to that for initializations of local variables at the top of functions. The most important consideration is that initializations inside loops are carried out at the start of *each iteration*. They are identical to assignment statements at the start of the loop. It is possible to initialize a variable to any expression, not necessarily a constant expression (even one involving the iteration variable). For example, the for loop below has identical effect to the loop above:

```
for (i = 1; i <= n; i++) {
    int x = 0, j = i * 2;
    ...
}
```

4.7 The break statement

The break statement is used to exit from within loops and switch statements. The break statement always exits from the innermost loop or switch. Its syntax is:

```
break;
```

The break statement is most often used in switch statements to prevent "falling through" of cases in a switch statement. Usually every case ends with a break statement. This use of break with switch is discussed in a later section.

Inside a loop, break causes termination of the loop. Control is transferred to immediately after the loop. This is a form of unnatural exiting, as it exits from inside the loop, rather than at the end of the loop. It bypasses the normal loop condition.

4.8 The continue statement

The continue statement is used to skip part of an iteration of a loop. It begins the next iteration without completing the current iteration. It causes the condition to be tested again to determine whether or not to perform another iteration of the loop. Its syntax is:

```
continue;
```

The continue statement applies to all three types of loops, but not to switch, and always applies to the inner loop. When a continue statement occurs inside a for loop, the third expression is executed before the condition is retested. This allows the for loop to perform any operation to prepare for the next iteration. An example of the use of continue is given below:

```
for (i = 1; i <= 100; i++) {
    if (is_prime(i))
        continue;              /* skip all prime numbers */
    ...    /* rest of loop */
}
```

4.9 Infinite loops

Sometimes it is useful to use an infinite loop and these can be specified many ways. The two most common are:

```
        while (1)            for (;;)
```

The constant 1 is always true and hence the while loop will iterate forever. An empty for loop expression is true in C. When for loops are used as infinite loops the second expression must be empty (or 1), but the other two expressions can still be used.

The break statement can be used to exit from an infinite loop. Infinite loops inside functions can also be exited by leaving the function using the return statement, or leaving the whole program using a call to the exit library function.

4.10 Empty statements and empty loops

The empty statement, or null statement, is also a statement. The empty statement is just a semicolon by itself, or two braces with no other statements inside (i.e. { }). It performs no action, and finds its main use in empty loops.

An empty loop is simply an empty statement used as a loop body. Sometimes it is useful to do all the work inside a header of a `while` or a `for` loop, leaving the body of the loop empty. This is especially true of `for` loops, which are extremely flexible. This practice can make compact and efficient code, sometimes at the expense of readability. Some examples of empty loops are:

```
for (i = 0; i < n; printf("%d ", a[i++]))   /* Print an array */
    ;       /* empty loop */

while (!button_down())                       /* Wait for button press */
    ;       /* empty loop */
```

Unfortunately, the use of the semicolon does create one problem. Always be careful not to place semicolons after the header of a `for` loop (or after any form of control statement). This is quite a common error, accidentally creating an empty loop. It causes the `for` loop to be interpreted as an empty loop. The block after the `for` loop is executed only once (when the empty `for` loop has completed). For example:

```
for (i = 1; i <= n; i++);      /* INCORRECT */
    printf("%d ");              /* print out i */
```

is actually interpreted as:

```
for (i = 1; i <= n; i++)        /* count 1 to n doing nothing */
    ;       /* empty loop */
printf("%d ", i);               /* print out n+1 */
```

4.11 The switch statement

This construct is used to choose between a number of options, when the choice is based on a single integer or `char` value. The syntax is:

```
switch (expression) {
    case const_expr:    statements
    case const_expr:    statements
    case const_expr:    statements
    ...
    default :   statements
}
```

The expression of the `switch` can be any expression but its type must be an integral type: an `int`, `char`, or enumerated type. The constant expressions for each `case` should be the same type as the `switch` expression.

Each `case` can be an arbitrary constant expression. It must be constant so that the compiler can evaluate the expression at compile-time.

The `default` keyword indicates a special type of `case`. The `default` clause is executed if the value of the `switch` matches none of the constant expressions. It is optional and no default actions occur if it is left out. It is not a run-time error if there is no `default` clause and no `case` expression matches the value.

There may be as many `cases` as necessary, but all must have distinct values. The `cases` may be placed in any order, and `default` need not be the last (though this is most common). The only effect of the order of `cases` is on falling through (which is rarely used). A good example of the use of a `switch` statement is in the action to be executed based on a menu choice by the user. The `switch` statement below assumes that the user has input an integer indicating which action to take:

```
switch (choice) {    /* Choose operation based on menu choice */
    case 1:
        load();
        break;

    case 2:
        save();
        break;

    case 3:
        print();
        break;

    default:
        printf("Unknown menu choice\n");
        break;
}
```

Statements in a `case` need not be placed in a block (i.e. in braces). Syntactically, `case` and `default` are like labels, and there can be a sequence of statements after each `case`. Only those surrounding the entire `switch` statement are strictly necessary. Whether to include extra braces is a matter of style.

4.11.1 Multiple cases

Multiple `cases` are written as two `cases` one after the other. There must be colons after both `case` labels. However, no semicolon is necessary after the first colon (i.e. the empty case):

```
case 1:       /* Nothing */
case 2:
    ...   /* statements for 1 and 2 */
```

Another common style is to place both `case` labels on the one line:

```
case 1:   case 2:
    ...           /* statements for 1 and 2 */
```

The Pascal-like syntax shown below is not allowed, and produces a compilation warning on most compilers.

```
case 1, 2:       /* ILLEGAL */
```

4.11.2 Falling through and the break statement

Programmers new to C may get trapped into believing that a switch statement only executes one of the cases. This is not strictly true. However, most programs written in C are written to ensure that only one case is ever executed. To ensure this, the programmer must explicitly code a break statement at the end of each case.

Execution of a switch proceeds by evaluation of the switch expression, and then a branch to a particular case (or the default). From this case, the statements are executed, then the statements from the next case, and then the next. This is called *falling through*.

Falling through is most commonly prevented using the break statement. Placing a "break;" at the end of each case prevents falling through to the next. The break statement causes execution to transfer to directly after the end of the switch statement.

One way to understand falling through is to think of the cases as being a special type of label, and the switch statement just being a multi-way goto. When finishing one case, the next case label is just ignored. To exit the switch (and prevent falling through further) it is necessary to use break.

Falling through cases is one of the problems with C. It is hardly ever used, and one of the most common bugs is to accidentally leave out a break and allow falling through to occur. One method of prevention is to use a template for a switch statement, with breaks already inserted. This template is copied into your work file whenever adding a new switch statement. It is much safer (and quicker) than typing everything out again. Remember, one missing break is all it takes.

A break statement is not necessary in the last case of a switch, but is good practice. If you later add another case and forget to add the break in the case above, then the case will execute its code *and* the code for the new case.

4.12 Immediate program termination: exit, abort

The exit library function causes immediate termination of the whole program. It accepts a single integer argument and returns this value to the operating system or the calling program (i.e. to the program that is running your program).

```
exit(1);            /* Terminate with error */
exit(0);            /* Terminate successfully */
```

Under UNIX, this returned value can be used (in sophisticated programs) to indicate success or failure of your program (e.g. the value is used by the operating system shell). A returned value of zero means successful termination (no errors). Any non-zero value means failure, with the value indicating which type of error. It is the responsibility of the calling program to interpret this error number.

The return value is irrelevant unless your program is to be used as a software tool, and the issue can be ignored in most programs. The best policy is to always use exit(0). Returning a value using exit is identical to returning a value using a return statement in main.

The abort function is similar to exit in that it causes immediate termination of the program. However, unlike exit, it causes a core dump under UNIX and prints an error message under DOS. Technically speaking, the effect of `abort` is identical to that of sending a particular signal, `SIGABRT`, to the program. This signal causes the program to terminate with a core dump.

The `exit` library function causes a much cleaner termination than `abort`. For example, `exit` closes all open files. Hence, `exit` is much preferred to `abort` unless a core dump is needed under UNIX (e.g. to invoke a symbolic debugger), or the error message produced by `abort` is desired.

4.13 The goto statement and labels

The `goto` statement can be used to jump to any location in a function, with the restriction that `goto` cannot jump between different functions. The use of `goto` can always be avoided, and is almost always bad style. Novice C programmers should never use `goto`. However, there are rare situations when it can be useful and appropriate. The `goto` statement is sometimes used to leave deeply nested loops or to collect common code together (such as a "cleanup" code sequence prior to returning from a function). In such places `goto`s can be efficient and intuitive, though the point is a controversial one.

Despite the arguments against it, `goto` is supported in C. To use it you place a label before a statement and `goto` that label. Labels are identifiers followed by a colon, and not numbers as in some other languages. The syntax is:

```
goto label_name;
label_name:   statement
```

The `goto` statement can only be used to jump within the current function. It is not possible to jump from one function to another using `goto`. Hence, labels have scope local to the function in which they are placed. Labels do not need to be declared before use (though they must be declared in the same function). An example of the use of `goto` is shown below:

```
again:   scanf("%d", &x);
         if (x < 0) {
                printf("Enter a positive number: \n");
                goto again;
         }
```

There are no restrictions on where you can `goto` inside a function. For example, it is possible to `goto` the middle of a loop from outside, although this bypasses all initializations of local variables in the loop body and these variables may contain garbage values.

A label must precede a statement. A right brace is not a statement. For this reason, it is necessary to place a semicolon after the label and colon if the label is at the end of a function or loop (i.e. before a right brace). Remember that a lone semicolon is a statement — an empty statement.

```
goto end;
...
end: ;              /* Empty statement required */
}
```

4.14 Long branching: <setjmp.h>

It is not possible to jump between functions using goto. However, it is possible to jump between different functions in a limited way using special standard library functions declared in the standard header file <setjmp.h>. Long branching is typically used for immediately leaving a function to return to the main function (or another higher level function) without returning to all the intermediate functions. The main limitation of this form of long branching is that there can only be one destination at a time (i.e. the most recently executed setjmp function), although this destination can be reached from a number of places (i.e. different longjmp calls). The use of long branching can be a convenient method of handling exceptions, such as running out of memory. For most other purposes the use of these functions is not recommended because they can be even worse than goto.

To use these functions, you must include <setjmp.h>. This header, among other things, defines the type jmp_buf. The two functions used are:

```
int setjmp(jmp_buf env)
int longjmp(jmp_buf env, int val)
```

The setjmp function must be called to set up the place to branch to. Long branching with longjmp will return to the place where setjmp is called. A call to longjmp will not branch to a setjmp function unless that function has been called already.

When setjmp is called normally, it will return zero. When longjmp is executed, program execution transfers to just after the setjmp call, as if setjmp had just returned, this time with a non-zero return value from setjmp (set by the val parameter to longjmp). Standard C code for setting up a long branch is:

```
#include <setjmp.h>
jmp_buf env;              /* Declare global variable */

if (setjmp(env) != 0) {
    ...                   /* Exception handler here */
                          /* Program has longjmp'd to here */
}
else
    ...                   /* normal start of program */
```

Later in the program longjmp can be called to return to the location of the setjmp. All calls to the longjmp function must have access to the global variable env, as defined for the code above.

```
if (error)
    longjmp(env, 1);
```

The setjmp function initially saves the environment in the global variable, conventionally called env. Since longjmp must restore the same environment it needs to use the same global variable. The parameter, val, passed to longjmp sets the value returned by setjmp after a longjmp call, and must be non-zero. It can be used to indicate what type of exception occurred. The above code would need to be modified to retain the value returned by setjmp:

```
if ((temp = setjmp(...)) != 0) {
    ...                     /* type of exception held in temp */
}
else
    ...                     /* Normal program start */
```

In fact, the ANSI standard disallows the assignment of the return value from `setjmp` to a variable, but the above code will work in most implementations.

The call to `setjmp` should be inside the `main` function, or, at least, higher in the function call hierarchy than any `longjmp` call. Values of global variables are as they were when `longjmp` was called. An important restriction is that the exception handler cannot rely on any values of local variables.

4.15 Exercises

1. Why are the braces necessary in the `if` statement below? What happens if they are left out?

    ```
    if (x > y) {
        temp = x;           /* Swap x and y */
        x = y;
        y = temp;
    }
    ```

2. What is wrong with the program fragment below? Examine the behavior of the code by using it in a small program. Fix the error and explain what caused the incorrect behavior.

    ```
    scanf("%d", &x);
    if (x = 0)
        printf("Error: You cannot enter zero\n");
    else
        printf("1/x = %f", 1.0 / x);
    ```

3. Write a program that asks the user for three integers and then prints out the maximum. *Hint:* The calculation of the maximum should be a number of `if` statements (two is enough).

4. Write a program that calculates the sum of a list of integers entered by the user. The program should first prompt the user for how many integers are in the list, and then prompt the user for exactly that many integers. *Hint:* Use a `for` loop.

5. Modify the previous program so that the user is not asked how many integers are in the list, but enters −1 when the end of the list is reached. *Hint:* Use a `while` loop. Why is a `while` loop more natural than a `for` loop?

6. What is the main difference between the `do` loop and the `while` loop? Is the `for` loop like the `while` loop or like the `do` loop?

7. Write a program that uses an infinite loop to continually print a message onto the screen. How do you stop the program running forever? *Hint:* On many systems the two keys *control* and *c* will interrupt execution.

8. What is the advantage of declaring variables after the left brace of a loop block? If these variables are declared with an initialization, when is this initialization performed?

9. Modify the while loop below so that it doesn't use the break statement. It is easiest to modify the code to use a do loop. Why is this?

```
while (1) {                    /* Infinite loop */
    scanf("%d", &x);
    if (x < 0)
        break;                 /* exit while loop */
}
```

10. What is the error in the switch statement below? Fix the error and incorporate the switch statement into a small program that asks the user for a grade and outputs a response.

```
switch (ch) {
    case 'A':
        printf("Excellent\n");
    case 'B':
        printf("Good\n");
    case 'C':
        printf("Satisfactory\n");
    default:
        printf("Unsatisfactory\n");
}
```

Chapter 5
Structured types

Structures are groups of smaller elements stored together as a single item, and referenced via a single variable. They correspond to "records" in some languages, such as Pascal. Structures are used to store related data together so as to be conveniently used as a group. For example, when implementing a mailing list it is convenient to store people's names and addresses together. Structured variables are defined in C using the keyword: `struct`. An example of a `struct` declaration is given below:

```
struct  employee {
    char    name[10];
    int     salary;
};
```

This example declares a structured type "`struct employee`", which contains two members: `name` and `salary`. The first member is a string and the second is an integer.

The identifier `employee` is called a *tag name* for the structure. There are three types in C that require the use of a tag name: structures, unions and enumerated types. In all cases, the tag name must be used in combination with the keyword `struct`, `union` or `enum`.

The declaration above declares a new type, but does not define any variables of this type. Variables of this type can be defined using:

```
struct employee x, y;
```

Note that the `struct` keyword is necessary and "`employee x, y;`" would be incorrect. This declaration must appear after the `struct` type declaration as given above.

The two declarations given above can be combined into a single declaration. The declaration below serves two purposes: it declares "`struct employee`" as a type, and defines variables `x` and `y` as that type.

```
struct   employee {
    char      name[10];
    int       salary;
} x, y;
```

Note that if the variables x and y are the only variables that need to be defined of this type, the tag name employee can be left out. The declaration becomes:

```
struct   {                      /* employee left out */
    char      name[10];
    int       salary;
} x, y;
```

5.1 Accessing members

A struct type can have any number of members declared between the braces. Members may be of any type, including simple types, other structs, pointers, and arrays. The declarations of members have identical syntax to ordinary variable declarations. The names given to members by these declarations are used to reference the individual elements within the structure. Individual members can be accessed using the "." operator. This operator can be used on either the left- or right-hand side of an assignment to set or access values of members. For example:

```
struct employee manager;          /* declare variable 'manager' */

manager.salary = 50000;           /* Set the salary */
strcpy(manager.name, "John");     /* Set the name */
if (manager.salary > 40000)       /* Access the value of salary */
    ...
```

Members can also be accessed via a pointer to the structure using the -> operator. The above examples converted to use pointers would be:

```
struct employee manager;          /* declare 'manager' as a struct */
struct employee *ptr;             /* declare 'ptr' as a pointer */

ptr = &manager;                   /* Set ptr to point to manager */
ptr->salary = 50000;              /* Set the salary */
strcpy(ptr->name, "John");        /* Set the name */
if (ptr->salary > 40000)          /* Access the value of salary */
    ...
```

5.2 Operations on whole structures

Some important operations are permitted on structures as a whole. These operations allow structures to be treated as a single entity. Structures can be:

- Assigned as a whole
- Passed as arguments to functions
- Returned from functions

However, whole structures cannot be compared in any way, not even for equality. If this is required, special functions must be written to compare the fields individually. Some examples of legal uses of structures are shown below:

```
struct employee x, y, z;

x = y;              /* Copy whole structure */
z = fn(x, y);       /* Passed to and returned from function */
```

Individual fields in structures can be used in any way that is legal for the type of that field. Fields of a structure are treated as variables of their given type.

5.3 Name spaces

Different `structs` can use the same names for fields. For example, many different `struct` types can have a `data` field. It is also legal to have a local variable declared with the same name as a `struct` field name. Any possible ambiguity is resolved by the compiler. Hence the C code below is correct:

```
struct employee {
    int data;
} n;

struct employee2 {
    int data;              /* Same field name is ok */
} n2;
int data;

data = 0;
n.data = data;
n2.data = n.data;
```

The use of identical names is not limited to `struct` fields, though this is its most common use. The term *name spaces* refers to uses of identifiers that do not collide with each other. There are a number of distinct name spaces in C. Each individual `struct` (or `union`) forms its own name space, containing only its field names. Labels for `goto` form a separate name space, as do the tags for `structs` (i.e. in `"struct employee"` the identifier `employee` is a tag). All other identifiers form the last name space.

5.4 Arrays of structures

Arrays of structures are defined with the same syntax as arrays of any type. The only difference is the two words `"struct employee"` to define the type that the array contains. An example declaration of an array of `structs` is:

```
struct employee arr[10];        /* array of 10 structs */
```

Indexing elements of the array uses the square bracket notation, as usual. Indexing into an array of structures retrieves an entire structure, just as indexing into an array of `int` retrieves an `int`. The examples below show how to access various elements of an array of structures:

```
    int her_salary;
    struct employee arr[10];
    struct employee n;

    n = arr[1];                    /* Copy whole struct */
    her_salary = arr[5].salary;    /* Get salary from 5th struct */
```

A short program is now presented that uses an array of `struct`s to maintain a payroll for a company. Each `struct` in the array contains the name of the employee and the salary. The program has two features: it allows new employees to be added, and allows printing of the full list of employees. Obviously, this is not a realistic payroll package because it does not store the payroll in a file.

The only trick used by the program is in the maintenance of the `num_employees` variable. This variable not only counts how many employees are stored in the table, but also keeps track of the next free `struct` for insertion of a new employee. The new entry can be stored at `table[num_employees]` because the other employees are stored in locations 0..num_employees-1.

```
/*-------------------------------------------------------------*/
/* PAYROLL: Manage a list of employees and their salaries      */
/*-------------------------------------------------------------*/

#include <stdio.h>
#include <stdlib.h>
#include <string.h>

#define MAX_EMPLOYEES   100    /* Maximum number of employees */
#define MAX_NAME_LEN    50     /* Maximum characters in a name */

struct employee {              /* Struct containing employee info */
    int salary;
    char name[MAX_NAME_LEN];
};

struct employee table[MAX_EMPLOYEES];   /* Table of employees */
int num_employees;                      /* Number of employees */

/*-------------------------------------------------------------*/
/* LIST_EMPLOYEES:  Print out the employees and their salaries */
/*-------------------------------------------------------------*/

void list_employees(void)
{
    int i;

    printf("\n\n           PAYROLL\n\n");
    printf("%10s    %10s\n", "Name   ", "Salary");
    for (i = 0; i < num_employees; i++) {
        printf("%10s       %d\n", table[i].name, table[i].salary);
    }
    printf("\n");
}

/*-------------------------------------------------------------*/
/*  ADD_EMPLOYEE: Get new information and store in the table   */
/*-------------------------------------------------------------*/

void add_employee(void)
{
    char name[MAX_NAME_LEN];
    int salary;

    printf("\n\nAdding new employee ...\n\n");
    printf("What is the new employee's name? ");
```

```
            scanf("%s", name);
            printf("What is the new employee's salary? ");
            scanf("%d", &salary);

               /* Add the information in the last unused struct */

            table[num_employees].salary = salary;       /* Store the salary */
            strcpy(table[num_employees].name, name);    /* Store the name */
            num_employees++;                            /* Increment counter */
      }
      /*-------------------------------------------------------------------*/
      main()
      {
            int choice;

            do {                                        /* List menu choices */
                  printf("\n\n        MENU\n\n");
                  printf(" 1.   Insert employee\n");
                  printf(" 2.   List employees\n");
                  printf(" 3.   Quit\n");
                  printf("\n");

                  printf("Enter your choice: ");        /* Prompt the user */
                  scanf("%d", &choice);                 /* Get the choice */

                  if (choice == 1)
                        add_employee();
                  else
                  if (choice == 2)
                        list_employees();
            } while (choice != 3);                      /* Until quit is chosen */
            exit(0);
      }
```

5.5 Unions

A `union` is another structured type that has syntax identical to `structs`. In almost all situations, the only difference is the replacement of the keyword `struct` with the keyword `union`. The `union` is a special type of structure, used to save memory by overlaying the storage of different variables. Any `union` variable has size large enough to accommodate the largest member of the `union`. The example below shows how to declare a `union` type that at any one time contains either an `int` variable or a `float` variable:

```
union node {
    int int_value;
    float float_value;
};
```

A `union` can be used when a number of different cases require storage of different data, and no two cases can exist at once (i.e. they are mutually exclusive). In this situation it can be useful to overlay the storage of the different data formats.

It is the programmer's responsibility to make sure that the data in the `union` is always used correctly (i.e. that the program is always using the correct type of data). There is no automatically maintained type tag (a variable indicating what type is currently stored). It is the programmer's responsibility to create and correctly use a type tag, if required. Sometimes other information (instead of a tag variable) is used to know what type of information is currently stored in the `union`.

Because there is no checking, `union`s can be used to coerce types. This is compiler-dependent, and very bad style. It is not necessarily equivalent to type casting.

All fields in a `union` are overlayed. To create a structure with some overlayed and some non-overlayed (i.e. a variant record), it is necessary to use a `union` inside a `struct`, as below:

```
struct variant_record {
    int data;                    /* Not overlayed */
    union variant_part {
        int i;                   /* Overlayed */
        float f;
    } un;                        /* un is member of struct */
} str;
```

In this case, accessing the overlayed variables requires the use of two levels of the `str.field` membership operator:

```
x = str.un.i;          /* Two levels of membership */
```

Note that it is possible in some non-ANSI implementations to use *anonymous unions* instead of this double level of membership. To use this "feature" it is necessary to make the names of the `union` fields distinct from other field names. The `union` inside the `struct` should have no field name (i.e. no "un" in the above example). It may also be necessary that the `union` be the first field of the `struct`. The use of anonymous unions is not recommended because they abuse a non-standard feature of the compiler and are non-portable.

5.6 Bit-fields

Bit-fields are a special type of field in a `struct` or `union`, and are mainly used to reduce space usage. They allow the number of bits needed for a field to be specified. When a number of different bit-fields are in the same `struct`, the compiler packs them into words, so as to minimize space. Most commonly bit-fields are used in `struct`s containing a large number of boolean variables. The example below declares two boolean variables, `visited` and `active`, and an `id` field which must be a small integer:

```
struct node {
    unsigned int    visited:1;
    unsigned int    active:1;       /* active = 0 or 1 */
    unsigned int    id:5;           /* id = 0..31 */
};
```

The field names are used exactly as any other field. The compiler automatically generates code to extract the required bits. Care is required when assigning values to the fields because no bounds checking is performed on values stored in bit-fields to check if the value is small enough to fit into its allocated number of bits.

The type of a bit-field can only be `int`, `signed int` or `unsigned int`. The type cannot be an enumerated type. The type should be "unsigned int" unless negative values are needed. Numbers are stored in the specified number of bits in 2's complement representation if they are a `signed` type. Using `int` or `signed int` wastes one bit of information to store the sign of the number. If you accidentally forget to declare the bit-field as `unsigned`, errors can occur because a large positive value stored in there will cause an overflow, and the stored value may become negative.

Bit-fields with no field name are taken to be padding. For example:

```
unsigned int : 3;          /* 3 bits of padding */
```

The dummy field width of zero can be used to force word alignment at the next word boundary.

It is illegal to take the address of a bit-field with the address operator (`&`). Even so, bit-fields are an l-value as far as the compiler is concerned.

There are a lot of picky details about bit-fields. Much about them is not defined by the ANSI standard. Code written using them can be non-portable unless care is taken. To write portable code, access bit-fields only through the field names. Additionally, do not assume that binary data files containing these structures can be ported across to different machines. When the new machine uses the C code to access the elements, its compiler may have placed the bit-fields in different order. Implementation-dependent details causing these problems include whether fields can overlap word boundaries and whether the field ordering is left-to-right or right-to-left.

5.7 Enumerated types

Enumerated types are specified by the keyword: `enum`. They are used to enumerate a subset of integers (or characters), and are quite similar to definition of constants using `#define`. They can be more convenient than `#define` in that the values are automatically generated, but do not have the same flexibility. For example, enumerated values cannot be added together without receiving a compilation warning.

The syntax for declaring enumerated variables is almost identical to that for `structs` and `unions`:

```
enum tag_name { list_of_names } variable_list;
```

When the variable list is omitted, this declares a new enumerated type "enum tag_name" which can be used to declare variables of that type. When the tag name is omitted, the variables are declared as an anonymous enumerated type, and no new variables can be declared of that type (i.e. only those in the variable list are declared as that type).

When both the tag name of the enumeration and the variable list are omitted, the definition only defines the constants inside the braces. It defines them as enumerated constants of an unspecified type.

Inside the braces is a list of the constant names (separated by commas) that are to be defined as members of this enumerated type. These constants are defined starting at zero and incrementing left-to-right (i.e. 0,1,2,...). The value of the constants may be changed anywhere in the list by assigning a constant expression to them. This sets the current name to be this value, and begins incrementing from that value (e.g. `PAWN=1` below restarts the count at 1). Constants need not have successive values and more than one name can have the same value. Some examples of `enum` declarations are:

```
            /* Declare "enum shape_type" as a type */
enum shape_type { CIRCLE, SQUARE, ELLIPSE, RECTANGLE };
            /* Declare "enum piece_type" as a type */
enum piece_type { PAWN = 1, BISHOP = 3, KNIGHT = 3, ROOK = 5,
                  QUEEN = 9, KING = 999 };
       /* Declare "enum white_space" as a type and    */
       /* declare variables x, y as type "enum white_space" */
enum white_space { SPACE = ' ', TAB = '\t', RET = '\n' } x, y;
```

Enumerated types can be used as a simple method of declaring symbolic constants without using `#define` or the `const` qualifier. The omission of both the tag name and the variable list declares the enumerated constants as an anonymous type, and allows these constants to be used as symbolic constants. Most compilers will not produce warnings about combination of these constants with integers.

```
enum { DOG = 1, CAT = 2 };   /* symbolic constants: DOG, CAT */
```

On compilers that do produce warnings, enumerated types allow closer type checking. This can be double-edged in that it can detect bugs, but can also give annoying compile-time type warnings between `int`s and enumerated types (requiring type casting to correct). Some compilers allow the suppression of warnings (e.g. "cc −w" on UNIX) but this is not recommended because useful warnings may also be ignored, and it is better to use the correct enumerated types in declarations.

5.8 More types with typedef

Some simple examples of `typedef` declarations for simple types and arrays were given in Section 2.7. For examples of these `typedef` declarations are:

```
typedef int data_type;        /* data_type is int */
typedef int array_type[5];    /* array_type is array of 5 int */
```

The `typedef` specifier can also be used to define new types equivalent to `struct`, `union`, or `enum` types. This has the advantage that the new type name need not be prefixed by a `struct`, `union` or `enum` keyword. Some examples of `typedef` declarations are:

```
typedef struct node {
    int data;
} node_type;            /* node_type is a struct type */

typedef struct node *node_ptr;    /* node_ptr is a pointer */
typedef enum {FALSE, TRUE} bool;  /* bool is an enum type */
```

These `typedef` declarations can be explained if you think of `typedef` declarations as special variable declarations, declaring a type name. A `typedef` declaration is identical to a variable declaration, except for the keyword `typedef` at the front. The identifier that would be the variable name in a variable declaration is the identifier that is the new type name in the `typedef` declaration.

The user-defined type names created by `typedef` can be used as if they were fundamental types. They can be used to declare variables and can be used in other `typedef` statements. Hence, the following variable declarations would be legal, assuming the `typedef` declarations above:

```
bool x = FALSE;
node_type n;
node_ptr p;
```

In the same way that it is possible to declare multiple comma-separated variables of different types in one declaration, it is also possible to declare multiple type names in one declaration. For example, the declaration below declares `node_type` as a `struct` type and `node_ptr` as a pointer to `struct`:

```
typedef struct node node_type, *node_ptr;
```

This notation is compact, but can reduce the readability of the program.

5.9 Self-referential structures

Self-referential structures are slightly more complicated because they contain a definition that refers to the current type. The declaration below declares `node` as a self-referential structure that could be used to define a linked list of integers:

```
struct node {
    struct node *next;    /* self reference */
    int data;             /* data field */
};
```

The use of `typedef` is quite common. The declaration below declares `node_type` as equivalent to "`struct node`" and `node_ptr` as equivalent to "`struct node*`" (i.e. a pointer to a `struct`):

```
typedef struct node {
    struct node *next;
    int data;
} node_type, *node_ptr;  /* define node_type and node_ptr */
```

There is a trap that many programmers fall into when using `typedef` to define a self-referential structure:

```
typedef struct node { /* INCORRECT - won't compile */
    node_ptr  next;   /* can't use node_type or node_ptr */
    int data;
} node_type, *node_ptr;
```

The two `typedef` names, `node_type` and `node_ptr` cannot be used to declare the `next` pointer, as they are not yet declared when the fields of the structure are examined. Instead, the type "`struct node*`" must be used for a pointer to the `struct`.

The type of the field should be known when the field's type is evaluated. There is one exception — pointers to undefined structures are permitted (i.e. variables of type "`struct unknown_type*`"). This allows the definition of *mutually recursive structures*; i.e. two structure types, each with a pointer to the other type of `struct`:

```
struct node2 {
    struct node1 *next;    /* ptr to as yet undefined type */
    data_type data;
};

struct node1 {
    struct node2 *next;
    data_type data;
};
```

5.10 Exercises

1. Assuming appropriate declarations of `str` as a `struct` type, could the statement below be legal in some program? In other words, is it legal to use the same identifier for two purposes?

   ```
   data = str.data;
   ```

   What are the name spaces in C? Can two different `struct` types both use the same name for a field? If so, can the field have a different type in both `struct` types?

2. What is the difference between a `struct` and a `union`? What is the purpose of the `union` data type? When can a `union` be used?

3. What is the purpose of bit-fields? What types are permitted?

4. Add a `delete_employee` function to the program in Section 5.4. *Hint:* This function will need to decrement the number of employees, and also shift a number of structures down so as to overwrite the one being deleted.

5. What are the values of X and Y in the following `enum` declaration?

   ```
   enum { X, a = 3, Y };
   ```

6. Use `typedef` to define `arr_node` as an array of ten structures, each containing an `int` field named `id` and a `float` field named `value`.

Chapter 6
Strings

It is often useful to program with strings of characters. For example, a person's name is a string of characters. Unfortunately, there is no specific named type "string" supported in C. However, arrays of `char` are supported by library functions and are usually referred to as strings. Strings in C are arrays of `char` *terminated by a zero character*. Hence, strings are often referred to as being "null terminated" or "zero terminated", and the zero character is called by many names: "zero byte", "zero character", "terminating zero", "null byte", "null character", "terminating null". Although this byte is often referred to as a "null", it is important not to confuse this with `NULL` (which is a pointer constant).

When using string variables there are two possible approaches — arrays of `char`, and pointers to `char`. The simplest and safest choice is to use arrays of `char`, and this will be the first approach examined in this chapter. The use of arrays is simpler to understand and avoids many of the pitfalls of using pointers. Fortunately, arrays of `char` are very flexible and there are very few occasions where we need to use pointers. Later sections of the chapter examine how pointers to `char` can be used to represent strings. Note that the reader may need to examine some of the material on pointer variables in Chapter 8 before attempting the section on pointers to `char`.

6.1 Simple strings: arrays of char

This section examines the implementation of strings as array variables. Strings in C are arrays of characters with the special feature that they are terminated by a zero character. When stored in fixed size arrays of `char`, strings can be thought of as having varying length (depending upon where the first zero character appears), but with a maximum length equal to the size of the character array (actually one less than the array size because of the need to store the null terminator).

Since strings are declared as arrays of `char`, it is possible to use array indexing to access individual characters of the string. For example, the program below builds a string one character at a time, and then prints the string using the `%s` option to `printf` (which is specifically intended for strings):

```c
#include <stdio.h>

#define STR_LEN 20          /* Maximum length of the string */

main()
{
    char str[STR_LEN];      /* String with maximum length 20 */
    str[0] = 'H';
    str[1] = 'e';
    str[2] = 'l';
    str[3] = 'l';
    str[4] = 'o';
    str[5] = '\0';          /* Add terminating zero character */
    printf("%s\n", str);    /* Print the string using %s */
}
```

This method of building a string is cumbersome and there is a much better method using standard library functions (discussed in the next section).

Note how the terminating zero character is specified as '\0'. The backslash is very important, as '0' specifies the ASCII equivalent of the decimal digit zero, and not the zero byte. An equivalent method of specifying the zero byte is to use the integer constant zero:

```c
str[5] = 0;      /* Add terminating zero */
```

However, the use of '\0' is better style because it indicates clearly that the value is a character, and not an integer, thus improving readability.

Another method of giving a string a value is to permit the user to input a value. The scanf function can be used to input entire strings. The %s option will skip any initial whitespace characters, and then read a string of characters up to the first whitespace character (i.e. space, tab or newline). The program below asks for the name of the user, which is read into a string using scanf and then output again using printf:

```c
#include <stdio.h>

#define STR_LEN 20          /* Maximum length of the string */

main()
{
    char str[STR_LEN];              /* String with maximum length 20 */

    printf("What is your name? ");  /* Prompt the user */
    scanf("%s", str);               /* Input the string */
    printf("Hello %s\n", str);      /* Print the response */
}
```

Note that there is no & on the str argument to scanf because strings do not require the computation of the address (i.e. passing an array passes the address of the first element). Note also that the program above does not restrict the length of the input string and the program has undefined behavior if the user types more than 19 characters (20 characters is too large because of the terminating zero that is added automatically by scanf). One solution is to use a field width specifier in the format string to limit the number of characters stored in the string: "%19s" (however, this is a poor solution to the problem of incorrect input).

Another method of giving a string a value is to *initialize* the array variable. If the string is too long, the compiler will generate a warning message during compilation. The initializer should be a string constant, as below:

```
char str[20] = "Hello";
```

Note that there is a convenient method of allowing the compiler to count exactly how many characters are required by the array. The declaration:

```
char str[] = "Hello";
```

will allocate exactly 6 bytes for `str` (five letters plus the terminating zero).

6.2 String library functions: <string.h>

The string library functions are declared in `<string.h>` which should be included using `#include`. The most commonly used functions are shown in Table 6.1. All parameters for these functions are string types — either `char[]` or `char*`.

Table 6.1. Common string functions

Function	Meaning
char *strcpy(dest, source)	Copy source to dest
char *strcat(dest, source)	Concatenate source onto dest
int strlen(s)	Find length of s
int strcmp(s1, s2)	Compare two strings

6.2.1 Copy, append and string length: strcpy, strcat, strlen

The `strcpy` function copies the second string over the top of the first string (i.e. copies source to dest in the prototype above). The terminating zero is also copied. No memory is allocated for dest, nor is there any check if source is too long to be stored in dest. Hence all calls to `strcpy` must ensure that dest has enough space to store the new string.

The return value of `strcpy` is dest which is the first argument to `strcpy`, but this return value is usually ignored by calling `strcpy` as if it were a `void` function. Most compilers permit the programmer to discard the return value, but strict compilers and the `lint` checker will complain. To avoid warning messages from strict compilers or `lint`, the return value can be discarded explicitly using a type cast to `void`:

```
(void) strcpy(...);
```

The `strcat` function is similar to `strcpy` except that it *appends* source onto the end of dest. The terminating zero of the original string in dest is overwritten by the start of source, and a new terminating zero is added to the end of dest after source has been appended. As was the case for `strcpy`, dest must have enough space to store the new string. The return value of the `strcat` function is always dest and this is usually ignored.

The `strlen` function returns the length of the string not counting the terminating zero. `strlen(NULL)` is undefined.

The example below uses `strcpy` to copy the string constant `"Hello"` into a string variable. The new string is then output and its length is calculated using `strlen`. Finally, another string `" World"` is concatenated using `strcat` and the new string printed.

```
#include <stdio.h>
#include <string.h>            /* Use string library functions */

main()
{
    char str[20];              /* String with maximum length 20 */
    int len;

    strcpy(str, "Hello");           /* str = "Hello" */
    printf("%s\n", str);            /* Print str */
    len = strlen(str);              /* Calculate length */
    printf("The length is %d\n", len);  /* Print the length */
    strcat(str, " World");          /* Append " World" */
    printf("%s\n", str);            /* Print str */
}
```

The `strlen` function calculates the length as 5, because it does not count the terminating zero. The assignment statement:

```
str = "Hello";           /* INCORRECT */
```

would be incorrect because array variables cannot be assigned values. An assignment statement cannot replace the `strcpy` call.

6.2.2 Comparing strings: strcmp

The `strcmp` function is another important string function, and is used to compare two strings. It can be used to determine whether two strings are exactly the same, and also whether one string comes before another string in alphabetical ordering. The `strcmp` function takes two arguments and returns zero if they are equal, and a non-zero value if they are not equal. Hence, the method of comparing strings for equality is to use `strcmp` directly in a conditional test, as in:

```
if (strcmp(str1, str2) == 0)
    printf("The strings are equal\n");
```

If it is only necessary to know whether two strings are equal or different, the return value can be compared with zero as above. However, if it is necessary to know the order of the two strings, a non-zero value can be examined more carefully. If it is less than zero then the first string comes before the second, and if it is greater than zero the second string comes before the first. Note that the return value is not merely 0, 1 or −1, as is assumed by some novice C programmers.

Because the return value of `strcmp` must be tested a number of times, it is common to assign it to a temporary variable, thus avoiding the inefficiency of multiple calls to `strcmp`. The program below asks for two strings and then performs a number of comparisons on them:

```
#include <stdio.h>
#include <string.h>          /* Use string library functions */

main()
{
    char str1[20], str2[20];     /* Two string variables */
    int ret;

    printf("Enter two strings: ");   /* Prompt the user */
    scanf("%s%s", str1, str2);       /* Read the 2 strings */

    ret = strcmp(str1, str2);        /* Compare the strings */

    if (ret == 0)                    /* Check for equality */
        printf("Strings are equal\n");
    else
        printf("Strings are different\n");

    if (ret < 0)
        printf("%s is before %s\n", str1, str2);
    else
    if (ret > 0)
        printf("%s is after %s\n", str1, str2);
}
```

6.2.3 Limited length functions: strncmp, strncpy, strncat

The library also defines three functions similar to strcmp, strcpy, and strcat that take an extra int argument, n, the number of characters, as shown in Table 6.2.

Table 6.2. Limited length string functions

Function	Meaning
int strncmp(s1, s2, n)	Compare at most n characters
char *strncpy(dest, source, n)	Copy at most n characters
char *strncat(dest, source, n)	Append at most n characters

The strncmp function compares at most n characters and returns zero if the first n characters are equal. The strncpy and strncat functions copy at most n characters to dest, and return their first argument. One very dangerous feature of these functions is that although strncat will correctly add a terminating zero to the end of dest, the strncpy function does not add a terminating zero if the length of source is greater than n (this is consistent with using these functions for strings with no terminating zero, as discussed in Section 6.6).

6.2.4 Miscellaneous string functions

There are a number of other useful string functions declared in <string.h>. In the discussion below, s1 and s2 have string type, c is a char, and n is an int. The remaining functions are listed in Table 6.3.

The strchr function returns the address of the first occurrence of character c in s1, or NULL if there is no such occurrence. The strrchr function returns the address of the *last* occurrence or NULL if c is not in s1. The strpbrk function returns the

Table 6.3. Other string functions

Function	Meaning
`char *strchr(s1,c)`	Find first occurrence of `c` in `s1`
`char *strrchr(s1,c)`	Find last occurrence of `c` in `s1`
`char *strpbrk(s1,s2)`	Find first occurrence of character from `s2` in `s1`
`int strspn(s1,s2)`	Length of prefix of `s1` using characters in `s2`
`int strcspn(s1,s2)`	Length of prefix of `s1` using characters not in `s2`
`char *strstr(s1,s2)`	Find occurrence of `s2` in `s1`
`char *strtok(s1,s2)`	Tokenize `s1` using characters from `s2` as delimiters
`char *strerror(n)`	Implementation-defined error message

address of the first occurrence in `s1` of any character from string `s2`, or NULL if there is no such occurrence. Note that the special calls `strchr(s, 0)` and `strrchr(s, 0)` can both be used to locate the terminating zero, but the zero that terminates `s2` is not considered one of the characters to be searched for by `strpbrk`.

The `strspn` function returns the length of the longest prefix of `s1` that contains only characters from `s2`. The `strcspn` function is similar, except that it looks for characters *not* in `s2`.

The `strstr` function searches `s1` for an occurrence of the entire string `s2` and returns the address of the first occurrence, or NULL if `s2` cannot be found in `s1`. In the special case where `s2` is the empty string (`""`), `strstr` returns `s1`.

The `strtok` function is used to break a string into tokens. This tokenization is achieved by multiple successive calls to `strtok`, where each call returns the next token. On the first of a series of related calls to `strtok`, the first argument `s1` must be the string to be tokenized, and the address of the first token is returned. On further calls to `strtok` the first argument must be NULL, and the address of the next token is returned. The address of a token returned is the address of the first character starting the token in `s1`. The end of the token is marked by a terminating zero which is added by `strtok` to overwrite the delimiting character (hence `strtok` modifies the string passed as its first argument). Every call to `strtok` must supply a string `s2` containing the characters that delimit tokens (note that `s2` need not stay the same in a series of calls). A token is defined as the longest string of characters that are not present in the delimiter string `s2`. The value NULL is returned if the string contains no more tokens. Below is an example of the use of `strtok` to print out the list of space-separated words in a string:

```
#define SEPARATORS " "          /* spaces separate tokens */
void print_tokens(char s[])
{
    char *token;            /* pointer to token */

    token = strtok(s, SEPARATORS);              /* get 1st token */
    while (token != NULL) {                     /* while more tokens */
        printf("The token is '%s'\n", token);   /* print the token */
        token = strtok(NULL, SEPARATORS);       /* get next token */
    }
}
```

The `strerror` function returns a pointer to a string representing the particular implementation's error message for error number n. These error messages are usually identical to those used by `perror` and are related to the error values in `<errno.h>`.

6.2.5 String functions in <stdio.h>: sprintf, sscanf

There are two other functions that are quite useful for programming with strings: `sprintf` and `sscanf`. These are both declared in `<stdio.h>` and not `<string.h>`. The prototype definitions are:

```
int sprintf(char *str, char *format, ...)
int sscanf(char *str, char *format, ...)
```

These functions are identical to the `printf` and `scanf` functions except that the output from `sprintf` is placed into `str` and the input characters for `sscanf` come from `str`. The powerful formatting of `printf` can be used to create a new string, and the input methods of `scanf` can be used to examine the data in a string. One simple task that these functions can perform is conversion between numbers and strings. The `sprintf` function can be used to convert integers or floating point numbers to their string equivalent, and the `sscanf` function can convert a string of digits to its numerical equivalent. Note that there are also functions declared in `<stdlib.h>` for the specific purpose of converting strings of digits to numbers: `atoi, atof, atol`.

6.3 Strings revisited: pointers to char

In previous sections we examined strings represented as arrays of `char`. There are actually two representations of strings: arrays of `char` and pointers to `char`. This section introduces the pointer representation and compares the two.

A string variable of type pointer to `char` is defined using the star notation:

```
char *str;
```

To define two pointer variables, a star is required before both variable names:

```
char *str1, *str2;
```

The type of a pointer to `char` is usually written as `char*`.

The main difference between the use of arrays and pointers as string variables is that arrays reserve memory for the string whereas pointers reserve no memory at all. Thus, if we assume that `str` is defined as above, it is wrong to access individual characters using `str[i]`, to copy a string into `str`, or to use `scanf` to place a string into `str`, *except* when `str` has first been assigned the address of a block of memory. Memory can be allocated using three main methods:

1. Dynamic allocation using `malloc`
2. Array string variables
3. String constants

The first method is the most common. The malloc library function is used to allocate a number of bytes for a string, and the pointer string variable is then almost identical to an array variable of that many bytes. For example, the code below assigns str the address of a block of 20 characters.

```
char *str;

str = malloc(20);          /* Allocate memory */
strcpy(str, "Hello");      /* Copy a string there */
```

However, this use of malloc is wasteful if the string being stored is shorter than 20 bytes. This is where one of the advantages of pointer string variables becomes apparent — the flexibility to allocate exactly the right number of bytes. The code below copies a string to a pointer string variable after allocating exactly the right number of bytes:

```
char *s;
char s2[20] = "Hello";

s = malloc(strlen(s2) + 1);  /* Allocate memory */
strcpy(s, s2);               /* Copy string */
```

Note that the "+1" extra byte is needed for the terminating zero.

The second method of allocating memory for pointer string variables is to assign the address of an array string variable to the pointer string variable. The pointer string variable can then be used as if it were an array string variable. The only drawback is the problem of *aliasing*, where two variable names can be used to refer to the one string (i.e. the pointer and the array variable both point to the same area of memory). This can lead the program to have unexpected behavior because copying a string to one variable changes another variable. The code fragment below illustrates how a pointer to char can access another array string variable:

```
#include <stdio.h>
#include <string.h>         /* define strcpy() */

#define STR_LEN  20         /* Length of a string */

main()
{
    char *str1;
    char str2[STR_LEN];

    str1 = str2;                    /* Make str1 point at str2 */
    strcpy(str1, "Hello");          /* Copy a string there */
    printf("str1 = %s, str2 = %s\n", str1, str2);
}
```

Because of aliasing (str pointing to str2), the strcpy function call unexpectedly changes the contents of str2. The output of the program is:

```
str1 = Hello, str2 = Hello
```

Note that the assignment statement setting str1 to point to str2 is only legal because str1 is a pointer. The reverse of this statement, str2 = str1, would be illegal because an array variable cannot be assigned a value. This is one of the main advantages of using pointers for strings — a string variable can point to a number of different string locations by assigning it different addresses.

The third method of allocating memory for pointer string variables is to assign them a string constant. String constants are automatically allocated memory by the compiler. For example, in the code fragment:

```
char *str;
str = "Hello";
```

the compiler allocates 6 bytes for `"Hello"` (5 letters plus the terminating zero), and assigns `str` the address of this memory. However, `str` cannot then be used exactly as an array string variable containing 6 bytes because string constants should not be modified (compilers are allowed to place string constants in read-only memory). `str` should be treated as a *non-modifiable* array string variable because it points to a string constant.

Nevertheless, one particularly good aspect of string pointers is that they can be assigned the values of string constants using the = operator. For example, the code fragment below shows a string pointer being used to store an error message. If an array of `char` were used, the assignment statements would have to be replaced by `strcpy` calls, which are much less efficient.

```
char *err_mesg;
if (err == SYNTAX_ERR)
    err_mesg = "Syntax error";
else
    err_mesg = "Type error";
```

6.3.1 Pointer differences

There are some important differences between arrays of `char` and pointers to `char` in string initializations. Initialized string variables can be declared by:

```
char str[LENGTH] = "First";
char *str2 = "Second";
```

There is a slight difference between the two initializations. In the first, `LENGTH` should be large enough for the string and the terminating zero, which the compiler automatically appends. A compilation warning is generated if `LENGTH` is not large enough to hold the string (except for a minor exception discussed in Section 6.6).

In the second case, the compiler automatically allocates exactly the right amount of memory for the string and the zero. However, the string `"Second"` is stored in a special area of memory which should not be modified by the program (i.e. it could be read-only memory). Hence, the string variable `str2` cannot have any of its elements changed after this initialization, whereas `str1` can be used normally.

Because of the dual nature of the string, as pointer or array, there are two types of "empty" strings. A `NULL` pointer is sometimes considered to be an empty string. The empty string `""` specifies a string containing only the terminating zero. Thus a pointer string variable can be "empty" in two senses — it can be `NULL`, or it can point to a string containing only the terminating zero. It is important to be aware of the difference.

6.4 Functions with string arguments

All of the string library functions can be applied to pointers to `char`, provided that the pointer has been allocated some memory to point to. Similarly, any function you may write to act on strings can accept either pointers to `char` or arrays of `char`. For example, consider the function below that counts the number of letters in a string:

```
#include <stdio.h>
#include <ctype.h>                  /* Declare isalpha() */
int count_letters(char s[])
{
    int i, count;

    count = 0;
    for (i = 0; s[i] != '\0'; i++) {    /* For all characters */
        if (isalpha(s[i]))                /* If a letter */
            count++;                      /* Increment counter */
    }
    return count;
}
main()
{
    char *s = "A string";
    char s2[] = "Another string";

    printf("\"%s\" has %d letters\n", s, count_letters(s));
    printf("\"%s\" has %d letters\n", s2, count_letters(s2));
}
```

The program above passes both types of string variable to the function `count_letters`. The function works correctly in both cases, producing the following output:

```
"A string" has 7 letters
"Another string" has 13 letters
```

Note the definition of the string parameter, `char s[]`, which declares s as an array of `char` (i.e. string) with unspecified size. The size of the string is not needed by the function. If an array size is specified, it is ignored by the compiler. Note also that the use of array indexing `s[i]` is legal on pointer variables, and the parameter could be declared as `char *s` with no need for changes to the function body.

6.5 String constants

String constants are special strings that can be used almost anywhere a string variable can be used. For example, the format strings for `printf` and `scanf` are string constants. String constants are delimited by double quotes. An example of a string constant is:

```
"Hello World\n"
```

String constants may contain escape characters such as \n in the example above. In fact, the only way to put a double quote inside a string constant is to use the escape \".

A string constant is stored as a list of characters plus the extra terminating zero character (which is automatically added by the compiler). The text characters and the terminating zero character are stored in a special area of memory reserved for string constants. This area is allowed to be read-only memory (in implementations that support it), and the characters in a string constant should not be modified. Note that the zero character is actually a zero byte and not the ASCII equivalent of the digit '0'. The empty string constant "" is stored as a single zero byte (its length would be zero if calculated by strlen).

A string constant in an expression evaluates to the *address* of the first character in the string constant, as stored in the special memory area. For example, when a string constant is used as a format string to printf, the address of the string constant is the value passed to printf. The type of a string constant is a pointer to char, qualified by const because it is (potentially) stored in read-only memory:

```
const char *
```

There is one important exception in the use of string constants. When a string constant is used to initialize an *array* string variable, the string constant is not stored separately. Instead, the string constant is merely a convenient notation for an initializer consisting of a list of characters, and these characters are stored directly into the space reserved for the array variable. The memory is like that of normal arrays and is not read-only. In other words, the two variable initializations below are equivalent:

```
char s[10] = "Hello";
char s[10] = { 'H', 'e', 'l', 'l', 'o', '\0' };
```

Both allocate an array variable with 10 bytes, where the first 6 bytes are taken up by the initial string value.

6.6 Omitting the null terminator

One method of reducing space usage is to omit the null terminator from strings. This is possible when strings are a fixed size, or are bounded by a fixed size. When strings are all a fixed size, there is no need for the null terminator at all. When strings are bounded by a fixed size, such as for identification codes of no more than 10 characters, the null terminator must appear if the string is less than 10 characters.

There are a number of differences when the null terminator is omitted. Output with printf must be qualified by a precision specification (e.g. %.3s in the program below), and the strn... family of <string.h> library functions must be used — strncpy to copy strings; stncmp to compare strings. Unfortunately, there appears to be no method of preventing scanf from adding the null terminator, and a null terminated string variable must be used for input, then copied to the non-null terminated string (using strncpy).

There is an important compiler initialization feature that provides some support for non-null terminated strings. If an array of char is initialized with a string constant that has exactly the correct number of characters (not counting the null character), then the null character can be silently squeezed out by the compiler. Note that non-ANSI compilers may not support this feature. Note also that this "nice" feature can also cause obscure bugs in programs where the null terminator is desired. A good compiler should produce a warning, but I've seen none that do!

An example of this feature appears in the program below, where the string constants have length 3 which is exactly the correct number of characters for the array. This program also uses precision of 3 in the format specification %.3s (%3s is wrong) to print out the strings.

```
#include <stdio.h>
#include <string.h>

#define NUM_DAYS   7        /* 7 days in a week */

char days[NUM_DAYS][3] = { "Mon", "Tue", "Wed",
                           "Thu", "Fri", "Sat", "Sun" };
main()
{
    int i;

    for (i = 0; i < NUM_DAYS; i++)      /* Print the days */
        printf("%.3s\n", days[i]);      /* Note:  %.3s */
}
```

6.7 Exercises

1. What is the value of `str[strlen(str)]` for any string?

2. What is the output of the following code fragment?

   ```
   char str[] = "Hello World";

   str[7] = '\0';
   printf("%s\n", str);
   ```

3. What is wrong with the use of the preprocessor to define a new "string" type as below? Does `typedef` suffer the same problem? *Hint:* What happens when declaring two string variables in the one declaration?

   ```
   #define string   char*
   ```

4. The statement below illustrates a natural use of the empty string. What is the purpose of the statement?

   ```
   printf("You have %d egg%s", num_eggs == 1 ? "" : "s");
   ```

5. What is wrong with the pointer string variable initialization below?

   ```
   char *s = 'c';
   ```

6. Use the library functions in `<string.h>` to write a function (or macro) to test whether one string is the prefix of the other. *Hint:* Use either `strncmp` or `strstr`.

Chapter 6

7. What is wrong with the following macro intended to test if one string is alphabetically before another?

    ```
    #define BEFORE(s1,s2)   (strcmp(s1,s2)== -1)
    ```

8. Given the declarations below, what is the value of the expressions s1==s2 and strcmp(s1,s2)?

    ```
    #define VALUE   "This is a string"
    char *s1 = VALUE;
    char *s2 = VALUE;
    ```

9. What is the difference between the two tests applied to the string variables below?

    ```
    char *s1, *s2;

    if (*s1 == *s2)
    if (strcmp(s1, s2) == 0)
    ```

10. What is the value of strlen("")?

11. What is the output of the following code fragment?

    ```
    struct {
         char *label;
    } x, y;

    x.label = malloc(20);            /* allocate memory */
    strcpy(x.label, "A string");     /* set string field */
    y = x;                           /* assign whole struct */
    strcpy(y.label, "Another string");
    printf("%s: %s\n", x.label, y.label);
    ```

    What is the (unrelated) problem with pointer string fields in structs when saving an array of structs to a binary file?

Chapter 7
Functions

For all but the smallest programs, it is infeasible to keep all of the statements in one block (i.e. all in `main`). Programs are most commonly written using a number of functions. Functions allow the program to be broken up into a number of sub-tasks, with a function for each task. Hence, the use of functions makes programs more logical and easier to write.

There is only one type of function in C, unlike Pascal with distinct "procedures" and "functions". All functions return a single value, of a type specified by the programmer. Procedure-like functions are declared as functions returning a nothing type, `void`.

Function declarations are the most important change made by the ANSI standard. The new method of declaring functions is called *prototyping*. This refers to the placement of parameter types inside the function header, as shown in all the examples below. Almost all the functions declared in this book use prototyping. The old non-prototyping method of function declaration is also briefly discussed in this chapter.

7.1 Defining functions

The best way to learn how to define functions is to look at some simple examples. The points to note are the declaration syntax (the function return type appears first, followed by the function name, and then the list of parameters) and the use of the `return` statement to return the function value.

The first example accepts two integer parameters and returns their sum:

```
int sum(int x, int y)
{
    return x + y;
}
```

Note that there are no semicolons after the parameter list or after the block (i.e. after the right brace).

The next example returns a boolean value (actually an `int`) indicating whether a character is a vowel:

```
int isvowel(char c)
{
    if (c == 'a' || c == 'e' || c == 'i' || c == 'o' || c == 'u')
        return 1;
    else
        return 0;
}
```

The next example is a procedure-like function that counts from one up to a specified number, n. The return type is `void` because it does not return anything.

```
void count(int n)
{
    int i;                      /* local variable */
    for (i = 1; i <= n; i++)
        printf("%d\n", i);      /* Print out i */
}
```

From these examples, it can be seen that the syntax for the definition of a function is:

```
return_type function_name ( parameter_list )
{
    local variable declarations
    executable statements
}
```

The type of result the function returns always starts the function definition. All `return` statements in the function should return values of this type. The return type can be omitted, defaulting to `int`, but this is bad style. Functions not returning any value (i.e. procedure-like functions) should be specified as returning the type `void`. The function return type can be any of the following types:

- Basic type— `int`, `char`, `float`, `double`
- Void type — return no value
- Enumerated type
- Pointer type
- Structured or union type

Note that a function cannot return an array type, although the effect can be achieved by storing an array as a field inside a `struct` and returning the `struct` type (but this is not recommended except in rare instances).

Braces surround the local variable declarations and the executable statements of the function. All local variable declarations must appear before the executable statements. The executable statements are ordinary C statements. There is no semicolon after the parameter list (i.e. not after the function header), or after the entire function (i.e. not after the last right brace).

The type, name, and parameter list are referred to as the *function header* and the statements inside the braces are called the *function body*.

7.2 Functions returning no value: void functions

Functions not returning any value are supported by C. They are declared only slightly differently to other "proper" functions. They are declared by specifying the function return type as `void`. `void` is a special type that indicates to return no function result.

```
#include <stdio.h>

void print_sum(int x, int y)           /* void function */
{
    printf("%d \n", x + y);
}

main()
{
    print_sum(3, 10);       /* Call the void function */
}
```

It is also possible, but not recommended, to leave out the return type in the declaration of the function. When this is done, the default type is `int`. Most compilers will allow a function returning `int` to be called as if it were a `void` function. Hence, the `print_sum` function could be declared as below:

```
print_sum(int x, int y)
{
    printf("%d \n", x + y);
}
```

The fact that it should return an `int` is ignored, and if an integer value is actually returned at run-time, it is thrown away. However, it is much better to declare the function of type `void`, than to use this default mechanism. The use of `void` allows better type checking by compilers. It also prevents good compilers (and `lint`) from complaining about an unused function value.

7.3 Functions with no parameters

Functions with no parameters are allowed and are declared by placing the keyword `void` in the parameter list, as below:

```
void mesg(void)            /* Accept no parameters */
{
    printf("Hello world\n");
}

main()
{
    mesg();                /* Call the function. */
}                          /* No arguments supplied */
```

7.4 Non-prototyping (non-ANSI functions)

Prototyping refers to the type of parameters being specified inside the parameter list, and is relatively new to ANSI C. Before prototyping appeared, a slightly different syntax was permitted for the definition of functions. Old-style declarations are usually referred to as "non-prototyping" declarations. Using this syntax, parameter names are listed in the parameter list, but their types do not appear with them. Instead, the types of parameters are listed after the parameter list, before the left brace, and have the same syntax as local variable declarations. Local variables can be declared as usual, after the left brace that starts the function. Non-prototyping functions can return any type and both `void` and non-`void` functions are supported. An example of a function definition using non-prototyping is:

```
void strncpy(s, d, n)
char *s, *d;
int n;
{
    int i;      /* Local variable */
    for (i = 1; d[i] != '\0' && i <= n; i++)
        s[i] = d[i];
    s[i] = '\0';
}
```

Note that if one of the variables declared in the function header is left out of the declaration list the header, its type defaults to `int`, and this is not a compilation error. Hence, the declaration of `n` in the example above is not strictly necessary.

Functions with no parameters can be declared in old-style C by leaving the parameter list empty (i.e. an empty pair of brackets). An example is:

```
void mesg()            /* No parameters */
{
    printf("Hello world\n");
}
```

Your compiler will still support the old-style declarations, but you should use prototyping if it is available. Do not use this old-style declaration syntax. Old-style declarations are mentioned here for a few reasons: (a) a great deal of C code has already been written using non-prototyping; (b) arguments to variable length argument list functions, such as `printf` and `scanf`, are treated in the same way as arguments to non-prototyped functions; (c) arguments in calls to functions that have not been defined are treated as arguments to non-prototyped functions.

The change to prototyping is not merely one of syntax. The two declarations are also treated differently by the compiler. The main difference is that in prototyping there is much stronger type-checking of parameters' types and number. Without prototyping there is no checking of parameter types or of the number of parameters. It is assumed that the programmer makes no mistakes and there are no warnings. Without prototyping, you must be very careful that the types of parameters in the function definition and the arguments to function calls are the same. If the types do not match, the parameters can be passed incorrectly, leading to run-time errors (often a cause of segmentation fault on UNIX machines).

The second difference with non-prototyping is the type coercions that are automatically carried out on function arguments. Small types, such as `char` and `short`, are automatically promoted to `int`, and `float` arguments are automatically promoted to `double`.

7.5 The return statement

When a function reaches its last right brace, it will terminate. When this occurs it does not return any value. This normal termination is only adequate for functions not returning any value (i.e. `void` functions).

The `return` statement is the only way to return a value from a function. If a non-`void` function does not encounter a `return` statement, it will still terminate as expected, but the returned value will be garbage. There is no default return value for any type of function.

The `return` statement can be used anywhere in a function. It can be placed at the end of the function to return the value and terminate normally. It can be used anywhere inside the function, to return a value and terminate the function immediately. Some examples of the use of `return` statement are:

```
return 10;
return x + y;
```

The `return` statement can also be used to immediately terminate a `void` function without returning a result, using the syntax:

```
return;
```

This use of `return` is useful for terminating a function from within the body of the function. For `void` functions there is no need for a `return` statement at the end of the function, as normal termination at the closing right brace is also adequate.

7.6 Local variable declarations

Local variables are declared at the start of each function block. They are exactly like ordinary variable declarations in `main`. In fact, declarations in `main` are just local variable declarations for the `main` function. The example below shows the definition of local variables of various types:

```
void fn(int x, char *s)
{
    int i;
    char *s1, *s2;
    int arr[10];

    ...     /* executable statements */
}
```

Local variables are not initialized automatically — they contain garbage values. Local variables do not retain their values between successive calls to the function. Every time a function is entered, its local variables again contain garbage. However, local variables can be explicitly initialized (discussed later).

Inner declarations "hide" outer declarations. Using the same name in a different scope level is not a compilation error. For example, consider what happens if a local variable in a function has the same name as a global variable. Inside the function, that name refers to the local variable, not the global variable. In fact, the global variable cannot be accessed inside the function because its name is hidden.

Function blocks are not the only place local variables can be declared. Variables can be declared at the start of any block. This includes loop blocks and blocks for `if` statements. In fact, variables can be declared after any left brace. As with function blocks, all variable declarations must occur before any executable statements. These variables have scope of that particular block. In other words, they can only be used up to the corresponding right brace. Inner declarations hide outer declarations — the same name can be re-used in inner blocks to refer to a different variable. For example, there are two `j` variables in the program below, and the compiler resolves confusion by examining in which block the use of `j` occurs. The program prints out "j = 2" ten times and then prints out "j = 1" once.

```
#include <stdio.h>

main()
{
    int i;
    int j = 1;

    for (i = 0; i <= 10; i++) {
        int j = 2;                   /* block-local variable */
                                     /* Hides outer j variable */
        printf("j = %d\n", j);
    }
    printf("j = %d\n", j);
}
```

7.7 Global variables

In addition to defining variables local to a function, it is also possible to define global variables that are accessible to every function. This can be a convenient method of communicating data between functions, or of allowing different functions to act on the same data structure. However, global variables should be used sparingly and local variables should always be used when only one function needs to use the variable.

Global variables are defined by placing variable declarations before all the functions, at the top of the file. A typical program using global variables is shown below. Note that instead of passing 10 as a parameter to the `squares` and `cubes` functions, the global variable `upper_limit` is set to 10.

```
#include <stdio.h>

int upper_limit;                    /* Global variables here */

/*--------------------------------------------------------------*/
/* SQUARES:  Print squares up to global variable upper_limit */
/*--------------------------------------------------------------*/

void squares(void)
{
    int i;                          /* local variable */

    for (i = 1; i <= upper_limit; i++) /* use global variable */
        printf("%d\n", i * i);
}
```

```
/*-----------------------------------------------------------*/
/* CUBES: Print cubes up to global variable upper_limit      */
/*-----------------------------------------------------------*/
void cubes(void)
{
    int i;                          /* local variable */

    for (i = 1; i <= upper_limit; i++) /* use global variable */
        printf("%d\n", i * i * i);
}
main()
{
    upper_limit = 10;               /* Set global variable */
    squares();
    cubes();
}
```

Note that although the definition of global variables at the top of the file is very common style, they can also be defined in the middle of a file, as long as they are not inside any function. In this case, the global variable must be defined before it is used.

7.8 Call-by-value parameter passing

Parameters are passed to functions using a mechanism called call-by-value (also called "pass-by-value"). The effect of call-by-value is that a function uses only a copy of an argument that it receives. It cannot change the value of the actual parameter outside the function. On entry to the function, a copy of the arguments is made for the function to act upon. Consider a simple example:

```
#include <stdio.h>

void fn(int a, int b)
{
    a = 1;
    b = 2;
    printf("a = %d,  b = %d\n", a, b);
}
main()
{
    int c = 3, d = 4;

    fn(c, d);
    printf("c = %d,  d = %d\n", c, d);
}
```

The call to the function inside main cannot change the values of c or d. Inside the function, it is possible to change the values of a and b, but this cannot change the value of c or d. The function uses an internal copy of c and d. When it is called, the arguments, c and d, are evaluated and the calculated values are copied into the variables, a and b. Hence, the output of the program is:

```
a = 1,  b = 2
c = 3,  d = 4
```

Call-by-value parameter passing is quite limiting in that a function cannot pass information back, except through its return value. However, the limitation can be overcome using pointers, as discussed in Section 8.4.

7.8.1 Arrays as an exception

There is an exception to call-by-value: arrays are said to be "passed by reference". The fact that arrays are passed by reference means that the elements of an array can be changed from inside the function. A local copy of the array is not used inside the function, and changes to the array elements inside are propagated to the array variable outside the function. C passes an array name as a pointer to the first element of the array. The function can use the pointer it receives to access the values outside the function. In the example below, the array variable b is passed as an argument to the function clear_array. This function changes the array elements of a, and this changes the values of the elements of b. Each assignment to an element of a is also an assignment to an element of b.

```
#include <stdio.h>

void clear_array(int a[], int n)
{
    int i;

    for (i = 0; i < n; i++)
        a[i] = 0;          /* Change elements outside */
}
main()
{
    int b[2] = { 1, 2 };            /* b is an array variable */

    clear_array(b, 2);              /* b passed by reference */
    printf("b[0] = %d, b[1] = %d\n", b[0], b[1]);
}
```

The output from this program shows that the array variable b has been cleared by the clear_array function:

```
b[0] = 0, b[1] = 0
```

It is possible to pass arrays by value by passing the array as a field of a struct (because structs are passed by value), but this reduces readability and is not recommended.

7.8.2 const parameters

A common use of the const specifier (see 2.8.3) is to inform the compiler that the value of an array parameter is not changed by the function. For example, the prototype for the strcpy library function could be:

```
char *strcpy(char dest[], const char source[]);
```

because the source string is not changed, whereas the dest string is changed.

The compiler should produce a warning message if statements inside the function body attempt to change the value of a `const` array parameter. However, the appearance of `const` before a function parameter is not a guarantee of non-modification. The compiler cannot check for all possible modifications and the compiler must either trust the programmer or generate annoying warnings about every possible modifications. For example, what should the compiler do if the `const` array parameter is passed as an argument to another function, possibly in a separate file, where its array parameter is not specified as `const`?

Most of the comments in this section apply also to *pointer* parameters, because of the close relationship between arrays and pointers. `const` can be applied to a pointer parameter to indicate that the value(s) at which the pointer is pointing will not change. For example, a prototype of `strcpy` equivalent to the one given above is:

```
char *strcpy(char *dest, const char *source);
```

7.9 Storage classes for variables

Declarations of local variables inside a function can be extended to specify the type of storage. This is called the *storage class* of a variable. There are three storage class specifiers relevant to local variables:

```
auto     register    static
```

In addition, `extern` is a storage class specifier relevant to external variables (see Chapter 13).

Storage class specifiers apply to all variable declarations. The `auto` and `register` specifiers apply to local variables in functions and to formal parameters of a function. The `static` specifier cannot be applied to the formal parameters of a function. Neither `auto` nor `register` can be applied to global variables. The use of `static` for declaring global variables has a totally different meaning to its use for local variables.

Only one storage class specifier is permitted per variable. The following declaration is illegal:

```
static register int x;          /* ILLEGAL */
```

7.9.1 The auto storage class

Ordinary local variables are created on entry to the function and destroyed on exit. On most machines, they are dynamically stored on the program stack. Local variables do not retain their value between successive calls to a function. Ordinary variables have a storage class of `auto`. However, because this is the default, the keyword `auto` is very rarely used.

7.9.2 The register storage class

Variables declared with storage class `register` are ordinary variables, except that their declaration gives a little extra advice to the compiler. The keyword `register` informs the compiler that a variable is used frequently, and tells the compiler to store the variable in a hardware register for faster access, if possible. The `register` specifier can only be applied to simple variables because of the practical limitations of hardware registers. The use of `register` gives the programmer some control over efficiency, though the compiler is free to ignore the advice if it cannot find an available register. In the absence of any `register` declarations, the compiler makes its own choices of variables to place in registers. Indeed, the compiler is in a better position to determine which variables should be in hardware registers, and may well totally ignore all `register` specifications.

As with ordinary non-`static` local variables, `register` variables do not retain their value between function calls. On entry to the function, they contain garbage values unless explicitly initialized.

The most common use of `register` variables is integer counter variables in `for` loops and pointer variables. The examples below specify that the variables i, j and ptr should be placed in registers:

```
register int i, j;
register struct node *ptr;
```

The code fragment above specifies that both i and j should be put in registers with greater priority than ptr. However, it is compiler-dependent which of i and j has priority because the order of processing variables in a single declaration is undefined.

A limitation of `register` variables that is occasionally important is that it is impossible to take the address of a `register` variable using the & address-of operator. Because the variable may be stored in a hardware register, the compiler cannot calculate the address, and produces a compilation warning for all such attempts (even if the compiler actually couldn't place the variable in a hardware register).

7.9.3 The static storage class: local variables

It is possible to specify local variables that are not stored on the stack, but are stored like global variables. When this is done, they do retain their value between calls to a function. These variables are declared as `static` variables. Any type of variable can be declared as `static`. All `static` variables are identical in effect to global variables except that they can only be accessed within a single function. The examples below show the declaration of `static` variables:

```
static int   x;
static int   arr[100];
static struct node n;
```

Most simple programs will have no need for `static` variables. They are special purpose variables, and should not be used without good reason. The only reason to use them is when a variable must retain its value between function calls.

Like global variables, `static` variables are not destroyed between function calls. Hence, they can be used to store permanent results. The only difference between `static` variables and global variables is that the names of `static` variables have local scope — they can only be accessed inside one function.

7.9.4 The static storage class: global variables

The `static` specifier may be applied to global variables, and to function declarations. This use of `static` relates to the issues of scope and independent compilation, and is separate from its use for local variables. This usage of `static` is only relevant when writing programs comprised of more than one file as covered in Chapter 13. The only reason the same keyword was used was to avoid adding another to the language. The effect of:

```
static int x;
```

where x is a global variable in a file, is to make the variable name available within the file, but not in other files. The scope of the variable name is restricted to a single file. Similarly the effect of:

```
static int fn(void)
{
    ...    /* function body */
}
```

is to make the function name unavailable to other files, but still global within the current file.

7.10 Variable initialization

C permits variables to be given initial values which is a very convenient feature. All simple types, including pointers and enumerated types, can be initialized (whether they be `static`, `auto`, or `register`). Similarly, all aggregates (i.e. arrays, structures and unions) can be initialized. However, non-ANSI compilers may disallow initialization of automatic aggregate variables.

7.10.1 Implicit initialization

Implicit initialization refers to the initializations that occur without the programmer explicitly requesting them. Global variables, `static` or otherwise, are initialized to zero if there is no explicit initialization. Local `static` variables are also implicitly initialized to zero, if there is no specified initialization. These initializations take place once only, at compile-time.

Neither `auto` nor `register` variables are initialized implicitly. They have garbage values if not explicitly initialized. Note that all local variables have storage class `auto` unless explicitly declared using a particular storage class specifier.

7.10.2 Explicit initialization

Explicit initialization refers to the programmer explicitly placing an initialization within the program. C allows programmers to initialize variables to any value. The syntax involves the addition of an assignment sign to the variable declaration.

The initializer must be a constant expression for global variables and `static` variables, so that it can be calculated at compile-time. These variables are only initialized once, at the start of the program. Hence, `static` local variables are not re-initialized each time their function is entered.

For `auto` (normal) and `register` variables, the initializer can be any expression (i.e. not necessarily a constant expression). These initializations are performed each time the function is entered (i.e. at run-time). They are equivalent to putting assignment statements at the start of the function block.

```
void my_fn(void)
{
    static int save_value = 0;  /* Once, at start of program */
    int x = 0;                  /* Each time function begins */
}
```

7.10.3 Simple variable initialization

Simple variables are initialized by adding an assignment sign and the expression in the declaration. The expression must be constant for `static` or global variables, but can be any expression for other local variables. Some examples of initializations are:

```
int x = 1;
int a = 1, b = 2, c = 3;
static int half = (10 + 20) / 2;   /* constant expression only */
int max = arg - 1;
char c = 'D';
char ch2 = '\n';
```

Initialization of enumerated types is just like that for other simple variables. Each variable is initialized to a single expression. The only restriction is that the type of the initializing expression should be the correct enumerated type. If not, compilation warnings are issued. Some examples of `enum` initializations are:

```
enum piece_type piece = PAWN;
enum name {Fred, Jill, Mary} man = Fred, woman = Mary;
```

7.10.4 Array initialization

Array initializations use a comma-separated list of constant expressions, inside braces. If the size of the array is omitted, the compiler will count the initializers and use this as the size. The examples below show initialization of a one-dimensional array:

```
int arr[3] = {1, 2, 3};          /* Size specified */
int arr[] = {2, 3, 5, 7, 11};    /* Size unspecified */
```

If the size is specified, but differs from the actual number of initializers, the compiler will complain if too many initializers are present. If too few, the extra elements are filled with zeros corresponding to the type of the array elements — either character zero, integer zero, floating point zero, or `NULL` (not necessarily equivalent to filling with zero bytes).

Note that the padding with zeros does not occur when no explicit initialization of any elements is present. In this case, the array variable is totally uninitialized and may contain garbage.

Multi-dimensional arrays can be initialized by nested sets of braces. The list of braces must be comma-separated. Only the first dimension can be omitted. If the first dimension is omitted, the number of initializers will be counted and used as the first dimension. Multi-dimensional arrays can also be initialized by a single list containing all the initializers in sequence (i.e. only one pair of braces). In the example below, all but the enclosing braces could be left out, but this is not very readable. The examples below show initialization of two-dimensional arrays:

```
int arr[3][2] = { {1, 2} , {1, 2} , {1, 2} };
int a[][3] = { {1, 2, 3}, {4, 5, 6} };
```

7.10.5 Pointer and string initialization

Pointers are initialized exactly as simple variables, except in the special case of pointers to characters (i.e. strings). The initializer must evaluate to a pointer type.

```
char *p = NULL;
int *q = &x;
```

A pointer to char can be initialized to point to a string constant. The string constant can contain escapes (e.g. \n). The compiler will automatically add a zero at the end of the string. Strings specified this way are stored in a specially allocated area and the pointer is initialized to the address of the string in this area.

```
char *p = "This is a string \n";
char *line = "";                    /* Initially an empty string */
```

An array of character pointers can be initialized by a list of strings. As with all arrays, if the size is omitted, the number of elements is counted. The example below initializes an array of strings using three string constants:

```
char *p[3] = { "string1", "string2" , "string3" };
```

A character array can be initialized to a string. In this case, the characters are stored in space allocated for the character array and not in a special area of memory, as was the case for pointers to char.

```
char str[] = "This is another string\n";
```

If the size of the array is specified, the initialization is like any other array initialization, and the number of characters is checked for correctness. Too many characters provokes a warning, but too few characters is ignored (extra space is padded with zeros).

7.10.6 struct and union initialization

A struct variable can be initialized by a list of comma-separated constant expressions inside braces. The expressions correspond to the fields, in the order that they appear in the struct declaration. If too many initializers are present, this is an error. If too few, the extra fields are filled with zeros corresponding to the type of the field — either character 0, integer 0, floating point 0.0 or NULL (not necessarily always zero bytes).

This padding with zeros does not occur when no explicit initialization of any fields is present. In this case, the `struct` variable is totally uninitialized and may contain garbage.

An automatic structured variable can also be initialized by a single non-constant expression that evaluates to a value of that structured type (e.g. a function returning that type of structure). However, many non-ANSI compilers will not permit this special form of initialization.

Arrays of structures are initialized like multi-dimensional arrays. They are lists inside lists. The nested braces are not strictly necessary, but are good style. Some examples of `struct` initializations are shown below:

```
struct node {
    int data;
    char label[50];
    struct node *next;
};

struct node temp = {100, "label1", NULL};   /* One struct */

struct node arr[5] = {                       /* Array of struct */
    {1, "big", NULL},
    {2, "Cat", NULL},
    {3, "hi there", NULL},
    {4, "variable\n", NULL},
    {5, "", NULL}
};
```

The syntax for `union` initialization is identical to that for `struct`s, except that only a single initializer is allowed in the list. Unions can be initialized to a value for their first member only. This initialization may be in braces, or may be a single expression. Initialization of `union`s is newly introduced by ANSI and older compilers may disallow it.

7.11 Exercises

1. Write functions for the following:

    a) The average of two numbers.
    b) The length of a line segment given two pairs of x and y coordinates.
    c) The maximum of 3 numbers.
    d) Find the next non-whitespace and non-digit character in the input stream.
    e) Sum the numbers from 1 to n.
    f) Count down from n to 1. Ensure that it does not loop infinitely on a negative argument.
    g) Return a boolean value indicating if its argument is prime (a prime number is divisible only by 1 and itself). *Hint:* Use the remainder operator (%).

2. Why is it not possible to define a `void` function `max(a,b,m)` such that the maximum is returned in m? Can the value of the parameter be changed for use within the `max` function itself (e.g. as a scratch variable)? Under what conditions are changes to a parameter propagated back to the argument in the function *call*?

3. What is the effect when a function with no parameters is called without brackets, as below:

```
void mesg(void)
{
    printf("Hello world\n");
}

main()
{
    mesg;       /* Call the function? */
}
```

4. Explain the differences between prototyping and non-prototyping definitions of functions. What are the advantages of prototyping? Does non-prototyping have any advantages?

5. What type promotions are automatically carried out on function arguments in calls to non-prototyped functions? How does this explain the fact that `printf` uses `%f` for both `float` and `double`?

6. Can a global variable be declared between functions, rather than just at the top of the file? When are global variables initialized? What is the difference between a local `static` variable and a global variable?

7. What is the difference between `static` local variables and ordinary local variables? What effect does the `register` specifier have? When are `static`, `auto` and `register` local variables initialized? Are `register` local variables initialized implicitly to zero?

8. Can a pointer variable be declared as a "`register`" variable? Can the address of a `register` variable be calculated using the `&` operator?

9. Given the array declaration and initialization below, write an expression using the `sizeof` operator that enables us to automatically compute the number of elements in the array:

```
int a[] = { 1, 3, 5, 7 };
```

Chapter 8
Pointers

Pointers are a special type of variable in C. This chapter examines many of the basic concepts when dealing with pointers, and some of their applications. Pointers are commonly used for overcoming the call-by-value problem, by simulating variable parameters (see Section 8.4).

A pointer variable can point to any type of data. Pointers may point to simple types, to structures or even to other pointers. Pointers to functions are also possible (see Chapter 14). A special type of generic pointer is also provided — the void pointer.

Pointers have a very special relationship with arrays. Arrays are implemented as pointers to the first element of the array. In many instances pointers and arrays can be used interchangeably, but there are some differences.

8.1 Declaring pointer variables

Pointer variables are declared using a star (*) before the variable name. The type that the pointer points to is the type before the star. Some examples of pointer declarations are:

```
char *s;              /* s is a pointer to char (a string) */
int *p, *q;           /* p and q both pointer to int */
struct node *ptr;     /* Pointer to struct node */
```

When talking about a pointer type it is common to include the star in the type description. For example, rather than saying that s has type "pointer to char", it is common to refer to the type as char*.

A star must appear before all names that are to be pointer variables. If the star is omitted, the variable is not declared as a pointer to the type. For example, the definition:

```
int *ptr, ptr2;    /* WRONG */
```

defines ptr2 as an int, not a pointer to int. The correct definition is:

```
int *ptr, *ptr2;   /* CORRECT */
```

8.2 Pointer operators

Pointers are variables in the ordinary sense. Hence, they can be assigned to each other, assigned values from expressions (of the correct type) and initialized. In addition to the usual operations, there are some operations that particularly apply to pointers.

The address operator (&) is used to set a pointer to point to a particular variable. This operator calculates the address of a variable, which can be assigned to a pointer variable. The pointer then points to the location containing the variable.

The indirection operator (*) is used to access the value pointed to by a pointer. This operator returns what a pointer is pointing to. The result of the indirection operator is an l-value, so it can be used on the left-hand side to assign a value to the variable where the pointer is pointing. Hence, the effect of the * operator depends whether it is on the left or right of an assignment statement. The code fragment below shows the use of the various pointer operators:

```
int value, data;
int *ptr;

ptr = &value;   /* Set ptr to point to value */
*ptr = 3;       /* '*' on left: set what ptr points to */
data = *ptr;    /* '*' on right: copy what ptr points to */
```

If the pointer points to a struct, the dereferencing operator (ptr->field) is used to access members of the structure pointed to. This operator is similar to the str.field operator for structs, but applies only to pointers to structs. The use of the -> operator is illustrated below:

```
int value;
struct node {
    int data;
} *ptr;

value = ptr->data;
```

8.3 NULL pointers

Empty pointers in C are indicated by zero. More commonly, the symbolic constant NULL is used. Empty pointers are often referred to as NULL pointers. This symbol is usually defined in the <stdio.h> header file by:

```
#define NULL 0
```

NULL is a special value for a pointer to hold, indicating that it does not point to the address of any variable. It is important not to dereference a pointer variable when it contains NULL (using either * or ->). This is a run-time error in most implementations, causing a segmentation fault under UNIX and unpredictable behavior on other systems. Hence, it is common to test if a pointer is NULL before dereferencing it:

```
if (ptr != NULL)
    *ptr = 1;               /* Store 1 where ptr points to */
```

8.4 Call-by-reference using pointers

Functions cannot normally alter the value of variables passed as arguments, because of the call-by-value parameter passing mechanism. To change the value of a variable outside the function, pointers must be used. The address of the value to be changed must be passed to the function as an argument. The address operator is used to pass this address. The function receives the address as a pointer variable. To change the value from within the function, the address pointed to by the function can be altered, by using the indirection operator (*). The get_max function below calculates the maximum of a and b and stores it in the address pointed to by max:

```
void get_max(int a, int b, int *max)      /* max is a pointer */
{
    if (a > b)
        *max = a;          /* Store result where max points */
    else
        *max = b;
}

main()
{
    int x = 1, y = 2, max;

    get_max(x, y, &max);                   /* Pass address of max */
    printf("Max is %d \n", max);           /* Print max */
}
```

When a parameter is being passed down more than one level to be changed, there is a slight difference. On the top level, the method is identical to that above. However, when passing the variable down another level there is no need to prefix it with an & in the argument list. The variable is already a pointer, and does not need & to find its address. The & would be wrong, as it would pass a pointer to a pointer. An example of the use of two levels of call-by-reference is shown below:

```
#include <stdio.h>

void change2(int *x)
{
    *x = 3;
}

void change(int *x)
{
    change2(x);                /* No & needed */
}

main()
{
    int x;

    change(&x);                /* & needed */
    printf("x = %d\n", x);
}
```

Since the use of the * and & operators can be annoying, the most common solution is to avoid the need for variable parameters. Instead, values are returned back as the return value of functions (using the return statement). Unfortunately, this is limited to one returned value per function. Another alternative to using pointers is to use global variables thus avoiding passing parameters. This is quite a feasible solution, but can lead to bad style if overused, making programs more difficult to debug and modify.

8.5 Generic pointers: pointers to void

Pointers to `void` are a special type of generic pointer, usually referred to as `void` pointers. They point to "nothing", or rather, something with no specified type. Note that `void` pointers should not be confused with `NULL` pointers — `NULL` refers to the *value* of the pointer variable, whereas `void` refers to the *type* of the pointer variable.

`void` pointers can hold the value of any pointer, no matter what type the pointer points to. They can be assigned to any type of pointer. When any assignment occurs, any needed type cast occurs automatically. Assigning another pointer to a `void` pointer (or vice versa) should not give a compilation warning.

`void` pointers cannot be dereferenced by the `*` or the `->` operators. `void` pointers cannot be incremented or involved in address arithmetic, because the size of the object they point to is unknown. These operations are meaningless, as the type of the object pointed to is "nothing". The `sizeof` operator can be applied to a `void` pointer — it returns the size of the pointer. The `sizeof` operator can be applied to type `void*`, but not to `void` which has undefined size.

`void` pointers are used when it is necessary to deal with pointers without knowing what type of object is being pointed to. Many of the standard library functions make use of `void` pointers. For example, `malloc` returns a `void` pointer that points to the memory it has allocated. The `malloc` function does not know the type of the object it has just allocated, so it returns a `void` pointer.

8.6 Dynamic memory allocation

C programs have access to a large block of free memory, called the *heap*. The actual size of the available memory depends on the system. This memory is available to a C program which can allocate itself chunks of memory from this heap. This is useful when a C program does not know beforehand how much data is being stored, and hence, how much memory is required. Instead of allocating a large array to cater for the worst case, the program can allocate itself blocks of memory as required. Common uses of dynamic memory include dynamic arrays (see Chapter 14), linked lists and binary trees.

One of the two standard library functions, `malloc` and `calloc`, is used to allocate a new dynamic memory block from the system heap (which one is largely a matter of preference). The blocks are returned to the heap for re-use using the `free` function, and existing blocks can be enlarged or reduced using the `realloc` function. The prototype definitions of these functions are:

```
void *malloc(int size);
void *calloc(int size, int number);
void free(void *p);
void *realloc(void *p, int new_size);
```

To use the dynamic allocation functions, it is necessary to include the standard header file `<stdlib.h>`. On non-ANSI compilers, with no such header file, the functions are sometimes declared in `<malloc.h>`. Omitting this file inclusion is usually not fatal and merely results in warnings about use of pointers with integers, as `malloc` is declared by default to return an `int`.

The dynamic allocation functions store important information in a few bytes before the address that is returned. Hence, the program should not alter any memory other than that specifically within the bounds of the block.

8.6.1 The malloc function

The `malloc` library function allocates the number of bytes specified as its argument, and returns a pointer to the allocated memory, or `NULL` if there was no available memory (system out of memory). It does not initialize the memory at all. Most commonly, the `sizeof` operator is used to determine how many bytes are needed, as in the example below, which allocating a dynamic `struct` variable:

```
node_ptr new_node;
new_node = malloc(sizeof(struct node));
```

For strings, the expression `strlen(str)+1` is often used to calculate the required size. The extra byte is for the terminating zero.

```
char *s;
char *s2 = "Hello World"
s = malloc(strlen(s2) + 1);    /* allocate enough to copy s2 */
strcpy(s, s2);                 /* copy s2 to s */
```

Some implementations support the `strdup` function which has the same effect as the two statements above. However, `strdup` is not defined in the ANSI standard library.

In non-ANSI code, the returned value of `malloc` is usually type cast into the required pointer type:

```
s = (char*)malloc(...);
```

but the use of the `<stdlib.h>` header file makes this type cast unnecessary because `malloc` is declared as returning a `void` pointer.

8.6.2 The calloc function

The `calloc` function takes two parameters, the number of objects and their size. A call to `calloc` is almost equivalent to a `malloc` call using the product of the two arguments, and a call to `calloc` with 1 as the number of elements argument is similar to a `malloc` call. The difference is that `calloc` initializes its allocated memory to all character zeros (`calloc` stands for "clear-and-allocate"). The `calloc` function can be used to define a dynamic array as below:

```
int *arr;
arr = calloc(100, sizeof(int));    /* dynamic array of 100 ints */
```

8.6.3 The free function

The free standard library function is used to release a memory block and return it to the heap so that it can be re-used by subsequent malloc or calloc operations. A pointer to the memory block is passed to free and free does not return any result. The free function is used as below:

```
free(ptr);
```

The free function can only be applied to memory that has been explicitly allocated by malloc or calloc (i.e. not to global variables). A call to free does not set this pointer to NULL (it cannot, because of call-by-value). No action is performed if NULL is passed to free.

8.6.4 The realloc function

There is also another standard library function to *change* the size of an allocated memory block: realloc. The realloc function is needed because two successive calls to malloc do not usually return contiguous memory — a second call to malloc cannot be used to increase the size of a block. The realloc function takes two arguments, the address of the existing block, and the new size required. It returns a pointer to the new block, or NULL if there is no more available memory. If the new size is zero, realloc performs the same function as free. If the address argument is NULL, realloc behaves like malloc.

The realloc function can only be applied to blocks of memory previously allocated by malloc, calloc or an earlier realloc call. If the new size is larger, realloc allocates a new block of memory and moves the old block to the beginning of the new block. The extra space is not initialized.

Care must be taken if there are a number of pointers to the original block. A call to realloc usually moves the block elsewhere, making these pointers no longer correct (they become dangling references). When the block is moved, the old memory block is freed to the heap as if by a call to free. The method of usage for realloc is:

```
ptr = realloc(ptr, new_size);
```

8.7 Incrementing pointers and address arithmetic

Pointers can be incremented or decremented using ++ and --. The increment is not by one byte. Instead, the pointer is changed by the size of the object it points to. If a pointer points to an integer, incrementing it will move it to the next integer. For a pointer to char the increment is by one character (i.e. one byte).

A common use of incrementing a pointer is traversing an array. For example, instead of using an integer index, i, in the for loop:

```
for (i = 0; i < n; i++)
    arr[i] = 0;
```

a pointer variable can be used. The advantage is efficiency; the disadvantage is reduced readability.

```
for (ptr = arr; ptr < arr + n; ptr++)
    *ptr = 0;
```

Increment and decrement on pointers are identical to using address arithmetic to add or subtract one. Note that address arithmetic is used in the second comparison expression of the `for` loop above (i.e. in the expression `arr+n`). It is legal to add integer quantities to pointers. This integer is the number of elements to move along. This value is implicitly multiplied by the size of the elements that the pointer points, and this multiplication gives the number of bytes to increment the pointer by. For example:

```
p += 10;
```

sets p to be the 10th element further along. Similarly, using the − or −= operators to subtract an integer from a pointer will move a pointer backwards a number of elements.

Another feature of address arithmetic is that two pointer values can be subtracted to give the number of elements between them (assuming both pointers point to the same array). The number of elements is a signed integer with negative values allowed. Both pointers must have the same type because otherwise the compiler cannot know which pointer type to use in the calculation.

Let us now rewrite the string function `count_letters` presented in Section 6.4 to use a parameter of type `char*` and increment this pointer using address arithmetic. Note that call-by-value prevents the increment of s from affecting the value of the address of any string variable passed to the function (although the characters in the string can be changed).

```
#include <ctype.h>              /* Declare isalpha() */

int count_letters(char *s)
{
    int count;

    count = 0;
    for (; *s != '\0'; s++) {   /* For all characters */
        if (isalpha(*s))        /* If a letter */
            count++;            /* Increment counter */
    }
    return count;
}
```

8.8 Pointers and arrays: the relationship

There is a close relationship in C between arrays and pointers. Array names are, in many ways, just pointers to the first element in the array. The array indexing operation is identical to a pointer expression involving address arithmetic. The following algebraic identities hold:

```
array[exp]   ==   *(array + exp)
&array[exp]  ==   array + exp
```

These relationships have a number of consequences. First, the commutativity of + means that exp1[exp2] is equivalent to exp2[exp1], as discussed in Section 3.15.

Another consequence is that, in many situations, pointers can be used instead of arrays. For example, it is legal to apply the array indexing operator (i.e. square brackets) to a pointer. For example:

```
x = ptr[3];                /*   i.e.   x = *(ptr+3)   */
```

sets x to equal the third element away from ptr, where ptr is pointing into an array.

When an array is passed to a function, the *address* of the first element of the array is passed. An array formal parameter is implemented as a pointer variable (i.e. a pointer pointing to the start of the array). This explains why arrays are passed by reference, not by value. A local copy of the array is not used inside the function. Instead, a pointer to the original array is used. Hence, any change to an element of the local array variable is actually changing the original array.

The differences between pointers and arrays are few. The main one is that an array name is not a variable, whereas a pointer is. An array name cannot be assigned to, or incremented, whereas a pointer can be. An array is similar to a constant pointer (e.g. int *const ptr).

There are also the differences between pointers and arrays in relation to initializations. Consider the two initializations:

```
char *p = "hello";
char arr[100] = "hello";
```

For the pointer, the string "hello" is stored in separate memory. Only the required number of bytes are allocated (six, because of the extra character zero added by the compiler to terminate the string). For the character array, 100 bytes are allocated, but only the first six are filled.

8.9 Exercises

1. What are the values of x and y after execution of the code fragment below?

    ```
    int x = 1, y = 2;
    int *p1, *p2;

    p1 = &x;
    p2 = p1;
    y = *p1;
    *p2 = 3;
    ```

2. If p and q are pointer variables, what is the difference between the comparisons p==q and *p==*q? What is the output of the code fragment below?

    ```
    int x = 1, y = 1;
    int *p1, *p2;

    p1 = &x;
    p2 = &y;
    if (p1 == p2) printf("The pointers are equal\n");
    if (*p1 == *p2) printf("The objects are equal\n");
    ```

Chapter 8

3. Why is it a dangerous error to return the address of an ordinary local variable as the value of a function?

4. The code fragment below allocates memory for a pointer and then stores the address of another memory block in the first one. How many calls to `free` will be required to return all the memory to the heap, one or two?

   ```
   p = malloc(sizeof(char*));
   *p = malloc(100);
   ```

5. Address arithmetic means that increment moves a pointer a number of bytes equal to the size of its data type. Hence, to access individual bytes in memory, a pointer to `char` can be used because `sizeof(char)` is 1. Write a program to examine each byte of a `float` variable after assigning it the value zero. Are all bytes zero? Note that this is implementation-dependent. *Hint:* Use `sizeof` to calculate the number of bytes in a `float` variable.

6. Do you need a type cast when converting from `void*` to another pointer type? Is the expression `sizeof(void*)` valid? Is incrementing a `void` pointer with `++` legal?

7. Could the statement below be legal in some program?

   ```
   x = p->next->next->data;
   ```

Chapter 9
Input and output

There are a number of very powerful standard library functions to handle input/output. They are declared in the standard library header file `<stdio.h>`. This chapter assumes that `<stdio.h>` is always included using:

    #include <stdio.h>

It is also assumed that input comes from the keyboard and output goes to the screen. Chapter 10 examines how to perform input/output to any file.

There are three basic methods of input/output, each with their own library functions:

1. Formatted
2. Line by line
3. Character by character

Formatted input/output is the most flexible, and the most commonly used. It allows integers, floating point numbers and character strings to be input or output in character form. Line by line output prints a string and a newline. Line by line input reads up to a newline, into a string. Character by character input/output allows one character to be output, or one character to be input.

9.1 Formatted output: printf

Formatted output is the most commonly used form because it is the most flexible. It is the only type of output that allows easy printing of numbers. Formatted output is specified by a call to the `printf` function.

The `printf` function allows the output of any string of characters mixed with any integers, real numbers or strings. The `printf` function accepts as arguments a *format string* followed by any number of arguments of any types (zero or more extra arguments). As we will see soon, each extra argument must have a corresponding format specification in the format string. However, let us first look at some examples where the only argument to `printf` is the format string:

```
printf("Hello World\n");     /* print text, and newline */
printf("Word");              /* print text, but no newline */
printf("\n");                /* print newline (go to next line) */
printf("\n\n\n\n\n");        /* print 5 blank lines */
```

Note that `printf` does not automatically output a newline. To go to the next line, it is necessary to explicitly use \n in the format string. This can be annoying at first, but is very flexible because it allows a sequence of `printf` calls to build a single output line, or a single `printf` call to output multiple lines. For example, the code fragment:

```
printf("1. ");
printf("Hello\nWorld\n");
```

produces the following output:

```
1. Hello
World
```

The percent character (%) is a special character in format strings. It indicates how to print one of the other arguments passed to `printf`. The format specifications using % must exactly match the number of arguments. The character following the % sign indicates what type of value is to be printed. For example, a %d indicates to print out the integer passed to `printf`. The `printf` call:

```
printf("%d %d\n", i, j);
```

will print the value of i, followed by a space, and then the value of j. Because all characters except % are copied to the output, we can make the output more readable using:

```
printf("i = %d, j = %d\n", i, j);
```

which produces the output:

```
i = 3, j = 7
```

Both `float` and `double` variables can be printed out using the format options %f, %e, or %g. All three options apply to both `float` and `double`. The three different options cause different output format for the `float` or `double` variable. The option %f outputs in the format xxx.yyy, %e in exponential notation, and %g chooses the most appropriate of these two representations. For example, if the number is very small or very large the %g uses exponential notation. Note that %g also has the convenient feature of deleting trailing zeros. For example, the code fragment:

```
double x = 3.14;
printf("%f,  %e,  %g\n", x, x, x);
```

produces the following output on my computer:

```
3.140000,  3.140000e+00,  3.14
```

Character string variables can be printed out using the %s format option (i.e. char* or char[] types). Single characters can also be printed by `printf` using the %c option. The examples below show the use of %s and %c specifiers:

```
printf("%s", str);                      /* print out a string */
printf("Hi there, %s \n", name);        /* be friendly */
printf("%c", ch);
printf("The letter is %c \n", ch);
```

A full summary of the possible format characters is given in Table 9.1. Some formats, such as %n and %p, are relatively new and not all implementations will yet support them. In the cases of %E, %G and %X, capital letters are used in the output (for the E in exponential format, and the hexadecimal letters). In other cases, the capital letter can be used instead of the lower case letter with no difference in the results, but this is not common style.

Table 9.1. printf format specifications

Specifier	Meaning
%d, %i	Decimal integer
%c	Single character
%s	String of characters
%f	Floating point (e.g. 45.307)
%e	Floating point exponential format (e.g. 4.5e+1)
%g	The "best" of %f or %e, depending on the value
%%	Percent character (no argument required)
%u	Decimal unsigned integer
%o	Octal integer
%x	Hexadecimal integer
%p	Pointer
%n	Store the number of characters written so far

The %p specification is a special option to print out memory addresses using an implementation-dependent format (usually decimal or hexadecimal). This provides a portable way of printing pointer values, whereas the previous method has been to print pointers as decimal integers using %d.

The %n specification does not produce any output. Instead, it stores the number of characters written so far into the address passed as the argument. Hence, its argument must be a pointer to int.

The %u specification is useful when dealing with unsigned variables but has no other special feature.

The %o specification prints an integer in octal, but without a leading zero. The %x specification prints an integer in hexadecimal (with no 0x prefix). Note that the %X specifier uses capital letters for hexadecimal digits. For example, the code fragment:

```
int i = 125, n;
int *p = &i;

printf("%d, %i, %o, %x, %X, %p%n\n", i, i, i, i, i, p, &n);
printf("n = %d\n", n);
```

produces the following output:

```
125, 125, 175, 7d, 7D, 7fffbe48
n = 31
```

Note that 31 is the length of the line of output produced because %n is the last specification.

The printf function is not a void function, though this is its most common usage. The return value of printf is an integer giving the number of characters output. If it is negative, there was an error. This return value is usually ignored, as in all the above examples.

9.1.1 Fancy formatting: field width and precision

The printf function is a very versatile function and this section examines the full extent of the formatting choices that are available. Between the percent character and the format specification character there can be a number of other format modifiers. The four types of modifiers are:

1. Flags
2. Field width
3. Precision
4. Type modifier

These modifiers appear after the % character in the order specified above. After the % character there can be a number of flags, a field width specification and a precision specification. All three fields are optional and independent of the others.

9.1.1.1 Flags

Formatting flags are placed immediately after the % character. Multiple flags can be placed in any order. The possible flags are given in Table 9.2.

Table 9.2. printf flags

Flag	Meaning
−	Left justification in field width
+	Prefix positive numbers with a + sign
space	Prefix positive numbers with a space
0	Pad with leading zeros
#	Alternate output form

A minus sign indicates left justification within the field width (the default is right justification). The printed value appears on the left, and enough spaces are added to the right to make up the field width.

A plus sign indicates that positive numbers be prefixed by a plus sign. A space flag indicates that positive numbers are printed with a space. Negative numbers are always printed with a minus sign. The presence of both plus and space flags causes the space flag to be ignored. Both plus and space format flags are useful to line up columns of figures because negative signs can cause formatting problems.

A zero character indicates that padding to the field width be with leading zeros.

A hash sign (#) indicates an "alternate" output form. A prefix zero is added for octal (%o); a prefix 0x or 0X for hexadecimal (%x or %X); %e, %f and %g have a decimal point even if there are no digits after it; and also for %g trailing zeros are not removed.

9.1.1.2 Field width

The field width specifies the minimum number of characters that are printed. If a printed value uses less than that number of characters, it is right justified in a field of that many spaces. If more characters than the field width are required, the field width is ignored.

Left justification can be specified using a minus sign flag immediately after the %. Hence, the program fragment:

```
char * s = "Hello";
int x = 23;

printf("%10d%10s\n", x, s);
printf("%-10d%-10s\n", x, s);
```

will produce the following output:

```
        23     Hello
23         Hello
```

If the field width is specified as *, the field width is calculated by the next argument — the argument before the one to be printed — which must be an int. Thus, an equivalent way to specify the field width for x in the code above would be:

```
#define FIELD_WIDTH    10

printf("%*d\n", FIELD_WIDTH, x);
```

9.1.1.3 Precision

A period begins the precision specification. The precision has a meaning that is dependent on the type of argument being printed. For %e and %f it represents the number of digits after the decimal point. A precision of zero causes the suppression of the decimal point and all decimal digits. For %g it represents the number of significant digits to be printed. For %d it represents the minimum number of digits to be printed. For %s it represents the maximum number of characters to be printed (extra characters are ignored). This is summarized in Table 9.3.

As for the field width, the precision can be a star, indicating that it be calculated from the next argument. In fact, both field width and precision can be computed from an argument using *.* in the format string, as in:

```
printf("%*.*s\n", field_width, precision, str);
```

Table 9.3. Effect of precision

Specifier	Effect
%e, %f	Number of digits after decimal point
%g	Number of significant digits
%d	Minimum number of digits (pad with leading zeros)
%s	Maximum number of characters from a string

9.1.1.4 Type modifiers

Just before the conversion character, there can be one of the characters h, l and L. The letter h before d, o, x or u indicates short or unsigned short. The letter l before d, o, x or u indicates long or unsigned long. The letter L before e, f or g indicates long double. These are summarized in Table 9.4.

Table 9.4. printf type modifiers

Letter	Effect
h	Specify short type
l	Specify long type
L	Specify long double type

9.2 Formatted input: scanf

The formatted input function is scanf. It performs the opposite function to printf, converting character stream input into different types and storing these converted values in variables. The format string is similar to printf. The percent sign is used to indicate what types of values to look for. The most commonly used conversions are given in Table 9.5. Some examples of the use of scanf are given in the program below:

```
#include <stdio.h>

main()
{
   int i, x, y;
   float val;
   char str[100];

   scanf("%d", &i);         /* read in integer */
   scanf("%f", &val);       /* read in floating point */
   scanf("%s", str);        /* read in string */
   scanf("%d%d", &x, &y);   /* read 2 space-separated integers */
   printf("i=%d, val=%f, str=%s, x=%d, y=%d\n",i,val,str,x,y);
}
```

The %d and %f specifiers work as expected. The %d specifier accepts an integer value, consisting of an optional sign and a string of decimal digits. The %f specifier accepts a floating point value in any of the formats output by printf (i.e. fractional or exponential). In both cases, initial whitespace is skipped — scanf will read past spaces, tabs and newlines to get to a number. However, it will not read past incorrect

Table 9.5. Common scanf conversions

Specifier	Meaning
%d	Decimal integer (`int`)
%hd	Decimal integer (`short int`)
%ld	Decimal integer (`long int`)
%c	Single character
%s	String of characters
%e,%f,%g	Real number (`float`)
%le,%lf,%lg	Real number (`double`)

characters, such as letters. These would cause `scanf` to terminate without storing any value in the current variable.

The `%s` specifier for reading character strings will only read in a sequence of non-whitespace characters. It will skip any initial whitespace, then read characters up to the next whitespace character (i.e. up to a space, tab or the end of the line). A terminating zero is then automatically added to the end of the string. The character string must have already been allocated memory because `scanf` allocates no memory.

All the corresponding arguments to `scanf` must be addresses. In the examples above, `int`s and `float`s have the address operator (`&`) before them to pass a pointer containing their address. It is very important never to forget to use `&`; otherwise the program may crash when it executes the `scanf` statement. Unfortunately, it is not a syntax error to forget the `&`. Note that it is incorrect to place an `&` before a character string variable, as it is already a pointer type (arrays are equivalent in this situation).

It is also important to use the correct option for the correct type. Using `%f` instead of `%lf` for `double` may also cause a run-time error because `scanf` will attempt to store a `float` value at the address pointed to by a pointer to `double`.

Two successive `scanf` calls can read from the same line of input (i.e. `scanf` does not scan each line, but only looks ahead a character at a time). Hence, to read in two space-separated numbers, two successive `scanf` calls can be used:

```
scanf("%d", &x);
scanf("%d", &y);
```

The `%c` option is used to read a single character. When using the `%c` option, whitespace is not skipped. Hence, all characters (even spaces, tabs and newlines) are found when using `scanf` to read a character at a time.

Whitespace in the format string causes the input to be read up until the first non-whitespace character, which is left in the input stream for the next call to `scanf` to read. Two consecutive whitespace characters have the same effect as a single whitespace character. The placement of whitespace in the format string is not very important for options such as `%d`, `%f` and `%s` where whitespace is ignored anyway. However, this use of whitespace in the format string is crucial for the `%c` option because it does not skip whitespace. The first non-whitespace character can be read using a space before the `%c` option:

```
scanf(" %c", &ch);
```

Without the space in the format string, `%c` will just read the first character, even if it is whitespace.

Other characters in the format string have a very special purpose: *character matching*. Characters that are not part of a format option (and are not whitespace) must match the next character of the input. If input does not match these characters, `scanf` terminates, leaving the character that failed to match in the input stream. Note that input can be forced to match a percent character by using `%%`.

Whenever `scanf` terminates (successfully or unsuccessfully), it returns the number of successfully stored variables (not the number of characters read in). The only exception to this occurs when `scanf` encounters end-of-file, in which case it returns `EOF` (usually −1). End-of-file can occur when the user presses `<ctrl-d>` under UNIX or `<ctrl-z>` under DOS.

Under UNIX, the action of `scanf` is complicated by line buffering — input is not passed to the program until RETURN is pressed. This means that input is only passed to the program a line at a time. The program cannot process any input until it has a whole line. The program will wait for RETURN to be pressed, even if `scanf` is examining input a character at a time.

9.2.1 Details of scanf conversions

The `scanf` function has a large number of options, and most of its options are rarely used. The full list of legal conversions is given in Table 9.6.

Table 9.6. scanf conversions

Specifier	Meaning
`%d`	Decimal integer
`%c`	Single character
`%s`	String of characters
`%e,%f,%g`	Floating point number
`%u`	Unsigned decimal integer
`%o`	Octal integer
`%x`	Hexadecimal integer
`%i`	Decimal integer (possibly octal or hexadecimal format)
`%p`	Pointer value
`%n`	Write number of characters read so far
`%[..]`	Scan set
`%[^..]`	Negated scan set

All the corresponding arguments to `scanf` must be pointers. Arguments to `%d`, `%i`, `%o`, `%x` and `%n` must have type `int*`. Arguments to `%e`, `%f` and `%g` must have type `float*`. Arguments to `%c`, `%s`, `%[..]` and `%[^..]` must have type `char*`. Arguments to `%u` must have type `unsigned int*`.

9.2.1.1 Type modifiers

If an argument of type `short`, `long` or `double` is to be evaluated, this information must be supplied to `scanf`. A letter h, l or L can be placed between the % and the conversion character. The letter h before d, i, o, x or u indicates that the object is a `short int`; l indicates that it is `long`. The letter l before e, f or g indicates that the object is a `double`; L indicates that it is `long double`.

9.2.1.2 Assignment suppression

Assignment of converted values to variables can be suppressed using a star character (*) between the % and the conversion character. This is called *assignment suppression*. In this case, no argument is needed and the field is processed and then simply skipped. This is useful when needing to ignore some fields of formatted data. The converted field is not included in the count returned by `scanf` (only *assigned* conversions are counted in the return value).

9.2.1.3 Field width

The maximum length of a value can be specified by placing an integer between the % and the conversion character. This specifies the maximum field width of the current conversion. The call to `scanf` will process at most this many characters (ignoring whitespace skipped at the start of a conversion). The examples below show the use of field width specifiers and assignment suppression:

```
scanf("%3d", &i);       /* Read at most 3 digits of an int */
scanf("%1s", str);      /* Read first non-whitespace character */
scanf("%*s %ld", &i);   /* Ignore a string, read a long int */
```

9.2.1.4 Scan-set conversions

The scan-set format options require closer examination. These are specified by pairs of square brackets. Any characters inside these brackets are included in the set of characters that is scanned. Any string of these characters is stored to the character pointer argument. The normal skip over whitespace is suppressed. The field ends when a character not in the set is found (or if the maximum field width has been specified). A terminating zero is appended to the string. Note that `scanf` will terminate unsuccessfully if no characters match this option.

The presence of a caret (^) as the first character causes characters *not* in the set to be scanned for. This action is identical to its use in UNIX regular expressions. In this case, the scan continues until a character in the set is found.

A caret (^) can be included in the set if it is not the first character. A left bracket ([) can be included normally. A right bracket (]) can be included if it is the first character after the [, or after the ^ in the negated case (e.g. %[]abc], %[^]abc]). In some implementations, ranges of characters can be specified as in %[a-z0-9], and the minus sign can be included if it is the first or last character. Other implementations may treat the minus sign as having no special meaning — the ANSI standard states that a minus sign in a scan-set conversion has undefined effect.

9.2.2 Handling incorrect input

The scanf function is not very forgiving if input does not match its requirements. It simply terminates, leaving the offending character in the input and returns the number of correct conversions carried out. The return value of scanf can be used to check for errors in input. For example, when waiting for an integer, if the user types a non-digit, scanf will return a count less than the number expected (i.e. less than that when all values are read). Similarly, when waiting for two integers (which must be space-separated), if the user places a comma between the two numbers, scanf will return an incomplete count.

The problem of incorrect input is particularly common in interactive input from a human. The limitations of scanf quickly become apparent, and my personal preference is to avoid using scanf by writing my own input function for each new task. Nevertheless, scanf can be used for interactive input if care is taken to examine its return value and to read over any incorrect input that appears. The program below shows one method of waiting for correct input of two integers using scanf:

```
#include <stdio.h>

main()
{
    int i, j, count;

    do {
        printf("Enter two space-separated integers: ");
        count = scanf("%d%d", &i, &j);
        if (count < 2) {                    /* Both numbers found ? */
            scanf("%*[^\n]");               /* Skip bad input */
            printf("Incorrect!\n");
            printf("Try again\n\n");
        }
    } while (count < 2);                    /* Until get valid input */
}
```

This example shows the two features of handling bad input. First, the return value of scanf is examined. If it is not 2, action must be taken to receive the input again.

Second, once bad input is identified, the rest of the input line is trashed using a second (complicated) call to scanf. The specification "%*[^\n]" skips all characters up to the newline but does not assign the value anywhere because * indicates assignment suppression. Without this second call to scanf, the program would loop infinitely when a letter was accidentally typed as input (because the letter would always cause %d to fail and would remain in the input — a bad input character is always left in the input).

9.3 Line input/output: gets, puts

The gets and puts functions are used for line by line input/output. Their prototype definitions are:

```
int puts(char *line)
char *gets(char *line)
```

The `puts` output function writes the string argument to output, and adds a newline. The `gets` input function reads input up to a newline, storing input in the string. It does not allocate any new memory. These functions are used as below:

```
puts("Hello World");            /* Print a line */
gets(str);                      /* Get an input line */
```

Note that error conditions are so rare that the return value from these functions is usually ignored. Errors are more common when input/output is related to a file, for which similar functions, `fgets` and `fputs`, are used. These are discussed in Chapter 10.

9.4 Character input/output: getchar, putchar

These functions are even more rudimentary than `puts` and `gets`. They allow input or output of a single character. This gives the programmer low-level control of input/output. The examples below demonstrate the usage of these functions:

```
putchar('h');                   /* print a "h" */
putchar('\n');                  /* print a newline */
putchar(ch);                    /* output a character variable */
ch = getchar();                 /* Get a character from the input */
```

The `putchar` function sends its argument to the output. The `getchar` function will read a single character from the input. The return value of `getchar` is actually an `int`, but the variable above receiving the result of `getchar` is defined as `char` type. Under some conditions, it may be necessary to use type `int` — see the discussion of `getc`. Again, error conditions are rare and usually ignored.

Note that on UNIX systems it is not normally possible to use `getchar` to implement a "press any key" facility. UNIX input is line buffered by the terminals. For example, try the following program on your system:

```
#include <stdio.h>

main()
{
    char ch;

    printf("Press any key to continue...");
    ch = getchar();
    printf("The key you pressed was '%c'\n", ch);
}
```

Under UNIX the terminal waits for the user to press RETURN before sending a single character. It is possible to alter this using advanced methods, but they are not covered here.

9.5 Exercises

1. What is the output of the following code fragment?

    ```
    printf("Hello");
    printf("World");
    ```

2. How do you print out a string variable? How do you print double quotes on either side?

3. How do you print out a percent sign using `printf`? What is the subtle bug in the incorrect method of printing a string given below?

    ```
    printf(str);
    ```

4. What is the output of code fragment below? How can it be abbreviated to one `printf` call?

    ```
    char s[100];

    sprintf(s, "%%-%ds %%-%ds\n", width1, width2);
    printf(s, string1, string2);
    ```

5. What is the meaning of a star (*) directly after a % character in a `printf` format specification? How many arguments to `printf` are needed to match the format string: `"%*d%d"`?

6. What is the error in the code fragment below which attempts to read the first non-whitespace character? How can `%c` be used to perform the task correctly?

    ```
    char c;

    scanf("%1s", &c);
    ```

7. What is the meaning of a star (*) directly after a % character in a `scanf` format specification? How many arguments to `scanf` are needed to match the format string: `"%*d%d"`?

8. How can `scanf` be used to read an integer in character form (i.e. a string of digits) when the next character after the digit need not be whitespace? How can `scanf` read an identifier (consisting of only letters, digits and underscores)?

9. Write a program that repeatedly asks the user for a *line* of input consisting of any number of integers, and then outputs the sum of the integers on each line. *Hint:* Why is `scanf` inappropriate for this?

10. (advanced) Why is the & not needed on string arguments to `scanf`? Why is there no need for different `printf` specification characters for `float` and `double` values, but `scanf` has `%e` for `float` and `%le` for `double`? *Hint:* See the discussion of argument promotion in Section 7.4.

Chapter 10
File operations

Many programs use files to store data on disk. Files allow the manipulation of large amounts of data and also allow data to be retained when a program is executed more than once. There are a number of standard library functions declared in `<stdio.h>` to allow a program to create, access and modify files, and this chapter examines all of them.

There are two main types of files, *text files* and *binary files*. Text files are made up of characters (usually printable) as would be created by an ordinary text editor. Binary files contain data stored in the internal form used by the computer. For example, a binary file of integers would allocate four bytes for each integer, just as the machine would. Binary files allow more efficient transfer of data between the program and the disk file because there is no need for conversion, whereas storing integers in a text file requires conversion between character form and internal form. Generally speaking, text files should be used for character data and binary files used for other types of data (e.g. integers, floating point values, `structs`).

There are two methods of accessing files — *sequential* and *direct access*. Sequential access refers to the method of reading a file from start to end without backtracking or skipping parts of it. Direct access refers to jumping to a particular location within a file and reading the data there. The most commonly used method is sequential access and the discussion of text files below assumes sequential access. Both sequential and direct access methods are discussed for binary files.

Input/output using the standard library functions in `<stdio.h>` is *buffered*. This means that any output to a file may not immediately be written to the disk file. Instead, the output functions fill up a buffer (in memory), only writing to disk when the buffer is full. In this way, only large blocks are written to the file, which increases efficiency (e.g. it avoids writing to the disk for every character output). Most of the time this is transparent to the user, but in some situations it can cause problems. For example, when a program crashes, not all of the output buffer may have been written and the contents of the output file may be misleading.

10.1 Text files

The standard library makes text file access similar to normal input/output as discussed in Chapter 9. The functions for file input/output are very similar to those for keyboard and screen input/output. In fact, for every function discussed in that chapter, there is an equivalent function to operate on files. The correspondence is shown below:

```
printf   →   fprintf
scanf    →   fscanf
gets     →   fgets
puts     →   fputs
getchar  →   getc
putchar  →   putc
```

The prototype definitions of the new functions are:

```
int fscanf(FILE *fp, char *format, ...)
int fprintf(FILE *fp, char *format, ...)
int fgets(char *str, int max, FILE *fp)
int fputs(char *str, FILE *fp)
int getc(FILE *fp)
int putc(int ch, FILE *fp)
```

The main difference between these functions and the functions discussed in Chapter 9 is the fp argument of type FILE*. This is called the *file pointer* corresponding to the particular file. The file pointer is a pointer to a FILE struct (an internal structure used by the library functions). FILE is declared in <stdio.h> and, hence, all file manipulations require the inclusion of the <stdio.h> header file.

The file pointer is the variable used to indicate which file is being accessed. This means that to access a particular file, there must be a way to associate a filename with that file pointer. This is achieved by *opening* the file. Removing this connection is called *closing* a file. These operations are achieved using the fopen and fclose functions discussed in the next section.

A special symbolic constant is used to indicate the end of a file. EOF is declared in <stdio.h>, most commonly with the value -1. To detect end-of-file, the return value from input functions must be carefully examined. For example, getc will return EOF when an end-of-file occurs. This causes a minor difficulty. Even though getc usually returns a character, EOF is not a character and hence getc has return type int. Assigning the return value of getc to a char variable is incorrect; the variable should be of type int.

10.1.1 stdin, stdout, stderr

When a program starts execution it always has three files already open. These files are defined by the names stdin, stdout and stderr, all of which are declared in <stdio.h>. These special file pointers are *constants* of type FILE*; they are not variables. The three constants are summarized in Table 10.1.

Normal keyboard input comes from stdin, stdout is the file that normal output goes to, and stderr is a special output file that is used to output error messages. Most of the time stderr will also go to the normal output stream with stdout. It is only when redirecting the output of the program that a difference arises (see Section 16.3.3).

Table 10.1. Standard FILE* constants

Name	Meaning
stdin	Standard input
stdout	Standard output
stderr	Standard error

Of the three constants, stdin, stdout and stderr, the most commonly used is stderr. It is useful when it is required that output be sent to stderr (e.g. debugging output). The constant stderr can be passed directly to output functions such as fprintf. A common use of stderr is for writing program error messages:

```
if (len >= MAX_LEN)
    fprintf(stderr, "String is too long\n");
```

10.1.2 Opening and closing text files: fopen, fclose

Before a file can be used it must be opened using the fopen library function. When a file is no longer needed it should be closed using the fclose library function. The prototype declarations of these functions are:

```
FILE *fopen(char *filename, char *mode)
int fclose(FILE *fp)
```

Opening a file checks that the file exists, checks that you have permission to access it and associates a file pointer with that file. The fopen function is used to open a file, and accepts a character string filename and a character string mode. The mode argument can be any of the strings listed in Table 10.2.

Table 10.2. fopen modes

Mode	Meaning
"r"	Read mode
"w"	Write mode
"a"	Append mode

If a file does not exist for write or append mode, a new file is created. If a file does exist for write mode, its existing contents are lost and the file is rewritten. The fopen function returns NULL if the file cannot be opened for any reason (e.g. file not found; permission denied). The example below shows how to check for errors when using fopen:

```
FILE *fp;                            /* file pointer variable */
char *filename = "myfile.dat";       /* name of the file */

fp = fopen(filename, "r");           /* Open file for reading */
if (fp == NULL) {
    fprintf(stderr, "Error opening %s\n", filename);
    exit(1);
}
...              /* File opened ok */
```

The above use of fopen is very common operation. It is common to see a few different, more efficient versions of the above statements used (though their use is not recommended because of the loss of readability). These alternatives use assignment inside a conditional expression:

```
if ((fp = fopen("myfile.dat", "r")) == NULL)
if (!(fp = fopen("myfile.dat", "r")))
```

It is possible to have more than one file open at a time — for this, more than one file pointer variable is needed. There is an upper limit on the number of files that can be open at any one time. The symbolic constant FOPEN_MAX, declared in <stdio.h>, represents this limit, which is usually at least 20. For most applications there is no need for concern, as only a few files are open at any one time.

To ensure that there are only a few files open, it is necessary to close files that are no longer needed. Opening another file using the same file pointer variable does not close the first one. Opening the same file again without first closing it is also incorrect. The library function fclose is used to close a file, as shown below:

```
fclose(fp);
```

Closing a file performs a number of tasks. It frees space in a system table to allow more files to be used (this is the reason for the limit on open files — the table has a fixed size). The call to fclose also flushes any output buffers, allowing other programs to access the file in its entirety. The fclose function returns zero for success; EOF on error (e.g. failure to write output when flushing buffers). In many cases, fclose is not strictly necessary, since files are automatically closed on program termination, but is good practice.

10.1.3 Text input/output: fprintf, fscanf, fputs, fgets, getc, putc

All of the input/output functions for the screen and keyboard have analogous functions for text files. For the most part, the details of the usage of these functions are identical to those for their equivalent functions discussed earlier in the chapter. The main difference is the need to remember the file pointer argument. An important difference appears in the return values of some of the functions. For proper error-handling, return values must always be checked.

The constant EOF is declared in <stdio.h> to be −1. Many of these functions return EOF for error conditions. Since −1 is not a legal char value, this explains why functions such as getc and putc have return type int, and not char. Note that because of C's automatic type conversions, the distinction between int and char in the *argument* to putc can usually be ignored. However, it is incorrect to assign the *return value* of putc to a char variable.

10.1.3.1 Formatted input/output: fprintf, fscanf

The functions for formatted input/output to text files are fscanf and fprintf. These functions are almost identical to the scanf and printf functions discussed in Chapter 9 and only a brief discussion is presented here.

The prototype declarations for `fscanf` and `fprintf` are:

```
int fscanf(FILE *fp, char *format, ...)
int fprintf(FILE *fp, char *format, ...)
```

The `fscanf` function returns `EOF` if an error occurs, or end of file is found; otherwise it returns the number of successful input conversions (as for `scanf`).

The `fprintf` function returns `EOF` if an error occurs; otherwise it returns the number of characters output — `printf` does the same, but its return value is usually ignored. In some environments, `printf` and `fprintf` merely return zero for success and negative for failure — this less strict assumption is more portable.

10.1.3.2 Line input/output: fgets, fputs

The functions for line by line input/output to text files are:

```
char* fgets(char *str, int max, FILE *fp)
int fputs(char *str, FILE *fp)
```

The `fgets` function returns `NULL` if an error or end of file occurs; otherwise the `char*` argument passed to it (i.e. the line read in).

There are a number of differences between `gets` and `fgets`. The obvious difference is the extra argument, `max`, limiting the number of characters transferred. The other crucial difference is that `fgets` retains the newline character from the end of a line. This can be deleted using:

```
if (line[strlen(line) - 1] == '\n')      /* If \n on end */
    line[strlen(line) - 1] = '\0';       /* Delete it */
```

The `if` statement is needed because there may be no newline on the last line of a file.

The `fputs` function returns `EOF` if an error occurs; otherwise non-negative. It is also different to the `puts` function in that it does not add a newline to the output. This behavior is consistent with `fgets` which does not delete the newline.

Below is a function that echoes a file line-by-line using `fgets` and `fputs`:

```
#define MAX   100      /* Maximum line length */

void output_file(char *filename)
{
    FILE *fp;
    char line[MAX];

    fp = fopen(filename, "r");         /* Open for reading */
    if (fp == NULL) {                  /* Error in opening file? */
        fprintf(stderr,"Error opening %s\n", filename);
        exit(1);
    }

    while (! feof(fp)) {
        if(fgets(line, MAX, fp) == NULL)   /* Read next line */
            break;
        fputs(line, stdout);               /* Output to screen */
    }
    fclose(fp);                        /* Close the file */
}
```

10.1.3.3 Character input/output: getc, putc

The functions for character by character input/output are:

```
int getc(FILE *fp)
int putc(int ch, FILE *fp)
```

The `getc` function returns `EOF` if an error or end-of-file occurs; otherwise the character read. The `putc` function returns `EOF` if an error occurs; otherwise the character just written.

There are also two functions, `fgetc` and `fputc`, which are identical to `getc` and `putc` except that `getc` and `putc` are macros, whereas `fgetc` and `fputc` are proper functions. The difference is only crucial in rare circumstances: if arguments to `getc` or `putc` have side effects, or if a pointer to one of these functions is required.

Given below is a function that reads in a file, character by character, outputting it to the screen. It uses `fopen` to open the file, `getc` to read each character and `putchar` to output them to the screen.

```
void output_file(char *filename)
{
    FILE *fp;
    int ch;                 /* int, not char */

    fp = fopen(filename, "r");      /* Open file for reading */
    if (fp == NULL) {               /* Error opening file ? */
        fprintf(stderr, "Error opening %s\n", filename);
        exit(1);
    }
    while ((ch = getc(fp)) != EOF) {  /* next char from file */
        putchar(ch);                  /* Output to screen */
    }
    fclose(fp);             /* Close the file */
}
```

End-of-file can also be tested by the function `feof`. This returns non-zero if end-of-file has occurred; zero if not yet end of file. In other words, it returns true if the end of the file has been reached. It can be used instead of testing for `EOF`, but using `EOF` is preferable. The modification to the above example to use `feof` is:

```
while (! feof(fp)) {            /* While not end of file */
    ch = getc(fp);
    putchar(ch);                /* Output to screen */
}
```

10.2 Error handling: ferror, perror

Many of the input/output functions return `EOF` on both end-of-file and error (not making a distinction between the two). The status of files can be tested fully using `feof`, and also `ferror`. Both are boolean functions, indicating the presence of end-of-file or an error condition, respectively.

Another standard library function, `perror`, can be used to print out an implementation-defined error message which appears on the `stderr` output stream. The `perror` function accepts a string argument which is printed followed by a colon and the system error message. This argument is your error message, to which the system appends its own. The argument to `perror` is often used to indicate the filename causing the error.

Using `feof`, `ferror` and `perror`, the error handling of the above example can be improved so as to output an error message to the screen. The program will read in a file, character by character, copying it to the screen. It handles errors by printing a system message prefixed by the filename of the offending file, and returning a boolean flag as its returned value.

```
void output_file(char *filename)
{
    FILE *fp;
    int ch;         /* Int, not char */

    fp = fopen(filename, "r");    /* Open file for reading */
    if (fp == NULL) {
        perror(filename);
        exit(1);                  /* Error opening file */
    }

    while ((ch = getc(fp)) != EOF) {  /* next char from file */
        putchar(ch);                   /* Output to screen */
    }

    if (ferror(fp)) {             /* EOF occurred due to error? */
        perror(filename);
        exit(1);
    }
    fclose(fp);     /* Close the file */
}
```

For greater control of error handling the type of the error can be discovered by examining the external `int` variable `errno` which is declared in `<errno.h>`. Note that this variable is examined by `perror` when it chooses the message to print. The value of `errno` can be compared to constants declared in `<errno.h>` to determine the type of error. For example, `EPERM` indicates permission denied and `ENOENT` indicates that there was no such file or directory.

There is also one other library function related to end-of-file and file errors. The function:

```
void clearerr(FILE *fp)
```

clears the flags indicating end-of-file and error that are stored in the file control block pointed to by the file pointer, causing `feof` and `ferror` calls for that file pointer to return false.

10.3 Binary files: fread, fwrite

The above sections have discussed input/output related to text files. Another common use of files is to store data in binary form. For example, an integer can be stored in binary form in a binary file, whereas it would be stored as a sequence of ASCII digits in a text file. Binary files are often more compact than text files, and are more convenient for storing large volumes of data (e.g. arrays of structs). However, data files generated as binary files are not portable, because of the system-dependent representation of integers and other data types. Never use binary files if data file portability is important — use text files.

Binary files are opened slightly differently to text files. This allows the operating system to distinguish between text and binary files. Some operating systems, notably UNIX, make no distinction between the two types of files, but using this quirk limits the portability of the program. Binary files are opened by appending a 'b' to the mode argument of fopen. The modes are listed in Table 10.3.

Table 10.3. fopen modes for binary files

Mode	Meaning
"rb"	Read binary file
"wb"	Write to binary file
"ab"	Append to binary file

Input and output to binary files are achieved using the fread and fwrite library functions. The prototype definitions of these functions are:

```
int fread(void *buffer, int size, int num, FILE *fp);
int fwrite(void *buffer, int size, int num, FILE *fp);
```

where buffer is the address of the data item(s), size is the size of each data item, num is the number of data items, and fp is the file pointer.

Both fread and fwrite return the number of objects successfully read or written. If this is less than the number requested, either end-of-file or an error has occurred. A few examples are given below:

```
int i, arr[MAX];

fwrite(&i, sizeof(int), 1, fp);         /* Write one int */
fwrite(arr, sizeof(int), MAX, fp);      /* Write array of int */
```

10.4 Direct access: fseek, rewind, ftell

Using only fopen, fread and fwrite functions it is possible to access value in a binary file in *sequential* order. This is satisfactory for many applications, but there are situations where we would like to access the 100th integer stored in a file. In a sequential binary file this would involve reading the first 99 integers before the desired value could be found. The use of *direct access* on binary files solves this problem by allowing the program to jump to any location in the file and then perform a fread or fwrite operation. For example, the 100th integer could be found at location:

```
99 * sizeof(int)
```

Because we can easily access any element in a file, using direct access is similar to maintaining an array on disk (although much slower).

To use direct access on a file, the file must be opened to allow both read and write operations. Direct access is specified using a plus sign in the mode field of fopen as shown in Table 10.4.

Table 10.4. fopen modes for direct access

Mode	Meaning
"rb+"	Open binary file for read/write
"wb+"	Create/Truncate binary file for read/write
"ab+"	Open/Create binary file for read/write at the end

The modes "r+", "w+" and "a+" are also legal, but are not frequently used. Using direct access on text files is not very common. Note that some non-ANSI implementations may specify direct access using "rw".

Note that append mode ("ab+") prevents the existing contents of the file from being overwritten. The contents may be read by direct access using fseek to get to the location, but all writes take place as if in normal append mode — sequentially at the end of the file.

Direct access to the file is achieved by moving to the required location using the function fseek, and then performing input or output using fread or fwrite. The library functions use a *file position pointer* to keep track of the current position in the file — the location where the next read or write will occur. This pointer is stored in the system table of open files. Do not confuse this pointer with the FILE* pointer which has a very different purpose (the file position pointer is used internally by the library; the FILE* pointer is used by the programmer to refer to a file). Hence, the main action of the fseek function is to set the file position pointer. The definition of fseek is:

```
int fseek(FILE *fp, long offset, int origin)
```

The fseek function returns zero for success; non-zero on error. The offset argument is a large (signed) integer indicating the number of *characters* to move from the origin. The origin is an int value of 0, 1 or 2 to indicate the beginning of the file, the current position or the end of the file. Three symbolic constants are defined in <stdio.h> to represent these values: SEEK_SET, SEEK_CUR and SEEK_END. The constants are summarized in Table 10.5.

If origin is the start of the file, the file position pointer is set to offset. If origin is the current position, the offset is added to the file position pointer. If origin is the end of the file, the offset is added to the location of the end of the file. Note that offset is a signed quantity and negative values are allowed, causing the position to move backwards from the origin.

The rewind function can be used to set the file pointer to the beginning of the file. It is functionally equivalent to fseek(fp, 0, 0). Its definition is:

```
int rewind(FILE *fp)
```

Table 10.5. fseek origin values

Name	Value	Meaning
SEEK_SET	0	Beginning of file
SEEK_CUR	1	Current position
SEEK_END	2	End of file

Direct access input/output consists of using fseek to get to the required location and then using fread or fwrite. Both fread and fwrite advance the file pointer to the next location, so that consecutive reads or consecutive writes can be performed without another call to fseek. However, reads and writes cannot be mixed without an intervening call to a file positioning function — fseek or rewind.

The current position of the file pointer can be examined using the function ftell. It returns the current offset from the beginning of the program, or –1 on error. Its definition is:

```
long ftell(FILE *fp)
```

There are two other library functions that can be used for positioning within a very large file. These functions are more general than the use of ftell and fseek. The functions:

```
int fgetpos(FILE *fp, fpos_t *ptr)
int fsetpos(FILE *fp, fpos_t *ptr)
```

can be used for large files where a long value is not large enough to hold the address of the current position in the file. The type fpos_t is a type declared in <stdio.h> to hold all possible file addresses. The fgetpos function stores the current file position in the address pointed to by ptr. The fsetpos function sets the current file position to be that stored in the address pointed to by ptr. The return value of both functions is zero on success, non-zero on error.

Presented below is an example of the maintenance of a database of records in a binary file, accessed using direct access methods. The program is a modification of the program in Section 5.4 to store the structs in a binary data file. The program illustrates a few design choices. It is necessary to store not only the records, but also the count of how many records are in the file. This is achieved by storing the count as a single integer at the start of the binary file, and storing records after it. This explains the calculation of an employee record address as:

```
sizeof(num_employees) + x * sizeof(struct employee);
```

The only other alternative was using another separate data file to hold the value of num_employees.

Note the use of the open_file and close_file functions. It would have been possible to open the file at the start of the program and close it at the end, but this creates problems if the program is aborted (any added employees would not be counted because the updated num_employees variable would not be stored on disk). Hence, the file is opened only when needed, and closed immediately after use.

```c
/*------------------------------------------------------------------*/
/* PAYROLL:  Employees and salaries in a BINARY DATA FILE           */
/*------------------------------------------------------------------*/

#include <stdio.h>
#include <stdlib.h>
#include <string.h>

#define DATAFILE        "employees.dat"
#define MAX_NAME_LEN    50          /* Maximum length of a name */

struct employee {                   /* Struct containing employee info */
    int salary;
    char name[MAX_NAME_LEN + 1];
};

int num_employees = 0;              /* Number of employees */
FILE *fp;                           /* Data file pointer */

/*------------------------------------------------------------------*/
/* PUT_REC:  Write out a struct to the binary data file             */
/*------------------------------------------------------------------*/

void put_rec(int x, struct employee *p)
{
    long location;

    location = sizeof(num_employees) + x * sizeof(struct employee);
    fseek(fp, location, SEEK_SET);
    fwrite(p, sizeof(struct employee), 1, fp);
}

/*------------------------------------------------------------------*/
/* GET_REC:  Read in the struct from the binary data file           */
/*------------------------------------------------------------------*/

void get_rec(int x, struct employee *p)
{
    long location;

    location = sizeof(num_employees) + x * sizeof(struct employee);
    fseek(fp, location, SEEK_SET);
    fread(p, sizeof(struct employee), 1, fp);
}

/*------------------------------------------------------------------*/
/* CLOSE_FILE:  Save counter to front of file and call fclose()     */
/*------------------------------------------------------------------*/

void close_file(void)
{
    rewind(fp);
    fwrite(&num_employees, sizeof(num_employees), 1, fp);
    fclose(fp);
}

/*------------------------------------------------------------------*/
/* OPEN_FILE:  Open the data file, read in counter                  */
/*------------------------------------------------------------------*/

void open_file(void)
{
    fp = fopen(DATAFILE, "rb+");
    if (fp == NULL) {
        fp = fopen(DATAFILE, "wb+");    /* Create new file */
        num_employees = 0;              /* No employees yet */
    }
    else    /* Opened file.  Read in counter */
        fread(&num_employees, sizeof(num_employees), 1, fp);
}
```

Chapter 10

```c
/*------------------------------------------------------------------*/
/* LIST_EMPLOYEES:  Print out the employees and their salaries      */
/*------------------------------------------------------------------*/
void list_employees(void)
{
    int i;
    struct employee temp;

    printf("\n\n          PAY ROLL\n\n");
    printf("%10s    %10s\n", "Name    ", "Salary");
    for (i = 0; i < num_employees; i++) {
        get_rec(i, &temp);
        printf("%10s        %d\n", temp.name, temp.salary);
    }
    printf("\n");
}

/*------------------------------------------------------------------*/
/*  ADD_EMPLOYEE: Get new information and store in the table        */
/*------------------------------------------------------------------*/

void add_employee(void)
{
    char name[MAX_NAME_LEN + 1];
    int salary;
    struct employee temp;

    printf("\n\nAdding new employee ...\n\n");
    printf("What is the new employee's name? ");
    scanf("%s", name);
    printf("What is the new employee's salary? ");
    scanf("%d", &salary);

        /* Add the information in the last unused struct */

    temp.salary = salary;              /* Store the salary */
    strcpy(temp.name, name);           /* Store the name */
    put_rec(num_employees, &temp);     /* Save new record to disk */
    num_employees++;                   /* Increment counter */
}

main()
{
    int choice;

    do {                                   /* List menu choices */
        printf("\n\n       MENU\n\n");
        printf(" 1.  Insert employee\n");
        printf(" 2.  List employees\n");
        printf(" 3.  Quit\n");
        printf("\n");
        printf("Enter your choice: ");     /* Prompt the user */
        scanf("%d", &choice);              /* Get the choice */

        if (choice == 1) {                 /* ADD EMPLOYEE */
            open_file();
            add_employee();
            close_file();
        }
        else if (choice == 2) {            /* LIST EMPLOYEES */
            open_file();
            list_employees();
            close_file();
        }
    } while (choice != 3);                 /* Until quit is chosen */
    exit(0);
}
```

10.5 Temporary files: tmpnam, tmpfile

It is common for a program to require a temporary scratch file. There are a number of functions related to temporary files. The two most commonly used are:

```
FILE *tmpfile(void)                /* Create a Temporary File */
char *tmpnam(char *name)           /* Create a Unique Name    */
```

The `tmpfile` function creates and opens a temporary file using the mode `"wb+"` (read-write binary direct-access file). The temporary file is automatically removed when it is closed or when the program exits. NULL is returned if the temporary file could not be created. The `"wb+"` mode is very general, and permits many different forms of access on the file. For example, the program can write to it sequentially, or can use direct access to seek to particular locations. The fact that the file is binary does not prevent it being used as a text file — a text file is a binary file containing only characters.

The `tmpnam` function creates a unique name, but doesn't open the file. It is the programmer's responsibility to create, open, close and remove the file. If the argument to `tmpnam` is NULL, `tmpnam` stores the temporary name in an internal `static` variable and returns its address — a second call to `tmpnam` will overwrite the first name. If the argument is not NULL, it must be a pointer to at least L_tmpnam characters (the constant L_tmpnam is declared in `<stdio.h>`). These characters are changed to become the new temporary name, and the return value is this string (i.e. the argument).

10.6 Removing and renaming files: remove, rename

The functions `remove` and `rename` are used to delete files or rename files from within a C program. Both return zero for success; non-zero on error. Their prototype definitions are:

```
int rename(char *old_name, char *new_name)
int remove(char *filename)
```

10.7 Character pushback: ungetc

The `ungetc` function is used to push one character back onto an input stream. The next call to `getc` will read this character (note that `getchar` is a macro that calls `getc` with file pointer `stdin`). The prototype definition is:

```
int ungetc(int ch, FILE *fp)
```

Character pushback is useful if the program needs to examine input to determine the course of action, but needs access to that character later on. In other words, in situations where too much input has been read in determining how much input is required. A good example of this would be in a lexical analyzer, that uses one-character lookahead to determine the current token.

Only one character push back is guaranteed though some implementations allow more. The EOF character cannot be pushed back. Some other file functions, such as `fseek`, will destroy the pushback if they occur before the `getc` call. The `ungetc` function returns the character pushed back (i.e. its first argument) or EOF on error.

10.8 Buffering: fflush, setbuf, setvbuf

The function `fflush` applies mostly to output files. It causes any output that is currently in the internal buffers to be written to the file. This output may be to the screen or to disk. The prototype definition of `fflush` is:

```
int fflush(FILE *fp)
```

The `fflush` function returns zero for success; EOF on error (e.g. failure to write buffered data to disk). Note that `fflush` does not close the file.

As an example, the statement:

```
fflush(stdout);
```

will write any output in internal buffers to the screen. Since `stdout` is usually line buffered (under UNIX), output will normally appear when a newline occurs. Hence, this function call will write any partially written lines, not yet terminated by a newline. Note that `scanf` flushes `stdout` before waiting for input. This allows for prompts on the same line as the input.

There are two functions for explicit control over the buffering performed on input/output to a file. The functions must be called before the first read or write on a file, and (obviously) after opening the file. The functions are:

```
int setvbuf(FILE *fp, char *buffer, int mode, int size)
void setbuf(FILE *fp, char *buffer)
```

The values for the `mode` parameter are declared in `<stdio.h>`: `_IOFBF` means full buffering, `_IOLBF` means line buffering and `_IONBF` means no buffering. The address passed to `buffer` will be used as the new buffer. However, if NULL is passed to `buffer` a new buffer will be automatically allocated. The `size` parameter specifies the number of bytes to be contained in the buffer. The return value of `setvbuf` is zero for success, non-zero for error.

The `setbuf` function is similar to `setvbuf` except that if `buffer` is NULL, buffering is turned off. If `buffer` is not NULL it is used as the buffer with full buffering and a buffer size equal to BUFSIZ (declared in `<stdio.h>`).

One use of `setbuf` functions is in debugging programs under UNIX. Changing buffering can avoid the problem of lost output when the program crashes (i.e. the output is still in the buffer when the crash occurs). The program lines:

```
#if DEBUG
    setbuf(stdout, NULL);
#endif
```

turn off buffering for standard output and ensure that all output appears immediately. This is equivalent to flushing the buffer with `fflush` after every call to `printf`, `puts` or `putchar`. Note that `stderr` is already unbuffered so that error messages appear on the screen immediately. Note also that buffering should not be disabled in the final program because buffering is more efficient (it is reasonable to assume that the default level of buffering is the most efficient level).

10.9 Redirecting input/output: freopen

The `freopen` function is used to "reopen" files. Its most common use is to redirect the standard I/O streams: `stdin`, `stdout` and `stderr`. When they have been reopened as a different file, any output to `stdout` from a `printf` will go to that file and any input from `stdin` will come from that file. However, this reopening of input/output streams is quite rarely used, because its equivalent can be achieved by using I/O redirection in an operating system command. The prototype definition of `freopen` is:

```
FILE *freopen(char *filename, char *mode, FILE *fp)
```

The first argument to `freopen` is the name of the file that is to be associated with the existing stream (the third argument). The mode is identical to that required by `fopen` (e.g. `"r"`, `"wb"`). `freopen` first closes the stream, if it can, and then attempts to open the file. If it cannot open the file, `freopen` returns NULL and the stream remains closed.

Below is an example of how to redirect both `stdin` and `stdout` from within a program. After redirection, `printf` becomes equivalent to `fprintf(out,...)` and `scanf` equivalent to `fscanf(in,...)`. Similarly, `putchar` and `puts` will send output to the file.

```
#include <stdio.h>
#include <stdlib.h>

main()
{
    FILE *in, *out;
    int i,n;

    in = freopen("infile", "r", stdin);      /* Redirect input */
    if (in == NULL) {
        perror("infile");
        exit(1);
    }

    out = freopen("outfile", "w", stdout); /* Redirect output */
    if (out == NULL) {
        perror("outfile");
        exit(1);
    }

    printf("Hello world\n");        /* Written to "outfile" */
    scanf("%d", &n);                /* Read from "infile" */
    for (i = 1; i <= n; i++)        /* for i = 1 to n */
        putchar(i + 'A' - 1);       /* Written to "outfile" */
    printf("\n");

    fclose(in);                     /* Close files when finished */
    fclose(out);
}
```

Note that the only reason the file pointers, `in` and `out`, are kept is to allow the files to be closed later using `fclose`.

10.10 Exercises

1. Write a program that asks the user for a filename (of a text file), then opens the file and prints out the entire contents to stdout. Make sure your program does not crash if the file cannot be found. *Hint:* Common C idiom for reading every character from a file is:

   ```
   while ((c = getc(fp)) != EOF)
       putchar(c);
   ```

2. Modify the program of the previous exercise so that it counts the number of characters, words and lines in the file. Consider a "word" to be a sequence of characters separated by whitespace.

3. Write a program that prints out the length of the longest line in a file. *Hint:* The simplest method of examining a file a line at a time is to use fgets.

4. What is the output of the following code fragment?

   ```
   fputs("One", stdout);
   fputs("Two", stdout);
   ```

   What happens if the program is changed to use puts instead of fputs(...,stdout)?

5. Write a program to encrypt a file with a character string key using exclusive-or (i.e. the ^ operator). The encrypted version should be written to another file. The user should be asked for both filenames. Write a companion decryption program. *Hint:* Encryption can be achieved by iterating repeatedly through the characters in the key, applying exclusive-or to the key character and the next file character. Exclusive-or is its own inverse, so that encryption with the same key is equivalent to decryption.

6. Write a pair of companion functions to store and read 20 integers in a *sequential* binary data file. *Hint:* You should only need to use fopen, fread and fwrite.

7. What is the effect of the statement: fflush(stderr)?

Chapter 11
The preprocessor

The preprocessor is the first phase of a C compiler. It is very similar to a macro preprocessor for an assembly language. The purpose of the preprocessor is to modify the C program before the C compiler compilation phase acts upon it. The preprocessor performs no error checking and no generation of code. All it does is take the original C program text file, and return the modified program text. The C preprocessor performs a number of functions:

- Symbolic constants
- Macro expansion
- File inclusion
- Conditional compilation

After all this has been done, the compilation phase of the C compiler acts on this modified text, generating code and checking for syntax errors. The preprocessor is a very powerful tool, but because it blindly performs substitutions without any error checking, some tricky errors can creep into a program that makes use of the preprocessor.

In many implementations, the preprocessor can be accessed as a separate software tool. This can be useful as it allows you to examine the output produced by the preprocessor and diagnose any problems with macro usage. Under UNIX, the C preprocessor is called cpp (for "C preprocessor"). and can be applied as a filter to any file(s) using the −E option to cc. This causes the resulting text file to go to standard output, and no further compilation occurs (i.e. only the preprocessor phase occurs). The UNIX preprocessor can also be accessed directly (usually /lib/cpp) but be careful not to apply cpp to multiple files since the second file is considered an output file and will be overwritten! This problem does not occur when cpp is accessed through cc. To find out more about the UNIX C preprocessor, read the manual entries for cc and cpp.

11.1 Preprocessor directives

The programmer uses the preprocessor by placing special lines in the C program. These lines contain *preprocessor directives* which instruct the preprocessor to performs various tasks. Directives begin with a hash sign (#). The full list of preprocessor directives is given in Table 11.1.

Table 11.1. Preprocessor directives

Directive	Meaning
`#include`	Include a file
`#define`	Define a symbolic constant or macro
`#undef`	Undefine a symbolic constant or macro
`#ifdef`	Conditional compilation — if macro defined
`#ifndef`	Conditional compilation — if macro not defined
`#if`	Conditional compilation — if expression non-zero
`#else`	Conditional compilation — else clause
`#elif`	Conditional compilation — else if
`#endif`	Conditional compilation — end of block
`#line`	Line numbering
`#error`	Error message
`#pragma`	Implementation-specific effect

The hash sign must be the first non-whitespace character of the line (only spaces or tabs before it). Whitespace is also allowed after the '#', just before the directive name. However, common style is to avoid whitespace both before and after the hash sign. Some examples of common directives are:

```
#include <stdio.h>    /* Include "stdio.h" system header file */
#define MAX 10        /* define MAX as a symbolic constant */
```

Comments are allowed on preprocessor lines. They are no different to ordinary comments. The preprocessor ignores them, even if they appear on a `#define` line as part of the replacement text.

11.2 Including files: #include

Other files can be included in the current file using the `#include` directive. When it occurs, the specified file is included where the line appears. When it has been included, the preprocessor moves on to the next line of the original file.

Nesting of file inclusion is allowed — an included file can include another file and so on. There may be some implementation-defined limit on the depth of nesting but this rarely causes problems. Infinite loops in file inclusion, such as when two files include each other, are not always detected (it depends on the compiler). Some compilers may use the limit on the depth of nesting to detect such infinite loops.

There are two different formats for `#include` with the delimiters around the filename being the only difference. The format for including standard header files is the delimiters < and >. The format for including files from the current directory uses double quotes as delimiters. The two notations are:

```
#include <stdio.h>              /* from system directory */
#include "mydefs.h"              /* from current directory */
```

Files included with `#include` are commonly called header files. By convention they have the filename suffix ".h". These files commonly contain information such as symbolic constant definitions, `typedef` declarations, `extern` declarations and forward declarations of functions. Including a header file in each C file removes the need for these definitions in each file. It also makes organizing multiple files much easier (no need to change each file). The use of header files for large programs is discussed more fully in Chapter 13.

The standard header files (e.g. `stdio.h`) are stored in the directory "/usr/include" on UNIX. Under DOS the directory containing include files will depend on your compiler — consult your compiler documentation. There is nothing special about these standard header files. They are ordinary C program text and it can be quite interesting to examine them.

Full path names are also allowed in the `#include` directive. For the `<file.h>` notation, the filename is appended to the system directory containing include files to give the complete filename. In other words, the path is relative to the system directory (e.g. `/usr/include` under UNIX). For example, the directive:

```
#include <sys/file.h>
```

will include the file "/usr/include/sys/file.h" under UNIX.

For the "file.h" notation, the path specified is either from the current directory (i.e. relative), or absolute (if it starts with a slash under UNIX or a backslash under DOS). This is consistent with normal directory usage. Some examples of more general filenames are:

```
#include "mydir/mydefs.h"         /* relative path */
#include "/user/cpcg/mydefs.h"    /* absolute path */
```

The filename for the `#include` directive can also be specified as a preprocessor macro. This feature allows the specification of filenames via macro names (allowing easier modification). If neither of the two `#include` notations are present, macro expansion occurs on the directive line. The line must expand to yield one of the two notations above. An example of this is given below:

```
#define MYDEFS   "/user/cpcg/mydefs.h"
#include MYDEFS                  /* CORRECT */
```

However, macros are not expanded when the filename is already in either of the two accepted forms. Hence, the following code fails to include `<stdio.h>`:

```
#define HEADER   stdio
#include <HEADER.h>               /* WRONG */
```

11.3 Macros and symbolic constants: #define

The preprocessor directive, `#define`, can be used to define both symbolic constants and parameterized macros. The symbol defined (i.e. the first parameter after the keyword `define`) can be any identifier. The identifier need not be all capitals, but this is common style. Some examples of the use of `#define` to define symbolic constants are:

```
#define TRUE 1
#define FALSE 0
#define MAX_SIZE 10
```

One or more spaces are needed after the identifier, followed by the replacement text. The replacement text is the rest of the line (up to the end of the line). The replacement text can be anything, though comments are deleted from it. The numerical examples as above are the most common.

There is no semicolon at the end of the `#define` line. Preprocessor lines are not C statements — they are preprocessor directives and do not need a semicolon at the end. In fact, any semicolon at the end of the line is assumed to be part of the replacement text and can lead to problems. For example, the macro definition and call:

```
#define max_size 10;     /* INCORRECT - no semicolon allowed */
x = max_size + 1;
```

expands to give the incorrect code:

```
x = 10; + 1;             /* extra semicolon */
```

Using `#define` for symbolic constants is a special form of a general substitution. As mentioned above, any replacement text is allowed. This means that an identifier in a program can be replaced by any text. Anything after the first space (after the identifier) is treated as replacement text. The replacement text is then anything up to the end of the line (except comments, which the preprocessor deletes).

If there is nothing after the identifier, there is no replacement text. When there is no replacement text, any occurrence of the symbol is effectively deleted (i.e. replaced by nothing).

This flexibility is useful because a symbolic constant can be defined in terms of another such constant. Another common example is to put type casting inside the replacement text. Hence, some more complicated examples of symbolic constants are:

```
#define MAX      (SIZE * 2 + 1)
#define true     (unsigned char)1
```

11.3.1 Parameterized macros

The `#define` directive is far more powerful than merely providing symbolic constants and text replacement. It can also be used to define parameterized macros. Some examples of parameterized macros are:

```
#define  sum(x, y)     ((x) + (y))
#define  cube(x)       ((x) * (x) * (x))
#define  print(str)    { printf("%s\n", str); }
```

The reasons for the masses of brackets in the first two macros are explained in the section on common mistakes with macros (Section B.11). Generally, if a macro is an arithmetic expression, it needs brackets surrounding the entire expression and around each occurrence of the parameter. Braces are good practice when declaring macros to imitate a void function (this is also covered in Section B.11).

There can be no spaces between the identifier (i.e. sum, cube) and the first left bracket. If there is a space, the preprocessor assumes that the left bracket is part of the replacement text (and that there is no list of macro parameters).

Spaces are allowed anywhere in the replacement text. Anything up to the end of the line is assumed to be part of the replacement text.

Macros can be *called* very much like a function call. In fact, the most common use of a macro is to imitate a function call. When a macro is called, it is expanded into its replacement text. Arguments in the macro call replace the parameters of the macro definition. The replacement is by direct text replacement (actually replacement occurs at the token level, but the effect is mostly identical). For example, when the macros above are called by:

```
c = sum(a, b);
y = cube(a);
print(argv[1]);
```

the macro calls expand to give the text:

```
c = ((a) + (b));
y = ((a) * (a) * (a));
{ printf("%s\n", argv[1]); }
```

Macros with parameters look like functions, because they require brackets for the arguments. Macros without parameters can be declared and used as if they had an empty parameter list. They are then used as if they were function calls with no parameters, as shown below:

```
#define  mesg()    printf("Hello world\n")
mesg();
```

Macro calls expand out into in-line code. There can be many copies of similar code throughout the expanded program. The advantage over functions is efficiency; the disadvantage is space wastage (the executable becomes larger).

11.3.2 Multiple line macros

Multiple line macro definitions are allowed, permitting very large macros. To specify multiple line macros, a backslash is placed at the end of each line, to indicate that the next line is also part of the macro definition. There is no backslash on the last line of a macro definition (because the next line is not part of the macro). For example:

```
#define swap_int(s1,s2)    { int temp;     \
                             temp = s1;    \
                             s1 = s2;      \
                             s2 = temp; }
```

is equivalent to:

```
#define swap_int(s1,s2)   { int temp; temp=s1; s1=s2; s2=temp; }
```

The backslash must be the very last character on the line. There must be *no spaces or comments* after the backslash.

Note that this use of a backslash to specify multiple-line macros is actually a special case of a general preprocessor facility, called *line splicing*, where the preprocessor will join any lines ending with a backslash, before performing any other processing on it.

11.3.3 Safe macro usage

There are many obscure problems that can occur because of poor use of macros. In particular, macros are not exactly equivalent to function calls, and these differences can lead to bugs. The main problem is that arguments to macros use exact textual replacement whereas an argument to a function is evaluated to a value before it is passed to a function. Thus if a macro uses the same argument twice, any side effect appearing in an argument will occur twice. For example, the macro definition and call:

```
#define cube(x)    ((x) * (x) * (x))
a = cube(b++);
```

expand out into code that increments b three times:

```
a = ((b++) * (b++) * (b++));
```

This problem and a number of other problems with macros are discussed fully in Appendix B. Although it is beneficial to understand the cause of the problems, there are a number of simple rules that can prevent most problems. These rules are summarized below:

- Don't place semicolons on the end of a macro definition.
- Bracket every occurrence of parameters in the macro replacement text.
- Bracket the entire expression in the macro replacement text.
- Avoid side effects to macro calls (and function calls!).
- Add braces around sequences of statements in macro replacement text.

Some examples of safe macro definitions are given below. Notice that macros that act like a function in returning a value require many brackets, whereas macros imitating void functions require braces.

```
#define inc(x)        ((x) + 1)
#define cube(x)       ((x) * (x) * (x))
#define print(str)    { printf("%s", str); }
```

11.3.4 Macro usage details

Macro names can be any identifier, and parameters to the macro are also identifiers. As with function calls, spaces are allowed between the macro name and the opening left bracket in macro *calls* (although some non-ANSI compilers may complain). However, no space is allowed between the macro name and opening left bracket in the macro *definition* (i.e. #define line). Spaces in the parameter list of a macro definition are ignored. Spaces in the argument list of a macro call are also allowed (i.e. before and after commas etc.). They are deleted before the text replacement takes place. Spaces in the middle of an argument are not deleted.

Replacement of macro parameters in the replacement text is by keyword matching. In other words, the parameters are only replaced by the argument text from the macro call if they are whole identifiers. If a macro parameter name appears as a string in the middle of a word, it is not replaced. The reason for this is that #define works on the token level, not directly at the text level. It looks for full identifiers, not just patterns of letters.

Also, parameters should not be replaced inside string constants. Although some older compilers permit expansion inside string constants, newer compilers should not allow it. There is a special preprocessor operator for this purpose — the stringize operator, #.

Macro definitions can contain calls to other macros. Macro names are expanded in the replacement text until there are no more names yet to expand, without restriction on depth of nesting of macro calls.

Definitions of a macro can include the same name. The name is expanded once only, so that infinite looping cannot occur. However, older non-ANSI compilers may have problems with self-referencing macro definitions. An example of a recursive macro definition is:

```
#define  if  if(             /* CORRECT */
```

These comments are also true of more general macro loops in macro definitions. The preprocessor keeps count of which names have already been expanded, and expands no name twice.

This "once only" expansion does not prevent macro *calls* making use of the same macro more than once. For example, if min is a macro, the statement below is correct:

```
y = min(min(a, b), min(c, min(x, y)));      /* CORRECT */
```

Macro names in another macro's replacement text are not expanded until the "outer" macro is called. For example, the code below will print out the value 2:

```
#define INNER   1
#define OUTER   INNER   /* INNER is inside OUTER's definition */
#define INNER   2
    printf("OUTER = %d\n", OUTER);
```

The main limitation of macros is that they cannot contain preprocessor directives. For example, the replacement text cannot contain a #include directive. Another limitation is that there is no method of specifying repetition in a macro expansion.

11.3.5 Example macros

Here are some examples of useful macros to show the many possible ways of using them, and to stir your imagination into finding more ways. The significance of the use of brackets, braces and the comma operator is discussed in Appendix B where common errors in macro usage are covered.

```
#define max(x, y)         ((x) > (y) ? (x) : (y))
#define min(x, y)         ((x) < (y) ? (x) : (y))
#define abs(x)            ((x) >= 0) ? (x) : -(x))
#define sign(x)           ((x) < 0 ? -1 : ((x) > 0 ? 1 : 0))

#define forever           for (;;)            /* Infinite loop */
#define repeat            do {                /* Pascal */
#define until(x)          } while (!(x))

#define TRUE      1
#define FALSE     0

#define line(x1, y1, x2, y2)   moveto(x1, y1), lineto(x2, y2)
#define line(x1, y1, x2, y2)   {moveto(x1, y1); lineto(x2, y2);}

#define swap(x, y)             {int temp; temp = x; x = y; y = temp;}
#define swap(x, y, TYPE)       {TYPE temp; temp = x; x = y; y = temp;}
#define swap(x, y, temp)       temp = x, x = y, y = temp

#define ctrl(x)           ((x) & 037)         /* e.g. ctrl('a') */

#define LEFT(ptr)         (ptr->left)         /* Abstraction */
#define RIGHT(ptr)        (ptr->right)        /* Abstraction */
#define DATA(ptr)         (ptr->data)         /* Abstraction */
```

11.3.6 Undefining and redefining macros: #undef

The `#undef` directive is used to remove a macro definition from an identifier. It applies to any definition made with an earlier `#define` directive; both symbolic constants and macro definitions. Its syntax is:

```
#undef name
```

If `name` is not already defined, the preprocessor should not produce a warning message. The directive simply has no effect in this case. Hence, there is no need to place a `#undef` directive inside a `#ifdef`-`#endif` pair.

The `#undef` directive is often used to redefine a macro name. The preprocessor should warn about redefinition of a macro name to a different value, and the usage below avoids this warning:

```
#undef name
#define name 10    /* redefine name */
```

11.3.7 The stringize macro operator (#)

This is a special operator that can be used only in macro definitions. It is used when it is necessary to place a macro argument inside quotes — for example, inside a `printf` format string. Consider the `assert` macro which takes an expression, and if false, prints an error message. One attempt to do this would be:

```
#define assert(EXP)    if (!(EXP)) printf("EXP is false \n")
```

However, this is incorrect because the identifier EXP is inside double quotes and will not be expanded (although some non-ANSI implementations still allow this expansion of arguments inside strings). The correct way to define this macro is:

```
#define assert(EXP)    if (!(EXP)) printf(#EXP " is false \n")
```

When the macro is called, the # operator expands out the parameter EXP and places quotes around it. The call:

```
assert(x != 0);
```

becomes:

```
if (!(x != 0)) printf("x!=0" " is false\n");
```

This leaves two string literals together. These two strings are concatenated by the compiler, and considered as if they were just one string. The desired effect is achieved:

```
if (!(x != 0)) printf("x!=0 is false\n");
```

Note that the # operator can only be placed in front of a macro parameter (not any identifier). If the argument to a macro call has any double quotes or backslashes, the preprocessor puts an automatic extra backslash before these characters (to make them into escapes).

Note that this example has a bug, and was presented only to show the concatenation of adjacent string literals. If the condition contains a % character (e.g. as the remainder operator), the `printf` call may crash (why?). A safe way to achieve the same effect is:

```
#define assert(EXP)    if (!(EXP)) printf("%s is false \n", #EXP)
```

11.3.8 The token pasting macro operator (##)

This is a special operator that can be used only in macro definitions. It is very, very rarely used. It is used when two tokens are to be joined together to make one token. However, it is not supported by most non-ANSI implementations. An example of the ## operator is a macro to declare a variable:

```
#define declare(x)      int var##x
```

The macro call:

```
declare(10);
```

becomes:

```
int var10;
```

The tokens "var" and "10" have been combined to make a single token. This is impossible without the ## operator, as the obvious try:

```
#define declare(x) int var x
```

places a space between var and 10. Another try:

```
#define declare(x) int varx
```

does not even expand the x because the x is part of a different token, and hence the 10 does not replace the x. Remember that macro parameter matching is based on whole identifiers, not on string matches.

11.4 Conditional compilation

The C preprocessor provides a very powerful compile-time feature called conditional compilation. This refers to the possibility of specifying which blocks of code from a program will be included in the current compilation. Conditional compilation achieves the effect of removing code lines by preventing them from being compiled. It allows blocks of code to be taken out or left in, depending on the value given to a macro name by a #define directive. The most common use of conditional compilation is for selectively including or omitting debugging code.

The preprocessor directives used by conditional compilation are listed in Table 11.2. In addition, the #define and #undef directives are important because many of the conditions tested depend on the definitions of macros and symbolic constants.

Table 11.2. Conditional compilation directives

Directive	Meaning
#ifdef name	Test if macro defined
#ifndef name	Test if macro not defined
#if const_exp	Test constant expression
#else	Begin else clause
#elif const_exp	Else if
#endif	End of conditional block

The three "if" directives all test for conditions which, if true, allow the following lines of code to be included, up to a corresponding #endif, #else or #elif. These clauses are very similar to the if-else statements of C. The constructs nest, and each if matches the inner endif. The dangling else ambiguity is resolved as usual — every else matches the closest if. An example of the use of conditional compilation is:

```
#ifdef UNIX
    version = "UNIX Version";
#else
    version = "DOS Version";
#endif
```

which decides which assignment statement to include based on whether the macro name UNIX has been previously defined by a #define directive (or a command line option to the compiler).

One minor observation can help ensure that the conditional code is correct. Every #if, #ifndef or #ifdef directive needs a corresponding #endif directive. Thus, counting the occurrences of both types of directives is a good simple check to apply to new code.

Each directive must be on a separate line. Comments are permitted on the end of directive lines. It is also possible to place extra text not enclosed by comment delimiters at the end of #else or #endif lines. Although this extra text is ignored, the use of this feature is not recommended, but is sometimes used as a comment mechanism in older code.

The #undef directive can also be of some use in conditional compilation. It can be used to "undefine" a name. It removes any previous definition, and the preprocessor then acts as if the name were not defined previously.

11.4.1 The #if directive

Whereas the #ifdef and #ifndef directives test whether the preprocessor has a record of a previous definition of a symbol, the #if directive evaluates a constant expression, and the following lines are included if the value of the expression is non-zero. The constant expression of #if is very flexible. All the arithmetic, logical, relational and bitwise operators are allowed. However, some features which the preprocessor cannot use are: the sizeof operator, enumerated constants and type casts. These restrictions make sense because the preprocessor, as the first phase of compilation, cannot be aware of types.

The expression of a #if directive can contain symbolic constants defined by #define, and even macros. These are replaced by their textual definition (which can contain further levels of definitions). Some example #if directives are:

```
#if MAX < 10
#if X < Y && DEBUG == 1
```

Any identifiers which have no macro definition default to zero (i.e. undefined names default to "0"). This has a useful feature in that the two directives below are almost identical in effect:

```
#if DEBUG
#ifdef DEBUG
```

When DEBUG is defined as 1 the two have the same effect. The difference occurs when DEBUG is defined as 0 (or as nothing). Thus, the method of removing the debugging code is different for the two versions: #ifdef requires the use of #undef; #if requires changing the definition to zero. Note that both alternatives work correctly if the #define line is simply deleted.

11.4.2 The defined operator

The `#if` expression can also use a special preprocessor operator "`defined`". It is a unary prefix operator and acts on symbols. It evaluates to 1 if the symbol is defined and 0 if not. It is not used very often because of the existence of `#ifdef` and `#ifndef`, but it can be used to test more than one symbol at a time. An example of the use of the `defined` operator is:

```
#if defined DEBUG && ! defined NO_DEBUG
```

11.4.3 The #elif directive

The `#elif` directive is very similar to an `else-if` sequence of C statements. Like `#if`, it requires a constant expression which is considered true if it is non-zero. The typical method of usage is:

```
#if exp1
    ...             /* block 1 */
#elif exp2
    ...             /* block 2 */
#elif exp3
    ...             /* block 3 */
#else
    ...             /* block 4 */
#endif
```

This has the effect of including block 1 if `exp1` is true, including block 2 if `exp1` is false but `exp2` is true, including block 3 if `exp1` and `exp2` are false but `exp3` is true, and including block 4 if all the expressions are false. Hence, only one of the four blocks can be included. Note that the `#else` clause is optional and no code would be included if `#else` were left out and no expressions were true.

Note that the `#elif` clauses can be replaced with `#else` and `#if` directives, but this would require additional `#endif` directives (to match the extra `#if` directives).

11.4.4 Leaving out code

Code that is temporarily unwanted can be left out in two ways. One way is to leave it inside a comment, called *commenting out*. However, comments do not nest, so any comments in the commented out code may cause a compilation error. A better way is to use conditional compilation to leave out code — I call it *preprocessing out*. This is achieved by using `#ifdef` with a symbol that is not defined, or, more commonly, using `#if` with the constant 0.

```
#if 0
    ...             /* lines of code to be left out */
#endif
```

11.4.5 Debugging code

During program development, it is useful to have debugging `printf`s in the program. Once the program is finished, they must be deleted. An easy way to prepare for their later removal is to use the preprocessor. Rather than actually delete the debugging statements, conditional compilation is used to leave them out of the compilation.

```
#ifdef DEBUG
     printf("Entered function: printout() \n");
#endif
```

The symbol `DEBUG` can then be defined by you in a header file during testing. When finished, delete its definition and recompile (or add an `#undef` directive and recompile). To limit testing to individual files, use different symbols for different files, or place the line:

```
#undef DEBUG
```

in files that don't need testing.

Note that it is also possible to use `#if` instead of `#ifdef`:

```
#if DEBUG
   ...
#endif
```

The main difference is that, when leaving the debugging code out, the symbol `DEBUG` can be defined as 0, instead of using `#undef`. This is particularly convenient when using a number of such symbols (e.g. for multiple levels of debugging), because it makes setting/clearing these flags a simple matter of changing a `#define` statement.

If special debugging functions are placed in the code, there is an alternative. Instead of making sure they are between a `#ifdef` and `#endif`, they can be left in the program as normal. When time comes to remove them, it is possible to eliminate them using macro expansion.

```
#ifndef DEBUG            /* if no longer debugging */
#define check(a, b)      /* check expands out to empty text */
#endif
```

If `DEBUG` is not defined, all calls to the `check` function are effectively deleted, by replacing them with whitespace during compilation.

In addition to a `#define` directive, the `DEBUG` symbol can usually be defined using an option to the compiler. Under UNIX this is the −D option to the `cc` compiler, as in:

```
cc -DDEBUG
```

which causes the preprocessor to act as if `DEBUG` were defined. It is also possible to give the symbol a particular value. If none is given, as above, the default value is 1. For example, to set `DEBUG` to the value 2, use:

```
cc -DDEBUG=2
```

This method can be convenient for a single file, and is especially effective when used in a `makefile`. To remove debugging code, a small change is made to the `makefile` and the whole program rebuilt.

11.4.6 Preventing multiple file inclusions

In large programs, it can be useful to ensure that a header file is never included more than once (preventing annoying compilation errors). One convenient way to do this is to add a few lines to the beginning of the header file.

```
#ifndef INCLUDE_TYPES
#define INCLUDE_TYPES
    ...         /* rest of "types.h" header file */
#endif
```

Note that a unique symbol is required for every header file this method is applied to.

11.4.7 Multiple versions

This example shows how to use checks for defined symbols to maintain a number of versions of a program. This can be used to aid portability to different systems, and is often seen in system code (e.g. standard library header files). However, the code can become very unmanageable if too many versions are maintained this way. An example of multiple nested `#ifdef` directives shows the type of problems:

```
#ifdef SYS_V
    x = 1;
#else
#ifdef BSD
    x = 2;
#else
    x = 3;
#endif   /* match ifdef BSD */
#endif   /* match ifdef SYS_V */
```

When the code involves some nested blocks of conditionally included code, some programmers use spaces after the hash and before the directive name to indent the code. The code becomes:

```
#ifdef SYS_V
    x = 1;
#else
#    ifdef BSD
        x = 2;
#    else
        x = 3;
#    endif        /* match ifdef BSD */
#endif            /* match ifdef SYS_V */
```

11.5 Other directives: #error, #line, #pragma

There are a number of miscellaneous preprocessor directives. These directives are rarely needed. First, the *null directive* refers to a # on a line by itself. It does nothing, and is ignored.

The #error directive causes the preprocessor to print a diagnostic error message, using the argument as part of the message. This is useful for trapping incorrect conditions in conditional compilation. Compilation is aborted when this directive is invoked. For example, it might be important that at least one of two symbols is defined, as in:

```
#if ! defined(UNIX) && ! defined(DOS)
#error  No version chosen. Define UNIX or DOS.
#endif
```

The #line directive is useful for utilities that create C code, such as yacc. It allows the compiler to generate error messages meaningful to the original text file, and not to the C source file created by the utility program. The #line directive has the format:

```
#line number "name"
```

which causes the compiler to think that the current line number is given by number and the current file is given by name. The filename is optional; if omitted the filename remains unchanged. Line number counting begins at the new number.

The #pragma directive is the standard way to introduce local non-standard directives. Unrecognized #pragma directives are ignored. This is intended to enhance the portability of C programs. Many implementations also support their own special directives (often not introduced by the #pragma directive). For information on local #pragma directives and non-standard directives consult your local documentation.

11.6 Predefined names: __LINE__, __FILE__

The preprocessor reserves a small number of symbolic names for special purposes. Each symbol is distinguished by having two underscores either side of a sequence of letters. These symbols cannot be undefined or redefined by the preprocessor. The full list is given in Table 11.3.

Table 11.3. Preprocessor predefined names

Name	Meaning
__LINE__	Line number of file being compiled
__FILE__	Filename of file being compiled
__STDC__	Standard C flag (1 if ANSI-compliant compiler)
__DATE__	Current date
__TIME__	Current time

The symbol __LINE__ is an integer representing the current line during compilation. The __FILE__ symbol is a string constant containing the filename of the current file. These are used, for example, in the assert macro which must print out which line of which file the assertion failed.

Compilers adhering to the ANSI standard are expected to define the name __STDC__ as 1, and non-ANSI compilers should leave it undefined. __DATE__ expands out as a string literal in the format "Mmm dd yyyy", such as "Jan 23 1990", and __TIME__ expands to a string literal in the format "hh:mm:ss". These symbols expand out into a string literal. Note that the symbols __DATE__ and __TIME__ may not be supported by non-ANSI implementations. Other non-standard symbols may also be available, depending on the implementation.

11.7 Exercises

1. Must a directive to the preprocessor have the # as the first character on the line? Are spaces permitted immediately after the # character?

2. What is wrong with the definition of the symbolic constant MAX given below? Will it cause compilation errors?

    ```
    #define  MAX = 10
    ```

3. Write macros for the following:

    a) The average of two numbers.
    b) The length of a line segment given two pairs of x and y coordinates.
    c) The maximum of three numbers.
    d) Find the next non-space character in the input stream.
    e) To determine if two strings are equal (using strcmp).

4. What are the # and ## preprocessor operators used for? Are they unary or binary? What is the result of the code below when passed through an ANSI standard preprocessor?

    ```
    #define set(n, x)   s##n = #x
    set(5, "Hello\n");
    ```

5. How do you "undefine" a macro defined previously by #define? Give an example where this would be useful.

6. What problem is there with the code segment below? How can it be fixed?

    ```
    #define max(x, y)   ( (x > y) ? x : y)
    a = max(b++, c);
    ```

7. Will the code segment below compile correctly if it is included in a small program? Assume that temp and temp2 are declared as int. If not, why not? If so, will it run correctly?

    ```
    #define swap(x, y)   {int temp;  temp = x; x = y; y = temp; }
    swap(temp, temp2);
    ```

8. Are there any problems if the directive #if 0 is used to remove a block of code that contains other #if directives?

9. What does the `defined` preprocessor operator test? Is it unary or binary? Can it be used in the replacement text for preprocessor macros? How can `#ifdef` and `#ifndef` be simulated using `#if` and the `defined` preprocessor operator?

10. Both `#if` and `#ifdef` can be used to include debugging code in a program. What is the difference between the two directives below? Is there a satisfactory method of removing debugging code if a program uses both `#if` and `#ifdef` in different places?

    ```
    #if DEBUG
    #ifdef DEBUG
    ```

11. How can preprocessor directives be used to give a default value for the symbolic constant `DEBUG` such that it can be overridden by a compilation option (e.g. cc −DDEBUG=0 under UNIX)?

Chapter 12
Standard library functions

All implementations of C come with a large suite of library functions that can be used in any C program. This chapter provides a brief introduction to the use of library functions defined in the ANSI standard library. The approach is intended to be a practical introduction and some of the more obscure details of the ANSI standard are not covered in full.

The standard library consists of a number of *header files*, each of which declares symbolic constants and function prototypes for a particular type of function. The full list of header files is given in Table 12.1.

Table 12.1. Standard library header files

File	Contents
`<stdio.h>`	Input/output and file operations
`<math.h>`	Mathematical functions
`<string.h>`	String functions
`<ctype.h>`	Character class tests
`<stdlib.h>`	Utility functions
`<assert.h>`	Assertions
`<setjmp.h>`	Non-local jumps
`<signal.h>`	Signal handling
`<errno.h>`	Error handling
`<time.h>`	Time and date functions
`<stdarg.h>`	Variable-length argument lists
`<stddef.h>`	Standard definitions
`<limits.h>`	Implementation-defined limits
`<float.h>`	Floating point arithmetic constants
`<locale.h>`	Locality issues (language, nationality, etc.)

A header file is included using the preprocessor directive:

    #include <file.h>

which usually appears at the start of a C source file. Header files need not be included at the top of the file, but must (obviously) be included before the use of any functions or constants declared in the header file.

The ANSI standard states that header files can be included repeatedly and in any order. Repetitive inclusion allows, for example, the flexibility to include <assert.h> at various points in a program with different settings of NDEBUG to turn assertions on and off. However, note that some older implementations may fail on repeated inclusions.

Not all of the standard library functions are actually functions. For example, most of the "functions" in <ctype.h> are implemented as macros. When a facility is provided by macro, there must also be a real function with the same name and the same effect. This function can be accessed by undefining the macro name. Note that the reason for equivalent functions is not that the use of macros is dangerous (the library macro definitions should be completely safe), but because a pointer to a library function is occasionally needed.

Not all of the above header files are discussed fully in this chapter. By far the most commonly used library functions are those for input and output in <stdio.h> and these functions are discussed in full in Chapter 9. The file handling library functions (also in <stdio.h>) are covered in Chapter 10. All but a few of the string functions declared in <string.h> are covered in Chapter 6. The use of <assert.h> for adding debugging assertions is covered in Section 16.4. Non-local jumps using <setjmp.h> are covered in Section 4.14. Processing of signals under UNIX is discussed fully in Section 19.8. Error handling using <errno.h> is covered in Section 10.2 and with special reference to UNIX in Section 19.3. The definition of functions accepting a variable number of arguments using <stdarg.h> is covered in Section 14.6. Finally, the issues of standardizing a program to different localities, nationalities and cultures using <locale.h> are briefly covered, but are largely beyond the scope of the book.

12.1 Examining characters: <ctype.h>

There are a number of useful boolean functions for testing whether characters are in a particular class. In particular, the functions isalpha and isdigit are useful for checking if a character is a letter or a digit. The full list of functions and the character classes for which they test are shown in Table 12.2.

These functions return non-zero (not usually one) if the character is in the class, and zero if the character is not. The functions are usually implemented as macros in <ctype.h>, but there are equivalent functions that can be accessed by undefining the macro names (although this may not be true of non-ANSI implementations).

In addition to the testing functions, <ctype.h> defines two conversion functions for converting between upper and lower case letters:

    int tolower(int c)
    int toupper(int c)

Table 12.2. Character class functions

Function	Character class
`isalpha(c)`	Letter
`isdigit(c)`	Digit
`isalnum(c)`	Letter or digit
`islower(c)`	Lower case letter
`isupper(c)`	Upper case letter
`isxdigit(c)`	Hexadecimal digit (0-9, a-f, A-F)
`isspace(c)`	Space, '\f', '\n', '\r', '\t' or '\v'
`isprint(c)`	Printable character (0x20...0x7E ASCII)
`iscntrl(c)`	Control character (0...0x1F and 0x7F ASCII)
`ispunct(c)`	Printable characters except space, letter or digit
`isgraph(c)`	Printable characters except space

If their argument is not a letter, `tolower` and `toupper` return the character unchanged. If the argument is a letter, the functions return the letter in the correct case.

The reason for the use of `int` rather than `char` for the arguments and return values of the functions in this section is to allow them to act on `EOF`. In addition, the use of non-prototyping in older libraries meant that the arguments had to have type `int`.

12.2 Memory block functions: <string.h>

In addition to the string functions discussed in Chapter 6, the `<string.h>` header file also defines a number of efficient functions that are similar to the string functions. These functions do not treat character zero as the end of a string, but rather rely on an argument, n, to indicate how many characters are in a block of memory. Another difference is that the arguments are of type `void*` rather than `char*` and these functions need not only be applied to strings. In the definitions given in Table 12.3, s1 and s2 are of type `void*`, c is a `char` and n is an `int`.

Table 12.3. Memory block functions

Function	Meaning
`int memcmp(s1, s2, n)`	Compare first n characters of s1 and s2
`void *memcpy(s1, s2, n)`	Copy n characters from s2 to s1
`void *memmove(s1, s2, n)`	As for memcpy, but allow overlap
`void *memchr(s1, c, n)`	Find first occurrence of c in s1
`void *memset(s1, c, n)`	Set the first n characters of s1 to c

The `memcmp` function returns a value with meaning identical to the return value of `strcmp`. The `memcpy` function returns s1, which is usually ignored. The `memmove` function is identical to `memcpy` except that it permits copying between areas that overlap, acting as if an intermediate buffer had been used for the copying. The `memchr` function returns the address of the first occurrence of c in s1 or NULL if not found in the first n characters. The `memset` function returns s1, which is usually ignored.

12.3 Mathematical programming: <math.h>

The C programming language provides support for mathematical programming in its floating point data types and in the library functions declared in <math.h>. The C language provides two floating point data types and allows simple arithmetic operations to be performed upon these types. The standard library provides functions for calculating a number of common mathematical functions. The functions supported include the basic trigonometric, hyperbolic and exponential functions.

12.3.1 float and double types

The fundamental design of the C language provides support for mathematical programming in its two floating point data types, float and double. The difference between float and double is that double has greater precision (the word double stands for double precision). The type "long double" can be used for even greater precision. Information about the range and precision of float and double types can be found in the header file <float.h>. For example, the maximum and minimum values of the types are given as FLT_MIN, FLT_MAX, DBL_MIN and DBL_MAX, and the decimal digits of precision are FLT_DIG and DBL_DIG.

The C language allows floating point constants to be declared using decimal point notation or exponential notation. Some examples are:

```
0.0
3.14159
1e-10
1.3E+20
```

Note that 0 without the decimal point is an int constant, whereas 0.0 is a floating point constant.

Constants of type float, double or long double can all be declared. The default type is double, and float constants can be declared with a suffix f or F (e.g. 15.4F), and long double constants can be declared using the suffix l or L (e.g. 15.4L).

When writing mathematical programs it is preferable to use double rather than float, if the program needs to be portable to old versions of C. Non-ANSI C has the problem that all floating point arithmetic is performed in double precision (rather than single precision), even if both operands are of type float. This means that when adding together two float variables and storing the result in another float variable, the operands are first converted to double, then added together using double precision arithmetic and the result converted back to float for the assignment. This can adversely affect the results of numerical programs. Although the ANSI standard has resolved this problem by allowing float variables to use single precision arithmetic, the use of only double variables avoids the problem when using older generation compilers, thus improving portability.

Another reason for using double variables is efficiency. All the standard library functions declared in <math.h> accept double arguments and return a double result. The use of double variables prevents costly type coercions between float and double.

12.3.2 Error handling

All of the standard library functions declared in `<math.h>` share common behavior under error conditions. There are two types of errors: domain errors and range errors. A *domain error* occurs when the arguments are outside the range for which the function is defined. A *range error* occurs when the result either underflows or overflows (i.e. is too small or too large to be represented as a `double` value). The library functions use the symbolic constants `EDOM` and `ERANGE` defined in `<errno.h>` to indicate these error conditions. When a domain error occurs, the external variable `errno` (declared in `<errno.h>`) is set to `EDOM`, and the return value of the mathematical function is undefined. When overflow occurs the function returns `HUGE_VAL` (defined in `<math.h>`) with a positive or negative sign, as appropriate, and `errno` is set to `ERANGE`. When underflow occurs the function returns zero, but it is undefined whether `errno` is set to `ERANGE` (this is unsatisfactory because there is no portable way to detect underflow).

12.3.3 Linking math libraries

The use of mathematical functions may require the programmer to explicitly link the mathematical libraries. Under DOS there are usually options to set that define which libraries are linked by default. When using `<math.h>` under UNIX it is necessary to link the math library explicitly using the `-lm` option to `cc`. This option must be placed at the very end, after all the source files to be compiled:

```
cc file1.c file2.c -lm
```

12.3.4 Simple mathematical functions

The standard library for C defines a number of functions to calculate common mathematical functions. The library is not broad enough for the full range of scientific programming requirements (e.g. no complex arithmetic or matrix operations), but it does allow the most common mathematical tasks to be accomplished simply.

In the discussion below, all the mathematic functions return values of type `double`, and all arguments are of type `double` unless otherwise indicated. The math library defines a number of useful functions for common operations on floating point values; see Table 12.4.

Table 12.4. **Common mathematical functions**

Function	Meaning
`sqrt(x)`	Square root of x, $\sqrt{x}$
`fabs(x)`	Absolute value of x, $\lvert x \rvert$
`fmod(x, y)`	Floating point remainder of x/y
`ceil(x)`	Ceiling function, $\lceil x \rceil$
`floor(x)`	Floor function, $\lfloor x \rfloor$
`modf(x, double *int_part)`	Split x into fraction and integer

Standard library functions

The `sqrt` function returns a domain error when x<0. The `fmod` function returns the remainder of x/y ensuring that the return value has the same sign as x. The result of `fmod` is not defined if y=0.

The `floor` function returns the largest integer not greater than x, and the `ceil` function returns the smallest integer not less than x. Note that both `ceil` and `floor` return their integer value as a `double` value and not an integral type. The behavior of the floor and ceil functions can be illustrated by examples as below:

```
floor(1.4)   ==   1.0
floor(-1.4)  ==  -2.0
ceil(1.4)    ==   2.0
ceil(-1.4)   ==  -1.0
```

The `modf` function splits x into its fractional part and its integral part. The fractional part is returned as the `double` value of `modf` and the integral part is stored (as a `double` value) at the address passed to the `int_part` argument. Both integral and fractional parts have the same sign as x.

12.3.5 Trigonometric, hyperbolic and exponential functions

The <math.h> library defines the three main trigonometric functions as shown in Table 12.5. The arguments are in radians.

Table 12.5. Trigonometric functions

Function	Meaning
sin(x)	Sine of x
cos(x)	Cosine of x
tan(x)	Tangent of x

The three inverse trigonometric functions are also declared in <math.h>, as is another function for the inverse tangent of a quotient. These functions return the angle in radians. For the functions `asin` and `acos`, the argument must be in the range $[-1, 1]$ or a domain error will occur. The functions are given in Table 12.6.

Table 12.6. Inverse trigonometric functions

Function	Meaning
asin(x)	$\sin^{-1} x$ in the range $[-\pi/2, \pi/2]$
acos(x)	$\cos^{-1} x$ in the range $[0, \pi]$
atan(x)	$\tan^{-1} x$ in the range $[-\pi/2, \pi/2]$
atan2(x, y)	$\tan^{-1}(x/y)$ in the range $[-\pi, \pi]$

The three common hyperbolic functions are also declared in <math.h> using their traditional names; see Table 12.7.

Table 12.7. Hyperbolic functions

Function	Meaning
sinh(x)	Hyperbolic sine of x
cosh(x)	Hyperbolic cosine of x
tanh(x)	Hyperbolic tangent of x

There are a number of functions related to exponentiation and logarithms; see Table 12.8. The pow function returns a domain error if $x = 0$ and $y \leq 0$ or if $x < 0$ and y is a non-integer. The logarithm functions are only defined for $x > 0$, and return a domain error if $x = 0$ and a range error if $x < 0$.

Table 12.8. Exponential functions

Function	Meaning
exp(x)	e^x
pow(x, y)	x^y
log(x)	$\log_e x$
log10(x)	$\log_{10} x$

12.3.6 Floating point internal representation

There are two functions for dealing with the internal representation of floating point values; see Table 12.9. These functions assume that the radix of the representation is 2.

Table 12.9. Internal representation functions

Function	Meaning
ldexp(x, int n)	Value from mantissa and exponent (i.e. $x . 2^n$)
frexp(x, int *power)	Split x into mantissa and exponent

The frexp function splits x into a normalized mantissa in the range $[0.5, 1)$, and an integral exponent. The mantissa is returned as the double result of frexp and the exponent is stored in the address passed to power (as an int). If x is zero, both mantissa and exponent are returned as zero.

12.4 Utility functions: <stdlib.h>

The header file <stdlib.h> defines functions for a variety of tasks, including simple mathematical operations on integers, base conversion, dynamic memory allocation, random numbers, searching and sorting arrays. There are also a number of functions to operate on multibyte characters, but these functions are beyond the scope of the book.

12.4.1 Absolute value and remainder functions

The mathematical functions defined in Table 12.10 are for absolute value and for the remainder of integers.

Table 12.10. Simple mathematical functions

Function	Meaning
`int abs(int x)`	Absolute value of an `int`
`long labs(long n)`	Absolute value of a `long`
`div_t div(int x, int y)`	Quotient and remainder of x/y
`ldiv_t ldiv(long x, long y)`	Quotient and remainder of x/y

The types `div_t` and `ldiv_t` are declared in `<stdlib.h>` and both are a `struct` type with field names `quot` and `rem` representing quotient and remainder. The fields are of type `int` for `div_t` and type `long` for `ldiv_t`.

12.4.2 Converting strings to numbers

The `<stdlib.h>` header file defines a number of functions for conversion of strings of digits to the numerical value they represent. Note that the `sscanf` function is also capable of conversion, as discussed in Section 6.2.5. The simplest conversion functions are given in Table 12.11.

Table 12.11. Simple string conversion functions

Function	Meaning
`int atoi(char *s)`	Convert `s` to an `int`
`long atol(char *s)`	Convert `s` to a `long`
`double atof(char *s)`	Convert `s` to a `double`

The acceptable character sequences and the error-handling behavior for `atoi` and `atol` is identical to `strtol` (discussed below) and `atof` is identical to `strtod`. These three functions all return zero if no characters are recognized as part of the number represented by `s`. The strings for `atoi` and `atol` must contain only decimal digits, and a prefix `0x` or `0X` does not cause hexadecimal conversion to be used, nor does a prefix `0` cause octal conversion.

The more complicated base conversion functions are given below:

```
long strtol(char *s, char **end_ptr, int base)
unsigned long strtoul(char *s, char **end_ptr, int base)
long strtod(char *s, char **end_ptr)
```

These functions all ignore leading whitespace and the first inconsistent character ends the conversion. If `end_ptr` is non-`NULL`, the address of the character after the last character used for base conversion is stored where `end_ptr` points to (i.e. the address of the first character not used by the conversion is stored there). If no characters are recognized as part of a number, zero is returned and `s` is stored at the address pointed to by `end_ptr`.

The `strtol` and `strtoul` functions ignore leading spaces and permit the integer to be prefixed with a sign. These functions use `base` to determine what base the conversion is to use. The value of `base` can be at most 36 (10 digits and 26 letters). If `base` is in the range 2 to 36 inclusive it is used as the base for conversion. As a special case, a leading `0x` or `0X` is permitted if `base` is 16. If `base` is zero, the string `s` determines the base to be used for conversion: a leading `0x` or `0X` indicates hexadecimal, a leading `0` indicates octal, otherwise decimal is used. For bases greater than 10 the letters are used as digits and a letter may be of either case. Any digit or letter that is not valid for the specified base ends the conversion.

The error-handling behavior of the `strtol` function is to return `LONG_MAX` or `LONG_MIN` (defined in `<limits.h>`) for overflow, depending if the number was positive or negative, and set `errno` to `ERANGE`. The `strtoul` function can only overflow in the positive direction and returns `ULONG_MAX`. Note that an integral conversion cannot underflow.

The `strtod` function accepts a string of whitespace characters, an optional sign, a string of digits (that may contain a period) and an optional exponent part (`e` or `E` followed by an optional sign and a string of digits). Hence, `strtod` accepts all common formats of floating point numbers: `0.31`, `2.75e-25`, etc. The error-handling behavior of `strtod` is to return `HUGE_VAL` on overflow and return zero on underflow. For both underflow and overflow `errno` is set to `ERANGE`.

12.4.3 Dynamic memory allocation

The `<stdlib.h>` header file defines prototypes for the dynamic memory allocation functions. The behavior of these functions is covered fully in Section 8.6 and only a brief discussion is given here.

```
void *malloc(int size)
void *calloc(int number, int size)
void free(void *address)
void *realloc(void *old_address, int new_size)
```

Note that all the `int` arguments in the prototypes above are, strictly speaking, of type `size_t` as declared in `<stddef.h>`, but for all practical purposes `int` is equivalent.

The `malloc` function returns the address of an uninitialized block of `size` bytes from the heap or `NULL` if not enough memory is available. The `calloc` function is identical to the use of `malloc` below, except that `calloc` initializes all bytes to zero.

```
malloc(number * size)
```

The `free` function returns the block of memory to the heap, allowing it to be reused. The address passed to `free` must have been previously allocated by `malloc`, `calloc` or `realloc`.

The `realloc` function reallocates the block at `old_address`, which must have been allocated by one of the dynamic memory allocation functions, to have a new size, and returns the new address. The data at `old_address` is copied to the new address, but any new memory is uninitialized if `new_size` is larger.

12.4.4 Random number generation: rand, srand

There are two functions declared in `<stdlib.h>` related to random number generation (actually *pseudo*-random number generation). Sequences of calls to the `rand` function generate a sequence of random numbers, and the `srand` function is used to seed the random number generator. The function prototypes are given in Table 12.12.

Table 12.12. Random number functions

Function	Meaning
`int rand(void)`	Return a random number
`void srand(unsigned int seed)`	Seed the random number generator

The random numbers are from zero to `RAND_MAX` which is a very large integer constant defined by `<stdlib.h>`. The usual method of generating random numbers in a restricted range, such as 1..100, is to use the `%` operator:

```
n = rand() % 100 + 1;
```

Note that the starting seed is always 1, and hence, without any calls to `srand`, the same sequence of numbers will be generated each time the program is re-executed. A common method of ensuring different sequences each time the program is run is to seed the random number generator with a value based on the current time as defined by the `time` function declared in `<time.h>`:

```
srand(time(NULL));
```

Note that `time` actually returns type `time_t` as declared in `<time.h>`, but `time_t` is usually declared as `int` or `long` which is compatible with the requirement of an unsigned long argument to `srand`.

12.4.5 Sorting arrays: qsort

The `qsort` standard library function is an implementation of a sorting algorithm similar to quicksort and is declared in `<stdlib.h>`. The `qsort` function can be used to sort arrays of any type. The prototype definition is:

```
typedef int (*ptr_to_fn) (void *, void*);
void qsort(void *arr, int n, int size, ptr_to_fn comp_fn)
```

where the name `ptr_to_fn` is introduced for convenience. The first argument, `arr`, is a pointer to the first element of the array — the simplest method is to pass the array name as this argument (alternatively "`&arr[0]`" could be used). `n` is the number of elements in the array — that is, how many elements to be sorted. `size` is the size of each array element as computed by the `sizeof` operator — `sizeof(arr[0])`. Note that `sizeof(arr)` is wrong because it gives the size of the entire array, not the size of a single element.

The last argument, `comp_fn`, is a pointer to a function to compare two array elements. A pointer to a function may seem overly complicated, but a function name is equivalent to a pointer to a function. Hence this function name can be passed to `qsort`, and any complicated pointer-to-function declarations are avoided. The comparison function has two parameters (for two elements), and accepts the elements as *pointers* to an element (not as integer indexes into the array). The function must compare the two elements and return an integer that is:

<0, when the first is less than the second (x<y),
0, when the first is equal to second (x==y),
>0, when the first is greater than the second (x>y).

The first example sorts an array of integers. When the arrays elements are integers, it is possible to use subtraction in the comparison function:

```
#include <stdio.h>
#include <stdlib.h>

/*--------------------------------------------------------------*/
/* Comparison function required by qsort                        */
/*--------------------------------------------------------------*/
int  comp_fn(const int *first, const int *second)
{
    return *first - *second;        /* Subtraction */
}

main()
{
    int arr[5] = { 1, 3, 2, 0, 4 };
    int i, n = 5;                   /* Number of array elements */

    qsort(arr, n, sizeof(arr[0]), comp_fn);  /* Sort array */
    for (i = 0; i < n; i++)                  /* Print array */
        printf("%d ", arr[i]);
}
```

Note that the parameters of comp_fn are declared as const to indicate that the comparison function does not change the array elements. In the absence of const the compiler should produce a warning message.

Another problem is that the comparison function, as given above, is that it is non-portable to implementations where void* and int* are not equivalent. qsort always calls the comparison function with arguments of type void* and the argument passing will be wrong if int* is a different size. The more portable comparison function uses arguments of type void* and type casts them to the appropriate pointer type:

```
int  comp_fn(const void *first, const void *second)
{
    return *(int*)first - *(int*)second;    /* Subtraction */
}
```

Note that later code examples for both qsort and bsearch will ignore this portability problem for greater clarity.

As implemented above, the elements of the array are sorted in *ascending* order. It is possible to sort in descending order simply by reversing the sign of the return value of the compare function. For the comparison function above, the operands to the subtraction operator would be swapped.

Standard library functions

The next example sorts an array of structures. This requires a different comparison function which accepts pointers to structures. Again, it is possible to use subtraction because the key fields being compared are integers.

```
#include <stdio.h>
#include <stdlib.h>

typedef int key_type;              /* Type of key field */
struct element {
    key_type key_field;            /* Key field */
};

/*----------------------------------------------------------*/
/* Comparison function required by qsort (assumes int keys) */
/*----------------------------------------------------------*/
int comp_fn(const struct element *e1, const struct element *e2)
{
    return e1->key_field - e2->key_field;
}

main()
{
    struct element arr[5] = { {1}, {2}, {0}, {4}, {3} };
    int i, n = 5;                  /* Number of array elements */

    qsort(arr, n, sizeof(arr[0]), comp_fn);   /* Sort array */
    for (i = 0; i < n; i++)                   /* Print array */
        printf("%d ", arr[i].key_field);
}
```

For arrays where the key field is a string, the standard library function strcmp can be used as part of the comparison function. The strcmp function returns an integer consistent with the requirements of qsort.

```
int comp_fn(const struct element *e1, const struct element *e2)
{
    return strcmp(e1->key_field, e2->key_field);
}
```

A different comparison function is needed for every use of qsort on arrays of different types. This is slightly better than needing a separate sort function for each type of array.

12.4.6 Searching sorted arrays: bsearch

The bsearch library function is an implementation of a binary search algorithm and can be used to search *sorted* arrays of any type. For bsearch to perform correctly, the array must be sorted, and the sorted order (ascending or descending) must be consistent with the definition of the comparison function. The bsearch function is very similar, in definition and use, to the qsort library function discussed above. In fact, it is often possible to use the same comparison function for sorting and searching when both these standard library functions are used. Note that the portability problem involving void* and other pointer types applies to the comparison functions for both qsort and bsearch. The prototype for bsearch is:

```
typedef int (*fn_ptr)(void *, void*);
void *bsearch(void *key,void *arr,int n,int size,fn_ptr comp_fn)
```

The method of usage is usually:

```
result = bsearch(key, arr, n, size, comp_fn);
```

where `key` is pointer to the element to search for; `arr` is a pointer to the first element of the array; `n` is the number of elements in the array; `size` is the size of each element; and `comp_fn` is a pointer to a function to compare two elements. The details are very similar to those for `qsort` above, with the exception of the returned result. The result is a pointer to the element found, or `NULL` if the element was not found. It is important to realize the returned result is not the integer index into the array. If needed, the integer index can be calculated using address arithmetic:

```
index = result - arr;
```

The `key` argument must be a pointer to the type in the array. For example, when sorting an array of `int`, the `key` argument must be a pointer to an `int` variable containing the value to be searched for:

```
#include <stdio.h>
#include <stdlib.h>

/*-----------------------------------------------------------*/
/* Comparison function: arguments are pointers to elements   */
/*-----------------------------------------------------------*/
int comp_fn(const int *first, const int *second)
{
    return *first - *second;
}

main()
{
    int arr[] = { 1, 2, 3, 4};      /* Array of elements */
    int n = 4;                       /* Number of elements */
    int * result;                    /* Result returned */
    int int_to_find = 2;;

    result = bsearch(&int_to_find,arr,n,sizeof(arr[0]),comp_fn);
    if (result == NULL)
        printf("Not found!\n");
    else
        printf("Found it at index %d!\n", result - arr);
}
```

As another example, if searching an array of `struct`, key must be a pointer to a `struct`. In this case, it is necessary to ensure that there is a value in the key-field of the `struct` — a dummy `struct` must be set up to hold the key.

```
struct element arr[] = { {1}, {2}, {3}, {4} };
int n = 4;
struct element *result;
struct element key_node;    /* Dummy struct to hold key */
key_type key_to_find = 3;

key_node.key_field = key_to_find;    /* Set up dummy node */
result = bsearch(&key_node,arr,n,sizeof(arr[0]),comp_fn);
```

Usually, it is required for the elements of the array to be sorted in *ascending* order. However, it is possible to use the bsearch function on arrays sorted in descending order by reversing the sign of the return value of the comparison function.

12.4.7 System-related functions

Finally, the <stdlib.h> header file defines a number of miscellaneous system-related functions. The exit and abort functions causing immediate program termination are defined in Table 12.13 (see also Section 4.12).

Table 12.13. Program termination functions

Function	Meaning
void exit(int ret_value)	Exit normally
void abort(void)	Exit abnormally

The exit function allows normal program termination, and performs some cleaning up. All open files are flushed and closed, and ret_value is returned to the environment as the termination value of the program. Zero indicates successful termination and non-zero indicates failure (the symbolic constants EXIT_SUCCESS and EXIT_FAILURE are also available in <stdlib.h> for this purpose).

The abort function terminates the program abnormally and is equivalent to raising the signal SIGABRT. Under UNIX a call to abort causes the program to terminate with a core dump.

The atexit function registers a pointer to a function (or just a function name) as a function to be called on termination of the program via a call to the exit function. These functions (obviously) do not accept any arguments. Functions registered by atexit are called before exit closes files, and if more than one function is registered by atexit they are called by exit in the opposite order to the atexit calls (i.e. atexit stacks the functions). The prototype definition of atexit is:

```
typedef void (*ptr_to_fn)(void);
int atexit(ptr_to_fn p)
```

The atexit function returns zero on success and non-zero on failure.

The system and getenv functions are available in <stdlib.h> for interaction between the program and operating system. The prototype definitions are given in Table 12.14.

Table 12.14. Environment functions

Function	Meaning
`int system(char *s)`	Execute operating system command
`char *getenv(char *var_name)`	Get value of environment variable

The `system` function sends the string `s` to be executed as a command by the operating system. Under UNIX a call to `system` invokes a new shell to execute the command, and the return value of `system` is the return value of this shell. The function call:

```
system(NULL);
```

can be used to determine if there is an environment to process a command, and returns non-zero if so. The use of `system` under UNIX is covered fully in Section 19.2.

The `getenv` function returns the string value of the environment variable called `var_name`, or `NULL` if there is no such environment variable. The use of `getenv` under UNIX is covered fully in Section 19.5.

12.5 Times and dates: <time.h>

The standard library defines a number of functions that deal with the representation of times and dates. In particular, the current time can be found using the `time` function. The `time` function is declared as:

```
time_t   time(time_t *ptr)
```

where the type `time_t` is an integral type declared in `<time.h>` (often just `int`). If `ptr` is non-`NULL` the returned time is stored at the address contained by `ptr` in addition to being returned. The `time` function returns −1 if the current time is not available.

The integer returned by the `time` function is an internal representation of time and needs to be converted to a representation that humans can understand. One function to convert between this representation and real seconds is:

```
double difftime(time_t t2, time_t t1)
```

which returns the number of seconds, expressed as a `double`, that expired between the two times `t1` and `t2` (where `t2>t1`).

Another method of manipulating times is to use another `struct` type, `struct tm`, that is declared to represent time. This type is declared in `<time.h>` as:

```
struct tm {
    int         tm_sec;         /* seconds: 0..61 (2 leap seconds) */
    int         tm_min;         /* minutes: 0..59 */
    int         tm_hour;        /* hours since midnight:   0..23 */
    int         tm_mday;        /* day of month:  1..31 */
    int         tm_mon;         /* months since January: 0..11 */
    int         tm_year;        /* years since 1900 */
    int         tm_wday;        /* days since Sunday: 0..6 */
    int         tm_yday;        /* days from start of year: 0..365 */
    int         tm_isdst;       /* daylight savings time flag */
};
```

There are a number of functions for converting between the types `time_t` and `struct tm`:

```
time_t mktime(struct tm *ptr)
struct tm *localtime(time_t *tptr)
struct tm *gmtime(time_t *tptr)
```

The `mktime` function converts from the `struct tm` representation to the `time_t` representation. The return value of `mktime` is −1 on error.

Both the `gmtime` and `localtime` functions convert from the `time_t` representation to the `struct tm` representation. The difference is that `localtime` converts to the current time at the location that the program is being executed, but `gmtime` returns time as represented in Greenwich Mean Time. The pointers returned by `gmtime` and `localtime` point to internal `static` variables that are overwritten on each call. To retain the time structure it is necessary to copy it to a declared variable. The usual method of storing time in a structure is shown below:

```
struct tm time_value;
time_t t;

t = time(NULL);                    /* Get the time */
time_value = *localtime(&t);       /* Convert to struct */
printf("Day of month = %d\n", time_value.tm_mday);
```

Note that a pointer variable could be used if `localtime` were only being called once. A structure is better when calling `localtime` more than once because each call overwrites the previous values of the internal structure.

There are a number of functions to convert from the `struct tm` and `time_t` representations of time to a character string representation. Their prototype declarations are:

```
char *asctime(struct tm *ptr)
char *ctime(time_t *tptr)
int strftime(char *s, int max, char *format, struct tm *ptr)
```

The `asctime` function converts from the `struct tm` representation to a character string representation. It returns the address of a string stored in an internal `static` area, and is overwritten on each call to `asctime`. The string is in the form similar to:

```
"Mon Nov 23 12:00:00 1991\n"
```

The `ctime` function uses the same format as `asctime` but accepts an argument of type `time_t` rather than `struct tm`. The statement `ctime(t)` is functionally equivalent to `asctime(localtime(t))`. Thus, a quick way to print out the local time is:

```
time_t t;

t = time(NULL);                   /* Get the time */
printf("%s\n", ctime(&t));        /* Print in string form */
```

The `strftime` function is very similar to the `sprintf` function, in that it formats a string according to `printf`-like format specifications using the % character given in a format string. Characters other than % are copied from the format string to s, and format specifications using % are expanded using the time information in the `struct` that `ptr` points to. A terminating zero is appended to s by strftime. The max argument limits the number of characters that can be placed in s. The return value of strftime is the number of characters placed in s, or zero if more than max characters were available for placement in s. The format specifications available are given in Table 12.15.

Table 12.15. strftime format specifiers

Specifier	Meaning
%a	Abbreviated day name (e.g. Sun)
%A	Day name (e.g. Sunday)
%b	Abbreviated month name (e.g. Jan)
%B	Month name (e.g. January)
%c	Local date and time representation
%d	Day of the month (01..31)
%H	Hour in 24-hour time (00-23)
%I	Hour in 12-hour time (01-12)
%J	Day of the year (001-366)
%m	Month (01-12)
%M	Minute (00-59)
%p	AM or PM
%S	Second (00-59)
%U	Week of year, Sunday starting each week (00-53)
%w	Weekday starting from Sunday (0-6)
%W	Week of year, Monday starting each week (00-53)
%x	Local date representation
%X	Local time representation
%y	Year (00-99)
%Y	Year (0000-9999)
%Z	Name of time zone
%%	The % character

12.5.1 Processor time

Although all of the above functions have been related to external time, there is one function declared in <time.h> to examine processor time. The processor time used by the program since it began execution can be found by calling the clock function. Its prototype definition is:

    clock_t clock(void)

where clock_t is an integral type declared in <time.h>. The return value of clock is −1 if the processor time is unknown.

The value returned by clock is the number of clock ticks since the program began executing, which is not equivalent to the number of seconds. The number of seconds can be found using the symbolic constant CLOCKS_PER_SEC which gives the number of clock ticks per second and is defined in <time.h>. The example below shows the use of the `clock` function to print out the number of seconds of processor time that have been used by the program since it began executing:

```
printf("%d seconds used\n", clock() / CLOCKS_PER_SEC);
```

12.6 Signal handling: <signal.h>

This section examines the signal handling facilities defined in `<signal.h>`. Further information about signals, with particular emphasis on their use under UNIX, can be found in Section 19.8.

Signals can occur due to a number of internal causes (dependent upon the implementation): arithmetic overflows, division by zero, dereferencing a `NULL` pointer. Signals also occur due to keyboard interrupts, such as when the user types `<ctrl-c>`. The program can also send itself signals using the `raise` function which is declared in `<signal.h>`:

```
int raise(int sig)
```

The `raise` function returns zero for success, non-zero for failure.

Usually, most signals cause the program to terminate, but `<signal.h>` provides a method of trapping these signals by installing functions to handle signals. The `signal` function is used to install a handler:

```
typedef void (*ptr_to_fn)(int);
ptr_to_fn signal(int sig, ptr_to_fn handler);
```

where `ptr_to_fn` is not actually declared in `<signal.h>`, but added here for clarity.

The `signal` function installs a new handler function for the signal `sig`, and returns a pointer to the old handler function (or `SIG_ERR` on failure to install the handler). The special symbolic constant, `SIG_DFL`, can be used to reinstate the default system handler, and `SIG_IGN` can be used to ignore the signal completely.

There are many symbolic constants defined for all the various signals. The full list can be found by consulting your local documentation. Some common signals are given in Table 12.16.

Table 12.16. Common signals

Signal	Meaning
SIGSEGV	Segmentation fault (UNIX)
SIGFPE	Floating point exception
SIGINT	User types `<ctrl-c>`
SIGQUIT	User types `<ctrl-\>` (UNIX)
SIGTSTP	User types `<ctrl-z>` (UNIX)

Once installed, a handler function will be called whenever the trapped signal occurs. The same handler can be used for any number of signals, but each signal has only one handler at a time. The signal number is passed to the handler as its first `int` argument, allowing the handler to distinguish which signal it has been called for. When the handler returns, execution continues as before from where the signal occurred (although a signal on some versions of UNIX can affect some system calls).

12.7 Standard definitions: <stddef.h>

The header file `<stddef.h>` contains a small number of rarely used definitions. The types `size_t` and `ptrdiff_t` are defined, `NULL` may be defined (often as a `void` pointer constant with value zero) and a macro `offsetof` is defined to find the offset of a member of a structure.

The type `size_t` is used as the type returned by the `sizeof` operator, the type of arguments to `malloc`, `calloc` and `realloc`, and as the return type for a few library functions such as `strlen`. The type `size_t` is usually declared as `unsigned int`, but for all practical purposes, the type `int` can be used instead of `size_t` (i.e. unless dealing with huge sizes).

The type `ptrdiff_t` represents the type of the difference of two pointers when they are subtracted using the binary − operator. It must be large enough to hold any possible difference between two pointers, and the sign of the difference. It is usually `int` or `long int`.

12.8 System constants: <limits.h> and <float.h>

The header files `<limits.h>` and `<float.h>` both define symbolic constants for various values. The `<limits.h>` header file defines symbolic constants related to integral types. In particular, it defines `CHAR_BIT` as the number of bits in a `char`, and also defined various constants for the maximum and minimum values that can be represented by integral types. The symbolic constant names for maximum and minimum values are given in Table 12.17.

Table 12.17. Constants in <limits.h>

Data type	Maximum	Minimum
char	CHAR_MAX	CHAR_MIN
int	INT_MAX	INT_MIN
long	LONG_MAX	LONG_MIN
signed char	SCHAR_MAX	SCHAR_MIN
short int	SHRT_MAX	SHRT_MIN
unsigned char	UCHAR_MAX	−
unsigned int	UINT_MAX	−
unsigned short	USHRT_MAX	−
unsigned long	ULONG_MAX	−

Note that the minimum values of an `unsigned` type are obviously zero, and there is no need for a symbolic constant.

The `<float.h>` header file defines symbolic constants related to floating point types and floating point arithmetic. Some of the symbolic constants for `float` and `double` variables that are declared in `<float.h>` are given in Table 12.18.

Table 12.18. Constants in <float.h>

Constants	Meaning
FLT_MIN, DBL_MIN	Minimum value
FLT_MAX, DBL_MAX	Maximum value
FLT_DIG, DBL_DIG	Number of decimal digits of precision
FLT_EPSILON, DBL_EPSILON	Difference between two representable values
FLT_MANT_DIG, DBL_MANT_DIG	Binary digits in mantissa
FLT_RADIX	Radix (usually 2)

Note that there are also corresponding constants for the type long double: LDBL_MIN, LDBL_MAX, LDBL_DIG, LDBL_EPSILON, LDBL_MANT_DIG,

12.9 International programs: <locale.h>

The standard library provides support for programs being ported to different countries. These functions allow the programmer to write a program such that it adapts to the current country, by being sensitive to the environment in which it is executed. For example, a program can determine whether the character representing money is a pound sign or a dollar sign, and use the correct character in program output. Unfortunately, most of <locale.h> is beyond the scope of the book and only a brief summary is presented here.

When a C program begins, it starts by using a minimal environment. The locale can be changed by calling the setlocale function, declared as:

```
char *setlocale(int category, char * locale)
```

The second argument to setlocale is commonly "" (the empty string constant) or "C". The use of "C" sets the locale to the minimal C environment. The empty string "" sets the locale to be the system dependent local environment (which could just be the minimal C environment in an unsophisticated implementation).

The setlocale function returns a pointer to a string (in static storage) that describes the locale, or NULL if the requested locale is not available. This string can be saved by the program and used to reset the locale settings in a later call to setlocale. If the locale argument is NULL, the current locale is not changed.

The first argument to setlocale indicates which functions in the standard library should be affected by the change in locale. It is typically one of the symbolic constants defined in <locale.h>; see Table 12.19.

The various categories have different effects. LC_COLLATE affects special string handling functions such as strcoll which is identical to strcmp except that it can be used when the local alphabet is not compatible with ASCII (e.g. contains more than 255 letters) and each letter is represented by more than one byte. LC_CTYPE affects the <ctype.h> library and is useful when characters are not single bytes. LC_NUMERIC changes the standard library's treatment of numeric values, such as allowing input/output to use a different decimal point character. LC_MONETARY changes the relevant locale settings, such as the currency symbol.

Table 12.19. Locale categories

Constant	Area affected
LC_ALL	All relevant library functions
LC_COLLATE	String functions (e.g. strcoll)
LC_CTYPE	Macros in <ctype.h>
LC_NUMERIC	Numeric information
LC_TIME	Time functions (i.e. strftime)
LC_MONETARY	Monetary information

The <locale.h> header file also declares a structure containing much information about the locale (struct lconv), and a function to extract the current setting of the locale.

The localeconv function is used to access the current value of this structure. It returns a pointer to the current structure in static storage. Its prototype definition is:

```
struct lconv * localeconv(void)
```

The lconv structure contains fields of two different types: char* and char. The most useful fields of type char* are listed in Table 12.20. The reason that they are strings, when in many cases it would appear a single char is adequate, is to provide support for multibyte characters (e.g. large Asian alphabets that require a number of char values for each letter).

Table 12.20. String fields of lconv

Field name	Meaning
decimal_point	Decimal point character
positive_sign	Positive sign
negative_sign	Negative sign
currency_symbol	Currency symbol
int_curr_symbol	International currency symbol
mon_decimal_point	Decimal point for monetary quantities

In addition, to the char* fields, there are a number of char fields that contain boolean flags (i.e. they don't contain characters). Some of these fields are listed in Table 12.21. The values of boolean flags are non-zero if the requirement is true.

Table 12.21. Char fields of lconv

Field name	Meaning
p_cs_precedes	Positive sign precedes value?
n_cs_precedes	Negative sign precedes value?
p_sep_by_space	Space between positive sign and value?
n_sep_by_space	Space between negative sign and value?

12.10 Further reading

For further information on the ANSI standard library, the definitive reference is the ANSI standard (refer to the Bibliography for details of how to obtain a copy). An interesting book discussing both use and implementation of the standard library, including full C source code for all library functions, is the book by Plauger:

PLAUGER, P. J., *The Standard C Library*, Prentice Hall, 1991.

12.11 Exercises

1. Write a program to ask the user for a real number and then output its square root, ceiling and floor. Are there any special linkage requirements on your system?

2. Testing for equality of real expressions is poor programming practice. Real numbers have to be approximated on computers and apparently equal expressions may often differ by a small amount. Examine this behavior of float and double variables by coding up the mathematical identity: $\sin^2 x + \cos^2 x = 1$. Use the code fragment below to test this identity for various real values:

```
for (x = 0.0; x <= 10.0; x += 0.01) {
    if (sin(x) * sin(x) + cos(x) * cos(x)   != 1.0)
        printf("Not equal\n");
}
```

If real numbers behaved exactly on computers, the printf statement would never be executed. What happens on your system? Is there different behavior when x is float or double? Modify the program to print out the difference when the two expressions are not equal.

3. Write a function to generate random *real* numbers between 0 and 1 using the rand function. *Hint:* Use the RAND_MAX constant to scale the integer values generated by rand.

4. Find the largest value of x for which exp(x) is correct. *Hint:* Use bisection on the range 0..DBL_MAX; at each iteration calculate the mid-point and evaluate exp(mid); if it overflows then reduce the upper bound to mid; otherwise increase the lower bound to mid.

5. How can the memset function be used to initialize an array of integers to zero? How can memcpy be used to copy one array to another?

6. Write a program to print out the current time using ctime. Modify this program to calculate how many seconds of execution time it requires. *Hint:* Use the clock library function for the second part.

Part II
Advanced Issues

Part II
Advanced Issues

Chapter 13
Large programs

Using a single file for a whole program becomes unrealistic as the project size increases. The C language provides a powerful mechanism for grouping multiple files as a single program. At its simplest level, it involves breaking a program up into groups of functions. Each file contains one or more functions and these files are compiled separately, and linked together (using the *linker*) to produce a single executable. The effect is almost the same as one long file.

There are some minor difficulties in the use of global data and functions defined in other files. It is often necessary to maintain extra files, called *header files*, that keep common data needed by all the different C source files. It is important to organize these header files correctly.

13.1 Independent compilation

When programs get large they become difficult to manage. The best way to resolve this problem is to break the program into separate files. When breaking a program up into different files, different functions are placed in different files. The `main` function only appears in one file. By convention, the file containing `main` is often called `"main.c"`.

Although the main motivation for using independent compilation is reducing the complexity of organizing the program, there is the extra advantage of reducing the time required for compilation because each file is compiled separately and only files that are modified need be recompiled. Instead of creating the executable from the single source file, the compiler creates object files corresponding to each source file. These object files can be linked to make the final executable. Compilation time is reduced because linking is much faster than compilation. Object files do take up extra space on disk, leading to a tradeoff of space for time. Note that this gain only occurs during the development phase of the program, when most of the object files will be up-to-date. When compiling the entire project to rebuild all object files, compilation may take slightly longer than it would with a single file.

Each C source file is compiled to produce an object file. Object files have the suffix ".o" under UNIX and the suffix ".obj" under DOS. Naturally, the method of producing the object files depends on the programming environment. Similarly, the *linker* is different in the various environments. Under DOS the method of compilation will depend on the compiler being used. For example, Turbo C has much of the task automated through the use of "project" files. However, the method is standard under UNIX and is now discussed.

Source files are compiled independently under UNIX using the −c option to cc. For example, the command:

```
cc -c lib.c
```

produces the "lib.o" object file which can be linked with other object files to create the executable. In fact, cc is also used for linking the object files to make a single executable (the linker is called internally by cc). The following sequence of commands compiles the C source files, "lib.c" and "main.c" into the object files, "lib.o" and "main.o", and then links them to create the executable "a.out":

```
cc -c lib.c         # produce lib.o
cc -c main.c        # produce main.o
cc lib.o main.o     # link lib.o and main.o to create a.out
```

13.2 External variables

In Section 7.7 we examined the use of *global variables* which are variables that can be accessed by more than one function. In this section we generalize the use of global variables to allow these global variables to be accessed by functions in other files. When a function uses a variable defined in another file, this is called using an *external variable*. However, because the distinctions between global and external variables are minor (depending upon how many files a variable is used in), it is common just to refer to these variables as global variables.

The use of external variables in multiple files is quite similar to that for global variables in a single file. For example, suppose we wish to define an external variable max_len in one file and use it in another. The definition of max_len in the first file is just a definition of a global variable (outside of any function definition):

```
int max_len;
```

However, the second file cannot use max_len without declaring the variable as external to that file. This is achieved using the extern specifier. The declaration below must be placed at the top of the second file (i.e. it must appear before the first use of the variable):

```
extern int max_len;
```

It is incorrect to define max_len without the extern specifier in the second file, because this will lead to compilation errors (actually linkage errors) because of the multiple declarations of max_len. Thus, the general method of using external variables is that the variable must be defined globally in exactly one file, and then defined as extern in any other files that need to use the external variable. Note that initialization of the variable is allowed in the first definition, but not in any of the extern declarations.

13.3 Function prototype declarations

Functions should be declared before they are used. In a single file program, this is usually a matter of ordering the function definitions correctly. However, in larger programs, functions are spread over different files and it is necessary to declare functions used in other files. This section examines the use of *function prototypes* to provide the compiler with information about argument types and the function return value, so that compilation can proceed as if the functions were actually defined in the current file. Note that this type of declaration is called a "forward declaration" in some other programming languages.

Function prototypes have a simple syntax that is very similar to an ordinary function definition. The difference is that the body of the function is left out and a semicolon is placed after the function header (i.e. after the right bracket of the parameter list). A function prototype always ends with a semicolon. Hence, the syntax of a function prototype is:

```
type fn_name(parameter_list);
```

The parameter list can be an ordinary list of parameters as with any function definition. Alternatively, it can be a list of abstract type declarators (i.e. the name of the parameter is left out, only the type is put in the list). If parameter names are left in, they are ignored and do not have to match the parameter names used in a function definition later in the file. Both forms are syntactically correct and the choice is a matter of style — leaving the parameter names in is preferable because of the documentation benefits it provides. Some examples of function prototype declarations are:

```
int   max_int(int, int);                    /* parameter names out */
char *strcpy(char *dest, char *source);     /* parameter names in */
void  mesg(void);                           /* no parameters */
```

Function prototypes can also use the extern keyword as below. It is unnecessary, and the meaning is identical.

```
extern int max_int(int, int);
```

When ANSI C is not available, non-prototyping function prototypes are also possible. They are identical, except that the parameter list is empty. Some examples of non-prototyping function prototypes are:

```
int max();
char *strcpy();
```

Function prototypes can be left out in some special cases, though this is not recommended. When the compiler finds an unknown function, it automatically assumes it to have return type int (and defaults to non-prototyping for function arguments). Functions returning non-int types can cause errors if not properly declared by a function prototype, because, by assuming type int, the compiler may generate code for a type coercion. If it finds a definition of a function further in the file, the compiler will usually emit a warning message. However, if the function definition is in a different file, the error is not even detected, and can cause unpredictable run-time behavior.

13.4 Definition versus declaration

A *declaration* specifies the important information about a variable — its name and type. A *definition* specifies the same information, and also reserves storage space for the variable. Every definition is also a declaration, but not all declarations are definitions.

Declarations using extern are examples of declarations that do not define the variable (i.e. do not reserve memory). The corresponding definition is a variable declaration without the extern keyword. Function prototypes are declarations that do not define a function; an ordinary function definition is the corresponding definition. The difference between a declaration and a definition is shown below:

```
extern int x;          /* Declaration */
int x;                 /* Definition and declaration */

int fn(int y);         /* Declaration */
int fn(int y)          /* Definition and declaration */
{
    ...
}
```

A variable or function can be declared any number of times, but must be defined exactly once. All of the declarations must agree with other declarations and the definition. This means that it is possible to define a variable as extern any number of times, or declare a function (using a prototype) any number of times, provided all declarations have exactly the same type as the (single) definition.

Some non-ANSI compilers will remove the restriction of exactly one definition and will merge two definitions of the same name into the same location. This is a convenient, but dangerous practice. It permits global variable *definitions* in header files, but it is possible that two totally separate variables of different types, accidentally given the same name, are merged into the one location. The compiler (linker) should disallow the two definitions and provide an error message about "multiply defined symbols". This chapter assumes that multiple definitions are illegal.

13.5 Single file scope: static

The storage class specifier static has a special meaning when applied to global variables. As covered in Section 7.9.3, its meaning for local variables is that they retain their values between function calls. Global variables always retain their value, so the static specifier is not needed to indicate this. Instead, static applied to global variables restricts their *scope* to the file in which they appear. Global variables declared as static are only accessible to functions in the file they are defined in, and cannot be accessed by functions in other files. In other words, it is not possible to use a static variable in another file by declaring it as extern and then accessing it. Similarly, when `static` is placed before a function definition, it restricts the scope of the function name to the single file and that function cannot be called from another file.

The `static` specifier provides a limited feature for information hiding and is useful, for example, when setting up a library of functions. Functions in a library file may need to use a global variable, such as a hash table, which other files have no reason to access:

```
static node_ptr hash_table[SIZE];
```

Declaring the hash table as `static` makes it impossible for other files to access it and ensures that it cannot be corrupted by functions outside the file. The hash table is local to the functions in the file.

Similarly, a local function can be declared for use within the single file. This is useful for functions that are used internally, but need not be called by functions outside the file. For example, a symbol table implemented using a hash table may have a search function that is designed specifically for the delete function to find the element. There is no need for external functions to call this search function and the search function would be defined as below:

```
static int search_for_delete(char *key)
{
    ...    /* function body */
}
```

The possibility of specifying single file scope with `static` also allows the same names for global variables or functions to be used by different files without name collisions (i.e. multiply defined names).

13.6 Header files

When using multiple files, there is always information that is common to them. Files will need the same `#define` declarations and the same type declarations (i.e. `struct` definitions and `typedef` declarations). Rather than having duplicates of these in all the files, it is better to use a single header file containing all this information. This header file can be included in all the files that need it using `#include`. By avoiding duplication we have also allowed easier modification, since a constant or type declaration need only be changed in one place.

Although `#include` can be used to include any C code in the middle of a file, there are some guidelines for good header file usage. Header files should contain only:

- Constant definitions
- Type declarations
- Macro definitions
- Extern declarations
- Function prototypes

Header files should not contain any executable code (i.e. no function definitions). Header files should not define variables, but only declare them — every variable declaration should be an `extern` declaration. If the header file does contain variable definitions, this causes multiple definitions of the same symbol, which is a linkage error.

The organization of header files is a matter of style. Organize the header files in a manner that is logical to you, and (hopefully) to anyone else who may need to modify the program. For a small project, a single header file may well be adequate. For a larger project, there will be some header files that all C source files require, and other header files that are only needed by some of the C source files.

The example below examines the use of header files for constant declarations and type definitions. All header files have the filename suffix ".h". Although it is possible to call header files any name (because `#include` accepts any name) this convention is recommended because it allows some software tools to distinguish between C source files and header files (e.g. the `make` utility examined later in the chapter). Note that the:

```
#include "file.h"
```

notation is used in the C source files to include the header file, rather than the `<file.h>` notation which is used when including standard library header files.

```
/*-------------------------------------------------------*/
/* FILE: consts.h - constant definitions                 */
/*-------------------------------------------------------*/

#define MAX 10
...
```

```
/*-------------------------------------------------------*/
/* FILE: types.h - type definitions                      */
/*-------------------------------------------------------*/

typedef int data_type;
...
```

```
/*-------------------------------------------------------*/
/* FILE: main.c - C source : functions and executable code */
/*-------------------------------------------------------*/

#include <stdio.h>
#include "consts.h"
#include "types.h"
...
main()
{
    ...
}
```

This example demonstrates the use of header files for two purposes — constants and types. The following sections show the addition of more header files — to hold `extern` declarations of variables and function prototypes.

13.7 Header file of extern variables

As mentioned above, header files should not define global variables. Instead, header files should declare variables as external variables using `extern`. The definition of global variables (i.e. the declaration without the `extern` keyword) should appear in only one of the C source files. Commonly the file containing the `main` function is used for all global variable definitions (often called `"main.c"`). However, the only aspect preventing you from defining different global variables in different files is the confusion it may create.

One possible organization of header files is to create a file called `"extern.h"` to hold all `extern` variable declarations used in any of the C source files. Including this header file in a C source file *declares* all global variables, but does not *define* them. If there is no definition in any of the files, but only `extern` declarations (i.e. if you forget to define it in `"main.c"`), the symbol will be undefined — a linkage error.

In the example below, note the order of inclusion of `<stdio.h>`, `consts.h`, `types.h` and `extern.h`. The ordering is because types may need constants, and `extern` declarations may need the types.

```
/*------------------------------------------------------------*/
/* FILE: extern.h - declaration of all global variables       */
/*------------------------------------------------------------*/

extern  int    flag;     /* Declare the variable as external */
extern  float  x;
...
```

```
/*------------------------------------------------------------*/
/* FILE : main.c  - C source file containing main()           */
/*------------------------------------------------------------*/

#include <stdio.h>
#include "consts.h"
#include "types.h"
#include "extern.h"     /* included to ensure correct types */

int    flag;            /* Define the variable as global */
float  x;
...
```

```
/*------------------------------------------------------------*/
/* FILE: other.c - C source file containing other functions   */
/*------------------------------------------------------------*/

#include <stdio.h>
#include "consts.h"
#include "types.h"
#include "extern.h"   /* included to declare global variables */
...
```

The header file of `extern` declarations must be included in all files that do not contain the variable definitions. The header file should also be included where the global variables are defined (i.e. even in `"main.c"`). Though it is not strictly necessary because the definition also declares the variables, including the header file ensures that the definition and `extern` declaration have the same type. A compilation error is produced if the types differ. If the header file is not included, there is no way for the compiler to check for the correct types.

13.7.1 Preprocessor trickery

An alternative to the above method of defining all global variables in "main.c" is to use a preprocessor trick to cause the "extern.h" header file to both declare and define global variables. To achieve this, a file of extern declarations is maintained, similar to the declaration below:

```
extern int x;
```

The variables are not defined in the "main.c" file (or any file). Instead, the lines of code shown below are placed in the "main.c" source file (i.e. in one source file only).

```
#define extern            /* Replace "extern" with nothing */
#include "extern.h"
#undef extern             /* revert to no change for safety */
```

The first line defines the word "extern" to be changed to whitespace. In effect, every occurrence of extern in the header file is deleted. An extern declaration without the extern keyword is a definition. In all files except "main.c" the variable x is qualified by extern. However, if extern is replaced with nothing in "main.c" (using the code fragment above) the global variables are defined exactly once, as required.

The disadvantage of this method is that global variables cannot be easily initialized at compile-time. Initializations in the header file usually cause compilation errors when extern is not deleted, because extern declarations cannot initialize variables (though some compilers may be lenient). Initializations can be included with more fancy preprocessor usage, but the trouble tends to outweigh the gain. For example, the header file can check if extern is defined and include the initialization only if extern is defined (i.e. if extern is being removed).

```
extern int x    /* no semicolon */
#ifdef extern
  = 2           /* initialization */
#endif
  ;             /* semicolon at the end of the declaration */
```

Unfortunately, this mess is needed for each initialized variable. An alternative is to keep two alternate copies of the variable declarations in the one header file:

```
#ifdef extern
    int x = 2;
    ...     /* other variable definitions with initializations */
#else
    extern int x;
    ...     /* other extern declarations for these variables */
#endif
    ...     /* other extern declarations without initialization */
```

This method leads to the inconvenience of duplication (though non-initialized variables need not be duplicated). This duplication leads to the need to include "extern.h" twice in "main.c" (once with extern defined as nothing, once without) to check the consistency of the two versions.

13.8 Header file of function prototypes

Functions defined in one file can be called from other files. In the files not containing the function, there is a need for a function prototype to allow proper type checking. There is no strict need for a prototype in the file defining the function, but prototypes are strongly recommended here to remove the problem of (accidentally) using a function before it is defined.

The omission of function prototypes loses all type checking of functions arguments, and may cause compiler or run-time errors. It is very strongly recommended to maintain a header file containing a prototype for every function. If this header file is included, the compiler knows the types of the parameters, and can use full type checking on arguments. As with `extern` declarations, there is no strict need to include prototypes in the files where the functions are defined, but this is useful in checking that the declarations in the header file match the actual definitions.

```
/*-----------------------------------------------------------*/
/* FILE : fns.h - Function prototypes                        */
/*-----------------------------------------------------------*/

int  max_int(int a, int b);
...
```

```
/*-----------------------------------------------------------*/
/* FILE: other.c - C source file containing other functions  */
/*-----------------------------------------------------------*/

#include <stdio.h>
#include "consts.h"
#include "extern.h"
#include "fns.h"         /* include function prototypes */

int max_int(int a, int b)
{
    ...      /* etc */
}
```

```
/*-----------------------------------------------------------*/
/* FILE : main.c - C source file containing main()           */
/*-----------------------------------------------------------*/

#include <stdio.h>
#include "consts.h"
#include "types.h"
#include "extern.h"
#include "fns.h"         /* include function prototypes */

main()
{
    ...      /* etc */
}
```

13.9 Automatic generation of header files

Maintaining a header file of function prototypes can be annoying because every new function must be added to the header file. Under UNIX, the `grep` and `sed` utilities can be used to automatically extract all function definitions. If these utilities are not available in your environment, a small C program can be written to perform the same task. This section examines both approaches to writing your own small software tool to improve your programming productivity.

The idea of this section relies greatly on the use of consistent programming style in C programs. If your C functions are defined as below:

```
int fn(int x)
{
    ...    /* indented function body */
}
```

generating function prototypes is a simple matter of extracting the first line, and adding a semicolon to the end of the line. Hence, this section will assume that function definitions always start on the first character of a line. Furthermore, the entire list of function parameters must be placed on one line. It is also assumed that there are no comments in the middle of the parameter list (although comments are allowed after the closing right bracket). If these restrictions are not adhered to, some functions may be missed or the output of our software tool may become incorrect.

13.9.1 Using grep and sed

Where available, it is very convenient to use existing utilities. The method given below uses `grep` to extract lines that match the pattern of a function definition, and uses `sed` to add the semicolon on the end of the line (and some other tasks). The script file is shown below. The first line is a comment, but the rest of the script file is actually one very long pipeline. For simplicity, it has been split into a number of lines.

```
# Script file: extract function prototypes from C source file
grep '^[a-zA-Z][a-zA-Z0-9\* _]*(.*)[^\;]*$' $*            |     \
sed 's/[^:]*://g'                                          |     \
sed 's/\/\*.*$//'                                          |     \
sed 's/[ \t]*//'                                           |     \
sed 's/$/;/'                                               |     \
sed -e '/^switch[ ]*(/d' -e '/^return[ ]*(/d'                    \
 -e '/^static[ ]/d' -e '/^main[ ]*(/d' -e '/^if[ ]*(/d'          \
 -e '/^while[ ]*(/d' -e '/^for[ ]*(/d'                           \
 -e '/^else[ ]*if[ ]*(/d'
```

The script file can be explained in terms of each step. The `grep` utility is used to search for the pattern: a line starting with a letter, then containing only letters, digits, underscores, spaces and `*` (for pointer types) until a left bracket is found. The line must also contain a right bracket and have no semicolons.

Lines matching this pattern are then piped through `sed` to perform a number of changes. `sed` is used to delete the filename and colon added to the lines by `grep` (some versions of `grep` may not have this problem), then to remove comments and spaces after the right bracket and to add a semicolon to the end of the line. Finally, `sed` is used to delete lines which matched the pattern, but are not function definitions or would not be appropriate as function prototypes. For example, if an `if` statement begins at the first character, it will match the pattern. However, many of these checks could be omitted if you indent statements inside a function. There are two special cases which match the pattern but may not be appropriate as a function prototype — `static` functions and the `main` function. A header file that will be included in more than one source file should not contain prototypes of `static` functions — this will cause a compilation error because the function is not *defined* in every file. The `main` function also matches the pattern, but it is rather pointless to declare it in a header file, so it is removed from the output.

13.9.2 Equivalent C program

Although the regular expressions used by `grep` and `sed` look complicated, the actual working of the script file is quite simple. Hence, if `grep` and `sed` are unavailable it is not difficult to write a C program that does the same job. The equivalent C program is shown below. The `match` function performs the same function as the first `grep` command (finding candidate lines), the `ignore` function tests for a bad match, and simple matters such as the deletion of spaces and comments, and the addition of the semicolon are handled in the `main` function. The most difficult aspect of the program is the processing of the filenames passed as command line arguments using the `argc` and `argv` parameters to `main` (this is discussed fully in Section 14.2).

```
/*---------------------------------------------------------------*/
/* GET_PROTOTYPES.C:  Generate C function prototypes from C code */
/*---------------------------------------------------------------*/

#include <stdio.h>
#include <stdlib.h>
#include <ctype.h>
#include <string.h>

#define TRUE  1
#define FALSE 0

#define MAX_LEN  200         /* Maximum line length */

/*---------------------------------------------------------------*/
/* MATCH:  Returns TRUE if the line is a function prototype      */
/*---------------------------------------------------------------*/
int match(char *line)
{
    int i = 0;
    int found_right_bracket = FALSE;

    if (isalpha(line[0]) || line[0] == '_') {        /* identifier? */
        while (isalnum(line[i]) || line[i] == '*'    /* Skip to '(' */
               || line[i] == '_' || line[i] == ' ')
            i++;

        if (line[i] != '(')
            return FALSE;               /* Not a function definition */

        for (; line[i] != '\0'; i++) {
            if (line[i] == ';')         /* If it has semicolon */
                return FALSE;           /* it is a C statement */
            if (line[i] == ')')
                found_right_bracket = TRUE;
        }
```

```
            if (!found_right_bracket)
                return FALSE;
            return TRUE;
        }
        return FALSE;
    }
    /*--------------------------------------------------------------*/
    /* IGNORE: Returns TRUE if the line should be ignored           */
    /*--------------------------------------------------------------*/
    int ignore(char *line)
    {
        char *keywords[] = { "main", "static", "if", "for", "while",
                             "else", "switch", NULL };
        int i;
        char *pos;

        for (i = 0; keywords[i] != NULL; i++) {
            pos = strstr(line, keywords[i]);            /* Keyword in line? */
            if (pos != NULL                              /* Keyword not in */
                && (pos == line || isspace(pos[-1]))    /*    identifier */
                && ! isalnum(pos[strlen(keywords[i])])
                && pos[strlen(keywords[i])] != '_')
                    return TRUE;                         /* Yes - bad keyword */
        }
        return FALSE;
    }
    main(int argc, char *argv[])
    {
        int i, j;
        FILE *fp;
        char line[MAX_LEN];

        for (i = 1; i < argc; i++) {            /* For all filenames */
            fp = fopen(argv[i], "r");           /* Open the file */
            if (fp == NULL) {
                perror(argv[i]);                /* Error opening file */
                continue;                       /* Try next argument */
            }
            while (!feof(fp)) {
                fgets(line, MAX_LEN, fp);
                for (j = 0; j < strlen(line); j++) {    /* Kill comments */
                    if (line[j] == '/' && line[j + 1] == '*')
                        line[j] = '\0';
                }
                while (isspace(line[strlen(line) - 1]))
                    line[strlen(line) - 1] = '\0';      /* Kill end spaces */
                if (match(line) && ! ignore(line))
                    printf("%s;\n", line);              /* Print and add ';' */
            }
            fclose(fp);
        }
    }
```

The output from this new software tool can be redirected to create a file of function prototypes. Assuming you have called the tool headers, a common form of usage is:

```
headers *.c >fns.h
```

The generation of function prototypes can also be useful within a single file, where it can be useful to declare prototypes for every function at the top of a file (to avoid worrying about ordering the functions correctly). The script file above can be run on the one file, and the output included into the C source file. Note that when used this way, it may be desirable to allow prototypes of `static` functions, requiring a slight modification to the script file above. Alternatively, the C code version could be modified to accept an option indicating whether to include `static` functions.

13.9.3 Automatic generation of extern declarations

The automatic generation of `extern` declarations is more difficult. The aim is to have no `extern` declarations of variables in any file, but only the global variable *definitions*, from which the `extern` declarations would be automatically generated. One possible solution is using indentation, by assuming that local declarations are indented whereas global declarations start at the first column. If indentation cannot distinguish local and global declarations, the problem is much harder. A script file to find many global variable declarations is given below:

```
# Script file: extract Variable Declarations from C files
sed 's/\/\*.*$//'    $*                                           | \
sed 's/[ ]*$//'                                                   | \
grep '^[a-zA-Z][a-zA-Z0-9_]*[\* ][\* ]*[a-zA-Z][^()]*;$'          | \
sed 's/[^:]*://g'                                                 | \
sed 's/{.*}//g'                                                   | \
sed 's/=[^,;]*//g'                                                | \
sed -e '/^return /d' -e '/^typedef /d'                              \
-e '/^static /d' -e '/^register /d'                               | \
sed 's/^/extern /'
```

The first two `sed` commands remove comments and trailing whitespace from the lines. The main feature of this script file is the `grep` command which looks for an identifier followed by at least one space or star followed by a letter, and having no brackets on the line (to avoid function definitions) and ending with a semicolon. The next `sed` command fixes the output from `grep` (not needed in all versions). The next `sed` removes pairs of braces that would appear in array initializations (because the next step would fail on the commas in the initializer lists), and then the initialization is removed by deleting the = up to the first comma or semicolon. A number of inappropriate declarations are removed, such as `static` variables and `typedef` declarations. Finally, the keyword `extern` is added to the front of the line.

This script file works correctly for ordinary declarations and even for array or `struct` initializations on a single line, but there is a problem with removing multi-line initializations and extracting `struct` variable declarations because `grep` and `sed` work a line at a time. A possible solution is to use the `awk` utility or a C program to extract lines up to the closing semicolons. This is left as an exercise to the reader.

13.10 Header file organization

As mentioned earlier in the chapter, the organization of header files is a matter of style and there are many alternatives. The previous sections have examined the use of a small number of header files for any number of C source files, where each header file had a specific purpose — constants, types, `extern` declarations or function prototypes. Although this organization is satisfactory for small projects, larger projects need more care in organizing the various header files. Note that there is always a tradeoff between good header file organization and the practical problems involved in maintaining a project with too many files.

The most important aspect of header file organization is not related to the header files, but rather to the C source files that include them. The various functions in a large project should be grouped in files in a logical manner — related functions should be in the same C source file. When the functions are grouped properly, each file should be a logical unit, with as little dependence on other files as possible. (Here we see that we are aiming towards an approximation of the object-oriented approach that is used in C++!)

In a medium-sized project each major unit of the program should fit into a single C source file. This unit may then require two header files, one for its internal use and one to specify its interface with the other files. In this way we have hidden information about the internal workings of the unit from the other functions that make use of the unit. For example, consider a symbol table in a compiler that is implemented as a hash table. The C source file will contain the definition of the hash table (declared as a `static` variable), and all of the functions to access the hash table. The internal header file will declare the size of the hash table, the `struct` type contained in the hash table and other information. The interface header file will contain declarations of the search, insert and delete functions that access the hash table so that other files can make use of the symbol table. The organization is shown below:

```
/*-----------------------------------------------------------*/
/* FILE : symbol_table.c:   Symbol Table Functions           */
/*-----------------------------------------------------------*/

#include "symbol_table_internal.h"
#include "symbol_table_interface.h"    /* Consistency check */

struct hash_node hash_table[HASH_TABLE_SIZE];

int search(char *key) { ...   /* function definition */    }
int insert(char *key) { ...   /* function definition */    }
```

```
/*-----------------------------------------------------------*/
/* FILE : symbol_table_internal.h                            */
/*-----------------------------------------------------------*/

#define HASH_TABLE_SIZE   100
#define KEY_LEN            20

struct hash_node {
   char key[KEY_LEN];
   ...              /* Other data fields */
};
```

```
/*-----------------------------------------------------------*/
/* FILE: symbol_table_interface.h                            */
/*-----------------------------------------------------------*/

int search(char *key);        /* Function prototypes */
int insert(char *key);
```

Note that although the internal header will only be included by one C source file (i.e. `symbol_table.c`), its information should not necessarily be placed inside the C source file. It is better to separate the constants and types used by the symbol table from the C code for the functions, simply because it is more convenient to edit the (smaller) header file.

13.11 The make utility

In the UNIX environment, there is a utility to aid in the design and maintenance of multiple-file programs called "`make`". The `make` utility is often available under DOS, and, in fact, the functionality of `make` is often inherent in the compiler. For example, the use of "projects" in Turbo C means that the convenience of automatic program building is already available within the development environment and the `make` utility need not be used. However, using the `make` utility is practically a necessity under UNIX and we will discuss its use here. Most of the principles are the same in both UNIX and DOS versions. However, there are differences in the practical details, such as the different suffixes "`.o`" and "`.obj`" for object files.

Once set up, the `make` utility relieves the programmer of the burden of remembering which files need recompilation. The programmer need only type "`make`", and the files needing to be compiled are compiled automatically. The `make` utility examines the dates of modification of files, to see if they have changed, and recompilation occurs if so. For example, if a C source file has changed more recently than when the executable was created, that C source file needs to be recompiled and the executable rebuilt from the object files.

The disadvantage of using `make` is the need to create a special file in the directory, called "`Makefile`" or "`makefile`". This file is a text file that specifies which files of your program depend on other files (i.e. when a file is modified, which others need be recompiled). The `make` utility examines the "`makefile`" to find the dependencies — for example, the makefile specifies which C files are needed to build the executable.

13.11.1 The makefile

The `makefile` consists of two main types of lines — dependency lines and command lines. Dependency lines show the dependencies between files, and command lines are the commands that must be executed by the operating system to compile the files. Each dependency specification is only one line long and each command must be on a single line, but the use of a backslash as the last character on a line can allow extended lines for both types of lines. Multiple commands can be specified on successive lines (they are executed in sequence). Comments are specified by the # sign and extend to the end of the line. Blank lines are allowed in some places — they should not separate a dependency line from its commands, and should not separate lists of commands.

Dependency lines show the dependencies between files. They consist of a target file, a colon and a list of the files the target depends upon (i.e. those files that, when modified, need to be recompiled to create the target). Generally speaking, dependencies are those files that are included in the target (with `#include`). In addition, object files depend on their corresponding C source files, and the executable depends on all the object files.

Command lines are ordinary operating system commands that recompile the files, as would be typed at the keyboard. Command lines are indented by a tab, to indicate that they are not dependency lines. Consider the following simple `makefile`:

```
a.out: main.c lib.c defs.h
       cc main.c lib.c
```

The first line is a dependency line stating that `a.out` depends on the other three files. When you type "make", if any of the three files have been modified since they were last compiled, the command "cc main.c lib.c" is performed.

There is nothing special about the use of `a.out` — it is just the default executable generated by the `cc` compiler. Another name could be used, with the –o option to `cc`. For example, the `makefile` could be changed to:

```
ex: main.c lib.c defs.h
    cc -o ex main.c lib.c
```

The above examples do not use the `make` utility effectively. Everything is recompiled even if only one file is changed. A better `makefile` that only recompiles a C file if it has changed is shown below:

```
a.out: main.o lib.o defs.h
       cc main.o lib.o

main.o: main.c  defs.h
        cc -c main.c

lib.o: lib.c  defs.h
       cc -c lib.c
```

Note that `a.out` is the first dependency line. The `make` utility tries to create the first name in the file, which should be the executable.

Using the improved `makefile`, if either C source file is changed, it is recompiled using "cc -c", and then "cc main.o lib.o" is executed. The other C source file is not recompiled unless it has also been modified. If the header file "defs.h" is changed, both C source files are recompiled.

13.11.2 Built-in rules

For convenience, `make` has some built-in rules for compiling files with common suffixes. For example, `make` assumes that ".o" files depend on their corresponding ".c" files, and that they are to be recompiled using `cc` with the –c option. In fact, the default is often something like "cc -cO". Using the built-in rules, the above `makefile` can be made more concise:

```
a.out: main.o lib.o
       cc main.o lib.o

main.o: defs.h
lib.o: defs.h
```

Note that it is unnecessary to specify that the .o file depends on its corresponding .c file because of the default dependencies.

The makefile above has the same effect as the previous makefile, except that the default "cc -cO" is used instead of the explicit "cc -c". This default is often not satisfactory. For example, you may not wish to use the -O (optimize) option because it is slower, or you may wish to add the -g option for the debugger. There are two methods to define your own defaults. The first method is to add a line to the makefile to set the CFLAGS variable, which is used by make to specify the options to cc. For example:

```
CFLAGS = -g
```

sets the options to be -cg because the -c option is implicit.

The second method for defining your own defaults is to add a special dependency line to the beginning of the makefile. This line specifies the command to execute to create .o files from .c files:

```
.c.o:
        cc -cg $*.c
```

Note that the special macro $* stands for the name of the file (without the suffix). There are a number of special macros and you should consult your local documentation.

13.11.3 Defining variables in the makefile

The use of CFLAGS above is a special case of a more general facility provided by make. The make utility allows any variables to be assigned values. The values of a variable can be accessed using a dollar sign and either brackets or braces: $(VAR) or ${VAR}. Note that the brackets or braces can be dispensed with for variables with single letter names. For example, a common use of variables is to specify the object files as a variable:

```
OBJS = main.o file1.o file2.o file3.o file4.o
       file5.o file6.o file7.o file8.o

a.out:  $(OBJS)
        cc $(OBJS)
```

Variables can be used anywhere in the makefile, on both dependency lines and command lines. Conceptually, the make utility expands variables before any other processing. As another example, the OBJS variable could be used on the left side of a dependency line to indicate that all object files depend on a single header file:

```
$(OBJS): defs.h
```

13.11.4 Common target names

The make utility need not only be used for the creation of an executable. In can be used to execute any operating system command. For example, another common use of make is to remove object files after compilation, by defining the target name clean as below:

```
clean:
        rm -f ${OBJS}
```

After creating the executable using `make`, the programmer need only type:

```
make clean
```

to remove all of the object files.

Other common target names are "`all`" and "`install`" which allow an entire project to be made and/or installed using one of:

```
make all
make install
```

13.11.5 Options to make

When a `makefile` controls a large number of files, some of the options to `make` can be useful. Note that different implementations of `make` may have different options and this section considers only the traditional UNIX implementation. The important options for the UNIX version of `make` are summarized in Table 13.1.

Table 13.1. Common make options

Option	Meaning
-f	Filename of the `makefile`
-i	Ignore return values
-k	Continue on non-dependent files
-n	No execute — only print commands
-s	Silent mode — suppress printing of commands
-t	Touch files that need updating

The -f option specifies the file to be used instead of the default files "`makefile`" or "`Makefile`".

The -s option causes `make` to suppress the printing of the commands it executes. However, it does not suppress the output produced by the commands when they are executed.

The -n option displays the commands that `make` would normally execute, but does not execute them. This is useful to see which files would be recompiled.

When a change is made to one of the files that should require no recompilation (such as adding comments), the -t option can be used. This option touches (t for touch) those files that are out of date. In other words, it marks them as recompiled without actually recompiling them.

The -i option causes `make` to ignore the return results from the shell commands it executes. This explains how `make` knows to stop compiling when a syntax error occurs — because `cc` returns a non-zero value. However, there are cases when it is annoying to rely on these values (e.g. when a program is returning the wrong value). Note that it is also possible to prefix a particular command with a minus sign causing only that command's return value to be ignored.

After a major change to a number of the C source files, it is sometimes desirable to recompile the lot. The `make` command will do this, but has the problem that it will stop if one file has a syntax error. The `-k` option specifies that `make` continue with any other compilation not dependent on the file that had the syntax error. The file with the syntax error can then be fixed, and `make` executed again, this time only recompiling the offending file. This solves the problem of setting a large `make` in motion, walking away and later returning to discover a trivial syntax error in one of the first few files. Note that the `-i` option could be used to ignore the returned value, but this would lead to a pointless attempt to link the object files into the executable.

13.11.6 Header files with make

When using a large number of header files, it can be useful to keep them separate from the C source files rather than clutter up directories. Similarly, it is a good idea to create your own header files of frequently used declarations (e.g. your own boolean type) and keep them separate. A convenient way to do this is to place them all in one directory, and then instruct the C compiler to search that directory for header files. Under UNIX the `-Idirectory` option tells `cc` to look in "`directory`" for header files (note that there is no space between the `I` and the directory name). Non-UNIX compilers will usually support `-I` or a similar option.

When using `-I`, the `<file.h>` notation is allowed for your own header files. However, the `"file.h"` notation is adequate. The compiler will first search the local directory, and if the file is not there, it will search the specified directories. Because the system directory `/usr/include` is searched last (after all the `-I` directories), it is possible to redefine standard header files — for example, to create your own `<assert.h>` header file.

```
cc -I~/include -c main.c
```

This is a rather long command to type. More realistic is including this line in your `makefile`. Even more clever use of `make` would be the inclusion of the `-I` option in the definition of the operation to be performed on `.c` files. Note that the absolute pathname is necessary inside the `makefile` as the tilde (~) is not expanded within a `makefile` (because it calls `sh` and not `csh`).

```
.c.o:
    cc -I/users/spuler/include -cg $*.c
```

13.11.7 Related UNIX commands: touch, ls -t

There are a few other UNIX commands that can be used with `make`. The simplest is the use of `ls` to display the times of last modification. This is done using the `-t` option to `ls` (often combined with the `-l` option):

```
ls -lt
```

This displays the files ordered by time of modification, most recently modified at the top of the listing.

The `touch` command causes files to be updated (like the `-t` option). It sets the last modification date of the file. Touching a file is equivalent to loading the file into an editor and then writing it. The `touch` command can be used to directly control which files will be recompiled by `make`. Touching a C source file causes it to become "out of date". This causes recompilation of the C source file when `make` is called. Touching an object file causes the executable (i.e. `a.out`) to become out of date, causing recompilation of object files into the executable. To reset times so that no files need recompilation, touch the C source files, then the object files and then the executable. This is equivalent to "`make -t`".

```
touch *.c
touch *.o
touch a.out
```

In addition, `touch` can be used in conjunction with the `-t` option of `make` to solve a common problem. If all files depend on a header file and that header file is altered, all files are now "out of date" and would be recompiled by `make`. This is undesirable if this change should only cause one C source file to be recompiled (i.e. if the constant changed in the header file is only used by one C source file). Recompilation of the other files can be avoided by:

```
make -t
touch file.c
make
```

This updates all the files, then touches the C source file needing recompilation and then uses `make` to compile it and create the executable.

An alternative is to leave some header files out of the dependencies in the `makefile`. This assumes that the relevant source file or files will also be written (i.e. touched) if the header file is changed. This is somewhat dangerous in that the `makefile` is not strictly correct. A preferred approach is to have better organized header files so that a file only depends on those header files containing information used by it. Unfortunately, this is often impractical because it increases the number of files dramatically.

13.12 Creating your own libraries

Most C compilers perform compilation in two phases — compilation and linking. Compilation converts C source files into object files. Linking refers to the process of examining the object files created by compilation and matching references to functions in different object files, and then converting them into a single executable. This function reference matching also occurs with functions in the standard libraries, which are also stored as object files. For example, when your program uses `<stdio.h>` the linker examines your object files for all references to library functions. It then extracts the required functions from the object file for `<stdio.h>` functions. We refer to these object files containing library functions as *libraries* (they are also sometimes called *archives* under UNIX). Under UNIX the standard libraries are usually stored in the directory `/lib` and have the filename suffix "`.a`". Under DOS, the libraries have the filename suffix "`.lib`" but the directory containing them will depend on the compiler used.

On most systems it is possible to create your own libraries. The main reason for doing this would be when you have a number of functions that you would like to use in many different programs. Rather than compiling these functions with each program, it is easier to link the library with the object files for each program. A good example is writing a number of data structure functions that can be used in many programs. Under DOS the method of creating your own library will depend on the compiler you are using and you will need to examine its documentation. The method is standard under UNIX and we examine it now.

13.12.1 UNIX libraries: ar, ranlib

Libraries are created under UNIX using the `ar` utility. We will use `ar` to create a small library containing two files, "`f1.o`" and "`f2.o`". The source file, "`f1.c`", is shown below:

```
#include <stdio.h>
int mesg1(void)
{
    printf("Hello World from f1.c\n");
}
```

and "`f2.c`" is trivially different, containing the function `mesg2`.

Before creating the library, the object files must be generated. This is achieved using the `cc` compiler:

```
cc -c f1.c f2.c
```

Once the object files are available, they can be stored in a library. We will call the library "`my_lib.a`". A library must have the filename suffix "`.a`" under UNIX (a for archive). The UNIX command to create our library using the `ar` utility is:

```
ar ruvs my_lib.a f1.o f2.o
```

This will create a new library and add the object files to it. If the library "`my_lib.a`" already exists, any object files not already in the library or that have changed since the library was created will be stored in the library. Table 13.2 explains the meanings of the options given to `ar` above.

Table 13.2. Options to ar

Operator	Meaning
r	Replace files (or add if not already present)
u	Update — only replace files if changed
v	Verbose — print messages about files added
s	Symbol definition file created

The s option is an important one. It adds an extra file, called the *symbol definition file*, to the archive. This file is used by the linker (i.e. the linking phase in `cc`) to resolve external references. The `cc` compiler cannot use the library without this symbol definition file. Some implementations of UNIX do not have an s option to `ar` and use the `ranlib` utility instead. The two commands below are equivalent to the one above:

```
ar ruv my_lib.a f1.o f2.o
ranlib my_lib.a
```

The `ar` utility can also be used to look at what object files are contained in a library. The command below will list the object files in our library:

```
ar t my_lib.a
```

Once created, the library can be used by other programs. Consider another file called "main.c" which uses our library functions, as shown below. It is assumed that the file "my_lib.h" contains prototypes for the functions in the library, `mesg1` and `mesg2`. Setting up such a header file is good style when defining libraries.

```
#include "my_lib.h"

main()
{
    mesg1();
    mesg2();
}
```

This program can be compiled using the `cc` compiler by placing the library name as an argument. Note that the library name is only needed when creating the final executable and is not needed when creating object files with the −c option. One way to compile our program above using the library is:

```
cc main.c my_lib.a
```

The more common method of creating a multiple-file program that uses a library would be to create object files as usual, and then link them with the library:

```
cc main.o other_stuff.o my_lib.a
```

It is no coincidence that the library name is the last argument to the `cc` compiler in both examples above. It is very important that the library name appears after any file that uses its functions. This is because the linker resolves external references in a left-to-right manner (i.e. in the order of the files specified). If the library were placed first, as in,

```
cc my_lib.a main.c          # WRONG
```

there would be no unresolved references when the library is examined and no object files from the library would be linked. When compilation is finished, any functions called by "main.c" would be undefined and linking would fail with an error message.

If keeping the executable small is important, it is necessary to separate different functions into different files for storage in a library. The linker cannot access individual functions and can only access each object file. Hence, if an object file contains two functions and only one is referenced, both functions will be linked because the whole file is linked. However, if the functions were in separate files only those needed would be loaded. Note that it may be necessary to leave more than one function in a file when one function in the library requires another function in the same library.

13.13 Exercises

1. When an entire C program is in one file, what is the difference between `static` global variables and ordinary global variables? Does the `static` specifier affect the initialization of global variables?

2. Is the following code fragment legal in a C program? Try it in a small program.

   ```
   int x;
   extern int x;
   ```

   What if `extern` is replaced by `static`? What if `extern` is replaced by "static extern"?

3. What is the difference (if any) between the two function declarations below?

   ```
   extern int fn(void);
   int fn(void);
   ```

4. What is the difference (if any) between the inclusion or omission of parameter names in the two function declarations below? Which one is preferable?

   ```
   int fn(int x, char c);
   int fn(int, char);
   ```

5. Why shouldn't a header file contain a function *definition*? What happens if the function definition in the header file is declared as a `static` function? What should a header file contain?

6. This exercise introduces you to the use of independent compilation (i.e. multi-file programs). Write functions `square` and `cube` to calculate the square and cube of an integer, and store each in a separate file. Now use another file to store the `main` function which prints out the squares and cubes of the numbers from 1 to 10. How should the `square` and `cube` functions be *declared* in the main file? Find out how to compile multi-file programs on your system. How do you create object files? How do you link the object files to create the executable?

7. Use the `make` utility to compile a single file program — this is just a matter of making the executable depend on the source file and specifying the command to compile the program. Now use `make` to compile the multi-file program specified in the previous exercise. Next, create a header file containing the function prototypes for `square` and `cube`, and add the appropriate dependencies to the `makefile`.

8. Modify the previous exercises to place the `square` and `cube` functions into a *library*. Hence, the library should contain two object files. The `main` function (which prints out the squares and cubes of 1..10) should use the functions in this library by linking the library at compile-time. Compile and run the program. If the `make` utility is available, use a `makefile` to create the library and to compile the program. If the environment is UNIX, use the `ar` utility to examine the contents of the archives `/lib/libc.a` and `/lib/libm.a`.

9. Improve on either the script file or C program in Section 13.9 to remove the restriction that function definitions always start on the first character of a line.

10. (advanced) Develop a method of automatically extracting global variable definitions and placing them into a header file. The program should handle multi-line declarations and initializations, and be able to distinguish between local variable declarations and global variable declarations. It may be possible to use `grep` or other software tools for a reasonable solution, but to do so properly you will need to write quite an advanced C program to perform the task. For example, the partially developed method in Section 13.9.3 will fail on a number of special cases, such as:

```
char *s = "The string, has a comma";
```

where the comma in the string means that the rule "remove from = up to a comma or semicolon" fails to remove the entire initialization. To solve this type of problem, it is necessary to properly deal with programs on a token level, accounting for the presence of string constants, character constants, and comments.

Chapter 14
Functions and pointers revisited

The most important aspects of the use of functions and pointers have been covered in Chapters 7 and 8. This chapter examines a number of advanced aspects of their use. The four main topics are: the main function, recursion, variable argument list functions and dynamic arrays.

The role of the main function is examined fully, including its three arguments (argc, argv and arge), which are omitted from most programs. Arguments typed at operating system level to execute a program can be accessed using argc and argv arguments, and environment variables as defined in both UNIX and MS-DOS can be accessed using arge. The ability to examine command line arguments makes it possible to implement some quite sophisticated software tools in C. The design of a simple filtering tool is examined.

The definition of functions that accept a varying number of arguments (i.e. like printf and scanf) is examined in this chapter. There is a standard method of defining these functions with the <stdarg.h> header file, using the macros va_start, va_arg and va_end.

The definition and use of recursive functions is examined in this chapter. Recursion is a difficult concept for beginners to understand, but once mastered, it provides an elegant method of solution for a number of programming problems. Although criticized for their inefficiency, recursive algorithms can be very efficient in areas with an inherent recursive nature, such as binary trees.

A number of advanced uses of pointers are examined in this chapter. First, an advanced use of pointers is to point to functions, which allows functions to be passed as arguments to other functions! Pointers can also be used to remove the restriction on array index ranges to allow arbitrary lower and upper bounds, instead of the 0..n−1 range. In combination with malloc, pointers can be used to implement dynamic arrays — one-dimensional dynamic arrays are quite simple, but multi-dimensional dynamic arrays are very complicated. This chapter presents, as a special showpiece, a function that creates arbitrary-dimensional dynamic arrays with arbitrary index ranges.

14.1 The main function

All programs have at least one function, the `main` function, which is usually defined as below:

```
main()
{
    ...
}
```

This definition defines `main`, by default, to return `int`, and to accept no arguments (by non-prototyping definition). Possibly better is the use of prototyping in the definition:

```
int main(void)
{
    ...
}
```

which explicitly states that `main` will return `int`, and uses a proper prototyped definition of no parameters. Note that `main` could be defined as returning `void` if no exit status value is returned by the program (i.e. no `return` statement in `main`). However, most programmers still use the first simple definition because `main` is usually called from outside the program and the operating system doesn't care how `main` was declared in the program. The declaration is only important within the program, to allow the compiler to check consistency of usage.

14.2 Command line arguments

When a C program is executed at the operating system prompt, it is executed by typing the name of its executable (i.e. usually `a.out` under UNIX). After its name, arguments can be added and these are called *command line arguments*. For example:

```
a.out 10 100
```

has two command line arguments, 10 and 100.

There are a few differences between UNIX and DOS when considering command line arguments. The main difference is the convention for specification of options — under UNIX options are specified using a minus sign (e.g. `-c`), but DOS uses a forward slash (e.g. `/s`). This section will use the UNIX minus sign convention for options, but the change to DOS will usually be a matter of changing only one character!

The other small difference between UNIX and DOS is in the processing of special arguments, such as *regular expressions* (e.g. `*.c`). These are also called *wildcards* under DOS. Under UNIX, the shell expands out tildes (`~`) to their full path name, and regular expressions are expanded to a space-separated list of filenames. For discussion of how to handle regular expressions under DOS refer to your compiler's documentation — for example, Turbo C requires the linking of a special object file, `"wildargs.obj"`. Note that under both UNIX and DOS, any pipes or I/O redirections are processed by the operating system and the program need not worry about these special notations.

Simple arguments such as options (e.g. `-c` or `/c`) and filenames are not processed by the operating system. It is the program's responsibility to examine these filenames and options and act on them accordingly. No distinction is made between the two types —

Functions and pointers revisited   213

the program must examine each argument for the initial minus sign (UNIX) or forward slash (DOS) indicating that it is an option.

The C program receives command line arguments as arguments to the `main` function. The definition of the `main` function is modified to declare two parameters, conventionally called `argc` and `argv`. The names are merely tradition, standing for argument count and argument vector. The `argc` variable is the count of how many arguments there are; `argv` is an array of strings containing the arguments. The definition of `argv` involves the use of double indirection, since `argv` is defined as a pointer to a pointer to `char` (i.e. `char **argv`) or as an array of pointers to `char` (i.e. `char *argv[]`).

On entry to the function, `argc` contains the number of command line arguments. If `argc` is 1, there are no arguments. In general, there are `argc-1` arguments. The variable `argv` is an array of strings that contains these arguments in `argv[1]` through to `argv[argc-1]`. The value of `argv[0]` is the name of the current program (e.g. `a.out`). The program below can be used to examine how arguments are processed:

```
#include <stdio.h>

main(int argc, char *argv[])
{
    int i;

    printf("Program name: '%s'\n", argv[0]);
    if (argc == 1)
        printf("There are NO arguments\n");
    else {
        printf("There are %d arguments \n", argc - 1);
        printf("The arguments are: ");
        for (i = 1; i < argc; i++) {
            printf("%s ", argv[i]);
        }
        printf("\n");
    }
}
```

Note that the `for` loop starts `i` at 1 because `argv[0]` is the program name.

One extra useful condition is guaranteed on entry to the program. There is a sentinel value of NULL at the end of the argument vector — i.e. `argv[argc]` is NULL. This sentinel facilitates stepping along the arguments using `++` on the pointer `argv` when it is declared as `char **argv`. The normal traversal of the arguments using `argv` as a pointer is:

```
#include <stdio.h>

main(int argc, char **argv)
{
    printf("The arguments are: ");
    while ((* ++argv) != NULL)
        printf("%s ", *argv);
    printf("\n");
}
```

The use of the prefix `++` skips over the zeroth argument, which is the name of the program. Note that this method prevents multiple traversals of the argument list, unless the value of `argv` is saved before this loop and restored afterward.

As a simple example of how to process command line arguments, let us write a program that counts from one up to the number supplied as its argument. The code is:

```
#include <stdio.h>
#include <stdlib.h>

main(int argc, char *argv[])
{
    int i, num;

    if (argc < 2) {
        fprintf(stderr, "Argument needed\n");
        exit(1);
    }
    num = atoi(argv[1]);         /* string to int */
    for (i = 1; i <= num; i++)
        printf("%d ", i);
    printf("\n");
}
```

Note that the argument in `argv[1]` is in string form and must be converted to an integer value using the `atoi` library function.

14.2.1 An example: writing a filter

Have you ever tried to print an executable? The output contains control characters and escape sequences that do not print properly. This section examines the construction of a small software tool that filters files, only printing out the printable characters. This utility can be used to examine the characters in an executable without getting annoying garbage output.

```
/*------------------------------------------------------------*/
/* Filter - filters a file for printable characters */
/*------------------------------------------------------------*/

#include <stdio.h>
#include <stdlib.h>
#include <ctype.h>                  /* define isprint() */

main()
{
    int ch;     /* Must be int, not char, because of EOF */

    while ((ch = getchar()) != EOF) {   /* For all characters */
        if (isprint(ch))                /* if printable char */
            putchar(ch);                /* output it */
    }
    exit(0);
}
```

Note that the variable, `ch`, must be declared as type `int`, not type `char`, because EOF is a constant with the integer value −1 and this cannot be represented by a `char`.

Let us assume that the executable created is called `"filter"`. `filter` is quite limited because it does not accept filenames as command line arguments:

```
filter file            # NOT allowed
```

It must be executed using input redirection:

```
filter <file
```

or as part of a pipeline as in:

```
cat file | filter           # UNIX
type file | filter          # DOS
```

This restriction is quite annoying and it is very simple to modify `filter` to accept the filename as a command line argument. The modified version of `filter` checks to see if there is a command line argument; if so, this is assumed to be a filename. If there is no command line argument, `stdin` is used (as was the case in the first version). Recall from the previous section that `argc` is 1 when there are no command line arguments, and if `argc` is 2, there is one argument, passed in `argv[1]`.

```c
/*-----------------------------------------------------------------*/
/* Filter - filters a file for printable characters                */
/* Accepts filename as first argument; otherwise uses stdin        */
/*-----------------------------------------------------------------*/

#include <stdio.h>
#include <stdlib.h>
#include <ctype.h>

main(int argc, char *argv[])
{
    int ch;        /* Must be int; NOT char, because of EOF */
    FILE *fp;

    if (argc > 1) {                       /* command line argument? */
        fp = fopen(argv[1], "r");         /* Filename is argv[1] */
        if (fp == NULL) {
            perror(argv[1]);
            exit(1);
        }
    }
    else           /* No command line argument - do stdin */
        fp = stdin;
                        /*-----------------------------------*/
                        /* Opened File;  Now filter it       */
                        /*-----------------------------------*/
    while ((ch = getc(fp)) != EOF) {   /* Read a character */
        if (isprint(ch))
            putchar(ch);                    /* Print to stdout */
    }
    exit(0);
}
```

This improved version accepts both usage methods: the pipeline and a filename specified in the argument list. However, it does not permit easy action upon more than one file. The following implementation is far more advanced. It extends the above program to allow specification of multiple files. It also allows options to be given to the filter using the UNIX notation of minus signs. The options accepted by the new `filter` tool are given in Table 14.1.

Table 14.1. Options for filter

Option	Meaning
-l, -L	Print out all letters
-d, -D	Print out all digits

If there are no options, the default action is to print all printable characters (as in the previous version). If both -l and -d options are present, the filter will print both letters and digits. This multiple option can be invoked as -ld or -dl. Options can appear before, after or between filenames — all options are processed before any of the files are filtered. Thus, all the following formats are allowed:

```
filter file
filter -l file
filter -l -d file1 file2
filter -l file1 file2 -d
filter -ld file1 file2
filter -d <file1
```

Options are detected by their first character being a minus sign. Subsequent letters of the argument are examined for the option letters l, L, d and D. All arguments are examined and processed as options if the first character is a minus sign. The filenames are examined only after all options have been processed.

Filenames are detected by a non-minus first character. These files are opened and filtered according to the options specified. If there are no filenames found, stdin is used, allowing the filter to be used as part of a pipeline.

```
/*------------------------------------------------*/
/* Filter - filters a file for printable characters */
/* Accepts filename and options in command line    */
/*------------------------------------------------*/
/* Options:                                        */
/*       -l, -L     --> print if a letter          */
/*       -d, -D     --> print if a digit           */
/*       no options --> all printable characters   */
/*------------------------------------------------*/

#include <stdio.h>
#include <stdlib.h>
#include <string.h>
#include <ctype.h>

#define TRUE  1
#define FALSE 0

#define OPTION_CHAR  '-'          /* '-' for UNIX, '/' for DOS */

/*------------------------------------------------------------*/
/* Global Boolean Flags for Options                           */
/*------------------------------------------------------------*/

int have_options = FALSE;
int do_letters = FALSE;
int do_digits = FALSE;

/*------------------------------------------------------------*/
/* Look for command line options starting with minus signs    */
/*------------------------------------------------------------*/

void process_options(int argc, char *argv[])
```

```
{
    int i, j;
    for (i = 1; i < argc; i++) {                /* For all args */
        if (*argv[i] == OPTION_CHAR) {          /* Test 1st char */
            for (j = 1; j < strlen(argv[i]); j++) { /* For all chars */
                                                /* e.g. -ld */
                switch (argv[i][j]) {
                    case 'l':
                    case 'L':
                        have_options = TRUE;
                        do_letters = TRUE;
                        break;

                    case 'd':
                    case 'D':
                        have_options = TRUE;
                        do_digits = TRUE;
                        break;

                    default:
                        fprintf(stderr, "Bad Option: %s\n", argv[i]);
                        exit(1);
                }
            }
        }
    }
}
/*------------------------------------------------------------------*/
/* Function that filters the file and puts output to stdout         */
/*------------------------------------------------------------------*/
void filter(FILE *fp)
{
    int ch;     /* Must be int, not char */

    while ((ch = getc(fp)) != EOF) {            /* Read in from file */
        if ((!have_options && isprint(ch))
            || (do_letters && (isupper(ch) || islower(ch)))
            || (do_digits && isdigit(ch))) {
                putchar(ch);                    /* Print to stdout */
        }
    }
}

/*------------------------------------------------------------------*/
/* Process any filenames in the command line arguments              */
/*------------------------------------------------------------------*/
int do_files(int argc, char *argv[])
{
    int i;
    int files_done = 0;     /* Count of how many files in arguments */
    FILE *fp;

    for (i = 1; i < argc; i++) {                /* For all arguments */
        if (*argv[i] != OPTION_CHAR) {          /* Examine first character */
            files_done++;                       /* increment counter */
            fp = fopen(argv[i], "r");           /* Filename is argv[i] */
            if (fp == NULL) {
                perror(argv[i]);                /* File opening error */
                exit(1);
            }
            filter(fp);         /* Opened file; now Filter the file */
        }
    }
    return files_done;
}
```

```
/*--------------------------------------------------------------------*/
/*      Start of program execution.                                   */
/*--------------------------------------------------------------------*/
main(int argc, char *argv[])
{
    int count;

    process_options(argc, argv);     /* Do any options in command line */
    count = do_files(argc, argv);    /* Do any files in command line */
    if (count == 0)                  /* No filenames in command line? */
        filter(stdin);
    exit(0);                         /* Terminate successfully */
}
```

As implemented, the filter allows a very flexible option format. Many utility programs only allow options before all filenames. The first option not starting with a minus sign signifies that it and all subsequent arguments are filenames. This allows the option processing phase to be simpler and faster — all arguments are scanned only once.

You may wonder how the filter should handle options such as:

```
filter *.c
```

Fortunately, the program need not concern itself with regular expressions. Under UNIX it is the shell that handles these. Under DOS the compiler should handle these by inserting code before the `main` function is called (it may be necessary to set a compiler option — refer to your compiler's documentation). In both cases the regular expressions are expanded into a list of filenames which is passed to `filter`. Hence, `filter` need only handle options of the form:

```
filter file1.c file2.c file3.c
```

As we have seen, the detection and processing of options has increased the complexity of the program quite significantly. This is true for any reasonably sized software tool — the user interface is always a non-trivial part of the implementation.

14.2.2 The getopt library function

Although it is not part of the ANSI standard library, many implementations of C supply the `getopt` function to automate most of the details of testing for command line arguments. The `getopt` function is declared as:

```
int getopt(int argc, char *argv[], char *letters)
```

where `argc` and `argv` are the usual arguments to `main` and `letters` is a string containing all the letters that are legal options to the program.

The `getopt` function also uses a number of external variables, which should be declared as (some implementations require you to explicitly define them):

```
extern int optind;          /* Index into argv */
extern int opterr;          /* Error suppression flag */
extern char *optarg;        /* Argument for an option */
```

A sequence of calls to `getopt` is used to extract each successive option, and each legal option is returned by `getopt`. If `getopt` detects an illegal option it produces an error message on `stderr` and returns the character `'?'`. The error message can be suppressed by setting the boolean flag `opterr` to zero. When there are no more arguments, `getopt` returns `EOF`. Importantly, the first non-option command line argument ends the search for more options, thus disallowing options after the first filename. The `process_options` function from `filter` can be implemented using `getopt` as given below:

```
void process_options(int argc, char *argv[])
{
    char c;

    do {
        c = getopt(argc, argv, "lLdD");
        switch (c) {
            case EOF:           /* Finished */
                break;

            case 'd':
            case 'D':
                have_options = TRUE;
                do_digits = TRUE;
                break;

            case 'l':
            case 'L':
                have_options = TRUE;
                do_letters = TRUE;
                break;

            case '?':           /* Bad Option - do nothing */
                break;          /* getopt prints error message */

            default:            /* Should never reach here */
                fprintf(stderr, "Internal error\n");
                exit(1);
        }
    } while (c != EOF);
}
```

The `getopt` function has a facility for more complicated options than the simple −l or −ld type options. An option can be specified that requires an argument, such as the −D option to `cc`:

    cc −DDEBUG

Such option letters are indicated by placing a colon *after* the letter in the `letters` argument to `getopt`. When the option is found by `getopt`, the letter is returned by `getopt` and `optarg` is set to point to the string value of the argument. Note that the option can also have a space between the option letter and the argument. `getopt` would consider the two commands below would as identical:

    cc −DDEBUG
    cc −D DEBUG

The `optind` variable is used by `getopt` to keep track of which option it is up to. The fact that this variable is visible allows the programmer to redo all options by setting `optind` to 1, or to redo some options by saving and resetting the value of `optind`.

14.3 Exit status: return value of main

When a program terminates, it returns an integer value to the operating system indicating its *exit status* (successful or unsuccessful). Most programs ignore this issue, and rightly so! There is no need to worry about the return value if the program is being executed by the user from the command line.

The issue of the return value from `main` is only important if your program is to be used as a tool in the operating system environment. If your program is to be a useful tool it should return appropriate status values. The operating system and its many utility programs use the return value to indicate success or failure of a program. For example, the `make` utility examines the return value of `cc` to decide whether to continue — if `cc` terminates unsuccessfully, `make` prints out a message and stops. The return value can also be used in under UNIX in advanced shell or C-shell script files, or in a batch file under DOS. A very advanced use of the return value involves the UNIX process control function `wait` — the return value of `main` is the termination status of the process.

Conventionally, a returned value of zero indicates that the program completed successfully; any non-zero value indicates some type of error. Most commonly, a program will return either zero or one. The symbolic constants `EXIT_SUCCESS` and `EXIT_FAILURE` are also available in `<stdio.h>` to aid in writing portable code. Note that there is no common convention for returning particular non-zero integers for particular types of errors.

There are two ways to return a value from `main`. Since `main` is a function, the `return` statement can be used normally. The other alternative is to use the `exit` library function. A good program will have one of the following as its last statement before the last right brace:

```
return 0;          /* Terminate successfully */
exit(0);           /* Both are equivalent */
```

to indicate successful termination. This is good practice, but not strictly necessary.

14.4 Accessing environment variables

Programs running under both UNIX and DOS can access environment variables using a third parameter to the `main` function. By convention, this parameter is named `envp` or `arge`. This is a pointer to an array of strings of the form `name=value`, where name is the name of the environment variable and value is the string value of the variable. A sentinel value of `NULL` terminates the array of strings. The example below prints out all of these strings.

```
#include <stdio.h>
#include <stdlib.h>

main(int argc, char **argv, char **envp)
{
    for (; *envp != NULL; envp++) {
        printf("%s\n", *envp);
    }
    exit(0);
}
```

Executing this program on a UNIX system should give output similar to:

```
HOME=/users/mary
SHELL=/bin/csh
TERM=vt100
USER=mary
PATH=/usr/ucb:/bin:/usr/bin:/usr/local:/usr/new:.
MAIL=/usr/spool/mail/mary
```

Note that it is also possible to examine the values of environment variables using the `getenv` standard library function. In addition, some implementations of C support the `setenv` and `unsetenv` functions to change the environment (see Section 19.5). Some implementations also set an external variable, `environ`, to be equivalent to the value passed to the `envp` parameter to main.

14.5 Recursion

A recursive function is one which calls itself. C supports recursive functions without need for any special notation. Recursion frequently scares novice programmers, because it requires different logic to more common types of functions. However, once mastered, it can yield very concise and convenient solutions to some complicated problems.

If a recursive function calls itself, how does it ever stop? The answer is that it doesn't *always* call itself. There is a *base case* for which the function does not call itself. This base case is usually a simple case. More complicated cases are broken up recursively. Hence, problems for which recursion is applicable have some special features:

1. The problem has an easily solved base case, and
2. More complicated cases can be broken into similar sub-problems.

Thus recursive algorithms exhibit *problem size reduction*. A large problem is broken up into one or more smaller, *similar* sub-problems. The larger problem must be broken up into smaller sub-problems, so that the problems will eventually be reduced to the base case. If the sub-problems do not approach a base case, the recursion will be infinite. Hence, recursive algorithms often have the form:

> if (*base case*)
>   *solve base case non-recursively*
> else
>   *solve larger case recursively*

The most common simple example of a recursive function is the factorial function. The factorial of a number is the product, 1*2*3*...*n, with the special case that the factorial of 0 is 1 (because this is mathematically convenient). A recursive function to calculate the factorial of a number is:

```
int factorial(int n)
{
    if (n <= 1)
        return 1;
    else
        return n * factorial(n - 1);
}
```

This function has a base case and a more complicated case. The base case (actually two cases) is n=0 or n=1. These base cases can be trivially evaluated to 1. The more complicated case is n>1. To see how recursion can be applied, note that the product 1*2*3*..n, is equal to the product 1*2*3*..*(n-1) multiplied by n. Hence the larger case is solved recursively by multiplying n by the factorial of n-1 (which is a smaller similar sub-problem). The recursive function call is used to calculate the factorial of n-1.

Recursive functions are commonly used in the implementation of some tasks related to binary trees. For example, traversals of binary trees are usually performed recursively. The recursive function for an inorder traversal is:

```
void inorder(node_ptr root)
{
    if (root != NULL) {
        inorder(root->left);     /* left subtree recursively */
        visit(root);
        inorder(root->right);    /* right subtree recursively */
    }
}
```

As in many examples of recursive functions on binary trees, this example has a base case of root==NULL. No action is taken in this function when the base case is found.

14.5.1 Recursion versus iteration

Recursion refers to functions calling themselves. Iteration refers, in particular, to the use of loops, but the term can be used to refer to any non-recursive algorithm. Recursive algorithms are often considered to be inefficient compared to their iterative counterparts. This is often true to some extent, but there is another factor that can outweigh efficiency considerations — ease of programming. Recursive solutions offer quick, simple to write, convenient solutions to many programming problems. This is particularly true in areas with an inherent recursive nature. For example, binary trees are inherently recursive, because each sub-tree of a binary tree is also a binary tree.

Recursive algorithms can always be transformed into an equivalent iterative algorithm. However, this transformation often requires the use of a stack data structure. Note that recursive algorithms always implicitly use a stack — the stack of function invocations. When an iterative algorithm requires a stack, it is generally better to use the recursive algorithm (because the system's function call stack should be fast).

Some recursive algorithms can be transformed into iterative algorithms without the need for a stack. Iterative algorithms not requiring a stack are usually more efficient than recursive algorithms because the overhead of function calls is avoided. For example, an iterative version of the factorial function is easily written:

```
int factorial(int n)
{
    int i, result = 1;

    for (i = 1; i <= n; i++)
        result *= i;
    return result;
}
```

14.5.2 Tail recursion elimination

There is a very simple transformation that can be applied to many recursive algorithms to increase their efficiency. Function call overhead can be reduced by a significant amount with minimal cost. The method applies to any recursive function that calls itself as the very last executable statement. Consider what happens when the function calls itself as the last statement — the function calls itself, waits for the return and then exits. No work is done after the recursive call returns, so the current invocation of the function is no longer really needed.

The transformation involves replacing the recursive call at the end of the function with a jump to the top of the function — to the top of the current invocation of the function. This jump can take the form of a `goto`, but more commonly it is a `while` loop. The `inorder` function presented earlier can be rewritten to eliminate tail recursion.

```
void inorder(node_ptr root)
{
    while (root != NULL) {
        inorder(root->left);   /* left subtree recursively */
        visit(root);
        root = root->right;    /* do right subtree in loop */
    }
}
```

14.5.3 Hidden functions and interface functions

It is quite common for a recursive function to be hidden from the outer function calls. A recursive function is often used to do the hard work behind the scenes, with another function serving as an interface to it. Hence I will use the terms *hidden function* and *interface function* to describe these types of functions.

Consider the task of printing a binary tree. Conceptually it is a single task, but, in practice, to do it recursively requires two functions. The interface function performs some initial processing and then calls the recursive hidden function.

```
void print_tree(node_ptr tree)
{
    printf("***--- Binary Tree ---***\n\n");   /* Title */
    print_tree_hidden(tree, 0);
}

/*--------------------------------------------------------------*/
/* Recursive hidden function that does all the work             */
/*--------------------------------------------------------------*/
void print_tree_hidden(node_ptr tree, int indent)
{
    if (tree != NULL) {
        print_tree_hidden(tree->left, indent + 1);    /* left subtree */
        printf("%*d", indent * 5, tree->key_field);   /* indent key */
        print_tree_hidden(tree->right, indent + 1);   /* right subtree */
    }
}
```

In the preceeding code, the first (interface) function serves two purposes: it prints out the title, and it supplies the zero argument to the recursive function. The title cannot easily be printed from within the recursive function (because it would be printed every time the function was entered). The zero argument could be passed from outside as an argument to the `print_tree` function, but this is annoying as it is not related to the task of printing a tree. The detail that the `print_tree` function needs a variable to control indentation should be hidden from the outside use of the `print_tree` function.

14.5.4 Recursion and static local variables

Local `static` variables can be used to accomplish special tasks when used inside recursive functions. For example, incrementing a variable on entry to the function and decrementing it on exit effectively keeps track of the current depth of recursion. A simple way to trap infinite recursion is:

```c
void recursive_fn(void)
{
    static int depth = 0;   /* Initialize once at compile time */

    depth++;                /* Increment on function entry */
    if (depth > MAX_DEPTH) {
        fprintf(stderr, "Recursion too deep.\n");
        exit(1);
    }
    ...    /* Main body of recursive function */

    depth--;                /* Decrement on function exit */
}
```

The variable, `depth`, is initialized to zero at compile time. After that, the only operations upon it are increment when the function begins, and decrement when the function ends. It is not hard to see that this keeps count of the number of current invocations of a recursive function (i.e. the depth of recursion). Note that the decrement must take place every time the function exits, even if it exits using the `return` statement in the middle of the function.

The `indent` parameter of the function `print_tree_hidden` shown earlier is effectively a measure of the recursion depth. The `indent` parameter can be replaced by a `static` local variable. This removes the need for an interface function.

```c
void print_tree_hidden(node_ptr tree)
{
    static int indent = -1;    /* Initialized at compile time */
                               /* -1 so 1st call has indent=0 */
    indent++;
    if (indent == 0)
        printf("***--- Binary Tree --- ***\n\n");    /* title */
    if (tree != NULL) {
        print_tree_hidden(tree->left);
        printf("%*d", indent*5, tree->key_field);
        print_tree_hidden(tree->right);
    }
    indent--;
}
```

Local variables declared as `static` can be thought of as global variables with local scope. Because recursive functions call themselves and not other lower level functions, this "local scope" does not prevent lower level calls from accessing their value — they have access to the same variable. Note that because of the similarity between `static` and global variables, global variables could be used instead of `static` variables, and `static` variables are used only because they can be conveniently declared inside the function.

14.6 Variable length argument lists: <stdarg.h>

Functions can be defined in C to accept an unspecified number of arguments. Most C programmers *use* functions with a variable number of arguments all the time: `printf`, `scanf`. The `printf` function takes a variable number of arguments: the first is a format string, and then a varying length list of other arguments (of any type!). However, most C programmers have no need to *define* their own functions of this type.

The key to defining functions accepting variable length argument lists is the dot-dot-dot token (also called the ellipsis) which consists of three periods together. This is a special token indicating to the compiler that the length of the rest of the parameter list may vary. There must be at least one named parameter before the dot-dot-dot token. An example of the prototype declaration of a variable argument list function is shown below:

```
int printf(char * format, ... )
{
    ...    /* function body */
}
```

Note that "`...`" is the ellipsis token, and is actually part of the C code.

The body of the function must handle the varying length list of arguments. Unfortunately, much valuable information cannot be known inside the function. There is no way to determine the number of arguments sent to the function, nor to find the type of any individual argument. The size of each individual argument or even the size of the total block of memory for arguments is also unknown. The only information available to the function is a pointer to the block of memory holding the arguments (if there are any).

The type of the arguments must be available some other way. For example, in the function call:

```
printf("%d\n", i);
```

the `printf` function uses the `%d` in the format string to indicate that the first unnamed argument is an `int`. Because it has no way of checking types of arguments, `printf` must assume that the information given to it in the format string is correct. It cannot check whether the type is correct, or if too many or too few arguments have been passed to it. Strange results, often implementation-dependent, may occur when the information given to it is incorrect. For example, try:

```
printf("%d", 3.0);        /* INCORRECT */
```

where `printf` expects an `int` value, but actually gets a `double` constant. The call to `printf` prints out the `double` value as if it were the representation for an `int`, and the result is implementation-dependent garbage.

Assuming that the function can determine the types of arguments, the function must use the standard macros from the header file `<stdarg.h>` to extract the arguments. The macros in `<stdarg.h>` allow implementation of variable-length argument lists in a portable manner. This header file declares three macros:

```
va_start(ptr,var);
va_arg(ptr,type);
va_end(ptr);
```

The type `va_list` is also declared in this header file. It is a pointer type, usually `void*` or `char*`, which is used to point to the list of arguments.

To initialize processing of arguments, the macro `va_start(ptr,var)` is used, where `var` is the name of the last of the named variables. This variable is the first variable if there is only one named parameter before the dot-dot-dot (as in `printf` above). The `va_start` macro initializes the `ptr` to the first parameter after `var` in the argument list (i.e. to point to the first unnamed argument).

The `va_arg` macro is used repeatedly to extract the arguments. The macro call `va_arg(ptr,type)` always returns the next argument (i.e. the next unnamed argument). Its first call returns the first unnamed argument. The `va_arg` macro also increments the pointer to point to the next argument on the list. It uses `type`, a type name such as `int` or `char*`, representing the type of the argument being read, to indicate how big a step to take (based on the size of that type).

Before leaving the function, the `va_end(ptr)` macro must be called. This does some cleaning up, although on many systems this "cleaning up" is to do nothing. Even if the action is to do nothing, the macro call should be included for portability.

Multiple traversals of the argument list are permitted. The macro `va_start` can be used a second time to get a pointer to the argument list, and begin processing the list again.

A toy variable-arguments function is given below. It is similar to `printf`, except that the format specifiers and their values are passed as pairs of arguments in the argument list. The first parameter, `num`, is used to indicate how many arguments have been passed.

```
#include <stdio.h>
#include <stdarg.h>

void print(int num, ...)    /* num = number of (format,value) pairs */
{
    va_list ptr;            /* Pointer to argument list */
    int i;
    int format_char;        /* int because chars converted to int */
    int int_value;
    double double_value;    /* not float; floats converted to double */
    char *str_value;

    va_start(ptr, num);

    for (i = 1; i <= num; i++) {
        format_char = va_arg(ptr, int);     /* Get format char */
                                            /* Note: uses int, not char */
```

```
            switch (format_char) {
                case 'd':
                    int_value = va_arg(ptr, int);
                    printf("%d", int_value);
                    break;

                case 'f':
                    double_value = va_arg(ptr, double);    /* not float */
                    printf("%f", double_value);
                    break;

                case 's':
                    str_value = va_arg(ptr, char*);
                    printf("%s", str_value);
                    break;

                case 'c':
                    int_value = va_arg(ptr, int);          /* not char */
                    printf("%c", int_value);
                    break;
            }
            putchar(' ');          /* Add space between values */
        }
    }
    main()
    {       /*  4 arguments, types 'c' 'd' 'f' and 's'   */
        print(4, 'c', 'f', 'd', 2356, 'f', 0.035, 's', "HI THERE\n");
    }
```

This example serves to illustrate some of the common pitfalls of programming with variable arguments. Notice the absence of the type char. Because variable argument functions default to non-prototyping, all arguments of type char passed to the function are promoted to type int. All arguments of type char or short appear on the argument list as an int. Similarly, only double variables should be used — all float arguments are promoted to double type.

This function assumes that the first argument, num, is a correct indication of the number of arguments. If this number is incorrect, the print function cannot detect it. Extra arguments are ignored, but too few arguments will cause a crash. The problem is typical of all variable arguments functions.

14.6.1 Related library functions: vprintf, vfprintf, vsprintf

In addition to library functions that accept a varying number of arguments, there are some library functions that accept a pointer to the argument list. In other words, they accept a pointer of type va_list. The main examples are the functions equivalent to the three printf-like functions declared in <stdio.h>:

```
int vprintf (char *format, va_list ptr)
int vfprintf (FILE *stream, char *format, va_list ptr)
int vsprintf (char *s, char *format, va_list ptr)
```

These functions are useful when declaring your own variable argument list functions. They allow your function to perform some initial processing and then pass the rest of the arguments along to either vprintf or vfprintf for output. Alternatively, your variable argument list function could immediately pass all the arguments to vsprintf, and then make use of the string value returned, such as to print it onto a graphics screen — note that this could not be achieved using vprintf or vfprintf.

A useful example is to declare an error-handling function that allows arguments exactly like those to `printf`. The error-handling function below prints out the error message passed to it using `printf`-like format, and then terminates the program:

```
#include <stdio.h>
#include <stdarg.h>
#include <stdlib.h>

void error(char *format, ... )
{
    va_list ptr;

    va_start(ptr, format);
    fprintf(stderr, "INTERNAL ERROR: ");
    vfprintf(stderr, format, ptr);      /* rest of message */
    va_end(ptr);                        /* clean up */
    exit(1);                            /* Terminate program */
}
```

14.6.2 Old-style variable length argument lists: <varargs.h>

In non-ANSI versions of C where the header file `<stdarg.h>` is absent, similar macros are often declared in the header file `<varargs.h>`. These old-style macros have slightly different usage to those in `<stdarg.h>` and are therefore not compatible. The macros predate the ANSI standard and therefore their use is not encouraged.

Instead of named parameters followed by the dot-dot-dot token, these macros require the parameter list to be declared as `va_alist`. Then the macro `va_dcl` is placed as a non-prototyped parameter declaration. There are no named parameters and all parameters, even the very first (i.e the format string), must be extracted using the `va_arg` macro. Because there are no named parameters, the `va_start` macro has only one argument: the pointer to the argument list. As an example, the `error` function can be declared using `<varargs.h>` as shown below:

```
#include <stdio.h>
#include <varargs.h>      /* Instead of <stdarg.h> */
#include <stdlib.h>

void error(va_alist)
va_dcl                    /* no semicolon */
{
    va_list ptr;
    char *format;         /* format of printf */

    va_start(ptr);
    format = va_arg(ptr, char*);        /* Get format string */
    fprintf(stderr, "INTERNAL ERROR: ");
    vfprintf(stderr, format, ptr);      /* rest of message */
    va_end(ptr);                        /* clean up */
    exit(1);                            /* Terminate program */
}
```

Instead of using the dot-dot-dot token, these macros take advantage of a feature of non-prototyping — it does not check argument types or number. A variable number of arguments can be sent to the `error` function above because the number of arguments is not checked by the compiler.

14.7 Pointers to functions

Pointers to functions are a complicated aspect of the C language, and are not used in most ordinary programs. Pointers to functions are, in effect, pointers to the first executable instruction in a function and are implemented like all other pointer variables. They can be passed to other functions as arguments, and returned from functions as the return value. For example, the `qsort` (quicksort) and `bsearch` (binary search) standard library functions in <stdlib.h> require a pointer to a comparison function as one of their arguments, and the `signal` function in <signal.h> returns a pointer to the old handler function.

Pointers to functions are declared by a pair of brackets enclosing a star and the name of the pointer, followed by a list of abstract declarators (i.e. type expressions indicating the types of parameters). The first type is the type that the function returns (i.e. the function pointed to). Some examples of declarations of pointers to functions are given below:

```
int (*cmp)(int, int);
double (*ptr)(float, float);
```

The first declaration declares `cmp` as a pointer to a function which returns `int` and accepts two `int` parameters. The second declares `ptr` as a pointer to a function which returns `double` and accepts two `float` parameters. Complicated declarations such as these are also covered in Appendix C.

Most of the ordinary pointer operations apply to function pointers. The extra operation is that a function pointer can be "called". This causes execution of the function that the pointer points to. The arguments inside the brackets are passed to this function. The syntax for calling a pointer to a function is:

```
(*ptr)(argument_list);
```

An abbreviated form without the dereferencing star is also allowed:

```
ptr(argument_list);
```

For example, if `cmp` is declared as a pointer to a function, as above, the function to which it points can be called using two equivalent notations:

```
x = cmp(a, b);          /* both are equivalent */
x = (*cmp)(a, b);
```

The complicated declarations of pointers to functions can often be avoided by remembering that the name of a function can be used as a pointer to a function. Hence, the function name can be used as a pointer to a function (i.e. pointing to itself). However, the function name is not a variable and cannot be assigned a new value. A function name is effectively a constant of type pointer to function.

In cases where the complicated declarations are necessary, they can often be simplified by using an extra `typedef` name to break up the declaration. For example, it is possible to declare an array of pointers to functions using:

```
typedef (*ptr_to_fn)();
ptr_to_fn jump_table[10];
```

which first defines `ptr_to_fn` as a pointer to function type, and then uses the ordinary method of declaring an array variable using `ptr_to_fn` as the type contained in the array. This is far more readable than:

```
int (*jump_table[10])();
```

Presented below is a simple program illustrating the use of pointers to functions. The program prompts the user to choose a mathematical function from the menu provided and then prints out values of that function in a specified range. Rather than use five different C functions for printing out each different mathematical function, this program has one function to print out the values, and passes pointers to the mathematical functions to that function. Thus the `print_values` function is a general function to print out the value of any mathematical function passed to it. Using the same idea it would be possible to write general C functions to perform any operation on a mathematical function such as numerical integration or plotting the function graphically.

```c
/*--------------------------------------------------------------*/
/* Example of the use of Pointers to Functions                  */
/*--------------------------------------------------------------*/

#include <stdio.h>
#include <math.h>
#include <errno.h>

typedef double (*ptr_to_fn)(double);

/*--------------------------------------------------------------*/
/* Print function 'f' in a specified range with a given increment */
/*--------------------------------------------------------------*/
void print_values(ptr_to_fn f, double lower, double upper, double step)
{
    double x, result;

    for (x = lower; x <= upper; x += step) {
        result = f(x);              /* Call the function pointed to */
        printf("%f\n", result);
    }
}

/*--------------------------------------------------------------*/
main()
{
    int choice;
    ptr_to_fn jump_table[5];    /* Array of pointers to functions */

    jump_table[0] = cos;    /* Store pointers to functions in array */
    jump_table[1] = sin;
    jump_table[2] = tan;
    jump_table[3] = exp;
    jump_table[4] = log;

    printf("1. Cos\n");                 /* Print the menu */
    printf("2. Sin\n");
    printf("3. Tan\n");
    printf("4. Exp\n");
    printf("5. Log\n");

    printf("\nEnter your choice: ");
    scanf("%d", &choice);               /* Get the user's choice */

    print_values( jump_table[choice - 1], 1.0, 2.0, 0.1);
}
```

UNIX users should note that the −lm option is required by cc when <math.h> is included. Most importantly, the −lm option must be placed *after* all filenames. This is discussed further in Chapter 12.

14.8 Passing sub-arrays to a function

If a function accepts an array type, it is possible to pass it any array as an argument, or any pointer of the right type. In this way, it is possible to pass sub-arrays to a function by passing the address of a particular array element. A function to operate on a particular type of array can be written, and used to operate on various arrays.

```
void clear(int a[], int n)
{
    int i;
    for (i = 0; i < n; i++)
        a[i] = 0;
}

main()
{
    int a[100];

    clear(a, 10);            /* clear first ten, 0..9 */
    clear(a + 50, 10);       /* clear 50..59 */
    clear(&a[50], 10);       /* clear 50..59 (equivalent) */
}
```

It is also legal to pass multi-dimensional arrays to functions. However, the sizes of all but the first dimension must be specified in the function receiving the array. For example, to pass a two-dimensional array to a function, the function header would look like:

```
void fn(int a[][SIZE2]);
```

The reason for this restriction is that the compiler cannot determine the address of an arbitrary array element if it does not know the sizes of all but one of the dimensions.

Because the sizes of most of the array dimensions must be specified in the function declaration it is very difficult to write a function to act on sub-arrays of multi-dimensional arrays. For example, this idea would be useful to define library functions to operate on matrices with different dimensions. Ideally, we would like one function to calculate the determinant of a matrix for any dimension (i.e an n-by-n matrix where n varies). We would like the determinant function to look like:

```
double determinant( double matrix[][], int n);    /* ILLEGAL */
```

where the dimensions of the matrix are not specified at compile-time, but are specified at run-time by the n argument.

This is not possible because the second dimension (i.e. n) needs to be specified in the definition of the two-dimensional array, matrix. One solution is to declare matrices as arrays of size MAX-by-MAX where MAX is the largest possible value of n:

```
double determinant( double matrix[MAX][MAX], int n);
```

This solution is effective, but does waste a large amount of memory because every matrix must be declared much larger than it need be.

The other solution is to use dynamic multi-dimensional arrays as discussed in Section 14.10.3. When a matrix is created using the `create_array` function given in that section, the determinant function can be written as:

```
double determinant( double **matrix, int n);
```

and elements are referenced normally using two pairs of square brackets:

```
x = matrix[i][j];
```

14.9 Removing the 0..n−1 array index restriction

There is a trick available to change the index range of an array from 0..n−1, to an arbitrary range low..high. The method uses a pointer to the array, instead of the array variable. The pointer is set to point to an address before the array, using address arithmetic (i.e. subtracting an integer from a pointer). For example, the definition of an array b[1..10] is achieved by:

```
int a[10], *b;    /* a is ordinary array, b is the new one */
b = a - 1;        /* Set b to 1 element before a; b[1]==a[0] */
```

The pointer points to an element before the array. Referencing b[i] is the same as referencing a[i-1]. In effect, the whole array has been shifted down. The method can be generalized to any index range low..high, as shown below:

```
int a[high - low + 1], *b;
b = a - low;
```

The only disadvantages with this method are the need for an extra pointer variable, and that, strictly speaking, the technique defies the ANSI standard because it allows a pointer to point beyond an array's limits (it should work correctly on most machines). As with all arrays in C, there is no bounds checking on these array references, and the index must never be less than the lower limit or greater than the higher limit.

The removal of the index range restriction for *multi-dimensional arrays* is more difficult, and involves setting up additional variables containing arrays of pointers. For example, the two-dimensional array definition:

```
a[LOW1..HIGH1][LOW2..HIGH2]
```

can be achieved by using an array of pointers and another pointer variable:

```
int data_a[HIGH1-LOW1+1][HIGH2-LOW2+1];   /* data array */
int *ptr_a[HIGH1-LOW1+1];                  /* extra pointers */
int **a = ptr_a - LOW1;                    /* the array */

for (i = 0; i < HIGH1 - LOW1 + 1; i++)     /* set pointers */
    ptr_a[i] = data_a[i] - LOW2;
```

The pointers in `ptr_a` point to rows of the array `data_a`. Any references to the "array" element `a[i][j]` are translated into references to the array of pointers in `ptr_a` (i.e. `a[i]` becomes `ptr_a[i-LOW1]`) which in turn supplies the address of the row of the array, which is combined with the second index, `j`. For example, consider the declaration of `a[2..5][3..7]` and the array reference `a[2][3]`. The reference `a[2]` is equivalent to `ptr_a[0]` which contains a pointer that has been assigned the address of `data_a[0]-3` (i.e. 3 locations before `data_a[0]` using address arithmetic). Thus, the reference `a[2][3]` becomes `ptr_a[0][3]` which becomes `data_a[0][0]`. The pointers in `ptr_a` act as an extra level of indirection that define a mapping from `a[2..5][3..7]` to `data_a[0..3][0..4]`.

Although `ptr_a` has been set at run-time using a `for` loop in the above example, it is possible to initialize `ptr_a` at compile-time using:

```
int data_a[HIGH1 - LOW1 + 1][HIGH2 - LOW2 + 1];  /* data */
int *ptr_a[HIGH1 - LOW1 + 1] = {                 /* Extra pointers */
        data_a[0] - LOW2,
        data_a[1] - LOW2,
        data_a[2] - LOW2,
        /* etc */
};
```

The method can be extended to three dimensions by adding yet another layer of pointers. The new pointer array is a two-dimensional array of pointers.

```
int data_a[HIGH1-LOW1+1][HIGH2-LOW2+1][HIGH3-LOW3+1];
int *ptr_a2[HIGH1-LOW1+1][HIGH2-LOW2+1];   /* Extra pointers */
int **ptr_a1[HIGH1-LOW1+1];                /* Extra pointers */
int ***a = ptr_a1 - LOW1;                  /* The variable */

for (i = 0; i < HIGH1 - LOW1 + 1; i++)     /* Set 1st level */
    ptr_a1[i] = ptr_a2[i] - LOW2;
for (i = 0; i < HIGH1 - LOW1 + 1; i++)     /* Set 2nd level */
    for (j = 0; j < HIGH2 - LOW2 + 1; j++)
        ptr_a2[i][j] = data_a[i][j] - LOW3;
```

Again, it is possible to replace the `for` loops with array initializations. From the two-dimensional example, it can be seen that this is merely a matter of unrolling the loops into a list of initializers.

This method of using extra arrays of pointers is also useful for defining dynamic multi-dimensional arrays, which is the main topic of the next section. The specification of arbitrary index ranges for multi-dimensional dynamic arrays is also discussed.

14.10 Dynamic arrays

One restriction in declaring array variables in a program is that the size must be specified at compile-time. It is possible to declare arrays of dynamic size at run-time using the dynamic memory allocation functions. Once allocated, these arrays can be used like ordinary arrays.

The library function `malloc` is used to allocate memory for the dynamic array, and a pointer is set to point to this block of memory. The pointer points to the lowest (zeroth) element of the array (i.e. `p==&p[0]`). This pointer variable is then used as if it were an array variable. Note that pointers can be indexed using the square brackets notation, ptr[i]. An example illustrating the allocation of a dynamic array of n structures is shown below:

```
struct node    *p;       /* p is a pointer */
int n;                   /* n is the number of elements wanted */

p = malloc(n * sizeof(struct node));     /* allocate memory */
```

Note that the malloc function does not zero the bytes of memory that it returns, but calloc does. Except for the fact that calloc initializes the memory, calloc(x,y) is equivalent to malloc(x*y). An equivalent method of allocating memory using calloc would be:

```
p = calloc(n, sizeof(struct node));     /* allocate memory */
```

Once allocated, the size of the array can be increased or decreased using the realloc function. For a larger size, realloc allocates a new bigger block, and then copies the original data to the new block, and frees the original memory. The extra bytes in the larger block remain uninitialized.

```
ptr = realloc(ptr, new_size);
```

It is important to note that realloc may physically move the array and if there is another pointer to the original array, this pointer becomes a dangerous dangling reference.

One subtle difference between dynamic arrays and normal array variables is that because a pointer variable is being used, and not an array variable, this pointer can be changed (e.g. ptr++ is allowed, whereas arr++ is not). The pointer can be moved back and forth along the array if this is needed. With pointers into an array, negative subscripts into the array have meaning (e.g. ptr[-1] points to the element before the current one).

14.10.1 Multi-dimensional dynamic arrays

Using dynamic memory to store multi-dimensional arrays is a difficult problem to solve. The main difficulty is that malloc and calloc return blocks of memory with no structure, and it is difficult to impose the structure of a multi-dimensional array. It is only legal to use one dimension of indexing on the pointer to this block of memory. For example, if we wish to declare an array similar to arr[5][3] on the heap, we cannot allocate 15 integers, pass the address to a pointer and then use two levels of brackets on the pointer variable. Instead, it is necessary to map the two indices, x and y, to a single index, i. For the array arr[5][3] the mapping is:

```
i = x * 3 + y;
```

More generally, a macro for defining the mapping for two-dimensional arrays, using the indices and the number of rows and columns, is shown below:

```
#define MAP2(x1, x2, size1, size2)    (x1 * size2 + x2)
```

Note that size1 is not actually used, but is left there to avoid confusion. The size of the first dimension is not needed in any index calculations.

The MAP2 macro can be used for multi-dimensional dynamic arrays, as below. Unfortunately, the MAP2 macro must be used for every array reference. The code fragment below allocates a two-dimensional dynamic array and then uses the MAP2 macro to set all elements to zero.

```
int *p, num_rows = 5, num_columns = 3;
p = calloc(num_rows * num_columns, sizeof(int));
for (i = 0; i < num_rows; i++)
   for (j = 0; j < num_columns; j++)
      p[MAP2(i, j, num_rows, num_columns)] = 0;  /* p[i][j]=0 */
```

Similarly, macros can be defined for mapping three-dimensional and higher dimensional arrays to the one-dimensional array index. The macros for dimensions three and four are shown below, and macros for higher dimensions can be devised by following the pattern.

```
#define MAP3(x1, x2, x3, size1, size2, size3)        \
                 (x1 * size2 * size3 + x2 * size3 + x3)
#define MAP4(x1, x2, x3, x4, size1, size2, size3, size4)    \
         (x1 * size2 * size3 * size4 + x2 * size3 * size4   \
            + x3 * size4 + x4)
```

14.10.2 Two-dimensional dynamic arrays

Obviously the use of multi-dimensional dynamic arrays is cumbersome with the above method because the MAP macros must be placed inside the square brackets for every array reference. This section examines an alternative implementation of multi-dimensional arrays that allows the use of the ordinary notation for array referencing (i.e. a[i][j]). However, the method does cost some extra memory, and uses extra functions for creating and freeing the dynamic array.

The idea of the method is to create an extra layer of pointer values pointing into the original data array. To create the array a[5][3] an extra array of 5 pointers is created, and a is assigned to point to this array. The first pointer in the new array points to the 1st element of the 15 data elements (i.e. &a[0][0]), the next points to the 4th, the next to the 7th, the next to the 10th and the next to the 13th. Thus, the reference a[0][2] will first evaluate a[0] which contains the address of the first element of the array (i.e. &a[0][0]). Then the second index, 2, is added to this address to give the address of the third element of the array (i.e. a[0][2]). In this way, the first array index navigates through the auxiliary pointer array and the second index is an offset into the data elements.

To define a two-dimensional dynamic array (of any type) a pointer variable is defined with two stars:

```
int **a;
```

The function create_2d_array is called specifying the number of rows and columns in the array, and the size of the data elements, as below:

```
a = create_2d_array(num_rows, num_columns, sizeof(int));
```

When the dynamic array is no longer needed, it must be freed to the heap using the function `free_2d`. The `free` function declared in `<stdlib.h>` is not adequate for this purpose. The source code for `create_2d_array` and `free_2d` is shown below.

```
#include <stdio.h>
#include <stdlib.h>
#include <assert.h>

void *create_2d_array(int x, int y, int size)
{
    int i;
    void *main_array;           /* Array containing user's data */
    void **index_array;         /* Array used for indexing only */

    main_array = calloc(x * y, size);         /* data array */
    index_array = calloc(x, sizeof(void*));   /* pointer array */
    if (main_array == NULL || index_array == NULL) {
        fprintf(stderr, "\nOut of heap memory\n\n");
        exit(1);
    }
            /* Store addresses of rows in index_array */
    for (i = 0; i < x; i++)
        index_array[i] = (char*)main_array + i * y * size;
    return index_array;
}

void free_2d(void *p)
{
    free(((void**)p)[0]);     /* Free the data array */
    free(p);                  /* Free the index array */
}
```

There are a number of special features of the program because `void` pointers should not be involved in address arithmetic: the type cast to `char*` ensures that address arithmetic occurs in byte sized increments (because adding to a `char*` pointer adds bytes, whereas adding to a `void*` pointer is undefined), and the type cast to `void**` in `free_2d` prevents a compilation warning about dereferencing a `void` pointer.

14.10.3 Dynamic arrays of any dimension

The method used for two dimensions above can be generalized to allow dynamic arrays of any dimension. For three dimensions there is an extra block of pointers, giving two blocks of pointers and one block of data. Generally, for n dimensions there are n−1 blocks of pointers and 1 block of data. The above functions could be modified to three or more dimensions, but the approach taken here is to create a function that builds dynamic arrays of any size and dimension, specifiable at run-time!

The new implementation consists of one function, `create_array`, which accepts the dimension of the array, an array of integers representing the sizes of each dimension of the array, and the size of the data elements to be stored in the array (i.e. the `sizeof` operator applied to the data type). Thus, the implementation is slightly different from above in that the size of the data element has not been extracted by the preprocessor (because it couldn't be). Arrays of any type are supported. The `create_array` function returns a pointer to the array which is assigned to the array variable. The only differences between declaring arrays of different dimensions is the number of stars in the declaration of the pointer variable. The number of stars should equal the number of dimensions. Note that dynamic arrays defined using `create_array` can be returned to the heap by using the usual `free` function.

The implementation below packs all pointers and all data elements together in one large block of dynamic memory. The size of the block can be computed as the number of pointers multiplied by `sizeof(void*)` plus the number of data elements times their specified size. If the sizes of the array indices for an N-dimensional array are `x1`, `x2`, `x3`, ...`xN`, then the number of pointers at each level is `x1`, `x1*x2`, `x1*x2*x3`, etc., and there are `x1*x2*..*xN` data elements. Once the block is allocated, all the pointers are set to point into the next level down. The source code is shown below:

```
/*------------------------------------------------------------*/
/* Generalized Dynamic Array Generator - Any dimension!       */
/*------------------------------------------------------------*/

#include <stdio.h>
#include <stdlib.h>

#define SIZE(i) (ranges[i])    /* elements in ith dimension */

void *create_array(int dim, int ranges[], int data_size)
{
    int i, j;
    int bytes;              /* Bytes needed */
    int term;               /* Temporary */
    void **temp, **temp2;
    void *block_address;    /* Address of allocated block */

    term = SIZE(0);
    for (i = 0; i < dim - 1; i++) {
        bytes += term * sizeof(void*);    /* memory for pointers */
        term *= SIZE(i + 1);
    }
    bytes += term * data_size;            /* memory for the data */

    block_address = malloc(bytes);        /* Allocate the entire lot */
    if (block_address == NULL) {
        fprintf(stderr, "\nOut of heap memory\n");
        exit(1);
    }
                         /*----------------------------*/
                         /* Set up all the indirection */
                         /*----------------------------*/
    term = SIZE(0);
    temp = block_address;
    for (i = 0; i < dim - 1; i++) {       /* For all levels */
        temp2 = temp + term;
        for (j = 0; j < term; j++) {      /* For each pointer */
            *temp = temp2;                /* store address */
            temp++;
            if (i < dim - 2)              /* pointer to pointer */
                temp2 += SIZE(i + 1);
            else                          /* pointer to data */
                temp2 = (void**)((char*)temp2 + SIZE(i+1) * data_size);
        }
        term *= SIZE(i + 1);
    }
    return block_address;
}
```

```
main()
{
    int **a;                    /* 2 dimensions, 2 stars */
    double ***g;                /* 3 dimensions, 3 stars */
    int ranges[10] = {5, 3, 2};

    a = create_array(2, ranges, sizeof(int));      /* 5x3 array */
    g = create_array(3, ranges, sizeof(double));   /* 5x3x2 array */
}
```

The code for setting the pointer variables is a little tricky and requires explanation. The loop variable i counts the levels of pointer indirection and j counts the number of pointers at each level. At all times, temp points to the next pointer to be set. The pointer temp2 always points to the next address to be assigned to the pointer at temp. At the start of each level (each iteration of i) temp2 is assigned the address of the beginning of the next level. At each iteration of j, temp2 is incremented by a number of pointer values if it is pointing to pointers, or incremented by a multiple of the size of the array elements if it is pointing to data (i.e. if on the last level of indirection).

14.10.4 Specifying index ranges of dynamic arrays

The methods used earlier to remove the 0..n-1 restriction on single and multi-dimensional arrays can be applied to the definition of dynamic arrays. In fact, this can be achieved with only minor changes to the above function, create_array. Exactly the same method of creating multiple levels of indirection is used, but the actual addresses stored in these indirection levels are affected by changes to the index range.

The modified create_array function is shown below. The obvious trivial change to the function definition is that the ranges variable becomes a two-dimensional array to allow specification of lower and upper index ranges, rather than just the size. The SIZE macro is also changed to calculate the number of elements at each dimension from these two values. However, the main changes are the subtraction of the lower index range, as calculated by the LOW macro, from addresses stored in the pointer arrays and also from the address returned by the create_array function as the address of the newly created dynamic array variable. Note that an if statement is required for these subtractions because there are two possible types of data being pointed to: pointers of type void*, or the real data. These differences are highlighted by comments in the source code below:

```
/*---------------------------------------------------------------*/
/* General Dynamic Array Generator - Any dimension! Any Index Range! */
/*---------------------------------------------------------------*/

#include <stdio.h>
#include <stdlib.h>

#define LOW(i)    (ranges[i][0])            /* Low index range */
#define HIGH(i)   (ranges[i][1])            /* High index range */
#define SIZE(i)   (HIGH(i) - LOW(i) + 1)    /* Number of elements */

void *create_array(int dim, int ranges[][2], int data_size)
{
    int i, j;
    int bytes;
    int term;
    void **temp, **temp2;
    void *block_address;
```

```
            term = SIZE(0);
            for (i = 0; i < dim - 1; i++) {
                bytes += term * sizeof(void*);
                term *= SIZE(i + 1);
            }
            bytes += term * data_size;

            block_address = malloc(bytes);
            if (block_address == NULL) {
                fprintf(stderr, "\nOut of heap memory\n");
                exit(1);
            }
                                /*----------------------------*/
                                /* Set up all the indirection */
                                /*----------------------------*/
            term = SIZE(0);
            temp = block_address;
            for (i = 0; i < dim - 1; i++) {
                temp2 = temp + term;
                for (j = 0; j < term; j++) {

                    /* MAJOR DIFFERENCE: lower bound subtracted */

                    if (i < dim - 1)
                        *temp = temp2 - LOW(i);   /* LOW(i)*sizeof(void*) */
                    else
                        *temp = (char*)temp2 - (LOW(i) * data_size);

                    temp++;
                    if (i < dim - 2)
                        temp2 += SIZE(i + 1);
                    else
                        temp2 = (void**)((char*)temp2 + SIZE(i+1)*data_size);
                }
                term *= SIZE(i + 1);
            }
                    /* MAJOR DIFFERENCE: lower bound subtracted */

            if (dim == 1)
                return (char*)block_address - (LOW(dim - 1) * data_size);
            else
                return (char*)block_address - (LOW(dim - 1) * sizeof(void*));
        }
        void main()
        {
            int **a;                /* 2 dimensions, 2 stars */
            double ***g;            /* 3 dimensions, 3 stars */
            static int ranges[][2] = { {1, 5}, {1, 3}, {1, 2}};

            a = create_array(2, ranges, sizeof(int));      /* 5x3 array */
            g = create_array(3, ranges, sizeof(double));   /* 5x3x2 array */
        }
```

14.11 Exercises

1. Write a program to count the characters, words and lines in one or more files. It should accept filenames as arguments or read from stdin if there are no filenames. The program should print the appropriate filename when printing out the counts. Modify the program to accept the options -c, -w and -l, which modify its output to only output one of the counts. *Hint:* Define a "word" as a string of characters separated by whitespace.

2. Write a program that prints out the length of the longest line of a file. It should accept filenames as arguments or read from stdin if there are no filenames.

3. Write your own version of the getenv library function to read the value directly from the array of strings contained in the envp argument of main. *Hint:* The value of envp is also available through the external variable environ.

4. Write a variable arguments list summation function, sum, which accepts the number of integers to be added together as the first argument and adds the integers together. Some sample calls to sum are:

    ```
    x = sum(2, 100, 50);
    x = sum(5, i1, i2, i3, i4, i5);
    ```

    Why can't double variables be passed to sum? Consider modifying the sum function to add double variables together. Why would sum(2, 3, 3.14) fail to produce the correct answer?

5. Write your own minimal version of printf that uses only putchar for output. The function should support only %c, %d and %s. *Hint:* The printing of integers using %d requires the conversion of an integer value to a sequence of character digits.

6. Write your own minimal version of scanf using only getchar for input, and supporting only %c, %d and %s. Note that all arguments to scanf are pointers. *Hint:* The input of integers using %d requires the conversion of a sequence of digits to an integer value.

7. Extend the print_values function in Section 14.7 to allow the user to specify the interval of values to be printed. Allow the user to change the lower bound, upper bound and the step value.

8. Modify the print_values function to calculate the maximum value of the function across the specified interval.

9. Write recursive functions as specified below and test them in a small program:

    a) Print out a string in reverse.
    b) Print out a number a digit at a time (i.e. convert an integer to a list of character digits).
    c) Compute the sum of the numbers from 1 to n.

10. The inorder function presented in Section 14.5 has the inefficiency that no action takes place when the argument is NULL. An entire function call has occurred without any result. Modify the inorder function to remove this inefficiency.

11. Does the use of static variables for maintaining recursive depth meet problems if two or more recursive calls occur in sequence from within the same function? For example, this can occur in a tree traversal function.

12. Under what conditions would a return statement in the main function *not* be equivalent to a call to the exit library function? *Hint:* When will a return

statement in main fail to terminate the program?

13. Code up the first program in Section 14.2. Run the program with a number of different arguments, and examine the results. For example, try:

    ```
    a.out "this is an" argument
    a.out *.c
    ```

14. Write a non-recursive version of the factorial function. A stack should not be necessary. Should the iterative version be faster than the recursive one? Code up both versions and test their relative speeds. *Hint:* See Section 15.4 for hints on how to time programs.

15. Write a number of matrix functions assuming that the arguments have been created using the create_array function in Section 14.10.3. Using this implementation, the dimension of the (square) matrix can be passed as an integer argument to these functions. Some of the functions might be:

    ```
    TYPE determinant(TYPE **m, int n);
    void zero_matrix(TYPE **m, int n);
    void identity_matrix(TYPE **m, int n);
    void multiply(TYPE **m, TYPE **p, TYPE **r);
    ```

Chapter 15
Efficiency

Although C programs are generally quite fast, good programming techniques can lead to major differences in execution speed. This chapter examines a large number of techniques to speed up programs.

With cheaper memory, the amount of space a program uses is becoming secondary to its speed. This is particularly true of the UNIX system, where there is usually plenty of memory. However, in some situations (such as C programming on a personal computer) there is the need to conserve memory. A number of techniques for achieving this reduction are examined at the end of this chapter.

15.1 When to optimize

The speed improvement techniques in this chapter can be applied either as the programmer is writing the code, or after the development of the program. The first method is preferable because optimizing your program once it is working is a dangerous practice, likely to introduce new bugs. Hence, the first rule of program optimization probably should be:

Don't do it!

However, there are cases when extra speed is needed for a program and the techniques in this chapter can be used.

There are many methods to make programs run faster. Some methods yield large increases in speed, but many merely improve performance slightly. The techniques are separated into three categories:

1. Improvements to algorithms and data structures,
2. Code transformations, and
3. Methods specific to C programs.

Changes to the algorithms and data structures used by a program are the best way to achieve a large increase in speed. Code transformations are changes to statements in a program that improve the speed. These ideas can be applied to any procedural programming language and are not limited to use with C. The C-specific transformations are unlikely to give major increases in speed, except when they are applied to loops or functions that are executed very frequently. Since many of the code transformations and C-specific techniques sacrifice clarity of the program for a small increase in speed, it is only worthwhile applying these ideas to parts of the program that clearly need the extra speed.

There is almost always a trade-off between time and space when making programs run faster. Hence, most of the transformations below sacrifice space for extra speed.

15.2 The C optimizer

The first step to take when improving the performance of a program is to invoke the C optimizer that is available as an option in most compilers. This optimizer can be used for a good speed improvement that is simple to achieve and unlikely to introduce new bugs into the program (although some optimizers have been known to have bugs themselves). The improvement in speed is often quite noticeable, although this obviously depends on the implementation. In addition, some optimizers provide options to choose between optimization towards speed improvement or space reduction.

In the UNIX environment, the optimizer for the cc compiler is invoked using the -O option. The use of -O causes all executable code generated to be optimized, in terms of space and time. The program should run faster, and require slightly less space to run. Note that some UNIX implementations support a number of levels of optimization — refer to the manual entry for the cc compiler.

In other environments the method of invoking the optimizer will depend on the compiler used. Many compilers for IBM PCs provide a built-in optimizer that can be invoked from a menu entry. Consult your compiler documentation for information on how to use the optimizer.

15.3 Profilers for C

When improving a program's performance, it is useful to know where the speed bottlenecks are. There is a saying that 90% of the time is spent in 10% of the code. Hence, any speed improvement should aim to speed up the functions that are most frequently used. The programmer can often tell where the program is spending most of its time (e.g. one function is called by all others), but it is useful to have a software tool to analyze exactly where the program is spending its time. Many implementations of C come with a software tool called a *profiler* which is used to examine the performance of your program.

Under UNIX the standard profiling utility is called "prof". This utility calculates the percentage time taken by each function. This is valuable information when considering which functions to make more efficient. Other related utilities include gprof and pixie.

To use `prof`, compile the program with the -p option to `cc` and then execute the program. Provided the program terminates normally or via `exit`, a data file called `"mon.out"` will be generated. This file contains the data to be used by `prof` in preparing an execution profile for the program. To examine this profile, type the command:

```
prof
```

If your executable is not called `a.out`, but `my_prog`, say, the command is:

```
prof my_prog
```

This command will generate a profile of your program's execution and the functions that use the most time can be identified. Note that the percentages calculated are only approximate because the profiler uses sampling techniques during interrupts and these interrupts might not provide a fully accurate picture. For example, if the program has a very small and fast function, this function might be completely missed.

15.4 Timing C code

There are a number of reasons why it can be useful to time the execution of a program. Timing C code can be useful in determining which statements should be optimized whereas profilers may only indicate which functions are consuming time. Timing code can also determine the relative efficiency of various operations and give you valuable information about writing code for your machine (e.g. is shifting faster than integer multiplication?).

If the full execution time for a program is all that is needed, the UNIX `time` command can be used to calculate the time required by a program. There are two versions — a stand-alone utility in `/bin` and a command built into `csh`. The command to run is usually:

```
time a.out
```

A different executable name could also be used and command line arguments can also be specified.

If a more detailed speed analysis is needed, it is possible to add C code to your program to monitor its own performance. The basic idea is to use the standard library functions declared in `<time.h>` to monitor the time before and after an action. The most useful function is the `clock` function which counts the number of clock ticks since the program began executing. The `time` function which keeps track of the real calendar time could also be used, but it is not a true indication of processor time on a large multi-user system such as UNIX. The `clock` function is correct for both single user and multi-user systems.

The `clock` function returns a value of type `clock_t` (typically `long` or `int`) that counts the number of clock ticks. This value can be converted to seconds by dividing by the constant `CLOCKS_PER_SEC`, also declared in `<time.h>`. The basic idea of timing C code is to call the `clock` function before and after an operation and examine the difference between the number of clicks. The code below examines the relative speed of 10,000 shift and multiplication operations on `int` operands. On my system, multiplications on integers are approximately 50% more expensive than shifts.

```
#include <stdio.h>
#include <time.h>

#define ITERATIONS 10000

main()
{
    int i, x, y, z;
    clock_t before;             /* Save old value of clock() */

    before = clock();
    for (i = 0; i < ITERATIONS; i++)
        x = y << z;
    printf("%d Shifts took %f seconds\n", ITERATIONS,
                (double)(clock() - before) / CLOCKS_PER_SEC);

    before = clock();
    for (i = 0; i < ITERATIONS; i++)
        x = y * z;
    printf("%d Multiplications took %f seconds\n", ITERATIONS,
                (double)(clock() - before) / CLOCKS_PER_SEC);
}
```

15.5 Algorithm improvements

Changing the underlying algorithms used by the program is often the only real way to gain a large speed increase. In particular, the data structures used can often be modified to give a significant speed increase. Is there a better way to do what your program does? Is it doing too much unnecessary calculation? Although much depends on the programmer's ingenuity, there are some common techniques for improving performance of algorithms and their data structures.

15.5.1 Augmenting data structures

Instead of recalculating data every time you need it, a faster way is to store the data in the data structure. This saves the time of recalculation, which need be done only once. If the data ever changes, the calculations must be redone and stored again. Hence this method works best where data is unchanging.

As an example of augmentation, consider a `struct` defined to represent a line segment. The `struct` contains four fields, for the x and y coordinates of the start and end points:

```
struct line_segment {
    int x1, y1;             /* Start point */
    int x2, y2;             /* End point */
};
```

If the computation of the length of the line segment, using:

```
len = fabs((y2 - y1) * (y2 - y1) + (x2 - x1) * (x2 - x1));
```

is a common calculation, it can be beneficial to store the length of the line segment as an extra field in the `struct`:

```
struct line_segment {
    int x1, y1;           /* Start point */
    int x2, y2;           /* End point */
    double length;        /* Length of line segment */
};
```

Whenever this length is needed during calculation it is immediately available as a field member. However, it is important to be careful that there is no consistency problem (where the length field is not the true length of the line segment). The main danger is that the `length` field won't be recalculated every time one of the other fields change.

15.5.2 Storing precomputed results: table lookup

This method aims to replace frequently called costly function evaluations with table lookup (i.e. array references). For example, when calculating the square root of integers, it would be possible to precalculate a table of square roots of integers from 1 to 100. In the main calculations, a call to the `sqrt` function is replaced by a table lookup. The use of precomputation of the `sqrt` function (applied to integers) is shown below:

```
#define NUM   100             /* Precalculate to 100 */

double sqrt_table[NUM + 1];   /* Table of values */

void precalculate(void)
{
    int i;

    for (i = 0; i < NUM; i++)
        sqrt_table[i] = sqrt((double)i);   /* Use real sqrt */
}

double square_root(int n)
{
    return sqrt_table[n];
}
```

The precalculation uses two separate functions: one to perform the precalculation, and another to calculate the values. The `precalculate` function must be called once by `main`. Alternatively, every call to the `square_root` function could check a `static` boolean flag indicating whether the values have been precalculated yet, and call the `precalculate` function if not. Note that this use of precalculation is only worthwhile if some calculations are repeated (i.e. computing the same result).

A common example of precalculation is boolean functions on characters (e.g. `isupper`). To improve performance, it is possible to precompute an array of 256 bytes with 0 if `isupper` is false, and 1 if `isupper` is true. Then `isupper` is evaluated by indexing the character into the precomputed table:

```
#define isupper(ch)    precomputed_array[ch]
```

This is faster (and safer) than the use of a boolean expression such as:

```
#define isupper(ch)    ((ch) >= 'a' && (ch) <= 'z')
```

In fact, many systems implement this function and the other functions in `<ctype.h>` as a table lookup over the 256 characters (plus an extra one for `EOF`), with precalculated one *bit* per function — that is, a bit indicating `isupper`, another bit for `islower`, etc.

15.5.3 Lazy evaluation

This method is a slight amendment to precalculation or data structure augmentation. Instead of precalculating every result, results are calculated only as needed. To use this method, some way is needed of indicating whether a result is already in the table. When seeking a result, it is necessary to check if the required value is already present. If so, table lookup is used to get the result. If not, the value must be calculated, stored in the table and that entry marked as present.

The precomputation of `sqrt` in the previous section can be modified to become lazy evaluation by adding another array of boolean flags, indicating which of the square roots have been computed. When calculating a square root, the function checks if it has been computed, and calculates it if not.

```
#define NUM_PREC    100         /* Precalculate to 100 */

double square_root(int n)
{
    static double sqrt_table[NUM_PREC+1];   /* Table of values */
    static int precalc[NUM_PREC+1];         /* Array of flags */

    if (!precalc[n]) {                      /* precalculated? */
        sqrt_table[n] = sqrt((double)n);    /* Use real sqrt() */
        precalc[n] = TRUE;                  /* Mark as computed */
    }
    return sqrt_table[n];
}
```

The use of lazy evaluation is slower than complete precalculation if all of the values are eventually calculated (because of the overhead of checking whether calculation is needed). However, it can make the program faster overall if not all calculations are needed. Any unnecessary calculations are avoided.

15.5.4 Special solution of simple cases

When solving a problem, simple cases can often be solved by specially designed fast functions. These "special solutions" can involve table lookup of precalculated values (e.g. storing the first ten factorials in an array) or just a fast algorithm for small cases (e.g. sorting less than five numbers quickly).

In general, the special solution of simple cases will give some speed increase if the simple cases are fairly common. The advantage of simple case precalculation over full precalculation is flexibility — it is not limited to those values that can be stored in a fixed size table.

The use of table lookup for simple cases for the `factorial` function is shown below. The use of the method here gives speed increase for all cases, not just the simple ones, because the recursive definition of `factorial` eventually breaks the problem down to a simple case.

```
#define NUM_PRECALCULATED  5       /* How many precalculated */
int factorial(int n)
{
    static precalc[NUM_PRECALCULATED+1] = {1, 1, 2, 6, 24, 120};
    if (n <= NUM_PRECALCULATED)
        return precalc[n];
    else
        return n * factorial(n - 1);
}
```

15.5.5 Incremental algorithms

It is often easier to modify what has already been done than to start from scratch. This idea can be used to write faster algorithms. Changing an existing algorithm to use incremental calculations will usually require total redesign of the algorithm.

A simple example of an incremental algorithm is counting the number of symbols in a symbol table. The non-incremental way to count them is to traverse the symbol table, counting the number of entries. The incremental method is to keeping a running count — increment it when a symbol is inserted; decrement it when a symbol is deleted. The incremental method is better if the count will be required most times. If the count is not required, there has been some unnecessary overhead.

Another good example appears in graphics animation. When displaying a new screen it is usually more efficient to change the existing screen than to redraw the whole screen. The idea is to set only those pixels that need to be changed.

15.5.6 Combining tests using sentinels

Sentinels refer to a value placed at the beginning or the end of a list or array to indicate a special condition. Sentinels are most commonly used to indicate the end of data to be processed (e.g. the character zero at the end of character strings is a sentinel). In this way, a check for the presence of more data can often be omitted. Instead, the program must test for the presence of the sentinel in the input data which is faster in some situations. For example, a program using a buffer can use an end-of-buffer marker as a sentinel. In this way, the program need not check how many characters are left in the buffer each time. Instead, the program merely checks each time that the character returned is not the sentinel.

A clever example of the use of sentinels can be found in the sequential search algorithm applied to arrays. The simplest form of sequential search is:

```
int search(int a[], int key, int n)
{
    int i;

    for (i = 0; i < n && key != a[i]; i++)
        ;              /* empty loop */
    if (i == n)
        return -1;     /* Not found */
    return i;          /* Found the key */
}
```

The test for whether the whole array has been checked (i.e. i<n) can be eliminated by placing a sentinel at the end of the array. The sentinel's key value is set equal to the key being searched for. In this way, when the search reaches the last element, it will find the correct key. In other words, the sentinel fakes a successful search. After the search, the algorithm must check whether the value found was the sentinel, or a real success. Setting up the sentinel is the only overhead and this compares favorably with the removal of the test inside the loop.

```
int search(int a[], int key, int n)
{
    int i;

    a[n] = key;                  /* add sentinel to end of array */
    for (i = 0; key != a[i]; i++)
        ;           /* empty loop */
    if (i == n)
        return -1;    /* Not found. Found sentinel only */
    return i;         /* Found the key */
}
```

15.5.7 Eliminating tail recursion

Recursion is often a cause of inefficiency. When the recursion can be eliminated without the use of a stack, it is particularly worthwhile. If a stack is needed, there may be little gain — it depends on how efficiently recursion is implemented. An example of recursion elimination without the need for a stack is the elimination of tail recursion. Tail recursion occurs when the last action of the recursive procedure is to call itself. The simple modification changes this last recursive call to become a loop back to the top of the current invocation. For example, consider the preorder traversal of a binary tree. The simplest recursive algorithm is:

```
void preorder(node_ptr root)
{
    if (root != NULL) {
        visit(root);
        preorder(root->left);
        preorder(root->right);    /* Tail recursion here */
    }
}
```

Tail recursion can be eliminated by replacing the `if` statement with a `while` loop. The transformation effectively reduces recursion by half, as the second recursive call is eliminated. This reduction in recursion is achieved with virtually no extra overhead!

```
void preorder(node_ptr root)
{
    while (root != NULL) {       /* while loop replaces if */
        visit(root);
        preorder(root->left);
        root = root->right;      /* Move to right subtree */
    }
}
```

There are many examples of recursive algorithms to which tail recursion removal could be applied: quicksort, preorder and inorder traversals (but not postorder).

15.5.8 Integer arithmetic

Real arithmetic is slow compared to integer arithmetic. Hence it is favorable to replace real arithmetic by equivalent integer arithmetic. Real arithmetic can be replaced by integer arithmetic when only limited precision is required (e.g. 1-3 decimal places). To do this, work in integer units that are 10, 100 or 1000 times larger (for 1, 2 and 3 decimal places). In this way, the decimal places appear as the lower digits of the integers.

To convert the integer into its true integer and fractional parts is quite simple. To get at the fractional part, calculate the number mod 10, 100 or 1000 (using the % operator). To get the true integer part, divide by 10 or 100 or 1000 — remember that integer division truncates the fractional part.

A good example is: when working in dollars and cents, do all calculations in terms of cents (an integer). Then when printing it out, convert to dollars and cents using:

```
cents   = value % 100;
dollars = value / 100;
```

15.6 Code transformations

There are a number of methods of directly improving the efficiency of a program just by changing the source code slightly. These methods are quite general, and apply to many programming languages. The techniques covered are only some of the huge number of general transformations that can be applied to a program to make it slightly more efficient without changing its meaning. The area is a research field in itself. The main techniques have been covered above, but there are always more.

Some of the methods covered below come from the theory of compiler optimization (e.g. code motion, strength reduction on induction variables, sub-expression elimination). Hence, the compiler will often automatically perform these types of optimizations (when the optimizer is invoked). To some extent, this makes these transformations redundant. Even so, good programming practice is to avoid situations where these optimizations are needed on a large scale. The compiler does not look at the program as a whole and can miss some "obvious" optimizations.

15.6.1 Moving code out of loops

Because loops are frequently executed, they should be as fast as possible. There are a number of ways to make loops smaller and hence faster. The overall aim is to move as much code as possible out of the loop. Any expressions that are constant during a loop can be calculated before the loop, rather than recalculating inside the loop every time through. For example, the computation of pi*2.0 in the code:

```
for (i = 0; i < 10; i++)
    a[i] *= pi * 2.0;
```

is the same in each iteration because `pi` does not change. Moving this computation out of the loop makes the code more efficient:

```
scale = pi * 2.0;           /* move multiplication outside loop */
for (i = 0; i < 10; i++)
    a[i] *= scale;
```

A common example occurs with the condition of a `for` loop. The conditional expression in a `for` loop is evaluated at each iteration. Any constant contained in this condition should be evaluated outside the loop. For example, consider the code fragment:

```
for (i = 0; i < strlen(key); i++)
    hash += key[i];
```

The computation of the length of the string using `strlen` does not change, but is calculated at each iteration of the loop (each time the loop condition is tested). Efficiency can be improved by moving the computation of `strlen` outside the loop:

```
len = strlen(key);
for (i = 0; i < len; i++)
    hash += key[i];
```

15.6.2 Loop unrolling

One way to make loops more efficient is to reduce the number of times they are executed. This method does not actually reduce the amount of work done by the loop body, but decreases the number of variable tests in controlling the loop (i.e. reduces loop condition evaluations). Loops can be unrolled to any level. The extreme is when the loop is totally replaced by in-line code. This is the most efficient the loop can get (the loop variable is totally eliminated). For example, the loop:

```
for (i = 0; i < 5; i++)
    a[i] = 0;
```

can be replaced by five assignment statements:

```
a[0] = 0; a[1] = 0;  a[2] = 0;  a[3] = 0;  a[4] = 0;
```

In fact, this can be even more efficiently written as a single statement, by re-using assigned values:

```
a[0] = a[1] = a[2] = a[3] = a[4] = 0;
```

Even if the total number of iterations is not known at compile-time, loop unrolling can still be achieved by repeating the code inside the loop twice (and modifying the header of the loop). This causes the loop to be executed half as many times, and gains efficiency by eliminating some branch instructions and some control variable manipulations. For example:

```
for (i = 0; i < MAX; i++)
    a[i] = 0;
```

becomes:

```
for (i = 0; i < MAX; ) {
    a[i++] = 0;             /* Unrolled by a factor of 2 */
    a[i++] = 0;
}
```

In the example above, the array a will always be accessed an even number of times, because each iteration of the `for` loop accesses the array a twice. If MAX is an odd number, the second array reference in the last iteration will access an illegal array element. For example, if MAX is 3, the first iteration will access elements a[0] and a[1], the second (final) iteration will access element a[2] and then attempt to access element a[3]. However, the array contains only three elements, a[0], a[1] and a[2], and thus a[3] is an illegal array reference. A solution to the problem is to declare the array a to have an even size. One way to ensure that the array contains an even number of elements is to declare one extra dummy element:

```
int a[MAX + 1];
```

If MAX is odd this extra element prevents a bad array reference; if MAX is even the extra element is just wasted space.

Loops can be unrolled more than twice. The problem of odd sized arrays is more general, and can be eliminated by declaring the array to contain a number of extra dummy elements. It is also possible to use a special loop to handle the odd cases.

15.6.3 Strength reduction on induction variables

Strength reduction refers to replacing a multiplication by an addition or by a shift. More generally, it refers to replacing an expensive operation with a less expensive one. This is discussed in more detail in Section 15.7.1. This section examines the application of strength reduction techniques to a particular type of variable.

An induction variable is a variable that changes in an arithmetic progression during a loop. In other words, it is increased by a fixed number each iteration. The control variable of a `for` loop is often an induction variable incrementing by one each time.

If there is more than one induction variable in a loop, efficiency can be gained by removing all but one of them. Any constant multiple of an induction variable is also an induction variable. The aim is to replace this multiplication with an addition. Instead of the multiplication, the induction variable is initialized alongside the initialization of the original induction variable, and then incremented each loop iteration. For example, both i and x are induction variables in the loop below.

```
for (i = 1; i <= 10; i++) {
    x = i * 4;                  /* x = 4,8,...*/
    ...
}
```

It is possible to remove the multiplication operation, because x is actually increasing by a fixed amount each iteration.

```
for (i = 1, x = 4; i <= 10; i++, x += 4) {      /* x = 4,8,...*/
    ...
}
```

For the example above, we see that this optimization makes the code almost impossible to read. Hence, the use of strength reduction is only recommended when speed is very important. In addition, this improvement is commonly performed automatically by the C optimizer.

15.6.4 Common case first

When testing for a number of different conditions, it is best to test the most common case first. If it is true, the other tests are not executed. When using multiple if-else-if statements, place the common case first. For example, consider the binary search function:

```
if (key > a[i])
    ...
else if (key < a[i])
    ...
else
    ...                 /* equality */
```

Equality is least likely of all the three conditions, and hence it goes last. Greater-than and less-than are more common, so they go first.

The idea of common case first also appears in boolean expressions using && or ||. The short-circuiting of these operators makes them very efficient when the common case is first. For ||, the most likely condition should be placed first (i.e. most likely to be true). For &&, the most unlikely condition should be placed first (i.e. most likely to be false).

15.6.5 Simple case first

This method is similar to common case first — the idea is to test the *simplest* condition first. More complicated (and more time-consuming) computations can be avoided if the first test succeeds (or fails, depending on the context). This idea appears in two main situations: the if-if construct (nested if statements), and with the logical operators (&& and ||). The simplest test should be the first of a pair of nested if statements and should also be the first operand of a && or || operator. In the examples below, the subexpression x!=0 is evaluated first because it is the simplest and hence the least expensive to evaluate.

```
if (x != 0)
    if (expensive_fn(x) != 0)
        ...

if (x != 0 && expensive_fn(x) != 0)
    ...
```

15.6.6 Algebraic identities

The calculations in some complicated expressions can be reduced by transforming the expression into another equivalent form. The aim when using algebraic identities is to group the operations differently, to reduce the total number of arithmetic operations. Care must be taken to ensure that the new expression has equivalent meaning. For example, the short-circuiting of the logical operators can cause differences. Some useful algebraic identities are:

```
2 * x == x + x == x << 1
a * x + a * y == a * (x + y)
 -x + -y   ==   -(x + y)
(a && b) || (a && c) == a && (b || c)
(a || b) && (a || c) == a || (b && c)
!a && !b == !(a || b)
!a || !b == !(a && b)
```

15.6.7 Eliminating common sub-expressions

In a complicated expression, there are often repeated sub-expressions. These are inefficient as they require the computer to calculate the same value twice or more. To save time, calculate the sub-expression first and store it in a temporary variable. Then replace the sub-expression with the temporary variable. For example:

```
x = (i * i) + (i * i);
```

becomes:

```
temp = i * i;
x = temp + temp;
```

Note that:

```
x = (temp = i * i) + temp;         /* WRONG */
```

may fail because of its reliance on the order of evaluation of the + operator.

Common sub-expressions do not occur only in single expressions. It often happens that a program computes the same thing in subsequent statements. For example, in the code sequence:

```
if (x > y && x > 10)
    ...
if (x > y && y > 10)
    ...
```

the boolean condition x>y need be calculated only once:

```
temp = (x > y);
if (temp &&  x > 10)
    ...
if (temp &&  y > 10)
    ...
```

15.7 Efficiency in C

The techniques in this section are specific to the C language and many will not be applicable to other languages. The changes described below tend to bring about smaller changes in speed than the techniques covered above. Some techniques are just good practice — you should use them as you write code, rather than going back to change them later.

15.7.1 Good operator use

C's operators are usually implemented in the most efficient way possible. Hence, it makes good sense to use them where possible. The increment and decrement operators are often especially efficient, as they correspond exactly to low-level assembly language increment and decrement operations. The extended assignment operators are very efficient — never use x=x+2 because x+=2 is more efficient (it evaluates the address of x only once).

15.7.1.1 Replacing * with <<

The shift operators are often more efficient than multiplication and division. One optimization is to replace multiplication or division by a power of 2 with a bit shift. Left shift corresponds to multiplication and right shift corresponds to division (for positive numbers only, as discussed below). Note that this optimization is only possible for integer multiplication, because shift operators do not work with `float` operands. For example:

```
a *= 2;
```

can be replaced by:

```
a <<= 1;
```

It is important to be careful when making this modification. The operator precedence of << is different to that of *, so that changing:

```
x = a + b * 2;
```

to use the << operator, as in:

```
x = a + b << 1;
```

is incorrect. It is accidentally equivalent to:

```
x = (a + b) << 1;
```

The solution is to bracket the expression, and take no chances. In addition, note that multiplication by 2 is equivalent to shift by 1. The change above requires a different integer in addition to the change of operator.

Yet another caution is for replacing division with >> when dealing with negative integers. Although >> is fine for positive integers, it has undefined behavior on negative integers. Some machines will sign extend which means that the value of the sign bit is propagated right but remains the same and this is equivalent to division. Some other machines will pad the leftmost bits with zero which yields a positive integer and >> applied to negative integers is not equivalent to division. Even if it is correct on your machine, making use of this feature compromises portability.

15.7.1.2 Replacing % with &

Bitwise-and may be more efficient than the % operator, because % will implicitly perform a division. When finding the remainder from division by a power of 2, a bit mask can be equivalent. For example:

```
y = x % 16;
```

is equivalent to:

```
y = x & 0xF;
```

15.7.2 Using register variables

Declaring variables as `register` is a method of improving the speed of programs without sacrificing clarity. By placing the word `register` before variable declarations, the compiler is advised to store the variables in hardware registers, if possible. The compiler is free to ignore this advice if there are no available registers. The idea is that the programmer can indicate to the compiler which variables are most used. In the absence of any `register` variables, the compiler makes its own decisions which may or may not be good decisions — it depends on the heuristics used.

This method may cause some speedup, but if the compiler is clever it would have already chosen the most used variables to store in registers, and there will be no difference. No harm is done, and it can be worthwhile. A good habit to get into is declaring loop variables and pointers as `register` immediately (rather than going back later to change it). For example:

```
register int i, j;
```

Despite the advantages, do not declare too many variables as `register`. Only declare those that really are used most frequently as `register`. If too many variables are declared as `register`, the compiler cannot know which ones are the most frequently used.

Note also that there is one limitation of `register` variables — their address cannot be calculated using the address operator (&).

15.7.3 Exit early

Using `return` as early as possible in a function is efficient. It prevents unnecessary code being executed. Similarly, both `break` and `continue` are efficient, as no more of a loop is executed than is necessary. For example, rather than using a boolean variable to indicate the end of the loop, as in:

```
    done = FALSE;
    while (!done) {
        ch = get_user_choice();
        if (ch == 'q')
            done = TRUE;
        else
            ...     /* rest of loop */
    }
```

a `break` statement can be used to exit the loop immediately:

```
    while (1) {                    /* Infinite loop */
        ch = get_user_choice();
        if (ch == 'q')
            break;                 /* EXIT EARLY! */
        else
            ...     /* rest of loop */
    }
```

Unfortunately, the overuse of jump statements such as `break` and `continue` can make the control flow of a program unclear.

15.7.4 Passing pointers to structures

All variables except array variables are passed by value in C. This means that when calling a function, a copy of every variable is made and stored in the activation record for the function. Hence, if whole `struct`s are passed, whole `struct`s must be copied. More efficient is to pass the address of the `struct`, and use a pointer to this `struct` inside the function. This causes only one pointer to be copied.

The trap is that the safety of call-by-value is lost and changes made to the local variable also appear in the calling function (as passing is now by reference, and not by value). However, the compiler can be used to detect situations that may change the value simply by declaring the parameter as `const` (see Section 7.8.2).

15.7.5 Removing debugging code

Self-testing code whose only purpose is debugging checks should be removed from the final version of a program. This change is commonly forgotten and the program does not run as fast as it could. For example, it is common that assertions are left in the program by accident. These should be removed by defining NDEBUG before including <assert.h>:

```
    #define NDEBUG
    #include <assert.h>
```

Other types of debugging checks should also be removed. In particular, any debugging statements that produce output should be removed as unnecessary output will waste much processor time. If debugging code is properly placed in the program using conditional compilation (i.e. #if DEBUG), this is a minor change to the definition of a preprocessor symbol.

15.7.6 Pointers for array indexing

When stepping through an array of elements, it can be faster to use pointer variables. The calculation of the address of an array element, `arr[i]`, from the array name and an integer index can be quite slow. The index must be multiplied by the size of an array element and then added to the address of the array. The direct use of pointers removes the need for this calculation, as the address is just the value stored in the pointer variable (i.e. `*ptr`). For example, to move through a one-dimensional array of size `MAX` setting all elements to zero:

```
for (i = 0; i < MAX; i++)
    a[i] = 0;
```

becomes:

```
for (ptr = arr; ptr < a + MAX; ptr++)
    *ptr = 0;
```

Note that the expression `&a[MAX]` is equivalent to `a+MAX` and could also be used in the second `for` loop.

Pointers can also be used for traversing multi-dimensional arrays. The method is the same regardless of the dimension of the array. The expression `a+X_MAX` (where `X_MAX` is the number of elements in the first dimension) always calculates the address of the first byte *not* in the array. For example, the two-dimensional case is:

```
int a[X_MAX][Y_MAX];

for (ptr = arr; ptr < a + X_MAX; ptr++)
    *ptr = 0;
```

Note that because of how arrays are stored, the order in which the elements are visited is equivalent to two nested `for` loops shown below. Note also that the `for` loop above will work for arrays of dimension greater than two (assuming `X_MAX` to be the size of the first dimension).

```
for (i = 0; i < X_MAX; i++)
    for (j = 0; j < Y_MAX; j++)
        a[i][j] = 0;
```

15.7.7 Converting functions to macros

If the program has many levels of nested function calls it can often be speeded up by reducing the level of function calls. This is particularly true of frequently called small functions, where the time used by the function call can be a significant proportion of the function's time usage (the overhead of function call and return). An improvement in efficiency can be achieved by replacing the function call with in-line code. In this way, the overhead of the function call is eliminated. In C, the obvious method is to convert the function into a macro.

There are a few dangers in converting a function to a macro. The first is that any side effects in arguments of a call to the function can cause problems. If there are any side effects in arguments to a macro call, the results can be plagued with bugs. The second problem is that, if the function changes its parameters, these changes to arguments passed to the function will be propagated back to the calling function if the function becomes a macro. The power of call by reference is achieved without pointers, but the safety of call-by-value is lost.

Although the conversion of a function to a macro is more of an art than a mechanizable process, there are some common steps to follow. First, a few simple textual changes are needed:

- Delete the types of variables in the parameter list.
- Add a backslash at the end of each line.
- Add brackets around parameters in the replacement text.

The backslashes are needed to make a long function into a multi-line macro. The extra brackets around parameters prevent operator precedence problems.

The best functions to convert to macros are very simple ones. For larger functions, there are some major problems that must be addressed:

- The `return` statement
- Loops and `if` statements
- Local variables

The `return` statement does not work inside a macro. If the `return` statement is left in the macro, the `return` will leave the encompassing function, possibly even `main`!

Conversion of `void` functions is usually quite straightforward. The braces are left around the statements in the function. Local variables are left unchanged (they are still in a block). If the function uses `return` in the middle of the function, the control structure of the macro must be changed to give the same effect (using `if-else`).

Non-`void` functions present further problems due to the need to return a result. The entire macro must be an expression, as only an expression can return a result. A block cannot return a result. For simple functions the conversion can be quite easy, but for large functions it can be difficult or impossible. The whole structure of the function may need to be modified to overcome problems with local variables and general control structure.

Sequences of statements can be made an expression by use of the comma operator (i.e. replace each semicolon with a comma). Any `if-else` statement can be made an expression using the ternary operator. There is no obvious solution to removal of any loop or `switch` statement. If a function contains a loop, it should stay as a function!

The problems caused by the `return` statement are larger in non-`void` functions. The control structure must be modified so that the effect of an early `return` is achieved and this is more difficult because of the replacement of `if-else` statements by the ternary operator. Furthermore, if the function contains sequences the returned value must be computed as the last operand of the comma operator. Hence, it is much simpler to convert a non-`void` function if it contains no sequences of statements. For example, the `max` function:

```
int max(int a, int b)
{
    if (a > b)
        return a;
    else
        return b;
}
```

becomes:

```
#define max(a, b)   ((a) > (b) ? (a) : (b))
```

Local variables present a more difficult problem. A block cannot be an expression, so the containing braces of the function must be deleted. Local variable definitions are no longer syntactically legal. One partial solution could be to replace every occurrence of a local variable with the expression it evaluated.

15.7.8 Writing your own malloc function

The standard library functions declared in `<stdlib.h>` for dynamic memory allocation are very general, and hence, very slow. The `malloc` and `calloc` functions must be general to accommodate varying requests for differing size blocks and this generality makes it difficult for the allocation functions to be efficient. Writing your own allocation functions is a method of improving efficiency of your program. Furthermore, the new allocation functions can also contain debugging checks to spot obvious errors (this idea is considered more in Section 16.7).

The `malloc` and `calloc` functions must store information in each block so that the `free` and `realloc` functions know how large the block is (this is stored in a few header blocks just before the address passed back to the program). This all takes time, and a faster allocator can be implemented if the flexibility to re-use blocks of memory is abandoned. Note that this is a case of wasting space to gain a speed increase.

A good example of this situation is the symbol table in a compiler. The symbol table must store each of its symbols, of unknown length, in the table. Because the maximum number of symbols is unknown in advance, it is best to use dynamic memory. Rather than use `malloc` to allocate memory for the string storing each symbol, a new function `char_malloc` is used. The source code for this function is shown below:

```
/*-------------------------------------------------------------*/
/* CHAR_MALLOC.C:  Customized dynamic memory allocator for STRINGS  */
/*-------------------------------------------------------------*/

#include <stdio.h>
#include <stdlib.h>

#define BIG_BLOCK_SIZE 1024           /* Size of large memory blocks */

char *char_malloc(int size)
{
    static char *address = NULL;      /* Address of remaining memory */
    static int bytes_free;            /* Bytes remaining in block */
    char *temp;

    if (address == NULL || size > bytes_free) {
        address = malloc(BIG_BLOCK_SIZE);   /* Use the real malloc */
        bytes_free = BIG_BLOCK_SIZE;
    }
```

```
    temp = address;
    address += size;       /* Move to next free spot for next time */
    bytes_free -= size;    /* Count bytes remaining */
    return temp;           /* Return address of string */
}
```

The `char_malloc` function runs much faster than the `malloc` function because it performs much less computation. It works by allocating a very large block of memory, using the real `malloc` function, and then breaking off chunks of this block for each string. Although the call to `malloc` is slow, it is called infrequently and this does not greatly slow down the new allocator. The main disadvantage of the approach used by `char_malloc` is that memory for the strings cannot be re-used after it is no longer needed — that is, the strings cannot be freed. It would be possible to implement a `char_free` function but for `char_malloc` to re-use the small blocks of memory used for each string it would be necessary to maintain a list of free blocks and their sizes. The maintenance of this free list would defeat the purpose of writing a fast allocator.

The main difficulty in implementing `malloc` and `calloc` efficiently is that these functions must operate without knowledge of how many blocks will be requested, or of which different sizes will be requested. The programmer, however, will often know roughly how many blocks of the various sizes will be required, and can use this information to write a more efficient version of the allocation function for the particular program.

A good candidate for such an efficiency optimization is a program that only uses dynamic memory for one type of node, such as a binary tree implementation of a symbol table. The knowledge that only one size block will be required can be used to write faster node allocation and de-allocation functions. Instead of using `malloc` and `free`, the program can use the new functions, `new_node` and `free_node`:

```
node = new_node();      /* Allocate a node */
free_node(node);        /* De-allocate a node */
```

The disadvantage is the need for a call to a slow initialization function called `setup_heap`. However, the cost of a call to `setup_heap` should be overshadowed by the efficiency of `new_node` and `free_node` if they are called frequently enough. Assuming the binary tree nodes are of type "`struct node`", the `setup_heap` call looks like:

```
setup_heap(sizeof(struct node), ESTIMATED_NUM_NODES);
```

The improvement in efficiency using this method comes by initially calling `malloc` from `setup_heap` to allocate a large block, and then using the `new_node` function to break off chunks to use as nodes. Because the `malloc` function is not usually called by `new_node`, the `new_node` function can be very fast (indeed, it could be a macro).

The choice of the estimated number of nodes required by `setup_heap` is quite important. This estimate determines how big a block to allocate in `setup_heap`. If the estimate is too small, `new_node` will occasionally need to call `malloc` to allocate another large block, which is less desirable than a single initial call to `malloc` in `setup_heap`. If the estimate is too large, this wastes space and will also slow down the initial call to `setup_heap`. Hence, the estimate should be large enough to accommodate the most likely requirements of the program, but not a huge worst-case upper bound.

Chapter 15

The source code for the new functions is shown below. The only non-trivial details of the program are in the creation and maintenance of the free list. The `new_node` function takes the first node off the front of the free list, the `free_node` function adds the node to the front, and the `setup_heap` function initializes the free list using a single loop. The free list is implemented as a linked list, with the "next" pointers stored in the first word of each node. This can cause alignment problems if the size of requested blocks is an irregular number of bytes, but there is usually no problem if the requested size is the size of a `struct` variable, because such variables are always of a size that prevents alignment problems. However, if alignment is a problem, the free list could be maintained as a separate list in another block of allocated memory.

```
/*------------------------------------------------------------------*/
/*  EFFICIENT_MALLOC.C : fast dynamic allocation functions          */
/*------------------------------------------------------------------*/

#include <stdio.h>
#include <stdlib.h>

static int estimate;         /* estimated number of blocks */
static int block_size;       /* Size of the block */
static void *free_list;      /* Pointer to first free block */

/*------------------------------------------------------------------*/
/* Internal function to allocate big block, and thread the free list */
/*------------------------------------------------------------------*/

static void *allocate_large_block(int size, int number)
{
    void * address;
    void * temp;
    int i;

    address = malloc(size * number);     /* Allocate large block */

            /* Thread linked list of free blocks */

    for (temp = address, i = 0; i < number - 1; i++, temp += size) {
        *(void**)temp = temp + size;     /* Store next pointer */
    }
    *(void**)temp = NULL;                /* NULL on end of list */
    return address;
}

/*------------------------------------------------------------------*/
/* Initialize the heap for an estimated number of nodes             */
/* If more nodes are required, more memory is allocated later       */
/*------------------------------------------------------------------*/

void setup_heap(int size, int estimated_number)
{
    if (size < sizeof(void*)) {          /* room for 'next' pointers? */
        fprintf(stderr, "Block is too small\n");
        exit(1);
    }
    free_list = allocate_large_block(size, estimated_number);
    estimate = estimated_number;         /* Save for use in new_node() */
    block_size = size;                   /* Save the block size too */
}

/*------------------------------------------------------------------*/
/* Allocate new node of size requested earlier                      */
/*------------------------------------------------------------------*/

void *new_node(void)
{
```

```
        void *temp;

        if (free_list == NULL)           /* Need another big block? */
            free_list = allocate_large_block(block_size, estimate);

        temp = free_list;                /* Save the block address */
        free_list = *(void**)temp;       /* Get 'next' pointer in block */
                                         /* Update free list */
        return temp;                     /* Return the block address */
}
/*-----------------------------------------------------------------*/
/* Free one of the nodes for re-use by new_node()                  */
/*-----------------------------------------------------------------*/
void free_node(void *address)
{
        *(void**)address = free_list;    /* Add node to front of free list */
        free_list = address;
}
```

One minor disadvantage of this implementation is that the memory allocated by `malloc` is never properly freed using the `free` function. To overcome the limitation, it is necessary to maintain a list of the large blocks that are allocated and add another function to free all the large blocks. This function is called when *all* the nodes are no longer needed.

Another interesting point is that debugging checks could be added to these functions. This approach is discussed in Section 16.7. The extra checks need not slow down the final version of the program, if they are placed inside `#if`-`#endif` pairs to allow easy removal using conditional compilation.

15.7.9 Small improvements

There are any number of tiny changes that may improve performance slightly. My suggestion is not to bother with any that ruin the readability of the code. In many cases, a reasonable optimizer would make the changes automatically. Nevertheless, a few possible methods are presented.

15.7.9.1 Re-using assigned values

The assignment operator returns a value that can be used. It returns the value of its right operand (i.e. the value that was being assigned) but with the type of the left operand. It can be efficient on some machines to use the value of the assignment operator. For example, when setting two variables to the same value, it is possible to set both in one statement. The two statements:

```
i = VALUE;
j = VALUE;
```

can be abbreviated to:

```
i = j = VALUE;
```

Both variables are set to `VALUE`. Recall that the assignment operator is right associative, so that the above statement is equivalent to `"i=(j=VALUE);"`, so that `j` is set to `VALUE`, and then `i` is set to the result of the assignment (i.e. `VALUE`). This idea can be generalized to any number of variables, if they are all to be set to the same value and any expression can be used on the right-hand side.

Using the assigned value inside an `if` statement or loop condition is quite a common method of improving efficiency slightly. It is efficient as the value returned from the assignment is used directly in the condition, rather than needing to be accessed again. For example:

```
f = fopen(filename, "r");
if (f != NULL)
    ...        /* etc */
```

becomes:

```
if ((f = fopen(filename, "r")) != NULL)
    ...        /* etc */
```

Another form of this method is to avoid recalculating values by passing a function result directly to another function. For example, consider the code below which allocates `memory` for a string and then concatenates two strings into the location.

```
s3 = malloc(MAX);      /* Allocate memory */
strcpy(s3, s1);        /* Copy first string there */
strcat(s3, s2);        /* Append second string to first */
```

Although not used in the code above, the `strcpy` and `strcat` standard library functions both return a pointer to the newly modified string. Hence, the three lines above can be combined into a single statement:

```
s3 = strcat(strcpy(malloc(MAX), s1), s2);
```

The advantage is that the calculation of the address of `s3` need not be duplicated

15.7.9.2 int only, double only

Mixing of different types can cause the need for implicit type conversion (e.g. mixing `int`, `short` and `char`). These type conversions take up valuable execution time and can be eliminated by using only `int` variables, possibly leading to a small speed improvement.

In older non-ANSI compilers, all floating point arithmetic is carried out in double precision. This can lead to the need for type conversions from `float` to `double`, even if all variables are declared of type `float`! Using only `double` variables (and no `float` variables) can lead to slight improvement. The brute-force way to achieve this is:

```
#define float    double     /* All floats become doubles */
```

15.7.9.3 Copying arrays using memcpy

Rather than copy each element of an array, one at a time, in a loop, the `memcpy` standard library function can be used to copy the entire array in one statement:

```
memcpy(b, a, sizeof(a));                    /* copy array a to b */
```

15.7.9.4 Copying arrays using struct assignment

An alternative method of copying arrays is to make use of the fact the C permits `struct` assignments. This method is not portable, is very unreadable and uses pointers incorrectly by converting between two different pointer types. However, it can be faster than `memcpy` because it makes use of the assignment operator rather than calling a function. To copy an array using this method it is necessary to declare a new dummy `struct` type that is the same size as the array that is to be copied. Then we use type casting to fool the compiler into thinking it is copying `struct`s when really it is copying arrays. The method is illustrated below:

```
struct dummy_transfer {     /* The new struct type */
    int a[MAX];             /* This field gives the right size */
};
int a[MAX], b[MAX];         /* The array variables being copied */

assert(sizeof(struct dummy_transfer) == sizeof(a));
*(struct dummy_transfer *)a = *(struct dummy_transfer *)b;
```

The assignment statement first type casts both a and b to be pointers to the new `struct` type, and then dereferences these pointers so that the compiler believes it is assigning between two `struct`s. The assertion is a safety net to ensure that the copying statement will work, and requires that <assert.h> be included.

15.7.9.5 Copying structs using memcpy

The usual method of copying one `struct` to another is to use an assignment statement (i.e. "b=a;"). However, some older compilers do not permit assignment of whole `struct`s. If this is the case, the `memcpy` standard library function can be used, instead of copying fields one-by-one.

```
memcpy(&b, &a, sizeof(a));      /* copy struct a to b */
```

15.7.9.6 Removing tests for zero

Tests of equality with zero are redundant in C because the compiler always tests a conditional expression with zero. Zero is assumed to be false, and any non-zero value is true. This means that comparisons with zero as in the expressions:

```
if (x != 0)
if (x == 0)
if (ptr != NULL)
if (ch != '\0')
```

are redundant and can be replaced by `if(x)`, `if(!x)`, `if(ptr)` and `if(ch)`. However, these comparisons do represent good style and the optimizer will often remove the comparisons for you automatically. Any improvement in speed due to this method is likely to be negligible.

15.7.9.7 Packing boolean flags into integers

If a number of boolean flags must be checked at once it can be efficient to store them all as bits of an `int`. In this way, it is easy to check if any are true by comparing the `int` to zero. If the `int` is non-zero, the individual bits can be examined using bit masks. Accessing individual bits becomes more time-consuming, so this method is only worthwhile if individual bits are rarely examined (e.g. the bits indicate rare error conditions).

15.7.9.8 Most used struct field first

References to the first field of a structure can often be more efficient because there is no need to add an offset. Hence, the most used `struct` field should be placed first in the declaration.

15.7.9.9 Parameters as local variables

Parameters to functions can be used as if they were local variables. Because of call-by-value parameter passing, this does not change the values of any variables not local to the function. This method saves on initialization time, and on stack space. In the example below, to zero an array, the size is counted down, rather than having a local variable counting up.

```
void zero(int a[], register int n)
{
    while (n > 0)
        a[--n] = 0;
}
```

15.8 Space efficiency

In these days of cheap memory, memory reduction techniques are perhaps not as important as those for increasing speed. However, there are certainly situations when reducing space requirements is far more important than increasing the speed of a program. This section discusses a number of techniques for reducing memory requirements. Unfortunately, reducing space requirements can often lead to loss of speed. There is a trade-off between space efficiency and time efficiency.

Every C program uses memory for a number of different purposes, and each of these areas needs to be attacked separately. The memory usage of the program can be divided into the following memory sections:

- Executable instructions
- Static storage
- Stack storage
- Heap storage

The executable instructions for a program are usually stored in one contiguous block of memory. Static storage refers to memory used by global and local `static` variables, string constants and (possibly) floating point constants. Stack storage refers to the dynamic storage of non-static local variables. Heap storage refers to the memory that is dynamically allocated by the malloc and calloc standard library functions.

The memory requirements for the executable instructions are largely independent of the other memory areas, whereas the techniques for reducing the memory required for the other three areas are often similar. However, care must be taken that applying a technique to reduce data space does not increase the amount of C code too greatly, thus increasing the executable size.

15.8.1 Reducing executable size

The size of the executable obviously depends on the size of your C program. Hence, the obvious way to reduce executable size is to reduce the number of executable statements in your C program. This could involve deleting non-crucial functions from the program, although this is not often possible. The use of compile-time initialization of global and static variables instead of assignment statements is another means of reducing code size.

Another possibility is that your compiler may support an option that causes the optimizer to focus on space reduction. This causes it to generate executable instructions that are as compact as possible, rather than being as fast as possible. Consult your compiler documentation for information about the optimizer, if it exists.

The size of the executable depends not only on the C code, but also on the extra library functions that are linked by the linker. Although it may seem that the programmer has no control over this, there are some techniques for reducing the amount of linked code. The techniques depend largely on how "smart" your linker is — that is, whether the linker links only the functions you need. For example, a dumb linker might link the entire I/O library if one function is used, whereas a smart linker would only link that function used (and any extra code it might need). If the linker is dumb, there is little to do except avoid using the library functions completely and write your own non-portable machine-specific functions. If the linker is smart, executable size can be reduced by replacing large general purpose library functions with your own special purpose versions. For example, the printf and scanf functions are very large because of the need to handle a multitude of format specifications (especially real numbers). Executable size can be reduced by writing your own functions to perform I/O, using getchar and putchar as the basic I/O calls. For example, if you are only using %d in printf, you can avoid using printf by writing your own print_num function:

```
#include <stdio.h>

#define BASE 10        /* decimal numbers */

void print_num(int num)
{
    if (num < BASE)
        putchar(num + '0');              /* only 1 digit number */
    else {
        print_num(num / BASE);           /* do left digits */
        putchar((num % BASE) + '0');     /* do rightmost digit */
    }
}
```

This function can be used to perform all integer output, and `putchar` and `puts` can be used to output characters and strings (they are smaller than `printf`). Another possibility is writing your own minimal `printf` function that supports only those format specifications that you actually use.

UNIX programmers can also use the `strip` utility which strips symbol table information from the executable. However, this is more relevant to the amount of disk space the executable file uses than to the amount of memory it uses during execution. In any case, UNIX programmers are rarely short of memory.

15.8.2 General techniques for reducing data size

There are a large number of techniques for making the size of program data small. These techniques apply to all three types of memory — static, stack and heap storage. In some cases, a method may increase the memory storage in one area to decrease the memory usage in another, which is valid only if the total storage requirements decrease.

15.8.2.1 Different data structures

The program should be examined to determine if a large space reduction can be achieved by changing to different data structures. For example, the program could use arrays instead of linked lists or trees, which avoids the extra space due to pointer storage. However, this also wastes more space if the array is not full, and it is even better to use dynamic arrays, which do not waste any storage, as exactly the right amount of memory is allocated. Unfortunately, using different data structures can sometimes reduce the time efficiency of programs.

15.8.2.2 Recalculation

This is exactly the opposite of the data structure augmentation, storing precomputed results and lazy evaluation techniques for time efficiency. The idea is to store as little redundant information as possible. Whatever can be calculated from the existing data is recalculated each time. Naturally, this reduces the time efficiency of a program.

15.8.2.3 Unions

When using a lot of structures, space can be reduced by overlaying the data fields. This can only be done if the fields to be overlayed are mutually exclusive (i.e. they never have active data in them at the same time). C has a special data type for this purpose: the `union` (see Section 5.5).

15.8.2.4 Re-using space

One way to conserve memory is to re-use the space used by a variable. The `union` data type is a particular instance of this general idea. Another instance of this idea is re-using variables for different purposes. For example, rather than a number of functions each having a local temporary variable, `i`, they could all use the same global variable (although this is a very dangerous practice). As another example, if a program uses two similar arrays, it should be examined whether the two arrays can share the same storage (possibly as a `union`).

15.8.2.5 Small data types: short, char

Instead of using arrays of `int`s, use arrays of `short`, `char` or `unsigned char`. There is no problem with this method, provided large integer values are not being stored (e.g. larger than 127 for `char`, or larger than 255 for `unsigned char`). This technique is particularly worthwhile when applied to `int` fields in `struct`s or large arrays of `int`. Smaller local variables could also be declared as a smaller type, but this may increase the executable size due to type conversions. Note that speed can be compromised because of these conversions, regardless of which type of variable it is applied to. Similarly, use `float` instead of `double`, where the greater precision of results is not important.

15.8.2.6 Bit-fields in structs

When storing small integers in `struct`s, there is a way to specify exactly the number of bits required. These types are called bit-fields, and can only be used for fields inside `struct`s or `union`s. When using bit-fields, small integers or boolean flags are automatically packed into a `struct` or `union`. This reduces storage requirements significantly, but reduces speed because of the need to pack and unpack bits.

The type of a bit-field can only be `int` or `unsigned int`. It cannot be specified as `char`, `short` or an enumerated type. Unless the values can be negative, the field should be declared as `unsigned int`. If not, one of the bits will be used as a sign bit, limiting the values that the field can hold (and possibly causing errors if the integer overflows these limits).

To minimize storage, all the bit-fields should be one after the other. If not, the compiler may not pack them all into the same word. An example is given below where three fields are packed into seven bits:

```
struct node {
    unsigned int    active:1;       /* boolean flag (0/1) */
    unsigned int    visited:1;      /* boolean flag (0/1) */
    unsigned int    component:5;    /* 0..31 */
};
```

15.8.2.7 Packing

When dealing with large arrays of small integers, it can be more efficient to pack them together (i.e. more than one value per word). This is particularly true when the information is binary (true or false), because only one bit per value is needed. On some machines it can even be worthwhile to pack arrays of `char` into arrays of `int` — some machines use whole integers for the representation of `char`s. In-depth discussion of how to pack values together is avoided here.

Note that bit-fields are a form of packing provided by the compiler and are much easier to use. However, there are situations where bit-fields cannot be easily used, such as packing an array of boolean values (bits) into an array of `int`.

15.8.2.8 Reordering struct fields

Because of word alignment on some machines, the order of fields in a structure can change the size of a `struct`. This is only applicable to `struct`s containing different size fields. A general rule for minimizing the space is to order the fields, largest to smallest. This heuristic may not give the best ordering — examine the size of a few different orderings using the `sizeof` operator, if space is crucial. This is a machine-dependent optimization, and may not be effective on some machines.

15.8.2.9 Using malloc for character strings

A common space wastage occurs with structures containing strings. These are often declared containing arrays of `char`, as in:

```
char label[MAX];        /* Array of MAX characters */
```

If the strings are usually less than the maximum length, there is great wastage. A better method is to allocate exactly the right number of characters for each string. When storing the string, `malloc` is called to allocate the memory:

```
char *label;                    /* Pointer to the string */

label = malloc(strlen(s) + 1);  /* allocate memory */
strcpy(label, s);               /* store the new label */
}
```

One disadvantage of this method is the extra complications caused by strings stored separately to the `struct`s. Care must be taken as the labels are now pointers. This complicates operations such as saving and loading to/from a file, as problems with pointers must be resolved.

The method may also actually *increase* space usage (if strings are about MAX characters long) due to the extra memory used by `malloc` for each allocated block. One method of avoiding this is to use the `char_malloc` function in Section 15.7.8, but this will increase executable size.

15.8.3 Reducing static storage

Static storage refers to the memory for global and local `static` variables, string constants and (possibly) floating point constants. All of the general techniques discussed above can be used to reduce the size of the global and `static` variables. The requirements for string constants can be reduced if the compiler has an option to merge identical string constants (which arise quite frequently). Note that this can create problems if string constants are modified, although modification of string constants does defy the ANSI standard and should be avoided.

15.8.4 Reducing stack usage

Stack storage refers to memory storage used for function calls, and includes non-`static` local variables, function parameters and system information used to keep track of function calls. Hence, the basic methods of reducing stack storage are to use fewer and smaller local variables, to pass fewer and smaller parameters, and to reduce the total number of function calls. The size of parameters and local variables can be reduced using the general techniques discussed above. Another method of reducing the size of parameters is to pass pointers to `structs`. The number of parameters can be reduced by using global variables, or by packing a number of parameters into a `struct` and passing a pointer to this `struct`. The number of local variables can be reduced by re-using local variables, although this can introduce bugs if not enough care is taken. Common examples of reusable variables are scratch variables, such as temporaries or `for` loop index variables. Another method of reducing the number of local variables is to use parameters as if they were local variables (this is safe because of call-by-value).

Reducing the depth of function call nesting (especially by avoiding recursion) also reduces stack space requirements. This can be achieved by using preprocessor macros or explicit inline code (but this will increase code size). Naturally, recursion should be avoided as much as possible by using iterative algorithms or tail recursion elimination (see Chapter 14), but in situations where recursion does occur, there are some extra considerations for reducing stack usage. Since all non-`static` variables are saved on the function call stack, as many local variables should be specified as `static` as is possible. A variable can be made `static` if the value it has before a recursive function call is not used again after the recursive call has returned (i.e. it doesn't matter if the recursive call overwrites its value). Note that making a variable `static` changes the meaning of initialization and will usually require the initialization changed to an explicit assignment statement at the start of the function.

15.8.5 Reducing heap usage

The amount of heap storage used depends on the size of blocks, the number of blocks and how quickly allocated blocks are freed. The size of blocks can be reduced using the general techniques discussed above (e.g. packing, `unions`). The number of heap blocks affects heap usage in the obvious way (more blocks means more memory) and because of the fixed space overhead of a few hidden bytes to store information about the block (so that `free` can de-allocate it). When small blocks are used, it can be useful to pack more than one block together to avoid this fixed overhead. All allocated memory should be returned to the heap using the `free` function as early as possible. If memory is not freed, unused memory (called garbage) can accumulate and reduce the available memory.

15.9 Further reading

A good place to look for more discussion of efficiency is Jon Bentley's book: *Writing Efficient Programs*. This book is a treasure trove of practical techniques for speeding up programs and reducing the space usage of programs. The techniques are presented using a variant of Pascal and are easily applied to C.

The book by Plum and Brodie presents a number of techniques for improving the time and space efficiency of C programs. Many of the general techniques used by Bentley are covered, in addition to techniques specific to C.

Many of the code transformation techniques of this chapter come from the theory of code optimization in compilers. The classic reference for compiler design is by Aho, Sethi and Ullman, and this book contains a good chapter on code optimization.

One aspect of efficiency not really covered by this chapter is the choice of data structure for a problem. Knuth's book on data structures for sorting and searching presents much of this theory, and is also interesting in that it applies a number of efficiency techniques to the program code presented (e.g. use of sentinels; unrolling loops). All programs are presented in a mythical form of assembly language called MIX.

BENTLEY, Jon Louis, *Writing Efficient Programs*, Prentice Hall, 1982.

PLUM, Thomas, and BRODIE, Jim, *Efficient C*, Plum Hall Inc., 1985.

AHO, Alfred V., SETHI, Ravi, and ULLMAN, Jeffrey D., *Compilers — Principles, Techniques and Tools*, Addison-Wesley, 1986.

KNUTH, Donald E., *The Art of Computer Programming (Vol. 3): Sorting and Searching*, Addison-Wesley, 1973.

15.10 Exercises

1. (This exercise is possible only if a profiler is available.) Write a program to compute the sum of the squares and the sum of the cubes of 1 up to MAX. The program should use separate functions to compute the square and cube of a number. Generate a profile of execution. Which function takes up the most time? *Hint:* It may be necessary to make MAX quite large so that the program runs for long enough to allow a realistic profile to be generated.

2. The Fibonacci numbers are the sequence of numbers such that F_0 and F_1 are 1, and the rest of the sequence is generated by the recursive rule $F_n = F_{n-1} + F_{n-2}$. Write a recursive function to compute F_n directly from the base cases and the recursive rule. Now write a function to compute F_n that does not use recursion at all. Compare the execution times of both functions.

3. The process of loop unrolling in Section 15.6.2 can be carried out to any degree. However, it becomes impractical to overcome the problem of odd sizes by declaring arrays larger than necessary. An alternative is to use a short non-unrolled loop to handle the odd cases. Write a function as declared below:

    ```
    void clear_array(int a[], int n)
    ```

    that sets n array elements to zero. Use a loop that is unrolled *eight* times to do most of the work and then use a short loop to catch the extra cases. Compare the execution time of the function with that for an uncomplicated version of the function (i.e. call each function repeatedly to get an average time). How do the functions compare when n is large? What if n is very small? *Hint:* The unrolled loop can only set elements from zero up to, but not including, the highest multiple of 8 (why?), and the non-unrolled loop is used for the rest. The highest multiple of 8 can be computed by:

    ```
    max = n & ~ 07;       /* Highest multiple of 8 */
    ```

Efficiency   273

4. Yet another technique for speed improvement is *loop fusion*. This refers to the merging of similar loops so as to avoid some loop overhead. How can this technique be used to improve the following code fragment?

```
for (i = 1; i < 10; i++)
    a[i] = 0;
for (i = 0; i < 10; i++)
    b[i] = 0;
```

5. Most character strings differ at the first character. Use this fact to write a STRDIFF(s1,s2) macro (to compare two strings for inequality) that does not call the strcmp function for this common case.

6. A chess program displays the chess board on a graphics screen. After each move it re-displays the whole board. How can an incremental algorithm be used to reduce the time spent displaying the new board? How much improvement can be expected?

7. Write a small program to time float and double multiplication. Which one is faster? What can you say about your compiler based on this result? *Hint:* Don't just time one multiplication, write a loop which performs a number of multiplications and use the volatile qualifier to write it so that the optimizer can't move the multiplication operation out of the loop!

8. Compile-time initialization is more efficient that run-time initialization. How can compile-time initialization be used to avoid the call to the precalculate function in Section 15.5.2? How can local variable initializations be made more efficient, and when is this possible?

9. How is it possible to improve the efficiency of the statement below (regardless of whether x is a local or global variable)? *Hint:* See Section 2.3.2.

```
float x = 0;
```

10. Although it has a large number of opponents, the goto statement can occasionally be used to improve efficiency using the "exit early" idea. How can goto improve the speed of the code fragment below?

```
for (i = 0; i < X_SIZE && !error; i++)
    for (j = 0; j < Y_SIZE && !error; j++)
        if (a[i][j] == -1)
            error = TRUE;
```

11. A program that tests a large data structure generates a list of random numbers to insert (and then later delete). After seeding the random number generator using srand, the program repeatedly calls rand to generate a number which is inserted into the data structure. Because the program must later call a delete function with the same sequence of numbers, each random number is also stored in a huge array. Naturally, this involves massive space wastage. How can the huge array variable be dispensed with? *Hint:* The sequence of numbers generated by rand is not truly random and can be reproduced (how?).

12. When attempting to reduce the size of the executable, why is it usually foolish to replace `scanf` with a specially written function but still allow calls to `sscanf` or `fscanf`?

13. Implement sets of upper case letters (A..Z) as an array of boolean bits packed into an array of `unsigned char`. Provide an `insert_element` function to add a letter to a set and a `member` function to test if a letter is a member of a set. *Hint:* You will need to use an array of 4 elements (4 bytes makes 32 bits which is large enough for 26 values). Scaling the characters to the integers 0..25 should make it easy to determine the index of the array and the number of the bit (from which the bit mask can be generated by shifting a 1 into place).

Chapter 16
Debugging techniques

The detection and correction of errors in programs is usually called *debugging*. Debugging is a major problem when developing programs. For the most part there is no standard method of debugging programs and much responsibility rests on the programmer's creativity and ingenuity in finding the cause of a program's malfunction. However, there are a number of useful techniques that programmers can use to aid in the debugging of programs. A number of debugging tools, such as symbolic debuggers and source code checkers, can be used by the programmer. In addition, the programmer should ease the debugging task by making the program "easy" to debug. This can involve printing out important information at various points in the program or making the program apply checks upon itself.

Another important aspect of debugging is being aware of the common errors that a program can contain. There are a number of errors that occur frequently in C programs, and these errors are examined in Appendix B.

16.1 Symbolic debuggers

Almost all implementations of the C language come with at least one tool for debugging of C programs: a symbolic debugger. Typically, this type of utility allows the programmer to set breakpoints in the program and examine values of variables during execution. Some of the more common debuggers under UNIX are `adb`, `sdb` and `dbx`. Note that the use of these debuggers requires the $-g$ option be used with the `cc` compiler. These UNIX debuggers are reasonably good but tend not to be as useful as the multi-window debugging often allowed on smaller machines. Some features can be very cumbersome, and my personal preference is to avoid the use of UNIX debuggers, except to trace segmentation faults. Further information on the use of particular debuggers can be obtained from your local documentation.

UNIX debuggers are useful in tracking down a segmentation fault or arithmetic exception. When invoked after a crash, the debugger will examine the `"core"` file created by the crash, to pinpoint the problem. The fact that segmentation faults cause a core dump can be both useful and annoying. It is useful for use with one of the symbolic debuggers but it can be annoying because it is a large file that you must remember to remove, especially if you are close to your disk quota. A trick to prevent your program from dumping a core file when a segmentation fault occurs is to create a zero size file called "core" in the current directory and set its file protection flags so that it cannot be overwritten. A simple way to achieve this is:

```
touch core
chmod 000 core
```

16.2 The lint source code checker

The lint checker is a UNIX debugging utility that examines the C source code for "obvious" mistakes. Generally speaking, it finds very few of the large number of possible mistakes. Its major use in the past has been to find errors in type checking, particularly of function parameters. The introduction of prototyping compilers has reduced the importance of lint, but lint can still find type errors when using multiple files and independent compilation, whereas compilers fail to.

The lint utility also finds such things as variables not initialized before use, functions failing to return a value (i.e. falling through to the right brace) and functions used inconsistently.

In addition to potential bugs, lint examines the source for wasteful code. For example, lint finds statements not reached and variables declared but not used.

Some implementations of lint are not particularly useful. This is not because the messages produced are incorrect, but because of the deluge of distracting messages that appear, concealing any important messages. It becomes necessary to search through every single message for relevant problems, or to painstakingly modify your code to resolve each message (e.g. delete unused variable declarations).

More recent implementations have greatly solved this problem. A good implementation I have seen prints out only the important messages on a line-by-line basis, saving less dangerous warnings for a summary at the end (e.g. variables not used). This makes lint a very powerful tool without the annoyances. When a program doesn't run as expected, it is worthwhile to test the program with lint before using other debugging methods.

Let us briefly examine how to use lint. lint can be invoked on a single C file, or a number of C source files. When applying lint to only one file from a group of C files, the −u option can be used to avoid some useless messages. Some examples are shown below:

```
lint -u main.c
lint *.c
```

lint defines a preprocessor identifier "lint". This can be used to hide dubious lines of code from lint (i.e. to stop it complaining):

```
#ifndef lint
    ...      /* not checked by lint */
#endif
```

Directives can be given to `lint` from within the program. `lint` recognizes special comments, such as `/*NOTREACHED*/` and `/*NOSTRICT*/`. This is useful to, for example, reduce the level of checking for a particular declaration. For more information on these directives, refer to your manual entry for `lint`.

16.3 Debugging output

A very common method of debugging a C program is placing `printf` statements at strategic positions in the program, either to print out contents of variables, or to indicate entry to a function or loop. This output information is examined to determine the source of a bug.

The main problem with using debugging output is the need to remove these output statements when the program is complete. The preprocessor can be used to aid in the removal of these testing `printf`s. Instead of actually removing them from the source code, they are simply ignored during compilation using the preprocessor's conditional compilation directives (see Section 11.4). A preprocessor symbol (e.g. DEBUG) is defined or left undefined, according to whether debugging is required. The testing `printf` is then placed inside a preprocessor `#ifdef`-`#endif` pair:

```
#ifdef DEBUG
    printf("Entered function print_list\n");
#endif
```

When the program is compiled, the debugging `printf` is only compiled if DEBUG is defined. The DEBUG symbol can either be defined in a header file (which must be included in all files), or defined using an option to the C compiler (e.g. cc -DDEBUG under UNIX). More flexibility can be added by the use of different symbols, indicating different levels of debugging. Also, the `#undef` preprocessor directive can be used to remove debugging code from single files, by placing a `#undef` line just after the `#include` line that includes the file that defines DEBUG.

An alternative method is to use `#if` instead of `#ifdef`:

```
#if DEBUG
    printf("Entered function print_list\n");
#endif
```

The slight difference is that the symbol DEBUG can be `#define`'d to 0 in the header file, rather than the use of `#undef`. Debugging code can be removed by changing the number in a `#define` line from 1 to 0.

16.3.1 A debugging printf function

It becomes annoying to place `#ifdef`-`#endif` pairs around every debugging `printf` statement. A better alternative is to use the preprocessor to automatically delete every occurrence of the debugging `printf` statement using macro expansion, without the need to use a `#ifdef`-`#endif` pair. This can be partially achieved by using a different function for debugging output, which we shall call `dprintf`, and declaring it as a *macro*. The simplest form allows output of a single string:

```
#ifdef DEBUG
#define dprintf(x)  fprintf(stderr, "%s\n", x)
#else
#define dprintf(x)    /* Nothing: calls expand to empty text */
#endif
   ...
dprintf("Entered function print_list");
```

When DEBUG is defined, the dprintf call will expand into an fprintf call; when DEBUG is not defined, the dprintf call will expand into empty text (it is effectively deleted).

The method above has the limitation of only allowing one argument to dprintf. There comes a time when the flexibility of printf is desired in such debugging output. This is not so easily achieved because of the problem that printf accepts a variable number of arguments. There is no way to define a macro to accept a variable number of arguments. A gruesome way is to define a different macro for each number of arguments: dprintf1, dprintf2, etc. There are also a number of tricky ways by abusing the preprocessor, such as:

```
#ifdef DEBUG
#define dprintf  fprintf
#else
#define dprintf   (void)
#endif

dprintf(stderr, "Entered function: main %d %d \n", x, y);
```

This way works normally when DEBUG is turned on but when debugging is turned off, there is no function call. Each dprintf call expands to be a "do-nothing" expression consisting of brackets around an expression where the comma is now the comma operator. The above dprintf statement becomes:

```
(void) (stderr, "Entered function: main %d %d \n", x, y);
```

which should have no effect (unless there are side effects in the arguments). The "(void)" before the expression prevents compilation warnings about discarding a value. This method of eliminating the dprintf statement is not very efficient because the expression may still be evaluated at run-time, although any good optimizer should remove the statement. A slightly better alternative is:

```
#ifdef DEBUG
#define dprintf(x)  fprintf x
#else
#define dprintf(x)       /* expand to nothing */
#endif

dprintf((stderr, "Entered function: main %d %d \n", x, y));
```

The trick is the double level of brackets in the call to dprintf. The extra brackets are needed so that "fprintf x" expands out to have brackets around the parameter list. The preprocessor is smart enough to ignore commas within nested pairs of brackets, and when debugging is turned off the dprintf statements are totally eliminated by the preprocessor.

However, the use of double brackets is not very appealing and it would also be better to leave out the specification of `stderr` (possibly to allow an easy change from `stderr` to `stdout` for debugging output). The solution is to write your own variable arguments list function that calls either `vprintf` or `vfprintf` with its argument list. This is not difficult and the implementation of the `dprintf` function using the macros in `<stdarg.h>` is shown below:

```
#include <stdio.h>
#include <stdarg.h>

void dprintf(char *format, ...)
{
    va_list p;

    va_start(p, format);
    vfprintf(stderr, format, p);
    va_end(p);
}
```

Explanation of the use of the `va_start` and `va_end` macros in `<stdarg.h>` is given in Section 14.6. Unfortunately, when using this method, there appears to be no better way of automatically removing the `dprintf`s than using:

```
#define dprintf (void)
```

and allowing the optimizer to remove the useless code.

There is also a hack solution that uses a non-prototyped function declaration of `dprintf`. Using a non-prototyping definition of `dprintf`, there is no checking of function arguments and you can send as many or as few as desired. Any missing arguments will be garbage, but this is not a problem because, if correct, the format string will never cause `dprintf` to request their use. This method will usually fail for `floats` and `doubles` (`%f`), but it is successful for `%s` if pointers are compatible with `int`. This method has dubious portability, but as it is mainly used in the development phase of a program, portability considerations may not be important.

```
void dprintf(format, x, y, z, any, number)
char *format;
int x, y, z, any, number;
{
    fprintf(stderr, format, x, y, z, any, number);
}
```

Again, the only method of automatically removing the debugging code is:

```
#define dprintf (void)
```

16.3.2 Flushing output buffers

An important point to note is that output to `stdout` is line buffered under UNIX and many other systems. A line of output to `stdout` is not printed until a `\n` is sent to `stdout`. This means that if a program crashes (e.g. segmentation fault), any output in the buffers will not appear on the screen. For this reason, it is a good idea to have a `\n` at the end of every debugging `printf` — otherwise you may be misled as to the location of the crash. The simplest method of avoiding this problem is to use `stderr` which is always unbuffered so that error messages appear immediately. However, there are situations when it is important that output goes to `stdout`. In this case, one method of avoiding the problem of lost output is to use the `setbuf` library function declared in `<stdio.h>` to turn off buffering for `stdout`.

```
#ifdef DEBUG
    setbuf(stdout, NULL);
#endif
```

Alternatively, if you have defined your own debugging `printf` macro, modify it to flush output buffers each time using the `fflush` library function:

```
#define dprintf(str)    printf("%s\n", str), fflush(stdout)
```

16.3.3 Redirecting output

Output redirection is a convenient feature of both the UNIX and DOS environments that can be used to aid in debugging programs that use the debugging output method. When programs generate a large amount of output it can be very useful to redirect this output into a file. After program termination, the output text can be examined using any text editor. To redirect output to a file under either DOS or UNIX, use the notation:

```
a.out >file
```

If a large amount of debugging code is generated, serious consideration must be given to which output stream the debugging output will go to. Using `printf`, the output goes to standard output, `stdout`. If program generates non-debugging output itself, the debugging output can be sent to the standard error output, `stderr`. This is done by changing the `printf(...)` to `fprintf(stderr,...)`. The advantage of sending debugging output to `stderr` is that `stdout` and `stderr` can be redirected separately in most environments. The UNIX environment allows redirection of both output streams, and DOS allows `stdout` to be redirected to a file, whereas `stderr` is fixed to the console. For example, the output redirection shown above will redirect `stdout` to a file, and send `stderr` to the console in both UNIX and DOS environments.

Under UNIX there is a method of throwing away unwanted output. This can be useful to throw away all output to `stdout`, but allow messages from `stderr` to appear on the screen. The special file `/dev/null` is used for this purpose. Any output redirected to this file is thrown away. To throw away output to `stdout` use the command:

```
a.out >/dev/null
```

The `stderr` output stream can be redirected under UNIX, but not under DOS. When program output is to `stderr`, the usual redirection will not redirect the error messages. Only `stdout` will be redirected, and `stderr` will be sent to the terminal as usual. To redirect both `stdout` and `stderr` to the same file, use:

```
a.out >& file
```

Under UNIX, the two streams, `stdout` and `stderr`, can be separately redirected using one of the following notations:

```
(a.out > file1) >& file2    # C-shell (csh)
a.out > file1 2> file2      # Bourne-shell (sh)
```

16.3.4 Changing debugging output without recompilation

When using a symbolic debugger to test a program it can be useful to turn the extra debugging output on and off *during program execution*. Debugging output can be changed at a specified breakpoint in the program. This is facilitated by using a global variable instead of the preprocessor symbol, `DEBUG`. The symbolic debugger can then be used to physically access the location of this variable, and turn debugging on and off. The `#ifdef-#endif` pair is replaced by:

```
if (debug) {
    ...             /* Debugging code */
}
```

Even if a symbolic debugger is not being used, it is possible to alter the `dprintf` function discussed above to allow selective enabling and disabling of different classes of debugging output. There are three main methods of changing debugging output without recompilation:

1. Command line arguments
2. Environment variables
3. Debugging file

These three methods are particularly useful if the debugging `dprintf` statements have been classified into different classes. For example, level 1 could denote `dprintf`s about an insert function and 2 could denote those for a delete function. However, note that the use of different output classes means that the `dprintf` function must be modified to accept another argument, the debugging class.

Using command line arguments requires that the `main` function accept two parameters: `argc` and `argv`. These parameters are used to examine any command line arguments passed to the program (see Section 14.2). For example, the notation:

```
a.out 1 2
```

could be used to set the debugging levels 1 and 2 on (i.e. turn debugging on for both insert and delete functions).

Environment variables, if supported by the operating system, can be used to communicate with the program. The program could examine a single variable to determine what level to turn on (i.e. if the variable is set to 5, turn on up to level 5), or a number of variables could be examined (one per debugging level). The debugging output can be changed by altering environment variables using operating system commands (consult your local documentation).

Finally, a text file containing numbers indicating what classes of printout to enable could be examined at the start of program execution. The program would determine what flags are specified in this text file and set those debugging levels on. In this way it would only be necessary to change this data file to change the debugging output produced by the program.

16.4 Assertions: <assert.h>

The task of debugging can be made much easier by making the program apply tests on itself during program execution. A good way of testing conditions that should be true is the use of assertions. An assertion is made that a condition is true. If it is not true when the assertion is executed, the program prints out an error message indicating which assertion failed and then terminates.

Assertions should only be used to test conditions that should be true, but that might not be if there is a bug in the program. Assertions should not be used to test conditions about input data, because terminating on incorrect data is not very appropriate. In addition, assertions should never attempt to replace an exception-handler. For example, the use of assert to check that the return value of malloc is not NULL is bad style, because this problem will rarely occur during program development. A better solution is an exception-handler that attempts to keep the program running.

There is a standard library assertion macro, assert, defined in the header file <assert.h>. Use of this macro is highly recommended, as it is part of the standard library and its performance is quite adequate — it reports the line and the filename where the error was found (in some implementations, the failed boolean condition is also given in text form). The format of an assertion is just like a function call:

```
assert(condition);
```

The condition can be any arbitrary expression, even containing function calls. This expression is evaluated by the program at run-time.

A nice feature of assertions is that they produce a form of program documentation that is executable. For example, in the code below:

```
#include <assert.h>
if (color == WHITE)
    ...
else {
    assert(color == BLACK);
    ...
}
```

the assertion is similar to a comment stating that color must be BLACK in the else clause. The advantage over using a comment is that if, for some reason, color is neither WHITE nor BLACK, the assertion will detect this error.

When the final version of the program is being produced, the assertions should be removed from the code — this assumes that the final version will have no bugs! The assert macro uses the symbol NDEBUG (no debug) to inhibit assertions. If NDEBUG is defined *before* the line including <assert.h>, assertions become empty statements. NDEBUG can be defined in a command line option to the C compiler or using a #define line before the inclusion of <assert.h>. When assertions are disabled this way, all calls to the assert macro expand to an empty statement.

Where and how often to use assertions are a matter of style. Generally, assertions should be used for impossible situations only. One common use of assertions is to detect `NULL` pointer dereferences. For example, the code:

```
assert(ptr != NULL);
ptr->next = NULL;
```

prevents `ptr` being dereferenced if it is `NULL`. The advantage over just allowing a segmentation fault is that, although the program still crashes, at least the line number causing the crash is known.

16.4.1 Writing your own assert macro

There is nothing special about the `assert` macro in the standard library, and for some additional flexibility it is possible to define your own `assert` macro. For example, it would be possible to have the `assert` macro invoke an exception-handling routine rather than terminating. Another reason for using your own `assert` macro would be to prevent a core dump under UNIX by calling `exit` rather than `abort` to terminate the program (the standard library `assert` macro usually causes a core dump).

One way to define `assert` is shown below. The stringize preprocessor operator, `#`, is used to print out the offending condition in text form. If the stringize operator is not supported in the current implementation, it is not possible to print out the failing condition and the `assert` macro can only report that some assertion failed.

```
#define assert(exp) if (exp); else      \
                 printf("Assertion failed: %s\n", #exp), \
                 exit(1)
```

Defined this way a failed assertion will print the offending condition in text form (using the stringize preprocessor operator), and then terminate.

Note that to use your own `assert` macro, the file must be called `"assert.h"` and the `#include` line must be modified to become:

```
#include "assert.h"
```

Alternatively, it is often possible to leave the `<assert.h>` notation in the program and use a compiler option to cause the compiler to search another directory for header files before searching the system directory. The required compiler option is `-I` under UNIX and in many other implementations.

An improved version of `assert` would output the message to `stderr`, and output the line number and filename of the failed assertion (as done by the standard library `assert` macro). The line number and filename can be found using the special preprocessor macro names: `__LINE__` and `__FILE__`.

```
#define assert(exp) \
       if (exp); else     \
         fprintf(stderr,     \
             "Line %d, File '%s', Assertion failed: %s\n", \
                __LINE__, __FILE__, #exp), \
         exit(1)
```

If assertions are to be removed after program development, the preprocessor can be used to help. Using the method below, assertions will be ignored if NDEBUG is defined.

```
#ifndef NDEBUG
#define assert(exp)      /* etc. as given above */
#else
#define assert(exp)      /* do nothing */
#endif
```

16.5 Self-testing code

During the development of a program, it can be very useful to have the program check itself for errors. The program checks for any incorrect conditions, and if they occur, some action is taken. During program development, an appropriate action could be to print out an error message and terminate.

When program development is complete, these checks can be removed. Alternatively, the checks can remain, and a more useful exception-handling routine installed using the setjmp library function (see Section 4.14). Instead of exiting the program when a problem is encountered, this exception handler is called using the longjmp library function. Almost anything is better than a crash.

Complex data structures are good candidates for self-checking code. The program could perform consistency checks on the data structures, after each insertion and deletion. Often some extra data is useful to compare against. For example, an incremental count of names in a symbol table can be maintained by incrementing on insertion and decrementing on deletion. This count variable can then be compared against a function that counts the number of names actually stored in the symbol table data structure. This idea is illustrated below:

```
      insert(table, node);           /* Insert node into table */
#if DEBUG
      count++;                                /* update count */
      if (count != count_elements(table)) {   /* correct? */
         ...                                  /* error message */
      }
#endif
```

When this self-checking code indicates an error, the first place to look is in this self-checking code. It is at least as likely to be wrong as the data structure functions and nothing is worse than checking an entire insert function only to discover that the sense of the condition in the checking if statement was wrong!

16.6 Robust code

Some bugs can be caught with a little forward planning. The idea here is to not allow bugs to creep into programs by using techniques that are less error-prone. A simple safety net can be used even in simple expressions. Consider counting down from n to 0 by:

```
      for (i = n; i != 0; i--)
         ...
```

This relies on an important assumption: that n is not negative. If n is negative, an (almost) infinite loop occurs (overflow will finally cause i to become positive again). The problem is the test for *equality* with zero. A slightly safer method would be to use:

```
for (i = n; i > 0; i--)
    ...
```

The other aspect of robust code is to write programs that continue to function even after an error has occurred. A program should be able to recover from errors such as failure to write to a file, running out of memory for malloc or even a segmentation fault. File errors and lack of memory must be checked on each call to a file function or to malloc. The return value of these functions indicates the presence of a problem. A reasonably simple way to check for a zero return value from malloc (indicating failure to allocate memory) is given below. The action on failure in the macro given is to call a function that handles the exception, possibly by printing a message and restarting the program by jumping to the start using longjmp.

```
extern void *malloc_tmp;    /* temporary variable */
#define malloc(n) \
    ((malloc_tmp = malloc(n)) ? malloc_tmp : (void*)error())
```

Note that in non-ANSI compilers the definition of the macro in terms of itself is not possible, and a different macro definition is needed. Note also that the (void*) type cast is necessary because the ternary operator's return type depends on both the second and third operand. There is a minor problem with this method: the need to define the variable malloc_tmp only once. Hence one file (e.g. "main.c") should contain the global variable definition "void * malloc_tmp;".

A program can often continue even after a segmentation fault or arithmetic exception simply by trapping or ignoring the signals that these failures cause. This is discussed further in Section 16.8.

16.7 Encapsulating dynamic memory allocation

The use of the dynamic memory allocation functions, malloc, calloc, realloc and free, is fraught with danger because these functions perform no error checking. Problems that can occur are blocks being freed twice, blocks being freed that were never allocated by one of these functions (e.g. mistakenly freeing an array variable) and accessing a block that has already been freed (i.e. a dangling reference). These errors cause immediate problems, but there is one problem with less immediate consequences. If a program allocates many blocks of memory but never frees them, the program will eventually run out of available memory, and probably fail. This problem of the accumulation of unused memory (often called *garbage*) is called a *memory leak*.

One reasonably simple method of detecting problems with memory allocation is to add your own error-checking front end onto the existing functions, and such a front end is presented below. The front end maintains a list of allocated blocks, and when a call to free or realloc passes an address, these functions check that the address is of a block that is currently allocated. If the block's address is not on the list, this is an instance of one of the two problems above related to freeing a non-allocated block.

The implementation of the new memory allocation functions is quite straightforward. The new `malloc` and `calloc` functions store information about the allocated block on a linked list of blocks, as well as actually duplicating the functionality of the real functions (i.e. calling the real `malloc` or `calloc` to get the address of a new allocated block). Both `free` and `realloc` check that the address is actually an allocated block and terminate the program with an error message if it is not valid. If the address is valid, the block is removed from the list, freed using the real `free` function. The `realloc` function also allocates a new block in a manner identical to the new `malloc` function.

A function called `print_block_list` is provided that prints out the current status of the heap, indicating how many blocks are available. To detect a memory leak, this function can be called from the program being tested at the end of execution (e.g. as an `atexit` function). If any blocks are currently allocated, their source can be traced because the line numbers of the statements creating the blocks are recorded. Thus, to detect a memory leak, the last few lines of the `main` function might well be:

```
#if DEBUG_MEMORY
    print_block_list();
#endif
```

The `print_block_list` function can be called at any point in the program where information about the current state of memory allocation is useful.

Unfortunately, one common problem with memory allocation cannot be detected automatically using the method here. The use of wayward pointers from dangling references or array references out of bounds cannot be as easily detected as the freeing of unallocated blocks. To provide a partial solution, two functions are provided to check that pointers are valid. The `check_pointer` function checks if the pointer points to the start of some block and can be used to trap dangling references. The `check_address` function checks if the pointer is inside some block, and can be used to detect bad array references. However, it is the responsibility of the programmer to explicitly check every pointer dereference, which requires code such as:

```
#if DEBUG_MEMORY
    check_pointer(p);    /* Check p points to a valid block */
#endif
    *p = s;              /* Dereference p */
```

The addition of an error-checking front end causes errors to be detected, but does slow down the program and the error checking should be removed for the final version. Thus the front end should be easy to add to the program and easy to remove. A simple method of achieving this is to use the preprocessor to change all calls to `malloc`, `calloc`, `free` and `realloc`. The inclusion of the header file "my_malloc.h", as shown below, causes all calls to these functions to translate to the new functions `my_malloc`, `my_calloc`, `my_free` and `my_realloc`. Extra arguments are also added to pass the line number and filename to the new functions. The header file also defines the functions `print_block_list`, `check_pointer` and `check_address` for the programmer to use in the program.

Debugging techniques

```
/*-------------------------------------------------------------*/
/* MY_MALLOC.H: debugging dynamic allocation functions        */
/*-------------------------------------------------------------*/
#if DEBUG_MEMORY         /* Only include if DEBUG_MEMORY is set */

#define malloc(size)          my_malloc(size,__FILE__,__LINE__)
#define calloc(size,num)      my_calloc(size,num,__FILE__,__LINE__)
#define free(p)               my_free(p,__FILE__,__LINE__)
#define realloc(p,size)       my_realloc(p,size,__FILE__,__LINE__)

              /* check that p is pointing inside some block */
#define check_reference(p)    check_address(p,__FILE__,__LINE__)

              /* check that p is pointing to a block */
#define check_pointer(p)      check_valid(p,__FILE__,__LINE__,4)

void *my_malloc(int size,char *filename,int line);
void *my_calloc(int size,int num,char *filename,int line);
void my_free(void *p,char *filename,int line);
void *my_realloc(void *p,int newsize,char *filename,int line);
void print_block_list(void);
int check_valid(void *address,char *filename,int line,int type);
int check_address(void *address,char *filename,int line);
#endif
```

Note that the header file inclusion only sets the error-checking on if the preprocessor symbol DEBUG_MEMORY is defined before the inclusion of "my_malloc.h", and the error checking can be used in the manner:

```
#define DEBUG_MEMORY  1    /* 1 if want allocation debugging */
#include "my_malloc.h"
```

The error checking can be removed as simply as setting DEBUG_MEMORY to 0.

When the debugging is required, the source file containing the function definitions must be compiled and linked with the rest of the program. The source code for the function definitions is given below:

```
/*-------------------------------------------------------------*/
/*  MY_MALLOC.C: debugging dynamic allocation functions       */
/*-------------------------------------------------------------*/

#include <stdio.h>
#include <stdlib.h>
#include <string.h>
#include <assert.h>

#include "my_malloc.h"
#undef malloc
#undef calloc
#undef realloc
#undef free

/*-------------------------------------------------------------*/
/*  COMPILATION SWITCHES                                      */
/*-------------------------------------------------------------*/

#define EXIT_ON_ERROR  1    /* 1 if want to exit on error */
                            /* 0 if try to keep going */

#define MARK_INACTIVE  1    /* 0 if don't want nodes to be retained */
                            /* 1 if garbage from list nodes is ok */

/*-------------------------------------------------------------*/
```

```c
#define FALSE 0                     /* A pseudo-Boolean type, bool */
#define TRUE  1
#define bool int

/*--------------------------------------------------------------------*/

void print_block_list(void);
bool check_valid(void *address, char *file, int line, int type);
bool check_address(void *address, char *file, int line);
static void add_to_list(void *p,int size,char *file,int line,int type);
static void remove_block(void *address);
static void error(char *mesg, char *file, int line, int type);

/*--------------------------------------------------------------------*/

#define MALLOC    0         /* Possible values of 'type' field below */
#define CALLOC    1
#define REALLOC   2
#define FREE      3
#define USER_CALL 4                 /* User call from outside */

char *type_string[] = { "malloc", "calloc", "realloc", "free" };

struct node {
    char file[20];         /* Filename of allocation call */
    int line;              /* Line number of allocation call */
    int size;              /* Size of the allocated block */
    void *address;         /* Address of the real allocated block */
    int type;              /* Block from malloc, calloc or realloc? */
    bool active;           /* Flag if block currently active, or if */
                           /*          has already been freed       */
    struct node *next;     /* Linked list pointer */
};
struct node *list = NULL;   /* Head of linked list of header blocks */

/*--------------------------------------------------------------------*/
/* MY_MALLOC:  Front end to the malloc() library function            */
/*--------------------------------------------------------------------*/

void *my_malloc(int size, char *file, int line)
{
    void *p;

    p = malloc(size);               /* call the real malloc */
    if (p != NULL)
        add_to_list(p, size, file, line, MALLOC);
    return p;
}

/*--------------------------------------------------------------------*/
/* MY_CALLOC:  Front end to the calloc() library function            */
/*--------------------------------------------------------------------*/

void *my_calloc(int size, int num, char *file, int line)
{
    void *p;

    p = calloc(size, num);          /* call the real calloc */
    if (p != NULL)
        add_to_list(p, size * num, file, line, CALLOC);
    return p;
}

/*--------------------------------------------------------------------*/
/* MY_FREE:    Front end to the free() library function              */
/*--------------------------------------------------------------------*/

void my_free(void *p, char *file, int line)
```

Debugging techniques

```c
{
    if (!check_valid(p, file, line, FREE))
        return;
    remove_block(p);
    free(p);                /* Call the real free */
}

/*--------------------------------------------------------------------*/
/* MY_REALLOC:  Front end to the realloc() library function          */
/*--------------------------------------------------------------------*/

void *my_realloc(void *p, int newsize, char *file, int line)
{
    void *new;

    if (!check_valid(p, file, line, REALLOC))
        return NULL;        /* return NULL for bad reallocation */
    new = realloc(p, newsize);
    remove_block(p);
    add_to_list(new, newsize, file, line, REALLOC);
    return new;
}

/*--------------------------------------------------------------------*/
/*   ADD_TO_LIST:    Add new header node info onto linked list       */
/*--------------------------------------------------------------------*/

static void add_to_list(void *p,int size,char *file,int line,int type)
{
    struct node *new;

    new = malloc(sizeof(struct node));    /* Make new header node */
    new->address = p;
    new->size = size;
    strcpy(new->file, file);
    new->line = line;
    new->type = type;
    new->active = TRUE;     /* Has not been freed yet */
    new->next = list;       /* Add new header node to front of list */
    list = new;
}

/*--------------------------------------------------------------------*/
/*   REMOVE_BLOCK: Remove header node for a block, or mark inactive  */
/*--------------------------------------------------------------------*/

static void remove_block(void *address)
{
    struct node *prev, *temp;

    for (prev = NULL, temp = list;
         temp != NULL && temp->address != address;
         prev = temp, temp = temp->next)
        ;   /* empty loop */
    assert(temp != NULL);   /* always find the block on list */

#if MARK_INACTIVE
    temp->active = FALSE;   /* Dont really free the block, */
                            /*    just mark block as freed */
#else
    if (prev == NULL)       /* Delete block from the linked list */
        list = temp->next;  /* Delete from front of linked list */
    else
        prev->next = temp->next;  /* Delete from middle or end */
    free(temp);
#endif
}
```

290   Chapter 16

```c
/*-------------------------------------------------------------------*/
/*   ERROR:     Print out error message, filename, line number       */
/*-------------------------------------------------------------------*/
static void error(char *mesg, char *file, int line, int type)
{
    fprintf(stderr, "ALLOCATION ERROR:  %s\n", mesg);
    fprintf(stderr, "                   ");

    if (type != USER_CALL)
        fprintf(stderr, "Call to %s: ", type_string[type]);
    fprintf(stderr, "File '%s', Line %d\n", file, line);

#if EXIT_ON_ERROR
    print_block_list();
    exit(1);
#endif
}

/*-------------------------------------------------------------------*/
/*   PRINT_BLOCK_LIST:    Print current status of the heap           */
/*-------------------------------------------------------------------*/
void print_block_list(void)
{
    struct node *temp;
    int count = 0;

    fprintf(stderr, "\n         CURRENT HEAP STATUS \n");
    for (temp = list; temp != NULL; temp = temp->next) {
        if (temp->active) {
            count++;
            fprintf(stderr,
                "%s: Address %p, Size %d, File: %s, Line %d\n",
                type_string[temp->type],
                temp->address, temp->size, temp->file, temp->line);
        }
    }
    if (count == 0)
        fprintf(stderr, "No blocks on heap\n");
    fprintf(stderr, "\n");
}

/*-------------------------------------------------------------------*/
/*   CHECK_VALID:   Check an address to be freed is actually valid   */
/*-------------------------------------------------------------------*/
bool check_valid(void *address, char *file, int line, int type)
{
    struct node *temp;
    bool found_inactive = FALSE;

    for (temp = list; temp != NULL; temp = temp->next) {
        if (temp->address == address) {
            if (temp->active)
                return TRUE;
            else
                found_inactive = TRUE;
        }
    }

    if (found_inactive) {              /* Found block but already freed */
        if (type == USER_CALL)
            error("Pointer to block already freed", file, line, type);
        else
            error("Memory block freed twice", file, line, type);
    }
    else {                             /* Not valid (not on list of blocks) */
```

```
            if (type == USER_CALL)
                error("Pointer not an allocated block", file, line, type);
            else
                error("Block freed was never allocated", file, line, type);
    }
    return FALSE;          /* Not a legal block */
}

/*------------------------------------------------------------------*/
/*   CHECK_ADDRESS:    Check an address is IN one of the blocks     */
/*------------------------------------------------------------------*/

bool check_address(void *address, char *file, int line)
{
    struct node *temp;

    for (temp = list; temp != NULL; temp = temp->next) {
        if (temp->active && address >= temp->address
                         && address < temp->address + temp->size)
            return TRUE;                    /* Address is in this block */
    }

    /* Address is not valid */

    error("Pointer not inside block", file, line, USER_CALL);
    return FALSE;
}
```

16.8 Using signals for debugging

Signals are an advanced feature of C that can be used for debugging purposes. They are particularly useful under UNIX where they are always supported. The DOS environment supports the `SIGINT` signal for the keyboard interrupt `<ctrl-c>`, but does not support keyboard interrupts for `<ctrl-\>` or `<ctrl-z>`.

There are two ways that signals can be used for debugging. The first is to set up a signal handler for `SIGINT`, the interrupt signal generated by `<ctrl-c>`, so that this handler prints out debugging information whenever the user presses `<ctrl-c>`. The second use is for trapping segmentation faults, arithmetic exceptions and other fatal errors by trapping the signals that these errors produce. Before discussing these methods in more detail, a brief introduction to signals is given here. Signals are covered fully in Section 12.6 and Section 19.8.

The header file `<signal.h>` defines the `signal` function which is used to catch signals, and also defines symbolic constants representing every type of signal. The `signal` function is declared as:

```
typedef void (*ptr_to_fn)(int);
ptr_to_fn signal(int sig, ptr_to_fn handler);
```

such that it sets the signal handler for the signal specified as `sig` to be the function passed as the second argument. The second argument can also be one of `SIG_IGN` and `SIG_DFL` which are default handlers declared in `<signal.h>` that ignore the signal or reinstate the default handler, respectively. The return value of `signal` is the old handler for the signal or the special value `SIG_ERR` if the signal handler cannot be installed, but this return value is often ignored.

When a signal occurs, such as that generated by the user pressing <ctrl-c>, the handler is invoked for that signal. The handler executes and then returns to the last instruction executed to continue execution. Thus, signals are almost like interrupts, and it is this feature that the first debugging method makes use of.

16.8.1 Using keyboard interrupts

The code below illustrates how to set up a handler for the <ctrl-c> interrupt (i.e. the SIGINT signal). The debugging function prints out the data currently in the array (which must be a global variable to allow the handler to access it). Another possible debugging function would be print_block_list, as defined in the previous section, to print out the current status of the memory heap.

```
#include <stdio.h>
#include <stdlib.h>
#include <signal.h>

int arr[10];                  /* Array is Global variable */

void handler()                /* Non-prototyping stops type warning */
{
    int i;
                              /* Print out debugging info */
    for (i = 0; i <= 10; i++)
        printf("%d ", arr[i]);
    printf("\n");
}

main()
{
    int i;

    signal(SIGINT, handler);
    printf("Running ....\n");

    while (1) {
        for (i = 0; i <= 10; i++) {
            arr[i] = rand() % 100;
        }
    }
}
```

Note that the handler function is defined to accept no arguments using the non-ANSI style of function declaration to avoid annoying type warnings from the compiler.

Trapping SIGINT means that <ctrl-c> no longer stops the program. It can be stopped under UNIX using <ctrl-\>, but this causes a core dump. Under DOS the program can usually be stopped using another key sequence, such as <ctrl-break>. An alternative that would allow <ctrl-c> to still work would be to trap the SIGQUIT signal generated by <ctrl-\> or SIGTSTP generated by <ctrl-z>.

Unfortunately, there is one problem with this approach of using signals to dump debugging output. Although signals act mostly like interrupts, there are a few situations where the last instruction is not restarted. Some UNIX system calls, including read and write, will fail and return −1 and set errno to EINTR if they are interrupted by a signal. This means that when using this signal-trapping approach for debugging it is important to examine the return value of some functions for which the return value is usually ignored, such as input and output functions.

Finally, instead of using keyboard interrupts, a call to the `raise` library function generates a signal passed as its argument (i.e. `raise(SIGINT)` causes the same interrupt as `<ctrl-c>`). Thus, `raise` can be used to indirectly call the debugging function from within the program. However, this use of `raise` is not recommended because a simple function call to a debugging function is equivalent and far more readable.

16.8.2 Trapping segmentation faults

A bug in a program will often cause the program to crash. Under UNIX these crashes are usually either segmentation faults, arithmetic exceptions or bus errors. DOS implementations may support some of these signals (refer to your compiler documentation). Segmentation faults and bus errors can be caught because they generate the signals `SIGSEGV` and `SIGBUS`, respectively. Floating point arithmetic exceptions can be caught using the signal `SIGFPE`, and integer exceptions can be caught using the signal `SIGTRAP` (although `SIGTRAP` also has other meanings). Note that arithmetic overflow does not always cause an exception, and often cannot be detected.

Upon detection of these errors, the signal handler can choose from a number of actions. The handler can use `longjmp` to jump to a safe location (e.g. in the `main` function) where the program can continue. This improves the robustness of the program by preventing a crash, but recovery from the error may not be easy since the cause of the error is not known. Alternatively, the handler can change the program counter to skip over the instruction causing the error. This is very advanced and the reader is referred to the manual entries for `signal` and `sigvec`.

The most common choice of action is to print out some debugging information and terminate using `exit`. This is particularly useful during the development and testing of the program. The debugging information that can be produced depends on the program, and could include printing the current heap status (as in the previous section), displaying a data structure or printing an internal buffer. This use of catching signals is shown below, although no debugging information is actually printed:

```
#include <stdio.h>
#include <stdlib.h>
#include <signal.h>

void handler(int sig, int code, struct sigcontext *p)
{
    switch (sig) {
        case SIGFPE:
            printf("Floating point exception\n");
            break;

        case SIGSEGV:
            printf("Segmentation fault\n");
            break;

        case SIGTRAP:
            printf("Overflow or divide by zero error\n");
            break;
```

```
            case SIGBUS:
                printf("Bus error\n");
                break;
        }
                    /* Print debugging information here */
        exit(1);
}
main()
{
    char *p = NULL;

    signal(SIGSEGV, handler);    /* Segmentation fault */
    signal(SIGFPE, handler);     /* Floating point exception */
    signal(SIGBUS, handler);     /* Bus error */
    signal(SIGTRAP, handler);    /* Overflow or divide by zero */

    *p = 1;    /* Dereference NULL - causes segmentation fault */
}
```

16.9 Further reading

Although debugging programs is a huge area, there appears to be relatively little written about debugging C programs. The book by Anderson and Anderson contains a good chapter on debugging techniques under C, as does the book by Kochan and Wood. Koenig's book is also an interesting discussion of programming errors in C.

> ANDERSON, Paul, and ANDERSON, Gail, *Advanced C: Tips and Techniques*, Hayden Books, 1988.
>
> KOCHAN, Stephen G., and WOOD, Patrick H., *Topics in C Programming (revised edition)*, John Wiley and Sons, 1991.
>
> KOENIG, Andrew, *C Traps and Pitfalls*, Addison-Wesley, 1989.

16.10 Exercises

1. If the `lint` utility (or a similar source code checker) is available, run it on one or more of your own C programs. Explain the cause of all warning messages and modify the program so that no warnings are produced.

2. Write a `dprintf` debugging function that accepts an extra argument, the debugging *level*, thus allowing finer control over debugging output. Implement the debugging levels as an array of boolean flags, each set to true if that debugging level should produce output. How can you remove the debugging code (i.e. calls to `dprintf`) when it is no longer required?

3. (advanced) Design a method of controlling debugging output without recompilation by specifying debugging flags in a text file (one flag for each debugging level).

4. What is the difference between the use of `#if` and `#ifdef` for including or ignoring debugging code. What is the effect of each of the directives:

```
#if DEBUG
#ifdef DEBUG
```

with the following definitions of DEBUG?

a) No definition.
b) `#define DEBUG 1`
c) `#define DEBUG 0`
d) `#define DEBUG /* nothing */`
e) `#undef DEBUG`
f) `cc -DDEBUG`   (UNIX only)

5. Modify the dynamic memory allocation debugging functions in Section 16.7 to install `print_block_list` as an `atexit` function (try to do so in a way that does not require a program using these functions to call `atexit` explicitly).

6. The `strdup` function is a common library function (not included in the ANSI standard library) that should also be handled by the memory allocation encapsulation functions in Section 16.7. If it is supported by your system, write a function equivalent to the `strdup` library function and include it as a debugging function (and add a macro in the header file).

7. (advanced) The same approach used to encapsulate memory allocation can be used to trap another less common problem — running out of file pointers. A file pointer is used up when a file is opened using `fopen`, but not closed using `fclose`. If a program opens new files but does not close them, it can happen that a call to `fopen` will fail because no more file pointers are available. Design a suite of functions to replace `fopen` and `fclose` that detect this problem.

8. Consult your local documentation to determine what types of signals are generated for various erroneous situations. For example, do NULL dereferences, arithmetic overflows, or division by zero cause signals? Type in the program in Section 16.8.2 and add statements that purposely create these error conditions (e.g. keep adding to a number until it overflows).

Chapter 17
Program style

Style of programming is a very personal issue. People program differently, using variable names meaningful to them and different types of comments (or lack thereof). Despite these differences, there are a number of issues that are fairly standard throughout the C programming community. This chapter examines the stylistic choices available to C programmers when writing a program.

There are some "golden rules" for good programming. First and foremost, code should do what it is supposed to do (this includes agreeing with its documentation!). Well-written code should be modular, commented, structured and readable. It should make use of constants, user-defined types and have no huge functions. Although many important stylistic issues are examined in this chapter, one very important matter is not covered here — the organization of header files is covered in Chapter 13.

In addition to these guidelines for writing good programs there are a number of details about formatting C code that can go a long way towards making a program more readable. The main areas here are the use of indentation for major control structures and the use of spaces to separate operations in expressions.

Under UNIX there are a number of tools available to produce nicely formatted C code automatically. Some of these pretty printers are `cb` (stands for "C beautifier") and `indent`. However, be warned that there may be bugs in these tools which destroy your code. For example, my version of `indent` adds spaces around the minus sign in constants such as `3.0e-3`, and this change won't even cause a compilation error!

17.1 Comments

Comments are a very important part of the program. There is no completely accepted format for comments. One fairly common style of commenting is blocks of comments before functions. These are usually placed in blocks of stars or dashes to make them stand out. In addition, lines of stars or dashes are commonly used to separate major parts of the program.

Where to place comments in a program is a matter of preference. Good practice is to comment each major construct (i.e. `if` statement or loop). It is also worthwhile to comment each `else`, so as to know which `if` the `else` applies to:

```
if (x < y)
   ...
else    /* x >= y */
   ...
```

Special features of the program should be commented. For example, the use of falling through in a `switch` statement should be commented to indicate that it is not an occurrence of the "missing `break`" bug. Another special feature that should be commented is an empty loop because it might be an instance of the "accidental empty loop" bug:

```
for (sum = 0, i = 1; i <= n; sum += i, i++)
    ;      /* empty loop */
```

The semicolon is placed on a separate line to emphasize the use of the empty loop.

When commenting a line of code, there are a number of places where comments can appear. Comments should be placed at the end of the line of code, or on their own separate line (before the statement). Comments should *not* appear in the middle of a line or on a separate line *after* the statement. If comments are placed to the right of the code, readability may be better if the comments are not too close to the C code and if the comments line up at the left as much as possible. This means that the comments can be read separately to the code. Comments on their own line should be separated from the code by blank lines.

```
/* This comment is on a line by itself */

if (i > 0)      /* This comment is to the right of the code */
    i++;        /* This comment lines up at the left */
```

Longer comments are best handled as separate lines. For even better readability, longer comments can be placed in a box of stars or dashes, or enhanced with a column of stars:

```
/*-------------------------------------------------------*/
/*   This is a box of comments                           */
/*-------------------------------------------------------*/

/*  This is
 *  another common
 *  method of formatting
 *  large comments
 */
```

17.2 Indentation

Because the C compiler ignores whitespace, it is useful to add spaces or tabs to make a program more readable. Generally, the bodies of loops and `if` statements should be indented to show the control structure of the program. Hence, an `if-else` statement inside a `while` loop should look like:

```
    while (x > y) {
        if (x == 0) {
            printf("x == 0\n");
        }
        else {
            printf("x != 0\n");
        }
    }
```

The body of a function, including both the variable declarations and the executable code, should all be indented from the left margin. Instead of:

```
int count(int n)
{
int i;

for (i = 1; i <= n; i++)
    printf("%d\n");
}
```

use indentation to make the extent of a function immediately clear, as below:

```
int count(int n)
{
    int i;

    for (i = 1; i <= n; i++)
        printf("%d\n");
}
```

When indenting code there is a choice between the use of tabs and spaces. Tabs can cause the indentation to go too far inwards, although tab stops can usually be set to a small number of spaces to avoid this problem. Tabs can also cause problems when porting program text between machines, if the two machines have different tab settings. However, a tab is only one keypress per column, whereas spaces require more than one.

17.3 Braces

When writing C programs there is a choice to be made about the use of braces in major control structures. The most common C style, as used in this book, is to place the opening left brace on the same line as the keyword and line up the closing right brace with the C keyword (i.e. `if`, `for`, etc). An example of this formatting is shown below:

```
    for (i = 0; i <= 10; i++) {
        printf("%d\n", i);
    }
```

The other main alternative is to place the opening left brace on a new line, indented from the C keyword. The loop body and the right brace are then aligned with this left brace, as shown below:

```
    for (i = 0; i <= 10; i++)
        {
        printf("%d\n", i);
        }
```

Another variation is to align both braces under the keyword starting the construct and indent all the statements:

```
for (i = 0; i <= 10; i++)
{
    printf("%d\n", i);
}
```

A related issue is which style of braces to use for function definitions. The style used in this book is to place the left brace starting the function body on a separate line. However, some programmers prefer consistency with other blocks and put the left brace on the same line as the function parameters.

Another style issue about braces is whether to use them for single statements in an `if` statement or the body of a loop. For example, should a program use:

```
for (p = head; p != NULL; p = p->next) {
    visit(p);
}
```

when the braces are unnecessary and lengthen the source code? The alternative is:

```
for (p = head; p != NULL; p = p->next)
    visit(p);
```

Generally, I recommend the use of the unnecessary braces due to the prevention of problems with macros, and the ease of adding new statements to a block. However, it does make programs longer and sometimes less readable.

17.4 Blank lines

Blank lines are often used to aid readability by separating sections of the program. For example, blank lines will often separate `#include` lines, `#define` lines and `typedef` declarations placed at the start of a file, as below:

```
#include <stdio.h>
#include <stdlib.h>

#define MAX 10
#define MIN 0

typedef int data_type;
```

Blank lines also usually appear between function definitions, and can be used to space out large functions. It is good practice to surround long loops or large `if` statements with blank lines. One particularly important use of blank lines is in separating local variable declarations from executable statements in the function body.

17.5 Spaces

Another stylistic issue is how many spaces should be used in expressions. A particular example of this is the assignment statement, such as:

```
x = 3;
```

Without the spaces around the = operator, the statement looks untidy:

```
x=3;
```

If the expressions on either side of the assignment operator were more complicated, the spaces would be important to improve the readability.

The use of spaces in the assignment statement above is a special case of a general rule — all binary operators should have spaces around them. Thus all arithmetic operators, logical operators and relational operators should have spaces surrounding them. For example, a program should use a + b instead of a+b. Some examples of good spacing are shown below:

```
x = a + b;
if (x <= 10 && x >= 0)
```

As with all general rules, there are exceptions — the `str.field` and `ptr->field` binary operators should have no spaces around the "." or the "->".

Unary operators should have no space between the operator and the operand. Hence, the statements below illustrate correct spacing:

```
i--;
ptr = &i;
comp = ~x;
```

The ternary operator is also usually padded with spaces around the question mark and the colon, as shown below:

```
max = (x > y) ? x : y;
```

There are a number of other places where spaces are usually placed. There should be a space *after every comma* wherever a comma is used — function declarations, variable declarations, function argument lists, the comma operator, `enum` declarations:

```
void my_fn(int x, int y);    /* Space in parameter list */
int i, j;                    /* Space in variable list */
printf("%d\n", n);           /* Space in argument list */
enum {FALSE, TRUE} bool;     /* Space in constant list */
```

A space is usually placed after an `if`, `while` or `for` keyword as shown below:

```
if (x > y)
```

However, there should not be a space immediately after a function name in a function call (or a function definition).

The header of a `for` loop is another situation where spacing should be used. There should be a space after every semicolon separating the expressions, but not before the semicolons (like normal English usage):

```
for (i = 1; i < 10; i++)
```

Finally, in all large constructs there should be a space before the left brace:

```
if (...) {
for (...) {
```

The spacing guidelines are summarized below. Note that different programmers may use slightly different styles, but these guidelines are commonly practised.

- Spaces around binary operators (except . and ->).
- No spaces for unary operators.
- Spaces around ? and : for the ternary operator (?:).
- Spaces after commas in argument lists, parameter lists and argument lists.
- Spaces after keywords: `if`, `while`, `for`, `switch`, `do`.
- No space after function names.
- Spaces after semicolons in a `for` loop.
- Spaces before a left brace.

17.6 Variable names

Any names can be used in a computer program for variables and constants. However, there are some frequently used conventions. Symbolic constants (as in `#define`) are usually in upper case letters. Type names, as defined by `typedef`, often have the suffix "_t" or "_type" to distinguish them from variable names.

Variable names should reflect their use. A long name, such as one containing a number of words separated by underscores, is most useful. For example, use `high_score` rather than h.

Although the overuse of single letter names is not recommended, a single letter is often adequate for common types of variables. For example, using `i` for a `for` loop variable is common and convenient. Similarly, `p` for a much-used pointer variable is common. As long as there are not many of these variables in each section, there should be little problem with confusion.

It is good practice to use underscores or capital letters in long variable names for readability. For example, both the use of underscores in `first_node_of_list` and the use of capitals in `FirstNodeOfList` are easier to read than `firstnodeoflist`.

17.7 Multiple else-if statements

The `else-if` combination is a common construct that is not actually a part of the language, but a result of it. The indentation shown below is good style, as it indicates the control flow correctly:

```
if (c == 'a') {
    ...
}
else if (c == 'b') {
    ...
}
else if (c == 'c') {
    ...
}
else {
    ...             /* Default, none-of-the-above */
}
```

17.8 Efficiency and compactness versus readability

There are many ways to write C code. The two extremes are to write it to run very efficiently using compact expressions, or to write it nicely for the sake of readability. Generally, I recommend the latter approach because the improvements to efficiency are usually only marginal and are far outweighted by the problems of debugging unreadable code. This section presents some of the alternatives available when coding programs in C.

In C, it is often easy to do more than one action in one statement. However, it is easier to understand a program if all actions are separated. Hence there is a choice between separating logical actions for readability, or combining them for efficiency. For example, the statement:

```
y = x++;         /* Two actions combined */
```

is more readable when separated into two distinct statements:

```
y = x;           /* Separating the two actions */
x++;
```

Another common abbreviation is the omission of zero constants or NULL from comparisons. For example, there is the choice between the more readable statements:

```
if (ptr != NULL)
if (ptr == NULL)
```

and the more compact notation:

```
if (ptr)         /* if not NULL */
if (!ptr)        /* if NULL */
```

Another common use of terse notation is in the combination of assignments inside conditional expressions. For example, when opening a file using fopen it is possible to assign the file pointer to a variable as well as testing for the error condition, as below:

```
if ((fp = fopen("infile", "r")) == NULL) {
    ...   /* Error occurred */
}
```

The conditional test could be even further abbreviated by replacing the use of NULL with the ! operator:

```
if (!(fp = fopen("infile", "r")))
```

Naturally, the more readable alternative is:

```
fp = fopen("infile", "r");
if (fp == NULL) {
    ...   /* Error occurred */
}
```

When using loops there is often an alternative between placing some code in the loop body, or performing all computation in the loop header. For example, the readable method of computing the sum of numbers 1 to n is:

```
sum = 0;
for (i = 1; i <= n; i++)
    sum += i;
```

but it is also possible to perform all computations in the loop header, by using the comma operator and an empty loop as the loop body:

```
for (sum = 0, i = 1; i <= n; sum += i, i++);     /* empty loop */
```

The ternary operator (?:) makes it possible to write very terse code by replacing `if` statements with a single expression. For example, instead of:

```
if (x > y)
    max = x;
else
    max = y;
```

the ternary operator can be used to compute the maximum in one step:

```
max = x > y ? x : y;
```

All of the style choices covered in this section illustrate the flexibility of C. There is no generally accepted standard for writing C code and the programmer can choose a very readable style or a very terse style.

17.9 The goto controversy

To use `goto` or not to use `goto`, that is the question. There are arguments for and against, and supporters of both views! The `goto` statement is never "needed" in the strict sense, as the other loop constructs can be used to do anything that `goto` can. Overuse of `goto` can lead to hard-to-understand "spaghetti" code, with branches going all over the place. However, under some conditions `goto` can be more efficient and under a few conditions it can actually enhance readability!

The best answer to the question of whether to use `goto` is to use `goto` rarely. It is best used for exceptional conditions — for example, use `goto` to exit from a deeply nested statement when some special case is detected. This saves setting and checking a boolean variable at all the nested levels.

C has a number of control flow statements that are similar in effect to a `goto` statement. Notably, the `break`, `continue` and `return` statements all force a type of unnatural jump. Although the jump is more restricted than `goto`, the overuse of these statements can lead to the same problems as the use of `goto`. It is good style to use `break` and `continue` as little as possible. It can also be advantageous to have only one `return` statement per function, at the end of the function. When debugging the program it is useful to know where the value is being returned from and this is obvious when there is only one `return` statement.

17.10 Retaining unnecessary else clauses

The use of abnormal exiting of loops and functions using the `return`, `break` and `continue` statements and calls to function such as `exit`, can lead to control flow that is difficult to understand. For this reason, it is recommended to retain the `else` clauses of an `if`, even if the statements in the `if` end with a jump statement. This makes it clear to someone reading the program that the following statements never occur if the first statements are executed. For example:

```
if (x > y)
    return;
    ...             /* rest of code */
```

becomes:

```
if (x > y)
    return;
else {
    ...             /* rest of code */
}
```

Extra `else` clauses do not reduce the speed of the program. They enhance readability, and allow easier code maintenance. Admittedly, extra `else`s do make the source code longer, and require an extra level of indentation.

17.11 Boolean types

It is quite common for programmers to compensate for C's lack of a distinct boolean type by defining their own boolean type. Specification of variables as boolean is good documentation. For example:

```
typedef enum bool {false, true} boolean;
```

defines a `boolean` type, with constants `true` and `false`. Reasonable type checking is achieved because of the strict checking of enumerated types. Another alternative that does not give type warnings, but still gives the documentation benefits is:

```
#define false 0
#define true  1
typedef int boolean;
```

17.12 Global variables

Global variables should always be used in moderation, regardless of whether they are being used in one file or many files. Wherever possible, use function arguments and function return values to pass information between functions. For example, a very bad method of calculating the maximum of two values is shown below:

```
#include <stdio.h>

int x, y, max;              /* Global variables badly used */

void calculate_max(void)
{
    if (x > y)
        max = x;
    else
        max = y;
}
```

```
main()
{
    printf("Enter two numbers: ");
    scanf("%d%d", &x, &y);
    calculate_max();
    printf("The maximum is %d\n", max);
}
```

There is no need to use global variables at all. The equivalent program using argument passing and return values is shown below:

```
#include <stdio.h>

int calculate_max(int x, int y)       /* x and y are arguments */
{
    if (x > y)
        return x;                      /* Maximum is returned by function */
    else
        return y;
}
main()
{
    int x, y, max;                     /* Local variables */

    printf("Enter two numbers: ");
    scanf("%d%d", &x, &y);
    max = calculate_max(x, y);
    printf("The maximum is %d\n", max);
}
```

17.13 The preprocessor

The preprocessor is a very powerful tool but it too should be used in moderation. The organization of header files is an important style issue, which is discussed in Chapter 13. The main pitfall to avoid is including C source files inside another C source file. Header files should not contain executable code, or non-`extern` variable definitions.

There are some cautions that should be heeded about the use of macros defined using `#define`. Avoid the use of long multi-line macros — they are horrible to read! Do not use macros that contain jump statements such as `break`, `continue` or `return` statements. This type of macro makes the control flow of a program almost impossible to follow. For the same reason it is also best to minimize the number of macros that contain `if` statements or loops. Use macros for very simple functions only.

Because of the flexibility of the preprocessor, it is easy to make C code look like something totally different. For example, C code can easily be made like Pascal, using:

```
#define begin   {
#define end     }
#define if      if (      /* Self-reference is correct */
#define then    )         /* Closing the bracket in "if (" */
#define not     !
#define and     &&
#define or      ||
#define repeat  do {
#define until(x) } while (!(x))
```

This use of the preprocessor is not recommended and it can be justified only if no one else is ever going to look at your program. You could even trap yourself, because some of the properties of the operators are not the same in C and Pascal (e.g. short-circuiting of the logical operators).

17.14 Further reading

The classic reference on programming style, for any programming language, is the book by Kernighan and Plauger. Thomas Plum has written a book specifically on C programming style. The book by Pugh also had some useful discussion of C style.

> KERNIGHAN Brian W., and PLAUGER, P. J., *The Elements of Programming Style*, McGraw-Hill, 1974.
>
> PLUM, Thomas, *C Programming Guidelines*, Prentice Hall, 1984.
>
> PUGH, Ken, *All on C*, Scott, Foresman/Little, Brown Higher Education, 1990.

17.15 Exercises

1. When modifying a C program written by another person, should you adopt their style of braces and indentation, or use your own style?

2. A function returns a boolean value indicating whether a chess move is valid. Should it be called `checkvalid` or `isvalid`?

3. Which of the following methods of increment should be used?

    ```
    i++;
    ++i;
    ```

4. An empty loop can be specified as either `{ }` or `;`. Which is preferable, and why?

5. Should you use `#define` or `enum` to define constants for `MALE` and `FEMALE`? The alternatives are:

    ```
    #define sex_type int     /* use #define */
    #define MALE     0
    #define FEMALE   1
    typedef enum { MALE, FEMALE } sex_type;   /* use enum */
    ```

6. (UNIX only) Run one of your C programs through a C beautifier such as `cb` or `indent`.

7. What is stylistically wrong with the macro definition below?

    ```
    #define test(p)   { if (p == NULL) return ERROR; }
    ```

8. What is stylistically wrong with the macro definition below?

    ```
    #define isletter(c)   ((c >= 'a' && c <= 'z') \
                         || (c >= 'A' && c <= 'Z'))
    ```

Chapter 18
Portability

Portability refers to the ease with which a program can be moved from one type of machine to another. It is usually impossible to run the executable version on a different type of machine and the C code must be moved to that machine and compiled there. This is not as easy as it sounds because there are differences between compilers, libraries and machine hardware. This chapter introduces a few guidelines that can increase the number of machines for which your C programs will work.

Portability is a huge issue, encompassing areas such as operating system features and machine architecture — portability of C programs is not merely about the C language. For example, how do you compile a C program on a machine without a C compiler? However, these larger issues of portability are beyond the scope of the book.

Generally speaking, small C programs written without using obscure library functions or complicated bitwise operations will compile and run on most machines. Average mathematical or data-processing programs will run correctly on most machines. With the rapid increase in the popularity of C, there are fewer and fewer implementations that present major problems. Even so, portability is something that should be considered for any program that may need to run on more than one type of machine.

Under UNIX the `lint` utility is available to automatically detect a number of common non-portable conditions. All C files should be checked with `lint` before moving them to another machine. The `lint` utility is examined in Section 16.2.

There are three important issues in portability:

1. Will the program compile?
2. Will the program run?
3. Will data files be portable?

A program moved to a new machine may not even compile the new C compiler. Even if it does compile, it may not run correctly, either because of a difference in the environment or because the compiler has generated different executable code. Non-portability of data files refers to the problem that data files created by a program on one machine may not be usable on another machine — this is a particular type of run-time problem.

18.1 Compilation problems

When porting programs, it is sometimes a great effort just to get the program to compile. Problems are caused by differences between preprocessors, compilers and linkers. These problems are easily detected because of the compiler diagnostic messages produced, but the correction of the problem may not be so easy.

18.1.1 Non-ANSI compilers

The ANSI standard is still relatively new and older compilers won't accept some constructs defined by the ANSI standard. Fortunately, the number of such compilers is rapidly diminishing.

The main problem is that machines with old-style compilers will not accept prototyped function declarations. For this reason, if portability is important it can be worthwhile to write C functions using the older non-prototyping notation. For example, the ANSI-style function definition:

```
int sum(int x, int y)
{
    return x + y;
}
```

changes so that the types of the function parameters are declared after the function header, but before the left brace:

```
int sum(x, y)
int x, y;
{
    return x + y;
}
```

In addition, some less obvious aspects of C are newly defined by the ANSI standard, and may not be supported. Avoid aggregate operations such as passing whole `struct`s to functions (pass pointers instead), returning `struct`s from functions or assigning whole `struct`s. Avoid initializations of *local* arrays or `struct`s (the restriction usually does not apply to global or `static` arrays or `struct`s) — the problem can be overcome by declaring local variables as `static` if the initialization need take place only once. Non-ANSI C does not permit the initialization of any type of `union`.

A number of keywords are new to C and must be avoided — `const`, `volatile`, `signed`, `enum`. The `void` keyword is not known in older C and thus `void` functions should be declared as `int`, or left without a return type (to default to `int`), as shown below:

```
mesg()
{
    printf("Hello world\n");
}
```

Many non-ANSI compilers do not support the generic pointer type, `void*`, even if `void` functions are allowed. The type `char*` must be used instead of `void*`. Note that the use of `char*` may require more type casts between pointer types (to prevent compilation warnings) than was required for `void` pointers.

There are some other smaller changes. The type "`long double`" may not be available, although it should default to plain "`double`".

The escapes `\a` (bell) and `\v` (vertical tab) and hexadecimal escapes using `\x` may not be allowed in non-ANSI C.

Some uses of suffixes for numeric constants are new in ANSI C. The use of `u` or `U` for integer constants is new, as is the use of any suffixes for floating point constants.

The use of the address operator (`&`) to take the address of an array variable name or a function name is usually not permitted in non-ANSI C (whereas it is ignored by ANSI compilers).

The unary + operator is not supported in non-ANSI C.

The calling of pointers to functions without an explicit use of the * dereferencing operator is not portable to non-ANSI compilers.

String constants should not be modified because the ANSI standard permits compilers to store these constants in read-only memory (although many implementations do not actually store them in this type of memory).

The squeezing out of the null byte in string initializations is not supported in non-ANSI C (see Section 6.6).

Another problem with non-ANSI compilers is that the "standard" library may differ between compilers. The most used header files such as `<stdio.h>` should not cause a problem, but less common ones may differ. Some header files may not even exist on some machines. For example, non-ANSI compilers may not have `<stdlib.h>` or `<stddef.h>`. This topic is far too extensive to cover fully in this book.

18.1.2 Non-ANSI extensions

Many compilers support specialized features that are not included in the ANSI standard. For example, many compilers under DOS support keyword extensions such as:

```
near      far       huge
asm       cdecl     pascal
fortran   interrupt
```

If portability to a DOS environment is important, programs should avoid using these keywords as identifiers.

Naturally any inclusion of assembly language into a C program severely reduces portability, regardless of whether it is guarded by an `asm` command or not.

18.1.3 Identifier length and name spaces

The ANSI standard states that identifiers have at least 31 significant characters. For example, the names `head_of_list1` and `head_of_list2` are distinct. However, non-ANSI compilers may not distinguish between such large identifiers. Local identifiers, such as local variable names and `typedef` names should be unique in the first seven letters for good portability. The identifiers for global variables and function names should be unique when reduced to six characters and one case (upper case or lower case) because these identifiers are used by the linker which may be more restricted than the compiler.

Avoid using identifiers starting with an underscore. These names are reserved for use by the standard library, so use of these names risks portability problems with different header files.

Some ancient compilers use only one name space, so avoid using the same names for variables and `struct` fields. For even greater portability, avoid using the same name for any two objects in the program (e.g. ensure that all `struct` field names are unique), although this is rarely necessary.

18.1.4 Preprocessor considerations

The introduction of the ANSI standard has had some effect on preprocessor functions. Although preprocessors are gradually becoming more standard, there is a long way to go. Many older preprocessors require that the `#` be the first character on the line (not even whitespace before it). Some of the more recent extensions to the preprocessor should also be avoided, such as `#elif` (use `#else` and `#if` instead), `#error`, `#pragma`, the `defined` preprocessor operator (use `#ifdef` and `#ifndef`) and the `#` and `##` preprocessor operators. Choose carefully between the ANSI stringize operator, `#`, and the use of non-standard macro expansion within string literals. Similarly, macro expansion inside character constants is non-portable because an ANSI preprocessor should treat character constants as indivisible tokens. The concatenation of adjacent string literals, as is often used in combination with the stringize operator, should also be avoided. Line splicing (see Section 11.3.2) should not be used to split tokens (even in multi-line macros) except for string constants. Macros using their own name in the replacement text (i.e. recursive macros) will often cause an infinite loop in older preprocessors.

The predefined constants `__DATE__`, `__TIME__` and `__STDC__` should also be avoided as much as possible. The constants `__LINE__` and `__FILE__` are much less likely to cause problems. However, `__STDC__` can be important in determining whether various standard features are available:

```
#if __STDC__
    ...                 /* ANSI C */
#else
    ...                 /* Non-ANSI C */
#endif
```

18.1.5 Linker considerations

The linker is the program that links object files to create the executable. It is usually incorporated into the compiler, but a discussion of its particular problems is worthwhile. Some linkers will combine two definitions of a variable into one location. This is very convenient as it allows global variable *definitions*, as opposed to *declarations* (using the `extern` specifier) to appear in header files (for the difference between declarations and definitions, refer to Section 13.4). Relying on this convenient feature of merging definitions limits portability. The program will not compile on a machine with a linker that disallows multiple definitions. It is far better to always ensure that there is only exactly one definition of a variable. For more explanation of how to achieve this, refer to Chapter 13.

A related issue is that some compilers will allow `extern` declarations of variables to contain initializations (which are ignored). Use of this feature prevents compilation on machines that do not ignore the initializations.

18.2 Run-time problems

Even if a program compiles, it may not necessarily run correctly. This is a more dangerous situation than compilation problems because there are no warning messages produced by the compiler — the program might fail immediately or it might fail much later when a particular condition occurs. The problems are often very subtle, and can be very difficult to locate and correct.

18.2.1 Zero

Zero is a major problem for portability because it is an overloaded constant. One problem with zero is that padding with character zeros may not fill a block with floating point zeros. There are some rare machines in which the floating point number 0.0 does not have all bytes zero. Such machines create problems for portability.

This is a problem for `calloc`, which initializes memory with character zeros (zero bytes). Unfortunately, `calloc` cannot determine at run-time the type of the data it is initializing. On problem machines, `calloc` does not initialize floating point data to zero. Hence, it is more portable to use `malloc` and explicitly initialize the memory yourself. For the same reason, the use of `memset` to zero arrays (other than `char` arrays) suffers portability problems.

There is no problem with compile-time implicit initialization of `static` or global variables by the compiler. It is reasonable to assume that the compiler will know the machine's internal representation of the floating point zero and perform initialization correctly.

18.2.2 NULL pointers

On most machines, the address 0 is an invalid address. However, on the machines where this is not true it sometimes happens that NULL is not equal to zero, and NULL pointers do not have all bits zero (i.e. another number is used to represent the invalid address because zero is valid). On these machines, the constant NULL may not be defined to equal zero. This is a problem if you freely swap between pointers and integers, assuming that integer zero is the NULL pointer. It is important never to assume that NULL is equal to zero.

Another issue worth raising is that implicit comparison with NULL in the conditional test:

    if (ptr)

may be less portable than the explicit comparison:

    if (ptr != NULL),

A smart compiler on a machine with a non-zero `NULL` value could watch for pointer types used as conditional expressions, and thus change the implicit comparison so that it compares with the non-zero value of `NULL`. However, it could not catch problems of pointers mixed with `int`s in expressions.

Another issue with `NULL` is that when using non-prototyping notation on a machine where pointers and `int`s are not compatible, it is necessary to type cast `NULL` function arguments to the appropriate pointer type:

```
fn( (char*)NULL );
```

The problem is that `NULL` expands out as the constant 0, which will be treated as an `int`. Hence, if `int` is not compatible with pointers, the wrong sized argument is passed. Note that the problem does not occur with prototyped functions, nor with assignments or comparisons involving `NULL`, because of the automatic type conversions that occur in these situations.

18.2.3 Pointers and integers

On some machines, pointers and integers may not be compatible. Do not mix pointers and integers, not even with type casts! The same can be said of pointers and `long` integers because even they may not be compatible. Never treat pointers as if they are integers — do not involve pointers in any arithmetic expressions, other than those using proper address arithmetic.

The problem can appear by accident if you forget to include the `<stdlib.h>` header file when using the `malloc` library function. A common practice in the past was to type cast the return value of `malloc`. This often concealed the problem that `malloc` had not been declared by a header file, and that the compiler assumed by default that `malloc` was a function returning `int`. In ANSI C it should never be necessary to type cast the return value from `malloc` because it is properly declared in the `<stdlib.h>` header file to return type `void*`.

18.2.4 Mixing pointer types

It is non-portable to assume that different types of pointers will have the same size or representation. For example, `void*` may be a different size to other types of pointers, and this creates problems for the comparison function of `qsort` and `bsearch` (see Section 12.4.6 for discussion of the problem). Another problem is that pointers to data may be incompatible with pointers to executable code (i.e. pointers to functions). The type `void*` is intended to hold the value of any pointer to data, but may not be capable of holding pointers to functions. The pointer type `void(*)()` is capable of holding all pointers to functions.

18.2.5 Mixing signed and unsigned char

When using `char` variables for their usual purpose, there is no portability problem. However, when using `char` variables to hold bytes of memory, there can be problems for bytes greater than 127 (i.e. with the highest bit set). When accessing bytes from memory, always use the type "`unsigned char`". It is not portable whether a character is signed or unsigned by default. If it is signed by default, problems arise when performing manipulations on bytes, such as right shift and conversion to int. On machines where char is signed by default, converting character 255 to int will give −1. On machines where the default is unsigned, the conversion will give 255. Using an explicitly unsigned variable ensures that the result is 255.

18.2.6 Expressions

Operators such as integer division, integer remainder and right shift are not properly defined with negative operands. One possible solution is to use explicitly unsigned operands to these operators.

Expressions that rely on the order of evaluation of C's operators or on the order of evaluation of function arguments are non-portable. This problem is discussed in full in Section 3.19.

Bitwise operations rely on the internal representation of an integer. Although it is almost always 2's complement, there is nothing in the standard stating that it must be. Hence, to be completely safe, you should not use bitwise operations without great care. For example, left shift might not be equivalent to multiplication on machines where the representation is not 2's complement.

There is no portable way to check for arithmetic overflow *after* an operation, although a common method of detecting integer overflow is that the result has the wrong sign. However, clever techniques can be applied *before* the operation to detect the possibility of an overflow. For example, assuming x and y are both positive, the code below will detect the overflow of int addition:

```
#include <limits.h>

if (INT_MAX - y < x)
    overflow();
sum = x + y;
```

A program should not modify a string constant because the ANSI standard permits the compiler to place string constants in read-only memory. The most common situation where this can occur is the modification of a pointer string variable previously assigned the address of a string constant.

18.2.7 Sizes of types

The sizes of various types are implementation-dependent. Do not assume any fixed sizes for any of the simple data types. Use the sizeof operator rather than assume that int is four bytes. However, it is reasonable to assume:

```
sizeof(short) <= sizeof(int) <= sizeof(long)
```

No assumption should be made about the size of a pointer, though it is commonly at least the size of an int.

A common mistake in the use of bitwise operations is to reset bits using:

```
x &= 0xFFFE;
```

which assumes a 16 bit representation of `int`. The portable method is to use the bitwise complement operator:

```
x &= ~ 1;
```

18.2.8 Character sets

Is the character set of the machine ASCII or EBCDIC? This affects the portability of some operations on characters. Admittedly, most machines now use ASCII and this issue is becoming less important. Even so, with a little care it is possible to avoid relying upon the particular character set. Obviously, the first warning is to use character constants instead of hard-coding numbers — use `'A'` instead of 65.

Some comparison operations are not portable. Comparisons for equality or inequality are portable, but less-than or greater-than comparisons can be problematical. Do not assume that characters are ordered a particular way. It is reasonable to assume that all lower case letters `a..z` are ordered in ascending order, and also that all upper case letters `A..Z` are in ascending order, but do not assume that all lower case letters are after all upper case letters. The best way to make character tests portable is to use the standard library functions in `<ctype.h>`.

18.2.9 Bit-fields and unions

Bit-fields in structures are not portable if wrongly used. They should be accessed individually through the field names. It is non-portable to use bit-fields to access particular bits in a machine byte because the mapping of bit-fields onto bit positions is unspecified, and can be either left-to-right or right-to-left.

Unions are implementation-dependent if accessed the wrong way. It is important to know what type data is currently in the `union`, and only access the `union` using that type. One way of achieving this is to maintain a "tag" field which indicates what type of data is currently stored.

18.3 Data file portability

An important portability issue is whether data files generated on one machine will port to another. This is important when a file of data generated by a program must be moved to another machine.

Generally speaking text files will be portable; binary files won't. However, note that text files will have problems if machines use a different character set (e.g. EBCDIC instead of ASCII). The problem with binary files is more common. Not only might the sizes of the basic data types be different, but different machines format binary files differently. For example, a binary file of `ints` may not be portable because different computers store the most-significant and least-significant bytes in different orders. Similarly, files of `floats` or `doubles` will not be portable because the format of floating point numbers may be different. Files of `structs` won't be portable because the fields may be placed in a different order, or may have extra padding bytes because of alignment needs.

The only real solution is to use text files and store the data in character format. Unfortunately, this increases the size of data files and slows down the program because it must convert character data into the internal formats of integers or floating point numbers. Structured data must be rebuilt field by field, which is slow and prone to error.

An alternative solution is to design utilities that convert the data file between the text and binary file formats. These utilities are only used when porting the data file. When moving from machine A to machine B, one utility converts the binary data file on machine A to a text file. This text file is moved to machine B where the other utility converts the text file to a binary file. Because the second utility program has been compiled on machine B, the format of the generated binary file is correct.

18.4 Further reading

Portability is a large issue and this chapter cannot cover all the aspects. However, this chapter has touched on most of the major issues. Further information on portability can be found in the references listed below:

HORTON, Mark, *Portable C Software*, Prentice Hall, 1990.

JAESCHKE, Rex, *Portability and the C Language*, Hayden Books, 1989.

LAPIN, J. E., *Portable C and UNIX System Programming*, Prentice Hall, 1987.

RABINOWITZ, Henry, and SCHAAP, Chaim, *Portable C*, Prentice Hall, 1990.

18.5 Exercises

1. What is non-portable about the code fragment below?

    ```
    char c;
    while( (c = getchar()) != EOF)
        putchar(c);
    ```

2. What is non-portable about the code fragment below, where the `pop` function pops an integer from a stack data structure (accessed as a global variable)?

    ```
    result = pop() / pop();
    ```

3. A memory dump program is attempting to read byte values from memory through a pointer variable, `ptr`, and manipulating bytes using the variable, `x`, both declared as below:

    ```
    BYTE *ptr, x;
    ```

    What is an appropriate declaration of the `typedef` name BYTE?

4. What is non-portable about the macro definition for converting upper case letters to lower case?

    ```
    #define TOLOWER(ch)    ((ch) + 32)
    ```

5. What is non-portable in the following function that calculates a hash address in the range $0..TABLE\_SIZE-1$?

    ```
    int hash(char *key)
    {
        int i, sum = 0;

        for(i = 0; key[i] != '\0'; i++)
            sum += (i + 1) * key[i];
        return sum % TABLE_SIZE;
    }
    ```

6. If a non-ANSI compiler does not support `const` or `volatile`, what two lines can be added to a program using these keywords to make it compile? Can the same method be used to port programs using the DOS (non-ANSI) keywords `near`, `far` and `huge` to an ANSI compiler? *Hint:* Use the preprocessor.

7. The policy of ignoring unrecognized `#pragma` directives prevents many problems. However, consider what happens if two compilers use the same `#pragma` directive for different purposes. How can the use of `#pragma` be moderated so as to prevent this type of "misunderstanding"?

Chapter 19
UNIX systems programming

This chapter examines the art of programming on a UNIX system. The issues discussed here are important when developing any reasonable-sized tool to be used in the UNIX environment. All of the main issues are similar across different UNIX systems, but there are always differences. In some areas there are major differences, notably signals, and these will be pointed out. However, it is always good practice to check your local manual entries about any of the system calls mentioned in this chapter.

19.1 UNIX software tools

There is much more to UNIX than just a C compiler. The immense power of UNIX tools can be brought to bear on the task of C programming. The more familiar you become with these tools, the more trivial some tasks will become. Some of the tools that are particularly relevant to C programming are given in Table 19.1. Note that your local implementation may not support all of these.

Table 19.1. UNIX software tools

Tool	Meaning
cc	C Compiler
make	Compile multiple file C programs
lint	Check C programs for errors
ar, ranlib	Create archives (libraries)
prof, pixie	Profile of execution time
cb, indent	Pretty print C programs
cexpl, cdecl	Explain C declarations
vgrind	Typeset C programs
sccs	Version management for large projects
vi, ctags	Editor with some C support

Other commands can be very powerful. There are examples throughout the book of `grep` being applied to C programs (e.g. the automatic generation of header files in Section 13.9). The tools `sed` and `awk` are also very powerful. The `lex` and `yacc` utilities are available for writing compilers and compiler-like software tools.

Other features of UNIX can be used to great effect. Script files of commands are very useful. Redirection of input and output is a very powerful feature which can be combined with the common file manipulation utilities: `cat`, `more`, `wc`, `cp`, `mv`, `head` and `tail`.

19.2 Executing UNIX commands: system

The UNIX function, `system`, is used to execute UNIX shell commands from within a C program. Its prototype definition is:

```
int system(char *command)
```

The `system` function executes the command as if it had been typed at the keyboard. This allows a C program to do almost anything that can be done from the shell. For example:

```
system("ls");                    /* List the current directory */
system("cat /etc/passwd");       /* List password file */
```

Bourne shell (`sh`) is used and not C-shell (`csh`), but `csh` can be used by sending:

```
"csh -c 'command'"
```

as the argument to `system` (refer to the manual entry for `csh` for more explanation).

The use of `system` has some limitations. It invokes a new shell for every system call, and does not retain shell variables changed between calls. The most annoying aspect of this is that `cd` will not have effect over consecutive calls. A second system call will not have its current working directory updated, because this is stored in a shell variable. The `cd` command can only be used within the one system call. The correct way to use `cd` is shown below:

```
system("cd ..; ls");             /* CORRECT */
system("cd ..");                 /* INCORRECT */
system("ls");
```

The return value of `system` is the termination status from the sequence of commands executed (i.e. the value returned from the shell).

19.3 Errors: <errno.h>

All UNIX system commands can return error status for various reasons. When the return value of a command indicates the presence of an error, the exact nature of the error can be determined by examining the contents of the external variable, `errno`, declared in <errno.h>. This value can be compared with the predefined constants also declared in <errno.h>. The definition of `errno` in <errno.h> is usually:

```
extern int errno;
```

The `errno` variable contains an error code whenever a library function returns an error. Note that the `errno` variable is not cleared by successful calls to library functions and it is unwise to test `errno` when no error has been indicated, because any earlier error will still be in `errno` (i.e. do not test `errno` after a system call unless that system call indicates failure). The `errno` variable can be explicitly cleared by your program, but this is not usually necessary. The more common approach is to test `errno` only when an error has been indicated by the return value of a function.

The `perror` function can be used to print out the error that has occurred. It examines the value of `errno` and prints the corresponding message to `stderr`. The prototype definition of `perror` is:

```
int perror(char *prompt)
```

The `prompt` argument allows the user to send a message indicating the location of the error's occurrence or the file causing the error. A common use of `perror` is for error messages about files. It is common to pass the filename to `perror` to use as the text before the error message. For example:

```
char *filename = "data_file";
if ((fp = fopen(filename, "r")) == NULL)
    perror(filename);
```

will produce the following output when a permission-denied error occurs:

```
data_file: permission denied
```

For greater flexibility, the value of the external variable `errno` can be directly examined and compared to symbolic constants declared in `<errno.h>`. There is no need to declare `errno` because `<errno.h>` already does this.

19.4 Low-level file operations

All UNIX systems have the same operating system low-level functions for input and output. Implementations of the standard library input-output functions in `<stdio.h>` on UNIX systems must call these low-level functions. Other non-UNIX implementations do not necessarily support these functions, so the standard library functions are recommended for portability (i.e. `fopen`, `fprintf`, etc). However, there are some occasions when it is useful to use low-level input-output, such as handling input/output for programs that create new processes.

UNIX file operations are conceptually similar to those of the standard library. Files must be opened before use and closed after use. Files can be opened for input, output or both (direct access). The main difference is that instead of `FILE*` pointers, UNIX files are accessed using *file descriptors* of type `int`.

Another difference is that UNIX low-level input-output is not buffered; whereas standard library functions are buffered. This leads to a few minor differences (e.g. there is no equivalent to `fflush`).

The file descriptors in Table 19.2 are reserved. These are opened by default when UNIX creates a process (i.e. runs a program).

Table 19.2. Reserved file descriptors

Value	Meaning
0	Standard input (`stdin`)
1	Standard output (`stdout`)
2	Standard output (`stderr`)

19.4.1 Opening and closing files: open, close, creat

The function `open` is used to open files. It returns a non-negative integer file descriptor corresponding to the file; or −1 on error. The definition of `open` is:

```
int open(char *filename, int flags, int permissions)
```

The filename can be an absolute path or relative to the current directory. The variable, `flags`, is an `int` with each bit indicating the type of access. There are symbolic constants defined for their values — they are defined in either `<fcntl.h>` or `<sys/file.h>`, depending upon whether System V or Berkeley versions respectively is used (there is no standard because the UNIX functions are not part of the standard library). The most common values for `flags` are given in Table 19.3.

Table 19.3. Modes for open

Mode	Meaning
`O_RDONLY`	Open for read
`O_WRONLY`	Open for write
`O_RDWR`	Open for read and write

In addition, there are some other modifiers. These can be set as well as one of the above, using bitwise-or to pass both bits. Some of these modifiers are given in Table 19.4.

Table 19.4. Modifiers for open

Modifier	Meaning
`O_CREAT`	Create if not found
`O_APPEND`	Write at end of file
`O_TRUNC`	Truncate existing file (if found)

The `permissions` argument to `open` is only used when the `O_CREAT` flag is set. It specifies the file protection permissions that the file is created with (modified by umask). When `O_CREAT` is not used, the last argument is ignored. The first example opens a file for reading:

```
int in_fd;              /* File descriptor */
in_fd = open("infile", O_RDONLY, 0);    /* read only */
```

The second example opens a file for writing, and also specifies that the file should be created with permissions 0666 if it is not already present:

```
int out_fd;              /* File descriptor */
out_fd = open("outfile", O_WRONLY|O_CREAT, 0666);   /* write */
```

Note that the permissions are specified as an octal integer constant 0666, and not a decimal integer 666 — the prefix zero is very important.

An alternative method of creating a new file is to use the UNIX function `creat`. Some implementations of `open` did not support the `O_CREAT` flag; hence the need for `creat`. The `creat` function will create a new file or truncate an existing one. The `creat` function returns the file descriptor of the created/truncated file; or −1 if an error occurs. This file descriptor can then be used for `read` and `write` file operations. The definition of `creat` is:

```
int creat(char *filename, int permissions)
```

A file is closed using the `close` function. A program can usually have only a limited number of files open. The use of `close` frees a file descriptor for later use. The definition of `close` is:

```
int close(int fd)
```

19.4.2 Input and output: read and write

The UNIX functions to read and write blocks of data are:

```
int read (int fd, char *buffer, int num)
int write(int fd, char *buffer, int num)
```

These functions read or write a specified number of bytes to or from a buffer. The `read` function returns the number of characters read: zero if end of file was encountered; −1 on error. The `write` function returns the number of characters written. A write error is indicated by this count being less than `num`. Some implementations return −1 on error, but the "count less than num" condition is more portable.

19.4.3 Removing files: unlink

UNIX has a library function to remove a file, `unlink`, which is functionally equivalent to the `remove` function of the standard library. The definition of `unlink` is:

```
int unlink(char *filename)
```

The `unlink` function returns zero for success; −1 if the file did not exist or could not be removed. This is consistent with the return value of the `remove` function: zero for success, non-zero for failure.

19.4.4 Input/output redirection: dup, dup2

The `dup` function duplicates a new file descriptor from an existing one, such that they both refer to the same file. The `dup` function returns a new file descriptor; or −1 on error. The new file descriptor is the lowest integer value available. The most common use of this is to redirect stdin, stdout or stderr. The method of redirecting stdin is shown below:

```
#define STDIN 0
int fd;

fd = open("infile", O_RDONLY, 0);   /* Open new file */
if (fd < 0) {                       /* Check for error */
    perror("infile");
    exit(1);
}
close(STDIN);           /* Close stdin (temporarily) */
dup(fd);                /* Duplicate fd into stdin */
close(fd);              /* Close one file descriptor */
...                     /* stdin now comes from "infile" */
```

The call to dup will open stdin because 0 is the lowest available file descriptor (it has been closed by the close function in the previous statement). The close function is then used to close the original file descriptor referring to "infile". However, stdin still refers to "infile" because the file is not closed until all file descriptors referring to it have been closed.

There is usually another related function, called dup2, declared as:

```
int dup2(int oldfd, int newfd)
```

This function allows the programmer to specify the new file descriptor, rather than taking the lowest numbered one. If this new file descriptor is already in use, it is closed as if by the close function.

Another alternative that sometimes appears in existing code is to make use of the undocumented feature of open — returning the lowest available descriptor. Because the feature is undocumented, this usage is not recommended. The following sequence is sometimes used in old C code to redirect standard input:

```
close(0);
open("file", O_RDONLY, 0);
```

Note that processes with their I/O redirected can still access the terminal by opening the file "/dev/tty", and writing to it directly. This can be useful for sending messages to the terminal if stdout and stderr are both piped or redirected.

19.4.5 Direct access: lseek

Direct access under UNIX is similar to that performed using the standard library. The file is opened for read-write (O_RDWR), using open or creat, and lseek is used to move throughout the file (instead of fseek in the standard library). The definition of lseek is:

```
long lseek(int fd, long offset, int origin)
```

The interpretation of origin and offset is identical to that for fseek. An origin of zero stands for start of file; one for current position; two for end of file. The return value is the new file position; or −1 on error.

The `read` and `write` functions are used instead of `fread` and `fwrite`. Note that because input and output are not buffered, there is no need to flush any buffer between reads and writes.

19.5 Accessing the environment: getenv, setenv

The environment variables associated with a program can be accessed from within the program. The environment can be accessed via an argument to the `main` function (see Section 14.4), but the most convenient method is to use the `getenv` library function. Its definition is:

```
char *getenv(char *variable)
```

The `getenv` function returns a pointer to the string value of the environment variable passed as its argument, or `NULL` if the variable is not defined. An example of its usage is:

```
printf("Home is %s\n", getenv("HOME"));
```

Environment variables should not be confused with shell variables. Only those shell variables that have been *exported* will be available in the environment. Some variables such as HOME and USER are usually exported by default. Other shell variables must be explicitly exported to the environment. Bourne shell variables are exported using the `export` command. C-shell variables can be exported from within C-shell using the `setenv` command. Note that C-shell usually sets HOME, USER and PATH to always be equivalent to home, user and path, so that setting these variables within C-shell will affect the environment, but this is not true for all C-shell variables. Refer to the manual entries for `sh` and `csh` for more information.

Environment variables can be set to a value using the `setenv` system call (not to be confused with C-shell's `setenv` command). The prototype definition of `setenv` is:

```
int setenv(char *variable, char *value, int overwrite)
```

The first argument is the name of the environment variable, the second argument is the string value to be stored and the last argument is a boolean flag indicating whether to overwrite any existing value. If no variable is found, the variable and its value are added to the environment. If a variable is found and `overwrite` is zero, any existing value is not overwritten. If `overwrite` has any non-zero value, the existing value will be overwritten. The `setenv` function returns 0 on success and –1 on failure (e.g. not enough space to store a new variable).

Another UNIX library function, `unsetenv`, can be used to remove a definition of a variable from the environment. The prototype definition is:

```
void unsetenv(char *variable)
```

For more flexibility than that provided, the environment must be accessed directly, either through the `envp` parameter to `main` (see Section 14.4), or through the external variable, `environ`, which is defined for each process and is equivalent to `envp`.

19.6 File protections and access times

The UNIX system provides a number of functions for dealing with the protection bits associated with each file. These bits can be changed using the chmod system call. The owner of a file may be changed using the chown system call. The file creation mask, used by creat, may be changed using the umask system call. The state of the protection bits of a file can be examined using the access system call. The stat and fstat system calls can also be used to test file protections, but this is not all that they return. These functions can be used to obtain a great deal of other information about the file, such as its size, owner and times of last access/modification.

A process may examine, and sometimes set, its user identification number (uid). The uid of a process is an integer indicating a property of a process similar to the "ownership" of a file. The uid is usually the identification of the person running the program. The uids are the same integers as used in calls to the chown function. Your uid can be found by examining the /etc/passwd file for your login name, or by calling the getuid function in a C program executed by you. A process has two uids associated with it — the *real* uid and the *effective* uid. The difference is only important in special programs that run in set-user-id mode. There is also another pair of integer identification numbers — the group ids (gids). Most programs do not fiddle with uids or gids. Programs that do need to examine or change uids (e.g. to take security precautions) can use the multitude of functions for this purpose: setuid, seteuid, setruid, geteuid, getuid, getruid, getgid, setgid, setegid, and setrgid.

There are a number of functions related to security. The getpass function can be used to get the typed password from the user. The getpwent, getpwuid, and getpwnam functions can be used to examine the crypted version of the password. These functions simply examine the /etc/passwd file. The crypt system call can be used to perform the encryption of a password, returning the crypted version.

19.7 Process control

Processes are referred to by a process id number which is represented as an integer. This integer is unique — each process has a different process id. A process can determine its own process id using the getpid system call. Every process has a parent — the process that created it. The parent process pid can be found using getppid. The short program below illustrates the use of getpid and getppid:

```
#include <stdio.h>

main()
{
    printf("My process id is %d\n", getpid());
    printf("My parent's process id is %d\n", getppid());
}
```

New processes are created by the fork system call. The execve system call is often used to execute another command in place of the current process, and can be used in combination with fork to spawn a child process. Processes can terminate due to natural completion of the program or can be killed by another process using the kill system call.

19.7.1 Suspending a process: sleep

The `sleep` system call can be used to suspend a process for a specified number of seconds. The definition of `sleep` is:

```
int sleep(int seconds)
```

This call will delay for the specified time. The actual time may be as much as one second less than that specified, because of the granularity of the time intervals considered by `sleep`. The return value will be zero under normal termination; otherwise it is equal to the number of unslept seconds.

19.7.2 Changing current directory: chdir

The `chdir` system call is used to change the current working directory of a process. Subsequent `execve` and related calls will prepend this path to all names not beginning with /. Note that `execvp` and `execlp` search a number of directories on the path, only using the current directory when it is specified in the path. The definition of `chdir` is:

```
int chdir(char *path)
```

It returns 0 for successful completion; −1 for an error. An error can occur for many reasons; such as execute permission denied on a directory in the path.

19.7.3 Creating a new process: fork

The `fork` system call is used to create a new process. The call by itself simply creates two almost identical copies of the current process, both executing concurrently from the same point (i.e. the program counter has the same value). The main difference between the two processes is the return value from the `fork` function. In the new child process, the return value is zero; in the parent process the return value is the process id of the child. If the `fork` call fails, the return value is −1 and no new process is created. The normal procedure for creating a child is:

```
int pid;           /* Child Process id */

pid = fork();
if (pid == 0) {
    ...            /* Child */
}
else if (pid == -1) {
    ...            /* Parent Processes error */
}
else
    ...            /* Parent continues - successful fork */
```

The return value is not the only difference between parent and child after a call to `fork`. Naturally, the two processes have different process ids. Other differences are discussed in the manual entry for `fork`.

A simple example of the use of `fork` is given below. It creates ten children, each of which prints a message, pauses for one second, prints a second message, pauses again, then prints a message before exiting.

```
/*--------------------------------------------------------------*/
/*      FORK10.C:       Fork 10 child processes                 */
/*--------------------------------------------------------------*/

#include <stdio.h>
#include <stdlib.h>

#define NUM_CHILDREN   10

main()
{
    int i;
    int pid;

    for (i = 1; i <= NUM_CHILDREN; i++) { /* Fork 10 children */
        pid = fork();
        if (pid == 0) {                   /* Child here */
            printf("Child %d says Hi\n", i);
            sleep(1);
            printf("Child %d says Hi Again\n", i);
            sleep(1);
            printf("Child %d EXITING\n", i);
            exit(0);
        }
        else if (pid == -1) {    /* Parent handles fork error */
            perror("fork");
            exit(1);
        }
        /* Parent here, continuing... */
    }
    printf("Parent EXITING \n");
}
```

If you run this program and examine the output, the asynchronous nature of processes in execution may be shown — the messages may not appear in the order you would expect.

The `fork` function is not particularly useful by itself, so `fork` is usually combined with one of a number of execute function calls (e.g. `execve`, `execl`, `execvp`, etc.), to overlay one of the processes with another different executing process. Using this `fork` and `exec` procedure, a process can create a new child process. It is common to talk of a parent process *forking off* or *spawning* a child process.

19.7.4 Overlaying a new process: execve (and others)

There are a number of execute calls, of which `execve` is the most fundamental — all the others call it. The definition of `execve` is:

```
int execve(char *filename, char *argv[], char *envp[])
```

A call to `execve` replaces the current process with the specified executable — that is, it runs the specified file. The new executable is overlayed over the old one — there can be no return from a successful `execve` call. The only conditions under which `execve` returns are error conditions; the return value will be −1.

All variables are lost when `execve` is called. However, some process characteristics are retained across an `execve` call — most notably, open files and some signal characteristics. All open files will stay open, and both processes (parent and child) will be acting upon the same file (i.e. only one file pointer). Ignored signals remain ignored —

the signal mask is retained. However, caught signals are reset to their default action. User-id, group-id, `umask` and some other characteristics are also kept by `execve`.

There are a number of other execute calls that perform some processing before calling `execve`. These provide two basic interfaces: one is similar to `execve`; one is useful when the arguments are known in advance. The `execv` function is similar to `execve`, except that the environment is taken directly from the process instead of as an argument:

```
int execv(char *filename, char *argv[])
```

As with `execve`, this requires the construction of an array of strings to pass as `argv`. This is not always convenient and there are functions that automatically do this and then call `execve`:

```
int execl(char *filename, char *arg0, ..., NULL)
int execle(char *filename, char *arg0, ..., NULL, char *envp[])
```

By convention, `arg0` is the name of the program, often the basename of the full filename path (e.g. `rm` when `/bin/rm` is executed). Any number of arguments can be passed; these become the command line arguments passed to the new process. The list of arguments must be terminated by a `NULL`. This is a sentinel value indicating the end of the list. Some examples of calls to `execl` are given below:

```
execl("/bin/ls", "ls", NULL);
execl("/bin/ls", "ls", "-l", "-a", "makefile", NULL);
execl("a.out", "a.out", NULL);
```

In all the functions considered above, the filename must be specified as an absolute path (starting with /) or relative to the current directory. A slightly more convenient form is to search the `PATH` of the current process for the command to be executed, as is done automatically in the shell. There are functions of both forms to do this:

```
int execlp(char *filename, char *arg0, char *arg1, ..., NULL)
int execvp(char *filename, char *argv[])
```

This allows calls to dispense with the absolute pathname for common commands. The working of these functions is identical to that of the shell — both examine the `PATH` environment variable for the list of directories to search. Note that both Bourne shell and C-shell maintain the `PATH` environment variable. Some example calls to `execlp` are:

```
execlp("ls", "ls", NULL);
execlp("ls", "ls", "-l", "-a", "makefile", NULL);
```

19.7.5 Spawning a child process: fork and exec

One of the execute function calls can be used to replace the current process with another (by calling `execve` as the last command). However, the most common use of these functions is combined with `fork` to spawn a new child process. The simplest code sequence for this is:

```
if (fork() == 0)                    /* Child */
    execl("/bin/ls", "ls", NULL);
...                                 /* Parent continues */
```

This does not take into account error checking and the need to retain the pid of the child process. A more comprehensive method is:

```
int pid;              /* Child Process id */

pid = fork();
if (pid == 0) {                       /* Child */
    execl("/bin/ls", "ls", NULL);
    perror("ls");                     /* execl returns only if error */
    exit(1);                          /* child self-terminates */
}
else if (pid == -1) {                 /* Fork failed */
    perror("Failure forking ls");     /* Parent Processes error */
    exit(1);
}
...                                   /* Parent continues - successful fork */
```

Notice the error checking after the `execl` function call. There is no need to examine the return value of `execl`. If `execl` returns, its return value will be −1 and an error has occurred. When `execl` is successful, it does not return and the error checks are never executed.

Some versions of UNIX support the `vfork` function intended to replace `fork` when using the fork-exec sequence to spawn a child process. The `vfork` function is more efficient than `fork` because it does not create a copy of the current process's memory (which is going to be overlayed anyway). The differences between `fork` and `vfork` are discussed in the manual entry for `vfork`.

19.7.6 Waiting for child process termination: wait

When spawning a new process, the parent may either continue or wait for the termination of the child. The `wait` system call is used to wait for the termination of child processes. The most common definition of `wait` is:

```
int wait (unsigned int * status)
```

Note that some UNIX versions may use a different type for the parameter. For example, some versions may define a `struct` type with a number of named bit-fields to make it easy to extract particular bits of the termination status.

The `wait` function blocks until a child terminates, or a signal or error occurs. When `wait` returns successfully, its return value is the pid of the terminating child. When a signal occurs, `wait` either returns −1 and sets `errno` to `EINTR` or resumes, depending upon how signals are set. When there are no children to wait for, `wait` returns −1 and sets `errno` to `ECHILD`. Other error conditions exist and are discussed in the documentation on `wait` and `signal`.

The argument to `wait` is a pointer to a variable in which the termination status of the process is stored. If the status is not important, `NULL` can be passed to `wait` and no status is returned. This is useful when a process wishes to wait for its child process to terminate but does not care about the child's termination status.

A process can wait for one child process using a single call to `wait`, but this does not check that the child is the correct one. A better method is to store the child pid when fork is called, and compare this pid with that returned by wait when waiting for the child to terminate. This method is illustrated below:

```
#include <stdio.h>          /* define perror() */
#include <stdlib.h>         /* define exit() */
#include <sys/wait.h>       /* define wait() */

main()
{
    int pid, ret;

    pid = fork();
    if (pid == 0) {                 /* Child */
        execl("/bin/ls", "ls", NULL);
        perror("ls");
        exit(1);
    }
            /* Parent */
    do {                            /* until correct pid or error */
        ret = wait(NULL);
    } while (pid != ret && ret > 0);
}
```

A parent process can wait for all children to terminate by repeatedly calling wait — no children are missed. If a child dies between successive calls to wait, the next call to wait returns immediately with the terminated child's pid. In a sense, terminating child process ids are queued by wait. A simple method of waiting for all children is to repeatedly call wait until it returns the value −1. It is then necessary to examine errno to check that the error was ECHILD and not some other error.

```
#include <errno.h>

while (wait(NULL) > 0))
    ;           /* empty loop */

if (errno != ECHILD)
    ...         /* some strange error */
```

Another method is to count the number of calls to wait, such that wait is called once for each child (assuming the number of children is known). Still more precise is to examine each pid returned from wait against a list of known children.

The status returned by wait has two main components — the exit status of the process (as returned by the exit library function), and the termination status of the process (e.g. was termination normal or abnormal? did a core dump occur?). For more detailed information on the status, consult the manual entry for wait and the file <sys/wait.h>. Although the method of extracting the exit status is dependent on the version of UNIX, one method that works in most cases is:

```
unsigned int status;

wait(&status);
exit_status = status >> 8;
```

In some versions of UNIX the type of the argument to wait will be different. For example, it may be a pointer to a struct or union containing named bit-fields. Even in this case, accepting the value as an unsigned int (as above) will often work.

19.7.7 Creating pipes between processes

Most users will have no need to set up their own pipes, because the shell allows a very simple notation for specifying this (i.e. |). However, when writing programs that create multiple processes it can be useful to set up pipes between two processes. There are two methods for creating pipes between processes — using the popen and pclose library functions, or using the pipe system call. The use of popen and pclose is more high level and involves the use of file pointers of type FILE*, as used by the standard library functions in <stdio.h>. However, popen is quite restricted because one of the processes must be created by a UNIX command which is executed by a shell, whereas the pipe function allows full flexibility in the creation of the processes using fork.

19.7.7.1 The popen and pclose functions

The popen and pclose functions are declared in <stdio.h>. Their prototype declarations are:

```
FILE *popen(char *command, char *mode)
int pclose(FILE *fp)
```

The first argument to popen is the UNIX command that is to be executed. The popen function is similar to the system function in that this command is executed by creating a new shell. The shell is always sh, but it is possible to use csh by using "csh -c 'command'" as the string argument to popen (refer to the manual entry for csh).

The mode argument to popen is either "r" or "w" which indicates whether we are reading from or writing down the pipe between our process and the newly created process. If "r" is used, the output from the command is sent down the pipe and we can use fscanf(fp,...) to read this output. If "w" is used, any output using fprintf(fp,...) is sent as input to the new process. An example of the second situation is shown below, where our process generates a grep process to examine the output sent down the pipeline using fprintf:

```
#include <stdio.h>
#include <stdlib.h>

main()
{
    FILE *fp;

    fp = popen("grep hello", "w");    /* Open pipe for writing */
    if (fp == NULL) {
        perror("Failure in popen");
        exit(1);
    }
    fprintf(fp, "This line contains 'hello'\n");
    fprintf(fp, "This line doesn't\n");
    pclose(fp);
}
```

The output from this program is just the string sent by the first fprintf call:

```
This line contains 'hello'
```

The `popen` function returns `NULL` if the pipe could not be created. The `pclose` function returns −1 if the stream has not been opened by `popen`; otherwise it closes the pipe and returns the exit status of the command. Note that `pclose` call does not kill the child process and will hang if the child process does not terminate. In the example above, `grep` terminates because it detects end-of-file on `stdin` when `pclose` closes the pipe.

19.7.7.2 The pipe function

For more flexibility than that provided by `popen` and `pclose`, pipes are set up using the low-level `pipe` system call, declared as:

```
int pipe(int p[2])
```

The `pipe` system call returns an array of two file descriptors — writing down the pipe is performed into `p[1]`, and the contents of the pipe can be read from `p[0]`. It returns zero for successful creation; −1 for any error. A read on a pipe that has no processes writing to it (i.e. all write file descriptors closed) will return `EOF`. A signal is generated by a write with no one to read it.

The `pipe` function is used with `fork` to generate a communications channel between two processes. These processes could use the file descriptors returned by `pipe` (i.e. `p[0]` and `p[1]`), but it is more common to move these descriptors to replace `stdin` or `stdout`. In this way, output of one process is redirected through the pipe to be read by another process. This redirection is the action taken by the shell when it sets up a pipeline. The usual method of redirecting a pipe is:

```
int temp, p[2], pid;

temp = pipe(p);         /* Set up the pipe */
if (temp == -1) {       /* Check for errors */
    perror("Pipe failure");
    exit(1);
}
pid = fork();           /* Fork a child to read the pipe */
if (pid == 0) {         /* Child */
    close(0);                   /* Redirect stdin from pipe */
    dup(p[0]);
    close(p[0]);                /* Close pipe file descriptors, */
    close(p[1]);                /*   as no longer needed */

    execve(...);                /* Execute the child process */
}
```

In this example, the child reads its `stdin` from the pipe. The parent can send output to the child using the file descriptor `p[1]` (i.e. `"write(p[1],...);"`). Alternatively, the parent could redirect its own `stdout` into the pipe.

Now consider a more complicated example. The program below will `fork` off two children, creating a pipe between them. It is equivalent to the shell command:

```
ls -l | cat -n
```

where `ls -l` provides a long listing of the directory and `cat -n` prefixes each line with a line number.

```
/*------------------------------------------------------------*/
/* Pipe Test:    equivalent to command:   ls -l | cat -n      */
/*------------------------------------------------------------*/

#include <stdio.h>
#include <stdlib.h>

main()
{
    int pid1, pid2;   /* Process id's */
    int p[2];         /* Pipe descriptor */
    int ret;

    ret = pipe(p);
    if (ret < 0) {
        perror("Pipe failed");
        exit(1);
    }
                /* Parent forks first child */
    pid1 = fork();
    if (pid1 == 0) {    /* Child */
        dup2(p[1], 1);        /* Redirect stdout down pipe */
        close(p[1]);          /* Close pipe file descriptors */
        close(p[0]);

        execl("/bin/ls", "ls", "-l", NULL);     /* ls -l */
        perror("Execl failed");
        exit(1);
    }

                /* Parent forks another child */
    pid2 = fork();
    if (pid2 == 0) {    /* 2nd Child */
        dup2(p[0], 0);        /* Redirect stdin from pipe */
        close(p[0]);          /* Close pipe file descriptors */
        close(p[1]);

        execl("/bin/cat", "cat", "-n", NULL);   /* cat -n */
        perror("Execl failed");
        exit(1);
    }

                /* Parent */
    close(p[0]);                  /* Close pipe file descriptors */
    close(p[1]);
    while (wait(NULL) > 0)    /* Wait for all children to die */
        ;        /* empty loop */
    exit(0);
}
```

There are a few important points to note. First, the program uses dup2 to redirect input-output instead of the close-dup sequence. This is equivalent, but may not be supported by all implementations.

Second, note that the pipe descriptors are closed in a number of different places — because of fork there is more than one copy of the p array. There are two reasons for closing the pipe descriptors. The first reason is that it is simply good practice to close file descriptors that are no longer needed. The second, more compelling reason is that there must be only one file descriptor writing down the pipe (i.e. stdout of the first process). If other processes do not close p[1], when the first process terminates, the second process will not receive an `EOF` and will hang (there will still be some open file descriptors applying to the pipe). Closing `p[0]` is not as crucial, but is good practice.

Third, note the method for waiting for all children to terminate. The program simply waits until an error is returned, and assumes that error to be indicating that there are no more children. This is effective under normal circumstances, but a slightly better method would be to check if `errno` is `ECHILD`, or check the pid returned by `wait` each time to compare with `pid1` and `pid2`.

19.8 Signals: <signal.h>

Signals are a similar concept to interrupts. When a signal is sent to a process, the current processing is interrupted and a signal handler is executed. Most tasks do not require fiddling with signals — the shell takes care of it. However, signals can be used by small programs to perform the simple task of trapping keyboard interrupts (i.e. <ctrl-c>). Larger programs that create sub-processes may need to consider the larger issues related to signals.

The simplest example of a signal is the `SIGINT` interrupt signal generated by <ctrl-c>. This causes the currently executing process to be interrupted, and control returns to the shell. Keyboard interrupts are not the only type of signal. Signals are generated for a number of different reasons — keyboard interrupts, program failures (e.g. segmentation fault) and signals sent by other processes. Examine the file <signal.h> or the documentation on `signal` for a complete list — there are quite a few! The signals that are most commonly used are given in Table 19.5.

Table 19.5. Common signals

Signal	Value	Meaning
SIGHUP	1	Hangup — e.g. when a terminal hangs up
SIGINT	2	Keyboard interrupt from <ctrl-c>
SIGQUIT	3	Keyboard interrupt from <ctrl-\>
SIGKILL	9	Kill a process immediately
SIGALRM	14	Alarm timer signal; alarm went off
SIGTERM	15	Terminate a process; similar to `SIGKILL`
SIGSTOP	17	Suspend a process
SIGTSTP	18	Keyboard interrupt from <ctrl-z>
SIGCONT	19	Resume a process
SIGCHLD	20	Sent to parent when child dies

Signals 1..15 are supported by all versions of UNIX. Others may not be supported — consult your documentation. In some variants, `SIGCHLD` is called `SIGCLD`.

19.8.1 Trapping signals: signal

Signals can be caught within a Bourne shell script using the `trap` command and in a C-shell script using the `onintr` command (refer to the documentation on `sh` and `csh`, respectively). Signals can be caught in C using the UNIX system call, `signal`. Any use of signals requires the inclusion of the header file `<signal.h>` and this section assumes that it is always included.

Consider a simple example. To ignore the `<ctrl-c>` keyboard interrupt (the `SIGINT` signal), use the following `signal` call at the start of your program:

```
signal(SIGINT, SIG_IGN);        /* Ignore SIGINT */
```

Other signals that can be generated from the keyboard are `SIGTSTP` from `<ctrl-z>` and `SIGQUIT` from `<ctrl-\>`. Note that the particular mapping of keys onto interrupts may differ slightly — consult the manual entry for `tty` or `stty`. If required, these other key interrupts could also be ignored as above, to completely prevent a program from being stopped (be careful of locking yourself out).

Signals can be reinstated to their default action using `SIG_DFL`. For example, to no longer ignore `SIGINT`, the program would use:

```
signal(SIGINT, SIG_DFL);
```

The signal function allows most signals to be trapped (a few special signals can never be trapped — `SIGKILL` and `SIGSTOP`). Signals can be trapped by specifying they be ignored using `SIG_IGN`, or by specifying a handler function. The `signal` function does both. Its full prototype definition is:

```
typedef void (*ptr_to_fn)();
ptr_to_fn signal(int sig, ptr_to_fn handler);
```

where `ptr_to_fn` is used here for convenience, but not actually declared in `<signal.h>`.

Both `SIG_IGN` and `SIG_DFL` can be thought of as special types of signal handlers. They are special symbolic constants declared in `<signal.h>`, and can be applied to any signal. The default actions on different signals can be found in the manual entry for `signal`.

The definition of the handler function was non-prototyped above (i.e. `ptr_to_fn` was non-prototyped). The full prototype definition of a handler function is given below:

```
void handler(int sig, int code, struct sigcontext *context)
```

However, it is more common to define the function using non-prototyping and ignore the second and third arguments. This is particularly useful in improving portability, since the declaration of the third parameter varies across UNIX implementations. If a handler is used for only one type of signal, it does not even need the first argument.

A signal handler can simply return, and execution will continue from where it left off. Most system calls will resume properly, but some system calls will return an error if interrupted by a signal. The functions affected differ, but often include `read`, `write` and `wait` — consult your local documentation. Some implementations will permit the specification of the behavior using a special flag — consult the manual entry for `sigvec`. Should a system call return due to a signal, it will set `errno` to `EINTR`.

In most situations, a signal is an exceptional circumstance and simply returning is not correct. More commonly a signal handler will terminate the process with `exit`, or jump to a specified location using `longjmp`.

Here is a simple program that traps all the signals and prints out the number of the first signal received before terminating. Run it in the foreground to determine the signal numbers corresponding to <ctrl-c>, <ctrl-z> and <ctrl-\>.

```
#include <stdio.h>
#include <stdlib.h>
#include <signal.h>

#define NUM_SIGNALS  31       /* Consult local documentation */

void intr(sig)      /* Non-prototyping prevents type warnings */
int sig;
{
    signal(sig, intr);            /* Reinstate signal handler */
                                  /* required by some systems */
    printf("Signal is %d \n", sig);
    exit(1);
}

main()
{
    int i;

    for (i = 0; i <= NUM_SIGNALS; i++) {   /* For all signals */
        signal(i, intr);                   /* Install handler */
    }

    while (1)              /* Wait for a signal */
        ;/* empty loop */
}
```

Signals can also be sent to a process from the shell using the UNIX "kill" command. By default, kill sends SIGTERM (signal 15), but kill can send any signal using the number of the signal or its name as an option (e.g. "kill -9" or the C-shell equivalent "kill -KILL"). Remove the call to exit in the test program, recompile, and run the program in the background (not in the foreground because you can't stop it!) and then try to kill it this way. The normal "kill" will not stop it, but "kill -9" will. This is because SIGKILL (signal 9) cannot be trapped.

When a signal handler is called, further instances of the same signal are blocked. When the signal handler returns, the signal is automatically unblocked. Note that different signals may be delivered to the process while it is processing the first, causing their handlers to be invoked. Note that "blocked" is not the same as "ignored" (with SIG_IGN) in the sense that blocked signals are left pending and are delivered as soon as they are unblocked, whereas ignored signals are discarded. For more discussion of blocked signals, see the manual entries for sigpause, sigblock, sigvec and sigsetmask.

Some systems will reset a signal to its default value when it has occurred. This requires that a signal handler reinstate itself each time it is called, using signal. Although it may not be necessary on your system, following this policy improves portability. Note that in the examples considered reinstatement is unnecessary because the handlers were only to be executed once.

Up to now, the return value of signal has been ignored. It is −1 on error, but more importantly, it returns the *old* value of the signal handler for the specified signal (note that not all systems support this — consult local documentation on `signal`). This is useful for checking what signals have been modified. The most important example is what happens when a program is run in the background by the shell. The shell ensures that `SIGINT` is ignored when a process is in the background. Suppose the program needs to trap `SIGINT` when the program is run in the foreground. The simple call:

```
signal(SIGINT, handler);
```

will undo the good work of the shell when the process is run in the background — the signal was ignored, but will now be sent to the handler. The solution is to check the previous value of the handler for `SIG_IGN` and to only set the handler if it was not set to `SIG_IGN`. The obvious method is:

```
old_handler = signal(SIGINT, new_handler);
if (old_handler == SIG_IGN)
    signal(SIGINT, SIG_IGN);
```

This is effective, but it leaves the signal incorrect for an instant. The following piece of code achieves the same result without the potential for danger:

```
old_handler = signal(SIGINT, SIG_IGN);
if (old_handler != SIG_IGN)
    signal(SIGINT, new_handler);
```

This is usually abbreviated to remove the need for a temporary variable:

```
if (signal(SIGINT, SIG_IGN) != SIG_IGN)
    signal(SIGINT, new_handler);
```

19.8.2 Sending signals: kill

Signals can be sent to processes using the `kill` system call (not to be confused with the `kill` shell command). The return value of `kill` is −1 if an error occurred; zero otherwise. Its prototype is:

```
int kill(int pid, int sig);
```

This is most commonly used by a parent to send signals to its children, but signals can be sent to any process (within the restrictions of protection). A process can send itself signals since the pid of the current process can be determined using `getpid`. Some examples of the use of `kill` are:

```
kill(child_pid, SIGSTOP);    /* Suspend a child process */
kill(getpid(), SIGQUIT);     /* Commit suicide */
```

As an alternative to using `kill` with `getpid`, a process can send itself signals using the `raise` standard library function. This function is declared in `<signal.h>` and its prototype is:

```
int raise(int sig);
```

Its return value is zero for success, non-zero for failure.

19.8.3 Alarms using signals

One common use of signals is to set an alarm to go off after a predefined amount of time. The `alarm` function sets an alarm to expire after a number of seconds. Its definition is:

```
int alarm(int seconds)
```

As one example, this can be used to prevent infinite loops in programs. The program sets up an alarm to go off after some length of time (known to be greater than the maximum time required by the program). If the program does not terminate within the required time, the alarm will go off, sending a signal `SIGALRM` to the process. By default, this signal terminates the process. Alternatively, a signal handler could be set up to catch the signal.

19.8.4 Segmentation faults and other signals

A number of program faults will cause a signal to be sent to the process. For example, `SIGSEGV` is sent for a segmentation fault, `SIGBUS` for a bus error. By default, these cause termination of the program with a core dump. These signals can be caught like any other signal, but this is only used by advanced programs. Catching these signals allows for a more graceful crash when the program fails for some unknown reason (i.e. a bug).

19.9 Further reading

Naturally, there is much more that could be said about programming under UNIX. For example, this chapter has only discussed some of the many library functions that are standard for UNIX systems, but not incorporated into the ANSI standard library. There are a number of books in which I found useful discussions of UNIX. Kochan and Wood's book has two good chapters on UNIX specific issues. Kernighan and Ritchie have a chapter dealing with UNIX low-level I/O and other issues. Horspool discusses programming in a particular variant of UNIX called Berkeley UNIX. The books by Bourne and by Kernighan and Pike are classic references for UNIX material and cover many interesting topics. Lapin is another interesting book focusing on portability under UNIX.

> KOCHAN, Stephen G., and WOOD, Patrick H., *Topics in C Programming (revised edition)*, John Wiley and Sons, 1991.
>
> HORSPOOL, R. Nigel, *C Programming in the Berkeley UNIX Environment*, Prentice Hall, 1986.
>
> KERNIGHAN, Brian W., and RITCHIE, Dennis M., *The C Programming Language (2nd edition)*, Prentice Hall, 1989.
>
> BOURNE, Stephen R., *The UNIX System*, Addison-Wesley, 1983.
>
> KERNIGHAN, Brian W., and PIKE, Rob, *The UNIX Programming Environment*, Prentice Hall, 1984.
>
> LAPIN, J. E., *Portable C and UNIX System Programming*, Prentice Hall, 1987.

19.10 Exercises

1. Write a simple version of the `cp` command using only low-level I/O functions. Your program should not need to use any functions or symbolic constant declarations in `<stdio.h>` at all. *Hint:* How can the action of `getchar` or `putchar` be produced using only `read` and `write`? What are the file descriptors for standard input and standard output?

2. Write a version of the `cat` command using only low-level I/O functions. It should receive filenames as command line arguments, or read from standard input if there are no filenames.

3. Write a version of the `tee` command using only low-level I/O functions. The `tee` command copies standard input to standard output *and* to any filenames appearing as arguments. What is the maximum number of filenames that it can accept?

4. Write a program that double spaces (i.e. puts a blank line between every pair of lines) the output from a directory listing using "`ls -la`". The program should use `popen` with the "`r`" mode.

5. Write a small program that produces output to both `stdout` and `stderr`. Experiment with the use of output redirection in your shell (you may need to read the documentation on `sh` or `csh`). When you only redirect `stdout`, where does the output to `stderr` go? Redirect both `stdout` and `stderr` to a file. Can you redirect `stderr` to a file and `stdout` to the screen? How can you pipe both `stdout` and `stderr` to another command such as `cat` or `more`?

6. Type in the program in Section 19.8.1 and run it in the foreground to determine the signal number of the keyboard interrupts `<ctrl-c>`, `<ctrl-\>` and `<ctrl-z>`. Remove the call to `exit`, recompile and run it in the background (why not in the foreground?), then try to kill it using the UNIX `kill` command. *Hint:* Read the manual entry for `kill` to find out what option should be used.

7. Write a program that forks a child process (which goes into an infinite loop producing output), sleeps for 5 seconds, then kills the child process. What is the return value from `wait` if the program, after killing the child, sleeps for 5 more seconds (to ensure that the child is dead) and then calls the `wait` function?

8. Write a program that sets an alarm to go off in 5 seconds and then goes into an infinite loop. What happens on your system if the signal is not trapped? Modify the program to trap the signal. Your signal handler should output an appropriate message and then terminate.

9. (advanced) A UNIX shell is not a particularly mysterious program, although writing a full shell is by no means a small task. All the shell does is repeatedly wait for input and then execute the command. Write a simple shell that waits for input and then uses the `system` function to execute the command. Make sure it handles signals correctly *and* allows the user a method of exiting the shell (because `<ctrl-c>` will no longer exit). Why doesn't `cd` work correctly? Modify your shell to detect `cd` commands as a special case and use the `chdir` UNIX library function to execute them.

Appendix A
C for Pascal programmers

This section does not aim to provide a comprehensive summary of all the differences between Pascal and C. Instead, it shows enough of the language to allow programmers already familiar with Pascal to understand simple C programs.

Pascal programmers learning C will notice a lot of similarities. Both languages are structured languages. The basic control structures differ only in syntax details. The basic operators are mostly the same, with the annoying exception of the assignment operator. Major differences appear in C's extra operators, the handling of data types and in input-output. C does provide many extra features. For example, the convenient notation for incrementing variables is sadly missed by C programmers (forced into) programming in Pascal. However, these advantages do not come without some loss of Pascal's "niceness" as a programming language (e.g. there is no bounds checking on arrays).

A.1 Overall program structure

Consider the two programs given below to print out a variable. It is easily seen that the structure of C is less rigid. For example, comments replace the `program` keyword at the start of the program. There is also no equivalent to the `var` section for variable declarations and variable declarations simply appear before the executable code. The Pascal program is:

```
program print (input, output);
{This program prints an integer}

var
    x : integer;

begin
    x := 2;                          (* assign x the value 2 *)
    writeln('x = ', x);
end.
```

Its equivalent C program is shown below. The entry point to the C program is indicated as the `main` function. Braces replace the `begin` and `end` keywords (less typing!).

```
/* print   - this program prints out an integer */
#include <stdio.h>          /* include I/O library functions */
main()
{
    int x;                  /* declare x as an int */

    x = 2;                  /* assign x the value 2 */
    printf("x = %d\n", x);  /* print x, and go to next line */
}
```

As in Pascal, blanks, tabs and newlines are ignored by the compiler (except to delimit tokens). Keywords are reserved, though the list of reserved keywords is obviously different. Identifiers for variable names are the same (using letters, digits and underscores). Case of letters is significant in C — the two identifiers `temp` and `Temp` are totally different references.

Comments are identical to Pascal, except that they are delimited by the tokens `/*` and `*/`. There can be no spaces between the slash and the star. As in Pascal, comments can span multiple lines but cannot be nested.

Input and output is quite different, with `printf` instead of `write/writeln` and `scanf` instead of `read/readln`. Because of the major differences, the details of input-output are not covered here. Further explanation of input-output is given in Chapter 9.

A.2 Statements and blocks

As in Pascal, C programs consist of sequences of statements. Single statements in C are terminated by a semicolon. Sequences of statements can also be grouped to create a block. The keywords `begin` and `end` in Pascal are replaced in C by braces.

Semicolon usage is slightly different. The semicolon is a statement *terminator* in C, but a statement *separator* in Pascal. The distinction has no effect on single statements but the rules about semicolons and blocks are different. Blocks in C never have a semicolon after the closing right brace (i.e. no semicolon after the `end`). A semicolon is always needed before the right brace, to terminate the last statement of the block (i.e. always before an `end`). The need for semicolons is shown in the example below:

```
main()
{
    if (x > y) {
        a = 1;
        b = 2;       /* Semicolon required here */
    }                /* No semicolon here */
}
```

A.3 The if statement

The `if-then-else` statement of Pascal is replaced by the `if-else` statement in C. The word `then` is not used and it is not even a keyword in C. The other major difference is that brackets are needed around the `if` condition. Examples of an `if` and `if-else` statement are given below:

```
if (x > y)
    y = 3;
if (x > y) {
    temp = x;
    x = y;
    y = temp;
}
else {
    ...     /* else part */
}
```

The semicolon usage differences discussed above appear with the `if-else` statement, and this is a common cause of confusion for Pascal programmers. It is sometimes necessary to have a semicolon before an `else` (if the statement is not enclosed in a block). For example:

```
if (x > y)
    max = x;            /* Semicolon needed here */
else
    max = y;
```

Semicolons are not required before an `else` if the `if` statement is a block. This is consistent with a block never requiring a semicolon after its right brace.

```
if (x > y) {
    max = x;
}                       /* No semicolon here */
else {
    max = y;
}
```

A.4 Loops

`while` loops in C do not use the keyword `do`. As with `if` statements, the brackets are needed around the condition. An example of a `while` loop is:

```
while (x > y) {
    ...     /* loop body */
}
```

C's `for` loops are very different to Pascal's `for` loops. Whereas Pascal's `for` loop increments (or decrements) an integer variable through a fixed range, C's `for` loop is far more flexible. In fact, C's `for` loop is an extension of the `while` loop. Consider the Pascal `for` loop for counting from 1 to 10:

```
for i := 1 to 10 do
begin
    ...             (* body of loop *)
end;
```

The corresponding C `for` loop statement is:

```
for (i = 1; i <= 10; i++) {
    ...              /* body of loop */
}
```

This is identical to the sequences of statements:

```
i = 1;
while (i <= 10) {
    ...              /* body of loop */
    i++;             /* increment i */
}
```

The two semicolons in the `for` loop header separate the three actions. The first is the initializer, the second is the loop condition and the third performs the increment.

As with the `while` loop, the brackets around the loop header are necessary (i.e. brackets around the three expressions). The `do` keyword found in the Pascal `for` loop is not used.

C has a post-tested loop corresponding to Pascal's `repeat-until`. It is the do loop (also called the `do-while` loop). An example of a do loop is:

```
do {
    ...       /* loop body */
} while (x > y);
```

There are a number of differences. The first trivial difference is that the brackets around the condition of the `while` are needed. More importantly, the sense of the conditional test is reversed. In Pascal, the loop iterates *until* the condition is true. In C, the loop iterates *while* the condition is true.

The loop must contain a single statement or a block, unlike Pascal where a sequence of statements is allowed. This means that braces are needed after the `do`, and before the `while`. In Pascal terminology, a `begin-end` pair around the body of the loop is needed. The keywords `do` and `while` do not act like a `begin-end` pair (whereas the Pascal keywords `repeat` and `until` do).

A.5 The switch statement (replacing case)

Corresponding to Pascal's `case` statement is C's `switch` statement. Like `case`, it allows multiway branching based on any number of constants. Each choice in a `switch` statement is called a "case", just to add to confusion. Hence, `case` is a keyword in C, but with different meaning to its use in Pascal.

`switch` statements are more flexible than Pascal's `case` statement. Any constant expression can be a case, and default actions can be specified using the `default` keyword. The `default` clause is optional, and it is not a run-time error if no `case` matches the value. Instead of producing an error message, execution silently moves to the next statement after the `switch` statement. Multiple cases are specified by two `case` clauses, one after the other, not by a comma as in Pascal.

Unlike Pascal's `case` statement, C's `switch` statement does not necessarily execute only one of the options. Unless told otherwise, control branches to the first match, and then continues on down through all the other `case` clauses below that case. Fortunately, this dangerous *falling through* can be prevented by the break statement. The break statement is not really part of the switch statement, but it is used very commonly with switch. It is important to have a break statement at the end of every case clause. The example below shows the use of break in a switch statement:

```
switch (x) {
   case 1:
            ...              /* statements for 1 */
         break;
   case 2:
   case 3:
            ...              /* statements for 2 and 3 */
         break;
   default:
            ...              /* statements for all other values */
         break;
}
```

A.6 Operators

Replacing the Pascal assignment operator (:=) is the equals sign (=). This can cause confusion, as the equals sign is not the equality relational operator in C. The equality operator is two equals signs (==).

The arithmetic operators are mostly similar and are listed in Table A.1. Pascal's integer division operator div is replaced by /. The types of the operands determine whether the division is integer or floating point. Integer division truncates to integer type, as occurs with the Pascal div operator. Pascal's mod operator is replaced by the non-alphabetic % operator, which is functionally equivalent.

Table A.1. Arithmetic operators

Operator	Meaning
+	Addition
−	Subtraction
*	Multiplication
/	Division
%	Remainder (modulus)

The relational operators are very similar. The differences here are != replacing <> for "not equal", and == replacing = for "equal". The full list is given in Table A.2.

A major source of confusion is that the single equals sign is the assignment operator, not the equality relational operator. It is a bad error to use the assignment operator in an if statement, as below:

```
if (x = y)      /* INCORRECT - if x assigned y */
```

The logical operators and, or, not are replaced by non-alphabetic operators; see Table A.3. An important difference is that C supports no boolean type, instead using integer

Table A.2. Relational operators

Operator	Meaning
==	Equal
!=	Not equal
<	Less than
>	Greater than
<=	Less than or equal
>=	Greater than or equal

zero to represent `false` and any non-zero integer to represent `true`. Hence, these operators can be applied to any integral values.

Table A.3. Logical operators

Operator	Meaning
!	Not
&&	And
||	Or

The precedence of these operators makes more sense in C than in Pascal. The main difference is that relational operators (e.g. <, >) have higher precedence than the logical operators. For example, brackets are unnecessary around the *terms* in the expression below (although they are needed around the entire condition):

```
if (x == y && a > b)          /* if x equals y and a > b */
```

whereas the Pascal equivalent requires brackets:

```
if (x = y) and (a > b) then   /* Pascal equivalent */
```

A.7 Data types and variable declarations

The basic types are mostly similar, with different names:

```
integer  →  int
char     →  char           /* char is the same */
real     →  float/double
boolean  →  int            /* explanation below */
```

There is no boolean type in C and `int` variables are usually used to store boolean values. This is possible because the relational and logical operators return an `int` — 1 for true, zero for false. The logical operators also assume any non-zero integer is true, and zero is false, which is consistent with 1 for true and zero for false (but more flexible).

To Pascal programmers, variable declarations in C appear to be the wrong way around: the type name comes before the variable's name. Multiple variables can be declared to be the same type by placing commas between the variable names. Some examples of variable declarations are:

```
int      x;              /* x is an integer */
char     ch, ch2;        /* ch and ch2 are both characters */
float    a, b, c;
double   d;
```

Variable declarations do not have a special section (i.e. no var section). Instead, declarations simply appear before the executable statements.

A.8 Arrays

The *use* of arrays in C is very similar to Pascal, but the *definition* of arrays is different. Array elements are referenced by placing the index in square brackets, as in Pascal. Array variables are declared by square brackets *after* the variable name. There is no array keyword in C

Inside the square brackets is the *size* of the array, rather than the range of indices. There is no way to declare lower and upper index bounds (i.e. array[10..20] is impossible). The lower bound in an array is always zero and the range is 0..size-1. Declaring an array of size 10 declares ten locations, a[0] up to a[9]. Any reference to a[10] is not legal and will cause a program failure because there is no bounds checking on array references in C. Some examples of the declaration and use of arrays are given below:

```
int  a[20];    /* a is array of 20 integers, a[0],a[1],..a[19] */

a[i] = 0;      /* zero the ith element of array a */
a[i]++;        /* increment ith element of array a */
```

Multi-dimensional arrays are referenced by two sets of square brackets. The Pascal syntax of commas between the two indices is illegal. Multi-dimensional arrays are defined and used as shown below:

```
int b[10][20];      /* b is an array of integers, 10 by 20 */
z = b[x][y];        /* NOT b[x,y] */
```

A.9 Records

Records in Pascal become structures in C. The keyword is "struct". Declaration of struct variables is quite different, and is discussed more fully in Chapter 5. A simple example of the declaration of a record type, node_type, and the definition of a variable of that type, first_record is given below. The Pascal code is:

```
type
    node_type = record
        data : integer;
    end;

var
    first_record : node_type;    (* declare record variable *)
```

There are no specified type or var sections in C, and both types of declarations appear in the same place (i.e. before the executable statements in a function), with the typedef keyword indicating the start of a type declaration. Note how the type name appears before the variable name in the variable declaration, as with all C declarations. The C equivalent is:

```
typedef struct {            /* declare "node_type" as a type */
    int     data;
} node_type;

node_type first_rec;        /* declare struct variable */
```

Record and struct *usage* is very similar. The period is the operator to reference a field of a struct (i.e. str.field). struct variables can also be assigned to each other, passed to functions and returned from functions. However, structs cannot be compared as a whole using any of the operators; even == for equality is not allowed.

A.10 Pointers to records

Pascal's major use of pointers appears in dynamic data structures such as linked lists. Using pointers for this purpose in C is quite similar to the usage in Pascal. Pointers are used in C for a number of other purposes, but these uses will not be considered in this section.

The keyword nil in Pascal is replaced by NULL in C (all capital letters). Note that NULL is actually a symbolic constant for zero defined in <stdio.h> and this file must always be included when using NULL.

The Pascal heap management functions, new and dispose, are replaced by the standard library functions, malloc and free, which are declared in <stdlib.h>. These functions are discussed in Section 8.6.

To reference a field of a pointer to a struct (i.e. record pointer), the "->" operator is used instead of the paired Pascal operators "^.". To reference the entire element that a pointer is pointing to, use the prefix operator *, instead of the Pascal postfix operator ^ (i.e. *ptr instead of ptr^). Pointers to structs are defined and used as shown below:

```
struct node *p;             /* Declare p as a pointer */
struct node *p, *p2;        /* Declare p and p2 as pointers */

p->data = 0;                /* Set data field to 0 */
*p = *p2;                   /* Copy entire node of p2 to p */
```

A.11 Other types

Strings in C are defined as arrays of characters. There is no "string" type (as there is in some Pascal implementations). No operators apply to this type. Instead, standard library functions are available for the common string operations.

There are no sets in C. These must be implemented some other way — for example, by writing your own library functions to define the set as a new data structure.

Files in C are defined very differently. Instead of having a predefined type "file of" as in Pascal, C uses a number of standard library functions. For further discussion refer to Chapter 10.

Enumerated types are similar to Pascal, but the syntax is slightly different in C. They are discussed fully in Chapter 5.

Sub-ranges of integers are not supported in any form by C. The only choice is to use the superset type (e.g. `int` instead of `1..100`).

A.12 User defined types using typedef

There is no special "`type`" section in C programs (`type` is not even a keyword in C). Instead, you can define your own type names using the keyword `typedef`. A `typedef` declaration can occur anywhere that a variable declaration is allowed (i.e. before executable statements in functions), and `typedef` declarations can be mixed with the variable declarations in any order.

In a `typedef` declaration the new type name is always the identifier on the right of the declaration and this identifier is often in the middle of some other non-alphabetic symbols (e.g. square brackets on the right when declaring an array type). Some examples of `typedef` declarations are:

```
typedef int data_type;          /* data_type == int */
typedef int array_type[10];     /* array_type == array of int */

typedef struct node {
    int     data;
} node_type;                    /* node_type == struct type */

typedef struct node *ptr;       /* ptr == pointer type */
```

A.13 Functions and procedures

C has only one type of basic module: the function. Functions are declared quite differently to Pascal. The Pascal keyword "`function`" is not a C keyword. The return type of a C function appears *before* the function header. Parameter types appear *before* the parameter names (as with all C variable declarations). The example below is a function returning `int`, accepting two `int` parameters:

```
int my_fn(int x, int y)
{
    ...     /* local variable declarations */
    ...     /* executable statements */
}
```

In C there is no syntactic distinction between procedures and functions. Procedures are declared as functions returning the special type `void` (i.e. returning nothing). An example of a `void` function is:

```
void print_int(int x)
{
    printf("%d\n", x);          /* Print out x */
}
```

Functions that return a value use a different syntax to that in Pascal. In Pascal, the function's name is used like a variable. In C, the `return` keyword is used. This is a special statement that exits the function *immediately* and returns the expression. A function can be exited from the middle, and not just the end (as in Pascal). An example of a function using the `return` statement is:

```
int max(int x, int y)
{
    if (x > y)
        return x;
    else
        return y;
}
```

There is no need to use `return` in a `void` function, as the function will return automatically at the bottom (i.e. at the last right brace). However, `void` functions can use `"return;"` to exit from the middle of the function.

There is no equivalent to the Pascal `var` keyword in C. There is no easy way to specify whether a parameter is passed by value or passed by reference. The parameter passing mechanism is fixed. Arrays are passed by reference (i.e. variable parameters), and all other variables are passed by value. Because of the problems with variable parameters, C programs tend to make more use of functions and their return value. Variable parameters can be implemented in a special way using pointers (see Section 8.4).

A.14 Symbolic constants

Symbolic constants are defined by a special type of line in the program. These are called preprocessor directives. In C, lines with `#define` can occur anywhere in the program, on a separate line. This line indicates to the compiler to perform a substitution throughout the rest of the program. This substitution can be from any symbol to a number or a constant expression. Note that there must be *no semicolon at the end*. Some examples of symbolic constant declarations are:

```
#define  MAX     20
#define  TRUE    1
#define  MIN     (MAX / 2)
#define  TWENTY  (2 * 10)
```

The `#define` mechanism is much more powerful than Pascal's `"const"`. Any constant expression is allowed — in fact, any replacement text at all! Also possible are macros with arguments, but this is not discussed here (see Chapter 11).

A.15 Extra features of C

C has a number of features with no equivalent in Pascal. Some of the main features are:

- Variable initialization
- The `break` and `continue` statements
- The preprocessor
- Independent compilation
- Standard library functions
- Extra operators

All types of variables can be initialized at compile time to specified values — even structures and arrays. This is discussion in Chapter 7.

The `break` and `continue` statements allow advanced loop control. The `break` statement is used to exit from a loop immediately, and the `continue` statement is used to skip part of an iteration. These statements are covered in Chapter 4.

The preprocessor performs text substitution, file inclusion, macro expansion and conditional compilation. Any line starting with # is a preprocessor directive (e.g. `#include`, `#define`). The preprocessor is covered in Chapter 11.

Independent compilation refers to the fact that source files can be compiled individually and then linked together to form the executable. It is not necessary to have the whole program in one file. Programs can be broken into functions, and different functions stored in different files. This feature allows fast compilation of large programs, and better organization of functions. Independent compilation is covered in Chapter 13.

There are a large number of standard library functions that come with any C compiler. To use these, the program need only `#include` the appropriate header file. The standard library is covered in Chapter 12.

There are many different operators available in the C language. The most commonly used operators are the increment and decrement operators (++ and --) and the extended assignment operators (+=, -=, etc). Some examples of these operators are:

```
i++;        /* i = i + 1 */
i--;        /* i = i - 1 */
i += 10;    /* i = i + 10 */
```

There are also operators for acting on the bit representation of integers, a type conversion operator and a conditional operator that is similar to using an `if` statement.

A.16 Pitfalls for Pascal programmers

There a number of common pitfalls into which many Pascal programmers fall when converting to C. Some of the less dangerous ones are listed below:

- Using upper case letters — C is case sensitive.
- Variables declarations — "`x: int;`" is wrong.
- Missing brackets around boolean conditions for `if` and `while`.
- Adding `then` or `do` keywords to `if` and `while` statements.
- Referencing multi-dimensional arrays using `arr[i,j]`.

These errors are less dangerous because they cause compilation errors. There are a number of other errors that do not cause compilation errors, and may cause the program to fail at run-time:

- Assignment and equality — using `if(x=y)` instead of `if(x==y)`.
- Missing `break` statements in `switch` statements.
- Semicolons on `for` loops — "`for(...);`" creates an empty loop.
- Omitting brackets on calls to functions or procedures with no arguments.
- Thinking `arr[10]` means `arr[1]`...`arr[10]`.

Appendix B
Common errors in C

Every programmer quickly becomes familiar with the phenomenon of run-time errors. These are errors that cause the program to crash, hang or produce incorrect output. In C there are some very common mistakes that cause run-time errors and this section is intended to document the most common errors. Making the programmer aware of the errors will hopefully diminish their occurrence.

B.1 Off-by-one errors

A common example of off-by-one involves problems with array indices. Remember that arrays indices range from `0..n-1`, and not `1..n`. When counting elements in an array, there are `n` elements, but the highest index is `n-1`. If the size is confused with the highest index, the program is off-by-one.

Another example of off-by-one is whether to increment before or after an operation (i.e. prefix or postfix increment). Consider the `for` loop to copy a linked list into an array:

```
count = 0;
for (p = head; p != NULL; p = p->next)
    a[++count] = p->data;                  /* INCORRECT */
```

This is incorrect as the zeroth array element is missed. The problem is the use of the prefix ++ causing `count` to be incremented before its value is used for the array index. The correct statement uses post-increment:

```
    a[count++] = p->data;                  /* CORRECT */
```

Another example of a one-off error occurs in the use of arrays. Common style for setting or accessing all elements in an array is to use a `for` loop similar to:

```
for (i = 0; i < n; i++)
    a[i] = 0;
```

There are two ways this can go wrong — i can be initialized to 1, or the < operator can be mistakenly replaced with <=. In the first case, the zeroth array element is missed. In the second case, the array element a[n] is accessed, often causing a crash.

B.2 Expression errors

Expressions in C programs can become very complicated and are prone to error. The sheer number of different operators can cause confusion, and errors occur when operators are used improperly or are applied in the wrong order.

B.2.1 Assignment and equality (= and ==)

The most common error for beginning C programmers is to use the assignment operator (=) instead of the relational equality operator (==). The assignment operator is legal in if statements. It evaluates to the value of its right operand. In the example below, the value 3 is assigned to x, and the result returned is 3, which is always true. If instead there had been "if(x=0)" it would always be false, because the value of the expression "x=0" is 0, which is false. The problem is illustrated below:

```
if (x = 3)      /* INCORRECT */
if (x == 3)     /* CORRECT */
```

There is no easy way to avoid this error. Many compilers do not consider assignment in logical conditions to be an error and do not generate any warning. The only real solution is practice — get used to typing ==.

B.2.2 Confusing logical and bitwise operators (& and &&)

Another common mistake that novice programmers make with double character operators is using & or | (which are bitwise operators) instead of && or || (which are logical operators). This bug is not shown by the compiler, as it is not a syntax error. The erroneous use of bitwise operators can cause intermittent bugs. The difference between & and && does not always cause an error. The bitwise-and operator, &, causes a bit operation on each bit of its two operands, and returns the result, which can be any integer. The logical operator, &&, returns only two possible values — zero or one. It returns 1 (true) if both operands are non-zero, otherwise it returns zero.

If both operands are either zero or one, there is no difference between the result of & and &&. This is often the case in conditions such as (x==y)&&(z>3), because the relational operators return only zero or one. However, problems occur when using a non-zero value to indicate the truth of a condition. Incorrect results can occur below if & accidentally replaces &&.

```
if (flag && x > y)          /* if flag != 0  and  x > y */
```

If & replaces && here, the test is effectively a bit mask on the lower bit of flag. The test "(x>y)" returns 0 or 1 which is then used as a mask for the & operator. If, for example, flag is 2 (non-zero means true) the condition will return false anyway, because the lower bit is zero.

The only solution to this problem is to be aware of it, and get used to typing characters twice. The preprocessor could be used to help (e.g. `#define and &&`), but this is not recommended, mainly because it is not common practice.

B.2.3 Boolean expressions: De Morgan's laws

A common mistake for novice programmers is to incorrectly interpret complicated boolean expressions. Unless you are very familiar with the rules of boolean algebra, check them carefully. A good idea is to hand-evaluate a few cases to check that the condition gives the correct result.

One problem area involves the combination of `!` with either of `&&` or `||`. De Morgan's laws of boolean algebra are counter-intuitive. For example, do not be fooled into thinking that "not (A or B)" is the same as "not A or not B". De Morgan's laws state:

```
!(x || y)   ≡   (!x) && (!y)
!(x && y)   ≡   (!x) || (!y)
```

B.2.4 Real number errors: floats and doubles

Real numbers behave strangely on computers. They are rarely exactly as they seem. Results of computations always differ at the tenth or fifteenth decimal place. Guaranteed. The problems are due to the internal representation of real numbers. Computers can only store real numbers to a limited precision (i.e. a limited number of significant figures). Inevitably, roundoff errors occur in calculations. The most common mistake made with real numbers is comparing them for equality. For example, the `for` loop below checks for equality (i.e. not equal):

```
for (x = 0; x != 10 * inc; x += inc)
```

This could cause an infinite loop, because when x nears `10*inc`, it might not be exactly equal. The test for equality would fail, and the loop would continue infinitely, incrementing x further away from `10*inc` at each iteration.

Instead of comparing two real numbers for exact equality, programs should examine their difference. When the absolute value of this difference is smaller than some defined tolerance, consider them equal. A greater difference than the tolerance means not equal. The tolerance value should be very small (e.g. 0.00001). The `for` loop becomes:

```
for (x = 0; fabs(x - 10 * inc) > TOLERANCE; x += inc)
```

B.2.5 Operator precedence errors

The precedence of some operators is not as you might expect it to be and nasty bugs can creep in. The only real solution is to become more familiar with the precedence of various operators, but placing extra brackets causes no harm and does eliminate the problem.

When masking bits and then comparing them with a value, brackets are needed to ensure the correct ordering:

```
if (x & MASK != 0)          /* INCORRECT */
```

```
if ((x & MASK) != 0)        /* CORRECT */
```

Similarly, when testing a function return value by assigning it to a variable, brackets are necessary:

```
if (c = getchar() != EOF)      /* INCORRECT */
if ((c = getchar()) != EOF)    /* CORRECT */
```

When using the shift operators to replace multiplication or division, the low precedence of the shift operators causes problems:

```
x = a + b >> 1;         /* INCORRECT */
x = a + (b >> 1);       /* CORRECT */
```

The use of increment or decrement operators with either of the pointer dereference operators is quite dangerous. There are always two interpretations, depending on whether brackets are used.

```
++p->len;    /* Increment p->len */
(++p)->len;  /* Increment p, then access p->len */
*p++;        /* Increment p, then access what p points to */
(*p)++;      /* Increment what p points to */
```

The last two statements illustrate a common error: the use of *p++ is incorrect when trying to increment what p is pointing to.

The high precedence of the type cast operator means that care is necessary when using it in expressions. For example, when trying to convert the result of x/y to int, the code below is incorrect:

```
z = (int)x / y;        /* INCORRECT */
```

The correct method is to use brackets:

```
z = (int)(x / y);      /* CORRECT */
```

B.2.6 Null effect operations

This error refers to use of operators where the returned result is ignored. It can occur due to a major misconception about some operators, or because of operator precedence problems. For example, the statements below have no effect:

```
x << 1;        /* INCORRECT */
~x;            /* INCORRECT */
```

The first statement is an attempt to double x using bit shifting, and the second is an attempt to complement x using the one's complement operator. Unfortunately, the << operator in the statement "x<<1;" does not affect x at all. Instead, the statement merely evaluates the value of x doubled and then "throws away" this value because it is not used. Compilers usually do not complain about throwing away values because it is commonly used in function calls (e.g. the printf function always returns a value, but this value is rarely used) and the statements above are executed normally (although they actually do nothing at all). The correct statements are:

354   Appendix B

```
x <<= 1;
x = ~x;
```

Another common example occurs when Pascal programmers call a function with no arguments and omit the empty pair of brackets, as below:

```
fn_name;            /* INCORRECT */
```

This is interpreted as a null effect statement that simply calculates the address of the function, rather than calling the function.

Another example of the problem, related to operator precedence, occurs in the statement:

```
*ptr++;             /* INCORRECT */
```

The intention is to increment what `ptr` is pointing to, but operator precedence causes ++ to be evaluated first, followed by the dereference operator. Hence, `ptr` is incremented, and the dereference operation has no effect (the value of what `ptr` points to is calculated and then thrown away). Brackets are needed to enforce the correct precedence.

UNIX programmers have a partial solution: the `lint` checker will find most instances of this error.

B.2.7 Side effects and short-circuiting

In expressions that use the binary logical operators (|| or &&) or the ternary operator (?:) can have problems if the sub-expressions contain *side effects*. Side effects are operations that either affect a variable, consume input or produce output. Thus, the increment and decrement operators and the assignment operators all cause side effects because they change a variable. A function call can be a side effect if it consumes input, produces output, changes one of its arguments or alters a *global* variable.

The problem is that C uses *short-circuiting* in the evaluation of the binary logical operators and the ternary operator. This means that not all sub-expressions in an expression with these operators is always executed. If a sub-expression containing side effects is not executed, the (usually important) effect of these side effects is lost. For example, in the expression:

```
if (x < y && printf(...))
```

if the first term (x<y) is false, the call to the `printf` function is not executed and no output is produced.

The only real solution is to avoid the use of side effects in boolean expressions. This is quite reasonable since such expressions are bad style anyway. The problem of short-circuiting and side effects is also covered in Section 3.19.1.

B.2.8 Order of evaluation errors

Order of evaluation errors are a complicated problem and are covered fully in Section 3.19. This error occurs in statements such as:

```
a[i] = i++;
```

The problem here is that i has a side effect applied to it and is also used without a side effect. Because the order of evaluation of the = operator is unspecified in C, it is undefined whether the increment side effect occurs before or after the evaluation of the i in the array index.

Fortunately, order of evaluation errors can be avoided by the simple policy of performing side effect operations in separate statements. For example, never increment a variable inside a complicated expression or in a function argument. The correct way to rewrite the above statement is:

```
a[i] = i;
i++;
```

B.2.9 Type conversion problems

The large number of type conversions performed implicitly by the compiler leaves room for error. Be careful when mixing real and integral types because conversion from a real to an integer truncates to the nearest integer. Similarly, conversion from double to float, or from one integral type to a smaller integral type, may lose information.

The type qualifiers signed and unsigned can also lead to problems. In particular, char variables are often implicitly signed char, and conversion of a character in the range 128..255 to an integer can yield a negative number. All common alphanumeric characters fall into the range 0..127 and present no problem. However, when accessing bytes (i.e. characters in the range 0..255), the type "unsigned char" should be used.

The unsigned qualifier can be a problem when dealing with negative values. For example, in the code below:

```
unsigned int x = 0;
int y = -1;

if (x > y)
    printf("x > y \n");
```

the operands of > are converted to the "larger" type — in this case, unsigned int. Hence, −1 is converted to an unsigned quantity, yielding a very large value.

B.3 Type errors

Although C compilers type-check most uses of variables, there are still some areas where the compiler ignores types. For example, when non-prototyped function declarations are used the compiler does not check the types of arguments passed to functions (to permit compatibility with old C code). Similarly, arguments to variable-length argument list functions such as printf and scanf are not checked (because the compiler cannot check them).

B.3.1 Wrong types to printf or scanf

The compiler cannot type-check arguments to functions with a variable number of parameters, such as printf and scanf. Even worse, functions with variable parameters cannot themselves check for correct types. If the wrong types are passed to printf or `scanf`, a number of different run-time errors can occur. The most harmless problem is that a meaningless number will be printed (i.e. garbage as output). The worst that can occur is a segmentation fault or some other abnormal termination.

A particular instance of wrong types to `scanf` is forgetting the `&` in front of the arguments. This causes the wrong type to be passed. Instead of a pointer to the variable being passed, the variable's value is passed as if it were a pointer value. This is usually an illegal address and a dereference of this address inside the `scanf` function will cause undefined run-time behavior.

B.3.2 Non-prototyping problems

Prototyping refers to the placing of types of parameters inside the parameter list. With non-prototyping, the types are specified in a list after the end of the parameter list. In compilers that do not support prototyping (or if you choose not to use prototyping for some reason), there is no checking of the types of arguments passed to functions. If the types are not consistent, or if the wrong number of arguments is passed to a function, this usually causes some form of run-time error. The most common error on large systems is the notorious "segmentation fault".

If the program crashes for some reason, one of the first things to check is the types and number of function arguments. Be careful to check for `&`'s on arguments that need them, as this form of type mismatch error is a common problem. To summarize, check for:

- Wrong types of arguments
- Wrong number of arguments
- Missing `&`'s on arguments

Note that non-prototyping problems also occur if a function is used before it has been declared. For this reason it is good practice always to have forward declarations (i.e. prototypes) for all functions at the top of the file. This problem is particularly common when using independent compilation.

B.3.3 Problems with independent compilation

The use of separate files for different functions can lead to a number of problems with types. The basic problem is that C compilers assume the types of function names not already declared. When an undefined identifier is found used as a function name, the C compiler assumes that this function returns `int`. If the function (as defined in another file) does not return `int`, there can be problems. For example, consider a function returning a `short`, but not declared in the current file. If the returned value is assigned to a variable of type `short`, the compiler thinks that an `int` function is being assigned to a `short` variable. It may generate some code to perform the type conversion from `int` to `short`. This type conversion code is the problem. When the program runs, the function actually returns a `short`. This `short` is treated as an `int`, and the type cast is applied, leading to incorrect results.

A similar problem can occur if a function is used before its declaration in the same file. This is not as dangerous because a compilation warning is usually generated about a "redeclaration" of a function.

Another problem is that when a function name is not defined in the current file, the compiler assumes non-prototyping for the function's parameters. With non-prototyping it then performs no type checks on arguments passed to the function. This can lead to the problems of arguments not matching the types of parameters (or the wrong number of arguments passed), as discussed above.

Further problems occur if an `extern` variable is declared incorrectly (i.e. to the wrong type) in any file. The compiler cannot detect the incorrect use of types, as it deals with each file separately.

A similar problem is that of accidentally declaring two global variables, or two functions with identical names, in different files. The compiler cannot usually detect the multiple declaration, unless its linker is smart. The linker differs between different machines. Some linkers will detect multiple declarations as an error, but other linkers will join the two declarations into a single location (i.e. the two variables refer to the same memory address). This can obviously cause incorrect results.

One partial solution to the problems of independent compilation (for UNIX users) is to use the `lint` checker, which checks for type problems over multiple files and is able to detect the errors discussed above. A better solution to these problems is to declare every variable or function used. The best way to do this is with a header file containing `extern` declarations of every global variable and predeclarations of every function. The header files are included into every other C file — even the files containing the actual definitions. Including an `extern` declaration or function forward declaration in the file containing the proper definition ensures that the header file and the definition are consistent. In this way, any difference in declarations is immediately detected as a compilation error. The proper organization of header files for independent compilation is covered in Chapter 13.

B.4 Flow of control errors

There are a number of common errors in the use of C's flow of control statements. Some of these errors are particularly hard to track down because control can pass through a function along many different paths and the error may only occur on one particular path.

B.4.1 Function return inconsistencies

There are a number of problems with the use of a `return` statement. A simple example of such an error is a non-`void` function with no `return` statement at all — obviously the function will return garbage. The same problem can occur in less obvious ways when a `return` statement is not found on some execution paths. The function exits at the closing right brace and returns garbage. For example, the function below returns a value only if the condition in the `if` statement is true:

```
int positive(int x)
{
    if (x > 0)
        return TRUE;
}
```

Another situation where a function may return garbage values is when an `int` function uses the `return` statement:

```
return;          /* return NO value */
```

The compiler may not produce an error message because non-ANSI C programs often used `int` instead of `void`.

B.4.2 Accidental empty loop

A common error with loops is to place a semicolon just after the header of a `for` or `while` loop. Syntactically, this is correct, so the compiler gives no error message. However, it changes the meaning of the loop. For example:

```
for (i = 1; i <= 10; i++);      /* Extra semicolon */
    ...         /* body of loop */
```

is interpreted as:

```
for (i = 1; i <= 10; i++)
    ;   /* empty loop */
    ...     /* body of loop - executed only once */
```

The effect of this is that the body of the loop is assumed to be an empty loop by the compiler. The block after the loop header (the real loop body) is executed after the loop has finished, and is executed only once. Worse still, the accidental empty loop may cause an infinite loop if the condition is not being changed in the header.

B.4.3 Missing break in a switch statement

Leaving out a `break` statement in a `case` clause causes execution to fall through to the next `case`. This causes the statements for more than one `case` to be executed. If a program appears to be doing two things when it should be only doing one, this could be the cause.

Another problem that can appear in a `switch` statement is failure to cover all cases such as a forgotten `case` or a missing `default` clause.

B.4.4 Non-initialized local variables

This problem occurs when a variable is used before it has been assigned a value, either by explicit initialization or an assignment statement. For example, the function below is incorrect because the local variable `sum` is not set with an initial value of zero:

```
int sum(int n)
{
    int i, sum;

    for (i = 1; i <= n; i++)
        sum += i;
    return sum;
}
```

The compiler does not necessarily initialize local variables to zero, although some compilers do. If not explicitly initialized, the values are undefined at the start of the function. One partial solution for UNIX programmers is that `lint` will detect most uses of local variables not previously set.

B.4.5 Unreachable statements

It is possible to have code in a program that cannot be reached under any circumstances. This type of code occasionally indicates the presence of a bug, but more commonly indicates that unnecessary code has not been removed. Good compilers should produce a warning message — the `lint` utility finds many instances of the error. One dangerous example of an unreachable statement is a missing `case` label at the start of a `switch`:

```
switch(x) {
    putchar('0');       /* Unreachable - missing case*/
    ....
}
```

B.5 Array index out of bounds

During execution, the C program does not check array references to determine if indices are too large for the array. A very common error is an array index passing the end of the array. This can cause other variables to be overwritten, crashing sooner or later. Most commonly, the mistake is that an array in C only extends from 0..n-1. Declaring an array of size n does not allow the index to be the value n.

B.6 Unclosed comments

In ANSI C, the presence of /* inside another comment does not start a nested comment; instead, it is ignored. Leaving a comment unclosed accidentally can comment out part of your code, without a compilation warning on many implementations. The /* of the unclosed comment matches the */ of a second comment, leaving out any code between the two. In the example shown below, only the first `printf` statement will be executed because the second is accidentally commented out:

```
printf("j = %d\n", j);    /* this is a comment - unclosed!
printf("i = %d\n", i);    /* this statement is commented out */
```

B.7 Passing structs by value, arrays by reference

Parameter passing can be very confusing in C. All `struct` variables and simple variables are passed by value, meaning that when a function is called, the arguments are copied and these copies are used inside the function. The original arguments cannot be changed within the function, and thus, the values of variables passed as arguments to a function cannot be changed by the function.

Arrays are the exception. When arrays are passed as arguments, the elements of an array can be changed inside the function. The reason for this exception is that arrays are considered to be pointers to the first element of the array. This distinction can cause errors when a function does modify its parameters (e.g. to use as working variables). Hence, the solution is never to modify function parameters.

B.8 Multi-byte characters

Because C compilers accept more than one character in a `char` constant, there are some common errors made by novices. The compiler does not complain about a space in a `char` constant, as below:

```
if (ch == ' A')              /* WRONG */
```

but interprets the code as testing whether `ch` is a space (on some machines).

Similarly, it is wrong to confuse string constants with `char` constants, as in the code below:

```
printf('Hello World\n');     /* WRONG */
```

B.9 Backslash in DOS filenames

A common error for UNIX programmers converting to DOS occurs when a DOS filename is encoded with its full path name. The apparently simple change of the slash character in UNIX filenames to the backslash in DOS filenames has a major danger — the backslash starts an escape. Hence, the filename below is wrong:

```
fp = fopen("c:\file.c", "r");      /* WRONG */
```

The backslash character starts the escape `\f`. The correct statement uses two backslash characters:

```
fp = fopen("c:\\file.c", "r");     /* CORRECT */
```

B.10 Pointer errors

Use of pointers can be fraught with danger. There are some common pitfalls to watch out for. Even experienced programmers have been known to fall for these.

B.10.1 Dereferencing a NULL pointer

A common error is to dereference a pointer that is NULL. This causes an immediate crash. It is one of the most common causes of a "segmentation fault" error on UNIX machines. Dereferencing a NULL pointer can occur with either of the two indirection operators (i.e. *p and p->field). It is most common when using dynamic data structures, but can occur any time you forget to set a pointer. An example is given below:

```
if (p->next != NULL && p != NULL)          /* WRONG ORDER */
```

When p is NULL, the first condition p->next is calculated first, causing a NULL pointer to be dereferenced. Simply reversing the order of the operands solves the problem:

```
if (p != NULL && p->next != NULL)          /* CORRECT */
```

If p is NULL, the first condition evaluates as false and the short-circuiting of the && operator causes the second condition to be skipped, avoiding the dereference of the NULL pointer.

B.10.2 Dangling references

Dangling references occur when a pointer points to the wrong place. More precisely, when it points to memory that is not at present controlled by the program. This is a common problem in algorithms involving linked data structures, where pointers point to blocks that have already been freed.

Another common occurrence is saving structures containing character pointers. If strings have been allocated using malloc, when saving the structs only the pointers are being saved and not the actual character strings themselves. When the structs are loaded back in, the pointers are dangling references and the strings have been lost.

B.10.3 Garbage

Garbage refers to memory allocated by malloc that no longer has any pointer pointing to it. It is unused by the program, and unusable by the program because malloc cannot find it. This problem in a program is often called a memory leak.

In a sense garbage is the opposite problem to dangling references — dangling references are pointers without allocated memory, garbage is memory without a pointer to it. The problem is not a major one unless memory is short. If memory is limited, then gradually accumulating garbage can lead to a program eventually running out of memory (and crashing if out-of-memory is not tested for). The only solution is to be careful to free memory as soon as it is no longer needed.

B.10.4 Freeing a non-allocated memory block

A bad error is to use free on a pointer to memory that has not been allocated by malloc or calloc. The effect of this is not defined, but usually causes a crash. A variable, such as a global array, cannot be freed to the heap. It was not dynamically allocated by malloc or calloc, and has the wrong format. Memory allocated by malloc has a special format — it has a few information bytes before it.

A special instance of this error is freeing a pointer twice. The first time is no problem, but the second time is an error — the memory is no longer allocated.

B.10.5 Not allocating enough memory

Problems occur if not enough memory is allocated for an object. Storing an object at this address may overwrite other variables, or cause a crash. An example of this is forgetting that a string has an extra zero at the end. If memory is not allocated for this extra character, there is the potential for a crash. For example, the use of `strlen` below is wrong. The `strcpy` function copies the terminating zero, but `strlen` does not count it.

```
len = strlen(str);
new_str = malloc(len);    /* INCORRECT - correct is len+1 */
strcpy(new_str, str);
```

B.10.6 Pointer and object confused

It is common to confuse a pointer with what it is pointing to. Assigning one pointer to another is not the same as assigning the items they point to. For example, if the statement "p=q" is used instead of "*p=*q", when *q is modified, *p is also modified (i.e. the value p points to is also modified). One common example of this occurs when copying character strings:

```
s1 = s2;              /* INCORRECT */
strcpy(s1, s2);       /* CORRECT */
```

B.10.7 Returning the address of a local variable

If a function returns the address of a local variable, this is a major error. Because the local variable is stored on the stack, when the function terminates that value is no longer defined. Any pointer that holds the address has become a dangling reference.

B.10.8 Returning the address of a static local variable

Consider a function, `str_label`, to allocate a new string label ten characters long. If the function allocates the string in a local variable and returns this temporary string variable, this is an instance of the previous error. The obvious method of resolving this problem is to declare the string array as `static`. However, this creates a different problem. The second time the function is called, the same pointer value will be returned, and the first label will be overwritten. All pointers will point to the same label. Changing one label will change them all. The only real solution to this problem is to use `malloc` to allocate some dynamic memory each time. However, note that many library functions use this method of returning the address of internal `static` storage, and this is satisfactory because the program using these library functions can make explicit copies of the values, rather than accessing them through the address returned.

B.10.9 Address arithmetic and incrementing pointers

When accessing bytes of data, it is common to use pointers to step through. It is important to remember that ++ and -- increment a pointer by a number of bytes (one or more) depending on the type of the pointer. Similarly, adding an integer to a pointer does not necessarily add that number of bytes — the change is implicitly multiplied by the size of the object the pointer points to (i.e. the type of the pointer). If access to memory at a byte level is needed, use pointers of type `char*` because the size of `char` is one byte.

B.11 Macro errors

Macros can cause two types of problems: compilation errors and logical errors. Compiler diagnostics due to incorrect macro definitions can sometimes be difficult to understand. This is because the compiler receives input after the preprocessor has done its substitutions. Comments have been deleted, and any macros or symbolic constants have been replaced by their corresponding text. Hence, the diagnostic lines printed up by the compiler (supposedly program lines) may bear no resemblance to your program.

The second problem with macros is a logical error. This occurs when the macro expansion is syntactically correct, but is not what was intended by the programmer. This kind of bug can be very difficult to track down. Many of the mistakes mentioned below do not cause a compilation warning. This makes them very dangerous.

B.11.1 Semicolons on the end of macro definitions

In a macro definition there should not be a semicolon on the end. The preprocessor replaces text exactly as it is asked to, and putting a semicolon on the end usually leads to there being an extra semicolon in the wrong place. For example, the code:

```
#define MAX  10;
x = MAX * 2;
```

leads to the incorrect statement:

```
x = 10; * 2;
```

In this example the extra semicolon causes "`*2;`" to be seen as a pointer dereference of the constant 2. As is the case with most instances of this error, this example causes a compilation error because the constant 2 is not a legal pointer type.

B.11.2 Spaces between macro name and left bracket

In a macro definition there cannot be any whitespace (spaces or tabs) between the macro name and the left bracket. Spaces indicate to the preprocessor where the replacement text begins. If there is space, the preprocessor assumes that the definition is for a parameterless symbolic constant and that the left bracket is part of the replacement text. For example, in the definition:

```
#define  abs (x) (x > 0) ? (x) : (-(x))
```

the identifier `abs` is replaced by:

```
(x) (x > 0) ? (x) : (-(x))
```

wherever it appears. As in most occurrences of this error, the above example will usually cause a compilation warning.

B.11.3 Operator precedence: brackets around parameters

When using macros with parameters, where the parameters form an expression in the definition, always place brackets around the parameter. Without brackets, problems occur due to operator precedence. To see this, consider the following example of an incorrect macro definition:

```
#define  cube(x)      x * x * x              /* INCORRECT */
```

The macro call:

```
y = cube(z + 1);
```

expands out as:

```
y = z + 1 * z + 1 * z + 1;
```

which is equivalent to the incorrect expression:

```
y = z + (1 * z) + (1 * z) + 1;
```

To solve this problem, place brackets around each macro parameter in the replacement text in the macro definition:

```
#define  cube(x)     (x) * (x) * (x)         /* CORRECT */
```

Then the macro call expands out correctly as:

```
y = (z + 1) * (z + 1) * (z + 1);
```

B.11.4 Operator precedence: brackets around expression

Although placing brackets around macro parameters solves most operator precedence problems, there is still one further safety measure needed. Consider the macros:

```
#define twice(x )     (x) << 1    /* INCORRECT */
#define inc(x)        (x) + 1     /* INCORRECT */
```

When called by:

```
z = 1 + twice(y);
p = 3 * inc(q);
```

these expand out to be:

```
z = 1 + (y) << 1;
p = 3 * (q) + 1;
```

which are equivalent to the incorrect expressions:

```
z = (1 + (y)) << 1;      /* Precedence of + higher than << */
p = (3 * (q)) + 1;       /* Precedence of * higher than + */
```

The solution to this problem is to place brackets round the entire expression in the macro definition. The examples become:

```
#define twice(x)    ((x) << 1)    /* CORRECT */
#define inc(x)      ((x) + 1)     /* CORRECT */
```

The calls become what was intended:

```
z = 1 + ((y) << 1);
p = 3 * ((q) + 1);
```

B.11.5 Side effects in macros

Macros are not function calls. If there is a side effect (e.g. an increment operator) in an argument passed to a macro call, it is possible that the side effect will occur more than once, or not at all. For example, consider the `cube` macro definition:

```
#define cube(x, y)    ((x) * (x) * (x))
```

When called with:

```
c = cube(a++);
```

the macro expands to:

```
c = ((a++) * (a++) * (a++));
```

and the side effect `a++` is executed three times.

The problem is even less obvious in macros like `min` and `max`, where the number of times a side effect occurs depends on the values of the arguments. For example, with the following definition of `min`:

```
#define min(x, y)    (x < y) ? x : y
```

the macro call:

```
c = min(a++, b);
```

expands out to give:

```
(a++ < b) ? a++ : b
```

where the `a++` side effect is executed twice if `a<b`, otherwise once.

In macros where each parameter appears only once, there is usually no problem. For example:

```
#define twice(x)    ((x) << 1)
```

has no problems, as any side effects are executed exactly once. However, some macros where parameters appear only once can still give trouble — if some parameters are not evaluated. Some side effects may not be executed at all. For example:

```
#define choose(x, y, z)     x > 0 ? y : z
```

Depending on x, any side effect of y or z may or may not be executed.

There is no easy solution. One solution is to use functions instead of macros when a parameter must appear twice in a macro, or when sometimes not all parameters are evaluated. Another incomplete solution is just to be aware of the problem, and to avoid side effects in macro calls.

B.11.6 Missing braces on multiple statement macros

If a macro contains more than one statement, it should have braces around it. Consider the swap macro below:

```
#define swap(x, y)    temp = x; x = y; y = temp    /* INCORRECT */
```

When called by:

```
if (a > b)
    swap(a, b);
```

the result is:

```
if (a > b)
    temp = a; a = b; b = temp;
```

which is (accidentally) equivalent to:

```
if (a > b) {
    temp = a;
}
a = b;
b = temp;
```

because only the first statement is considered to be the statement for the if.

There are a number of possible solutions. Placing braces around any sequences of statements prevents the problem:

```
#define swap(x, y) {temp = x; x = y; y = temp;}    /* IMPROVED */
```

This is satisfactory, but gives minor problems with the else statement, where the code below will cause a compilation error because of a semicolon after a right brace and before an else statement:

```
if (...)
    swap(a, b);    /* semicolon causes error */
else
    ...
```

Another solution is to use the comma operator. The comma operator joins two expressions together to make a single expression. In this way, the sequence is considered as a single statement, and both problems are resolved — the orginal problem with the if and the syntax error with the semicolon before the `else`.

```
#define swap(x, y)     temp = x, x = y, y = temp     /* CORRECT */
```

This solution is not possible if some of the statements are flow of control statements such as `if` statements, loops or `return`. In this case, a special form of `do` loop can be used:

```
#define swap(x, y)    do { temp = x; x = y; y = temp; } while(0)
```

This macro avoids syntax error problems with a semicolon before an `else` statement because the semicolon terminates the `do` loop statement. Note that the block of statements inside the loop is only executed once because `while(0)` is always false. A similar solution is to use an `if` statement with a condition that is always true:

```
#define swap(x, y)    if (1) { temp = x; x = y; y = temp; } else
```

This also works correctly because the semicolon ends the `if` statement. However, this method is slightly worse than the `do` loop because accidentally omitting the semicolon after the macro call may silently introduce a major bug (although some compilers will report an unreachable statement warning), whereas a compilation error occurs when the `do` loop form of the macro is used. One minor problem with both these solutions is that `lint` will warn about a "constant in conditional context".

A slightly different solution is to use a different style for all `if` statements and loops — use blocks instead of single statements. This is generally sound practice, and can be combined with any of the other solutions, just to be safe. Admittedly, this solution leads to longer programs (extra lines), and sometimes less clear programs.

B.11.7 Macros containing if: dangling else problem

Consider the (very simplified) `assert` macro:

```
#define assert(x)    if (!(x)) error()    /* INCORRECT */
```

When called by:

```
if (i == 1)
    assert(a > b);
else
    ...   /* etc */
```

it expands out as:

```
if (i == 1)
    if (!(a > b)) error();
else
    ...   /* etc */
```

This is equivalent to the code below, because an `else` matches the closest `if`. The dangling `else` is resolved by choosing the inner `if`. This is not what was intended by the programmer.

```
if (i == 1) {
    if (!(a > b))
        error();
    else
        ...         /* etc */
}
```

There are many possible solutions. The most obvious solution is to place braces around the replacement text. This solution is effective, but gives the minor problem with the syntax error before the `else` (discussed earlier).

```
#define assert(x) {if (!(x)) error();}   /* IMPROVED */
```

Another solution is to use an empty `else` clause, to make sure that the macro has an `else` to match the `if`. Note the added semicolon after the `printf`, before the `else`, and also the lack of semicolon after the `else`.

```
#define assert(x) if(!(x)) error(); else   /* CORRECT */
```

When an assertion is expanded out, the semicolon after the macro call's right bracket is immediately after the `else` keyword, creating an empty `else` clause.

Another similar solution is to reverse the sense of the conditional test to make sure that the macro has an `else` to match the `if`. The `if` part then does nothing, and the `else` does the work. Note the semicolon before the `else` and no semicolon after the `printf`.

```
#define assert(x)   if (x) ; else  error()     /* CORRECT */
```

Another solution involves converting the `if` statement into an expression using the ternary operator. Note that the second case, after the colon, is a dummy expression (i.e. the constant 1). If the `else` clause is used by the macro, this second case will be executed (and have no effect). If the macro passes back some other type (i.e. not `void`), replace "`void`" with that type.

```
#define assert(x)   ((void)(!(x) ? error() : 1))    /* CORRECT */
```

An obscure method of implementing the `assert` macro is to convert the `if` statement into an equivalent expression, using the short-circuiting of the logical operators to get the effect of the control flow of an `if` statement:

```
#define assert(x)   ((void)((x) || error()))    /* CORRECT */
```

If x is true, the short-circuiting comes into effect and the `printf` is not executed. The use of the ternary operator is just as effective, and the extra complexity of this method is hard to justify.

Another partial solution is to change your programming style instead of changing the macro definition — don't use single statements in `if` statements or loops.

B.11.8 Accidental macro expansion

Macro expansion occurs before any other phase of compilation. Consider what happens to the function definition below if "min" is already defined as a macro:

```
int min(int x, int y)
{
    ... /* etc */
}
```

The macro expansion occurs, leading to absurd syntax. This causes the compiler to output nonsensical error messages and garbled diagnostic lines. The solution is to un-define the macro name *before* the function definition using:

```
#undef min
```

The #undef line is also needed in any other file that *calls* the function.

A more dangerous problem is that if the macro is defined where the function is called, the macro will be invoked without problem, and the function will never be called! This is a far worse problem because it will not cause a compilation error. An example of this problem would be trying to define your own version of the getchar function. The problem is that getchar is actually a macro and will expand out before compilation — the new getchar function is never called.

Appendix C
Complicated declarations

C's type definitions are meant to mirror exactly the usage of the variable in the program. This is very convenient for the compiler, but not so easy for the programmer. C has been criticized at times for the over-abundance of brackets in variable declarations.

Because types are similar to expressions, complicated types can sometimes be clarified by thinking of the statement as if it refers to a variable. For example:

```
int *p;
```

means that (*p) is an int, so p must be a pointer to int.

The same rules of precedence apply to type declarations as to expressions. However, not all of C's operators are used in variable declarations. The operators used in type declarations are given in Table C.1.

Table C.1. Type operators

Operator	Meaning
*	Pointer indirection
[]	Array declaration
()	Function declaration

Brackets also appear to enforce precedence. To distinguish between these two uses of brackets, remember that function call brackets are a postfix operator (i.e. after the expression), whereas normal brackets surround the expression.

Another aspect of complicated variable declarations is that more than one type of variable can be declared in a single declaration. For example, the declaration:

```
int x, *p, fn(char);
```

declares x as an int, p as a pointer to int, and fn as a function returning int (with one char parameter). Note that the declaration of fn is actually a forward declaration of a function and not an ordinary variable declaration. Thus, a variable declaration consists of a base type (i.e. int in the example above) and then one or more comma-separated declarations.

C.1 Declarators and abstract declarators

Because of the close correspondence between type declaration and usage, type declarations often look very similar to expressions. The term *declarator* is the name given to the "type expression" that declares a type or a variable. For example, a typedef statement is a declarator that defines the name in that declarator as a new type name. Valid declarators are those that define legal types.

The term *abstract declarator* is used for expressions formed by a declarator with the variable name omitted. For simple declarations, these are just a type name (e.g. int). For more complicated declarations, the abstract declarator contains all the special symbols of the type declaration (i.e. brackets and stars). Some examples of abstract declarators are given in Table C.2.

Table C.2. Examples of abstract declarators

Abstract declarator	Meaning
char *	Pointer to char
char [10]	Array of 10 char
char []	Array of char (undefined size)
int *[]	Array of pointers to int

Abstract declarators are most commonly used in type casting. The expression inside the brackets must be an abstract declarator. Some types cannot be type cast to, so not all abstract declarators are valid here. If complicated types are used (e.g. pointers to functions), it is much better to use a typedef initially, and use this type name in the type cast.

Forward declarations of functions can also include abstract declarators to define the types of each parameter. These are forward declarations with the parameter names omitted. Some examples of the use of declarators in type casting and in function prototypes are shown below:

```
y = (int) x;                          /* int is a declarator */
ptr1 = (char *) ptr2;                 /* "char *" is a declarator */
int my_fn(int, int *, char []);       /* int, pointer and array */
```

When using complicated types, such as an array of pointers to functions, it is easier to break the declaration into two steps. An array of pointers to functions can be declared using:

```
typedef int (*ptr_to_fn)();
typedef ptr_to_fn arr_ptr_fn[10];
```

C.2 List of declarations

Rather than trying to work out how to declare a difficult type from the precedence of operators in a declarator, it is much easier to simply look up the declaration in a table. Table C.3 is such a table of declarations, and these can be used to form `typedef` declarations simply by placing `typedef` at the start of the declarations.

Table C.3. Variable declarations

Declaration	Meaning
`int x;`	`int`
`int a[SIZE];`	Array of `int`
`int *ptr;`	Pointer to `int`
`int *a[SIZE];`	Array of pointers to `int`
`int (*p)[SIZE];`	Pointer to array of `int`
`int fn(parameter_list);`	Function returning `int`
`int *fn(parameter_list);`	Function returning pointer to `int`
`int (*p)(parameter_list);`	Pointer to function returning `int`
`int *(*p)(parameter_list);`	Pointer to function returning pointer to `int`
`int (*(*p)(list1))(list2);`	Pointer to function returning pointer to function returning `int`
`int *(*(*p)(list1))(list2);`	Pointer to function returning pointer to function returning pointer to `int`
`int (*x[])(parameter_list);`	Array of pointer to function returning `int`
`int *(*x[])(parameter_list);`	Array of pointer to function returning pointer to `int`
`int (*(*x[])(list1))(list2);`	Array of pointer to function returning pointer to function returning `int`

In the examples with more than one parameter list, `list1` refers to the parameters to the function pointed to and `list2` refers to the parameters of the function pointed to by the return value.

On some UNIX platforms there is a utility called `cdecl` to explain complicated declarations. It can be used to convert English-like statements such as:

```
declare x as pointer to int
```

into the variable declaration `"int *x;"`, or can be used in reverse to convert C declarations into English.

Appendix D
Answers to short exercises

Chapter 1. Introduction to C

1. Only c) `for` and d) `2i` are not valid identifiers. `for` is a keyword (which are disallowed as identifiers) and `2i` begins with a digit which is illegal.

2. The semicolons are missing off the end of both statements.

3. No, nested comments are not permitted in C.

7. The crucial line in the program is:

   ```
   print_number(square(i));
   ```

8. The guess input function could be implemented as:

   ```
   int get_guess(void)
   {
       int temp;

       printf("Enter you guess: ");    /* prompt */
       scanf("%d", &temp);             /* get input */
       return temp;                    /* return guess */
   }
   ```

Chapter 2. Variable declarations and types

1. The default type of real constants is `double`. The type can be changed using suffixes. `1.0` is a `double` constant, `1` is an `int` constant.

2. Decimal is not possible. Only octal and hexadecimal are possible. Hexadecimal is indicated by a prefix of `x` (e.g. `\123` is octal and `\xFF` is hexadecimal). The single quote can be used as the escape `'\''` (or directly inside string constants). `'\0'` is the zero byte; `'0'` is digit zero (ASCII 48).

373

374   Appendix D

3.
```
#include <stdio.h>

main()
{
    char c;

    for (c = 'A'; c <= 'Z'; c++)
        printf("%d   =   %c\n", c, c);
}
```

4. Yes, the initialization is legal. x can be either local or global since the initializer is a constant expression.

5. No difference at all. The first declaration uses the fact that the type defaults to int.

6. 0 is the smallest value representable in an unsigned variable. No, there is the same number of distinct representable values. Yes, the smallest and largest representable values are different.

7. volatile informs the compiler that a variable is special and may be changed in ways that the compiler cannot control or predict. The compiler is prevented from reducing, increasing or delaying any references to the object as could happen through code optimization. For example, the time delay loop below uses volatile to prevent the compiler from optimizing the loop:

```
volatile int i;

for (i = 0; i < DELAY; i++)
    ;   /* empty loop */
```

8. const indicates that the value of a variable will be constant during program execution, permitting the compiler to store the variable in read-only memory. However, const variables cannot be used in constant expressions such as array sizes, case expressions and initializers for global and static local variables. Hence, the name const is misleading and is better understood as "read-only" than as "constant".

Chapter 3. Operators

1. No, there is no unary relational operator. The arithmetic operators have highest precedence, then the relational operators and then the logical operators.

2. The result type is int. The possible result values are 0 or 1 (false or true), although the *operands* to these operators need not be restricted to 0 or 1.

5. The expression can be abbreviated as below with the extra advantage of efficiency because the address of sum need not be calculated twice:

```
sum += i;
```

6. The precedence of the / operator is higher than that of + and the expression is interpreted as:

```
average = a + ( b / 2 );
```

8. There is no difference between ++i; and i++; as single statements. The output of the code fragment is:

    ```
    x = 0, y = 1
    ```

9. Short-circuiting of the && operator means that the increment to i does not occur if x<y is false.

11. ```
    #define NUM_BITS 32      /* Number of bits in an int */
    void binary_print(int n)
    {
        int i;
        for (i = NUM_BITS - 1; i >= 0; i--)
            if ((n & (1 << i)) != 0)
                putchar('1');
            else
                putchar('0');
    }
    ```

Chapter 4. Control statements

1. The braces are needed to group the three statements. Without them, only the first assignment statement is part of the if block and the code would be interpreted as:

    ```
    if (x > y) {
        temp = x;
    }
    x = y;
    y = temp;
    ```

2. The error is assignment in the if statement: if (x = 0). This causes the test to always evaluate to false, and hence compute the reciprocal of 0.

3.  ```
    max = n1;
    if (max < n2) max = n2;
    if (max < n3) max = n3;
    ```

6. The do loop is post-tested and the while loop is pre-tested. A do loop always executes the loop body once, whereas a while loop need not execute the loop body at all. The for loop is similar to while.

8. The advantage is declaring variables close to their point of usage (i.e. convenience). The initialization of *automatic* block local variables occurs each time the block is entered.

9. It is easier to use a do loop because scanf must be called at least once.

    ```
    do {
        scanf("%d", &x);
    } while (x >= 0);
    ```

10. The break statements are missing from each case.

Chapter 5. Structured types

1. Yes, assuming correct types. Local variables can be declared with the same name as fields of a structure. The four name spaces in C are a) labels (for `goto`), b) tags (for `struct`, `union` and `enum`), c) field names in each `struct` or `union`, and d) all other names. Two `struct` types can use the same field names and the types need not be the same.

2. A `union` overlays its fields, a `struct` doesn't. The purpose of a `union` is to reduce memory usage. A `union` can only be used when the requirements for storing data in each field are mutually exclusive.

3. Bit-fields reduce space usage by packing small integral values together. The permitted types are `int`, `signed int`, and `unsigned int`.

5. X = 0, Y = 4

6. `typedef struct { int id; float value; } arr_node[10];`

Chapter 6. Strings

1. The zero byte.
2. `Hello W`
3. In the declaration below, s has the correct type but s2 has type `char`, because a star is needed for each pointer variable. `typedef` does not have this problem.

    ```
    string s, s2;   /* both strings? */
    ```

4. States how many eggs you have, without incorrectly saying "you have 1 eggs".
5. Single quotes indicate a character constant, not a string constant.
6. ```
   #define prefix(str, s)   (strncmp(str, s, strlen(s)) == 0)
   #define prefix(str, s)   (strstr(str, s) == str)
   ```
7. It relies on the return value of `strcmp` being −1, whereas all that is guaranteed is that the return value will be less than zero.
8. The value of `s1==s2` depends on whether your compiler merges identical string constants, which would make the condition true. Obviously, `strcmp(s1,s2)` is equal to zero because the strings are equal.
9. ```
   if (*s1 == *s2)            /* Compare first characters */
   if (strcmp(s1, s2) == 0)   /* Compare whole strings */
   ```
10. The length of the empty string is zero.
11. The original value of `x.label` is overwritten by the `strcpy` to `y.label`, causing the output to be:

    ```
    Another string: Another string
    ```

    The problem is that `struct` assignment does not copy the string, but only the address of the string. Hence, after the assignment, both `x.label` and `y.label` point to the same memory location (i.e. the same string). Using an array string variable avoids this problem because `struct` assignment would copy the entire string. The problem of saving `structs` to a file is a separate problem — saving the `structs` does not save the strings at all because they are stored separately. An array string field would also prevent this problem.

Chapter 7. Functions

2. Call-by-value of `int` function arguments (and all non-array types) prevents their value being changed. Yes, it can be changed and used internally, but the outside is not affected. Changes to an `int` variable are never propagated to the argument, but they are propagated to the argument if the parameter is an array variable.

3. Without the brackets, the function is not called. The statement is a null effect statement. In fact, this usually causes a run-time error because the compiler does not produce a compilation warning, and the call to the function silently disappears!

4. Using prototyping, the number and types of arguments and parameters are checked, and arguments are promoted as if assigning from the argument type to the parameter type. Using non-prototyping, no argument checking occurs, and arguments are promoted up to `int` or up to `double`. Prototyping prevents errors caused by incorrect argument passing, but has the disadvantage that function prototypes need be maintained when using independent compilation of multi-file programs.

5. `short` and `char` are promoted to `int`; `float` is promoted to `double`. `printf` is a variable-argument list function and its arguments are treated like arguments to a non-prototyped function; thus `float` is promoted to `double` and `printf` needs only one format specification for both `float` and `double`.

6. Yes, there is no need for all global variable declarations to be at the top of a file, although it is common style. Global variables are initialized at compile-time. A `static` variable can only be accessed within the one function, whereas a global variable can be accessed from any function.

7. Ordinary local variables are created on entry to the function and destroyed on exit; values are not retained between function calls. `static` variables are created once at compile-time and always retain their value between function calls. `register` advises the compiler that a variable will be highly used and should be placed in a hardware register to improve efficiency. `static` variables are initialized at compile-time; `register` and `auto` variables are initialized each time their function (or block) is entered. No, initialization of `register` variables is identical to that for automatic local variables.

8. Yes. All integral types and pointers can be specified as `register` variables. No.

9. `sizeof(a) / sizeof(a[0])`

Chapter 8. Pointers

1. x = 3, y = 1

2. p==q tests if the pointers are equal; *p==*q tests if the values of the variables pointed to by the pointers are equal. The output of the program is:

    The objects are equal

3. Because when the function returns, the local variable is destroyed and the address is invalid. This practice causes undefined run-time behavior.

4. Two, of course, because the free function cannot know that the address of a second block is stored in the first. The number of free calls must always equal the number of malloc and calloc calls. The sequence of calls must be:

    ```
    free(*p);
    free(p);
    ```

6. No. Yes, sizeof(void*) gives the size of the pointer. No, incrementing a void pointer is illegal because the size of object pointed to is not known.

7. Yes, the example is correct as long as the next field is itself a pointer, as in the type declaration:

    ```
    struct node {
            struct node *next;
            int data;
    } *p;
    ```

Chapter 9. Input and output

1. HelloWorld

2. ```
   printf("%s",str);
   printf("\"%s\"",str);   /* use the \" escape */
   ```

3. printf("%%"); — %% is a special format option. The bug occurs if str contains a percent character, which is interpreted by printf as a request for arguments that are not present.

4. It prints two strings left-justified in their field width. It can be abbreviated by using a * as the field width for each string and placing width1 before string1 and width2 before string2.

5. It specifies that the field width appears as the next argument. Three, because %*d requires two — one for the field width and one for the integer value.

6. The method is wrong because %1s will store one character and then add a terminating zero, thus storing two characters at the address of c. The correct method is scanf(" %c"), where the space causes leading whitespace to be skipped.

7. A star signifies assignment suppression, so that the field is not stored to any variable. One, because the first specification is not stored in an argument.
   ```

8. ```
   char s[100];

   scanf("%[0-9]", s);         /* integer */
   scanf("%[_a-zA-Z0-9]", s);  /* identifier */
   ```

9. `scanf` is inappropriate because it can't easily detect the end of a line. The program should use `gets` to read the line of input into a string and then examine the string, converting the integers using either `sscanf` or `atoi`.

10. `&` is not needed for strings because the address of the characters in the string is already passed (as a pointer or array type). The difference between `scanf` and `printf` conversions occurs because of the conversions applied to non-prototyping arguments. `float` is promoted to `double`, but `float*` and `double*` as needed by `scanf` are not affected.

Chapter 10. File operations

4. The output is:

   ```
   OneTwo
   ```

   because `fputs` does not add a newline. If changed to `puts`, newlines are added to the end of each line.

7. `fflush` will flush all internal memory buffers. However, `stderr` is unbuffered by default and hence the statement has no effect.

Chapter 11. The preprocessor

1. No, not on standard compilers, although older compilers are often more restrictive. Yes, spaces are allowed after the #.

2. The = should not be there. Yes, it will usually cause compilation errors.

4. The # operator is used to create a string constant from a macro argument; ## is used to paste two tokens together. # is unary; ## is binary. The output from the preprocessor is:

   ```
   s5 = "\"Hello\\n\"";
   ```

5. Use the `#undef` directive. This can be useful, for example, to remove debugging code included using conditional compilation, or to access a real function hidden behind a macro definition.

6. The side effect `b++` is executed twice if x>y. The best solution is to change the macro *call*:

   ```
   a = max(b, c);
   b++;
   ```

7. Compiles, but produces wrong results.
   ```

8. Not usually, because these directives nest. However, the `#endif` matching the `#if 0` must appear after the `#endif` directives matching the `#if` directives in the ignored block of code (why?).

9. The `defined` operator tests if a preprocessor macro name is defined. It is a unary operator. No, it can only be used in the constant expression for `#if` or `#elif`.

   ```
   #if defined X      /* #ifdef X */
   #if !defined X     /* #ifndef X */
   ```

10. Both `#if` and `#ifdef` are the same if the symbol is defined as 1, or if the symbol is undefined. There are differences if the symbol is defined as 0, or with no replacement text. If both forms are used, the code can be removed by ensuring that DEBUG is never defined.

11. ```
    #ifndef DEBUG
    #define DEBUG 1     /* default value */
    #endif
    ```

Chapter 12. Standard library functions

3. ```
   double random_real(void)
   {
        return rand() / (double) RAND_MAX;
   }
   ```

5. ```
   memset(arr, 0, sizeof(arr));
   memcpy(arr1, arr2, sizeof(arr2));
   ```

Chapter 13. Large programs

1. None at all. No, it specifies scope, not initialization.

2. Yes, the code fragment is legal. Replacement by `static` will cause a compilation error about the multiple definition of x. `static extern` is a syntax error.

3. No difference in effect at all. The `extern` keyword is redundant.

4. No difference at all. Leaving names in is better style because the names are useful documentation.

5. It will introduce multiple definitions of the function, causing a compilation error (actually linkage error). A `static` function will not cause a compilation or linkage error, but will cause the same `static` function to be defined in each file where the header file is included, leading to multiple copies of the executable code for the function. A header file should contain *declarations* of functions (i.e. function prototypes), in addition to other non-executable code: preprocessor symbols and macros, `typedef` declarations, and `extern` variable declarations (but not variable *definitions*).
   ```

Chapter 14. Functions and pointers revisited

4. `double` variables can't be passed because there is no way for the function to know that an argument is not an `int`. `sum(2,3,3.14)` fails because 3 is an `int` constant and 3.14 is a `double` constant.

9.
```
void reverse(char *s)
{
    if (*s != '\0') {        /* base case: empty string */
        reverse(s + 1);      /* do rest recursively */
        putchar(*s);         /* print this character */
    }
}
```

10. The basic idea is to test for `NULL` before calling the function:

```
if (root->left != NULL)
    inorder(root->left);
```

11. No problems. Only one recursive call can be in effect at a time. The second call cannot occur until the first has returned.

12. When `main` has been called recursively.

15. The functions are actually quite simple because `create_array` has done all the work. For example, the identity matrix function is:

```
void identity_matrix(int **m, int n)
{
    int i, j;

    for (i = 0; i < n; i++)
        for (j = 0; j < n; j++)
            m[i][j] = (i == j) ? 1 : 0;
}
```

Chapter 15. Efficiency

2.
```
int fib1(int n)
{
    if (n <= 1)
        return 1;            /* F0=1, F1=1 */
    else
        return fib1(n-1) + fib1(n-2);  /* Fn = Fn-1 + Fn-2 */
}

int fib2(int n)
{
    int temp, large = 1, small = 1;   /* F0 and F1 */

    for (; n > 1; n--) {
        temp = large + small;    /* Fn = Fn-1 + Fn-2 */
        small = large;
        large = temp;
    }
    return large;
}
```

3. Unrolling is efficient if n is large, allowing a number of unrolled iterations. If n is too small, the overhead of setting up the loops becomes too costly.

```
void clear_array(int a[], int n)
{
    int i, max = n & ~07;      /* Highest multiple of 8 */
    for (i = 0; i < max; ) {
        a[i++] = 0;            /* Main loop */
        a[i++] = 0;            /* Unrolled 8 times */
        a[i++] = 0;
        a[i++] = 0;
        a[i++] = 0;
        a[i++] = 0;
        a[i++] = 0;
        a[i++] = 0;
    }
    for (; i < n; i++)         /* Do the odd cases */
        a[i] = 0;
}
```

4. ```
b[0] = 0;
for (i = 1; i < 10; i++)
    a[i] = b[i] = 0;
```

5. `#define STRDIFF(s1,s2) (s1[0] != s2[0] || strcmp(s1,s2) != 0)`

6. Re-display only those squares on the chess board that have changed in the move. The number of squares is usually two, and at most four (castling), so the method compares well with re-displaying 64 squares.

7. If `double` is faster than `float` then the compiler is non-ANSI because it converts `float` values to `double` before multiplying.

8. The array `sqrt_table` could be initialized with 100 `double` constants, possibly generated by another program! Use `static` local variables, but only where initialization need not be done each function entry.

9. `float x = 0.0;   /* use float constant */`

10. ```
for (i = 0; i < X_SIZE; i++)
    for (j = 0; j < Y_SIZE; j++)
        if (a[i][j] == -1) {
            error = TRUE;
            goto after;
        }
after:  ... /* etc */
```

11. Before the deletion phase, simply seed the random number generator again with the same seed value and use `rand` to re-generate the same sequence of numbers.

12. Since these functions are so similar, it is reasonable to assume that they will all use mostly the same executable code (possibly all calling an internal function). Hence, avoiding `scanf` but still using `sscanf` or `fscanf` will probably not reduce executable size greatly.

13. The basic type declaration for a set is:

    ```
    typedef unsigned char set_type[4];
    ```

    The code fragment below is used by both `member` and `insert_element` functions to calculate which element of the array is used and what the bit mask is.

    ```
    x = ch - 'A';           /* Convert to 0..25 */
    index = x / 8;          /* array index 0..3 */
    bitnum = x % 8;         /* bit 0..7 */
    mask = 1 << bitnum;     /* mask to get that bit */
    ```

    The two functions then make use of `index` and `mask` in similar ways:

    ```
    if ((set[index] & mask) != 0) /* member: test bit */
    set[index] &= mask;           /* insert_element: set bit */
    ```

Chapter 16. Debugging techniques

2. Removal of the `dprintf` calls depends on whether they accept a fixed number of arguments. If the number is fixed, the method of removal is:

    ```
    #define dprintf(level, format, arg1)   /* nothing */
    ```

    Otherwise, the only method is:

    ```
    #define dprintf      (void)
    ```

3. Setting the debugging flags is a simple matter of opening the debugging text file and reading in the numbers there. This should be done at the start of program execution, or every `dprintf` call can use a `static` boolean flag to indicate whether the file has been read yet, and read the file if not.

4. a) Both ignore the code (test is false).
   b) Both include the code (test is true).
   c) `#if` ignores the code; `#ifdef` includes the code.
   d) `#if` causes a compilation error; `#ifdef` includes the code.
   e) Both ignore the code.
   f) Both include the code (cc defines DEBUG as 1).

5. Use a `static` local variable in the `add_to_list` function, as below:

    ```
    static int installed = FALSE;

    if (!installed) {
        installed = TRUE;
        atexit(print_block_list);
    }
    ```

Chapter 17. Program style

1. Adopt their style to maintain consistent style in the program.
2. `isvalid` makes it clear that the function returns true if the move is valid, whereas `checkvalid` is vague. The use of `isvalid` is clear in conditions such as:

    ```
    if(isvalid(move))
    ```

3. Who cares?
4. `{}` may be preferred because it is obviously not an instance of the accidental empty loop error. However, the use of a single semicolon is a widespread practice.
5. `enum` is preferable in this case because the only tests of values of type `sex_type` will be for equality/inequality with one of the constants. If any less than or greater than tests were required, `#define` would be more natural.
7. Macros should not use flow of control constructs that make the flow of the resulting code non-obvious. In this case, it is difficult to see that the statement `test(ptr)` can actually cause the enclosing function to return. Macros should have semantics similar to function calls.
8. There is a library function, `isalpha`, declared in `<ctype.h>` that performs the same task and is more portable and more efficient. Don't reinvent the wheel.

Chapter 18. Portability

1. It assumes that `char`s are `signed` by default because of the comparison of `c` with `EOF` which has the value -1. `c` should be declared as `int`.
2. The result depends on the order of evaluation of the `/` operator, which is undefined. Each call to `pop` is a side effect because it modifies a global data structure used by the other call. Refer to Section 3.19 for more discussion.
3. `typedef unsigned char BYTE;     /* must be unsigned */`
4. The definition of `TOLOWER` assumes an ASCII character set.
5. A long key string could cause the local variable `sum` to overflow, thus becoming negative. The use of `%` on negative operands is undefined and may return a negative value (which is not a legal hash address). The local variable should be declared as `unsigned int`. Note that the function return value need not be `unsigned` (why?).
6. The method below works because the absence of these keywords is usually harmless:

    ```
    #define const      /* nothing */
    #define volatile   /* nothing */
    ```

    However, the method will fail on statements with no explicit type (defaulting to `int`) such as `"const x = 1;"`. The method is also valid for `near`, `far` and `huge` because these qualifiers can be omitted in most cases.

7. The only real solution is to hide `#pragma` directives inside pairs of `#if` and `#endif` directives, and this is only a partial solution because it requires modification of preprocessor symbol definitions to port the code.

Chapter 19. UNIX systems programming

3. The `tee` command can only have `FOPEN_MAX` files as arguments because it should read from standard input and then add to each file at the same time.
6. In the background it can only be stopped using "`kill -9`" or the equivalent command in C-shell: "`kill -KILL`". These commands stop the program because `SIGKILL` (signal 9) cannot be trapped.
7. The return value from `wait` will be the pid of the child process, even though the child died some time ago. In effect, the `wait` function *queues* the pids of terminating child processes.

Bibliography

I have read a large number of books before and during the writing of this book. There is no way I could list (or remember!) all of these. The ones I found most relevant and most useful are listed below:

AHO, Alfred V., HOPCROFT, John E., and ULLMAN, Jeffrey D., *The Design and Analysis of Computer Algorithms*, Addison-Wesley, 1974.

AHO, Alfred V., SETHI, Ravi, and ULLMAN, Jeffrey D., *Compilers — Principles, Techniques and Tools*, Addison-Wesley, 1986.

AMMERAAL, Leendert, *Programs and Data Structures in C*, John Wiley and Sons, 1987.

AMSBURY, Wayne, *Data Structures from Arrays to Priority Queues*, Wadsworth Publishing Company, 1985.

ANDERSON, Paul, and ANDERSON, Gail, *Advanced C: Tips and Techniques*, Hayden Books, 1988.

ATKINSON, Lee, and ATKINSON, Mark, *Using C*, Que Corporation, 1990.

BANAHAN, Mike, *The C Book*, Addison-Wesley, 1988.

BARCLAY, Kenneth A., *C Problem Solving and Programming*, Prentice Hall, 1989.

BARCLAY, Kenneth A., *C Problem Solving and Programming (ANSI edition)*, Prentice Hall, 1991.

BENTLEY, Jon Louis, *Writing Efficient Programs*, Prentice Hall, 1982.

BERRY, R. E., MEEKINGS, B. A. E., and SOREN, M. D., *A Book on C*, Basingstoke Macmillan Education, 1988.

BOURNE, Stephen R., *The UNIX System*, Addison-Wesley, 1983.

ESAKOV, Jeffrey, and WEISS, Tom, *Data Structures: An Advanced Approach Using C*, Prentice Hall, 1989.

FEUER, Allan R., *C Puzzle Book (2nd edition)*, Prentice Hall, 1989.

GEHANI, Narain, *C: An Advanced Introduction*, Computer Science Press, 1985.

GONNET, G. H., and BAEZA-YATES, R., *Handbook of Algorithms and Data Structures (2nd edition)*, Addison-Wesley, 1991.

HARBISON, Samuel P., and STEELE, Guy L. Jr., *C: A Reference Manual (3rd edition)*, Prentice Hall, 1991.

HOROWITZ, E., and SAHNI, S., *Fundamentals of Data Structures (3rd edition)*, Pitman Publishing, 1990.

HORSPOOL, R. Nigel, *C Programming in the Berkeley UNIX Environment*, Prentice Hall, 1986.

HORTON, Mark, *Portable C Software*, Prentice Hall, 1990.

JAESCHKE, Rex, *Solutions in C*, Addison-Wesley, 1986.

JAESCHKE, Rex, *Portability and the C Language*, Hayden Books, 1989.

KELLEY, Al, and POHL, Ira, *A Book on C (2nd edition)*, Benjamin/Cummings Publishing Company, 1990.

KELLEY, Al, and POHL, Ira, *C by Dissection*, Benjamin/Cummings Publishing Company, 1987.

KERNIGHAN, Brian W., and PIKE, Rob, *The UNIX Programming Environment*, Prentice Hall, 1984.

KERNIGHAN Brian W., and PLAUGER, P. J., *The Elements of Programming Style*, McGraw-Hill, 1974.

KERNIGHAN, Brian W., and RITCHIE, Dennis M., *The C Programming Language (1st edition)*, Prentice Hall, 1978.

KERNIGHAN, Brian W., and RITCHIE, Dennis M., *The C Programming Language (2nd edition)*, Prentice Hall, 1989.

KNUTH, Donald E., *The Art of Computer Programming (Vol. 3): Sorting and Searching*, Addison-Wesley, 1973.

KOCHAN, Stephen G., *Programming in ANSI C*, Hayden Books, 1988.

KOCHAN, Stephen G., and WOOD, Patrick H., *Topics in C Programming (revised edition)*, John Wiley and Sons, 1991.

KOENIG, Andrew, *C Traps and Pitfalls*, Addison-Wesley, 1989.

KORSH, James F., and GARRETT, Leonard J., *Data Structures, Algorithms and Program Style Using C*, PWS-Kent publishing, 1988.

KRUSE, Robert L., LEUNG, Bruce P., and TONDO, Clovis L., *Data Structures and Program Design in C*, Prentice Hall, 1991.

LAPIN, J. E., *Portable C and UNIX System Programming*, Prentice Hall, 1987.

MASTERS, David, *Introduction to C with Advanced Applications*, Prentice Hall, 1991.

MILLER, Lawrence H., *Advanced Programming: Design and Structure using Pascal*, Addison-Wesley, 1986.

MULDNER, Tomasz, and STEELE, Peter W., *C as a Second Language*, Addison-Wesley, 1988.

OGILVIE, John W. L., *Advanced C Struct Programming*, John Wiley and Sons, 1990.

PRESS, W. H., FLANNERY, B. P., TEUKOLSKY, S. A., and VETTERLING, W. T., *Numerical Recipes in C: The Art of Scientific Computing*, Cambridge University Press, 1988.

PLAUGER, P. J., *The Standard C Library*, Prentice Hall, 1991.

PLUM, Thomas, *C Programming Guidelines*, Prentice Hall, 1984.

PLUM, Thomas, and BRODIE, Jim, *Efficient C*, Plum Hall Inc., 1985.

PURDUM, Jack, *C Programming Guide (3rd edition)*, Que Corporation, 1988.

RABINOWITZ, Henry, and SCHAAP, Chaim, *Portable C*, Prentice Hall, 1990.

PUGH, Ken, *All on C*, Scott, Foresman/Little, Brown Higher Education, 1990.

REINGOLD, Edward M., and HANSEN, Wilfred J., *Data Structures in Pascal*, Little, Brown and Company, 1986.

ROHL, J. S., *Recursion via Pascal*, Cambridge University Press, 1984.

SCHILDT, Herbert, *C: The Complete Reference*, Osborne-McGraw-Hill, 1987.

SESSIONS, Roger, *Reusable Data Structures in C*, Prentice Hall, 1989.

SCHWADERER, W. David, *C Wizard's Programming Reference*, John Wiley and Sons, 1985.

SMITH, Jerry D., *Reusability and Software Construction: C and C++*, John Wiley and Sons, 1990.

STRAWBERRY SOFTWARE, *Accessing C: Tips from the Experts (2nd edition)*, Van Nostrand Reinhold, 1989.

STROUSTRUP, Bjarne, *The C++ Programming Language*, Addison-Wesley, 1987.

STUBBS, Daniel F., and WEBRE, Neil W., *Data Structures with Abstract Data Types and Pascal*, Brooks/Cole Publishing Company, 1985.

TENENBAUM, Aaron, LANGSAM, Yedidyah, and AUGENSTEIN, Moshe J., *Data Structures Using C*, Prentice Hall, 1990.

TONDO, Clovis L., and GIMPEL, Scott E., *The C Answer Book (2nd edition)*, Prentice Hall, 1988.

TRAISTER, Robert J., *Mastering C Pointers*, Academic Press, 1990.

VAN WYK, Christopher J., *Data Structures and C Programs*, Addison-Wesley, 1988.

WIRTH, Niklaus, *Algorithms and Data Structures*, Prentice Hall, 1986.

WORTHINGTON, Steve, *C Programming*, Boyd and Fraser, 1988.

Perhaps the most important reference is the ANSI standard, although the majority of people won't need to read it. The standard is more properly called American National Standard ANS-X3.159-1989 "Programming Languages—C", and has also been adopted as the international standard ISO/IEC 9899:1990 (which differs only in section and page numbering). The standard is not a public domain document and can be purchased from:

American National Standards Institute
1430 Broadway
New York, NY 10018
USA
(+1) 212 642 4900

and also from:

Global Engineering Documents
2805 McGaw Avenue
Irvine, CA 92714
USA
(+1) 714 261 1455
(800) 854 7179 (within USA and Canada only)

Within Australia, a version of the standard (equivalent to ISO/IEC 9899:1990) can be purchased from Standards Australia, and is called Australian Standard AS 3955-1991 "Programming Languages—C". The mailing address of the National Sales Centre is:

PO Box 1055
Strathfield 2135
AUSTRALIA
(02) 746 4600 (within Australia only)

Index

Symbols

| | logical or operator 35
| bitwise or operator 39
~ one's complement operator 39
! logical not operator 35
!= not equal relational operator 34
preprocessor operator 152
preprocessor operator 153
% modulus operator 31, 256
%= modulus assignment operator 38
& address operator 43
& bitwise-and operator 39, 256
&& logical and operator 35
(type) operator 44
* indirection operator 43
* multiplication operator 31, 255
*= extended assignment operator 38
+ addition operator 31
++ increment operator 36, 255
+= extended assignment operator 38
- subtraction operator 31
-- decrement operator 36, 255
-= extended assignment operator 38
-> structure pointer operator 43
/ division operator 31
/= extended assignment operator 38
2's complement 76, 313
< less than relational operator 34
<< left shift operator 41, 255
<<= extended assignment operator 43
<= less than or equal relational operator 34
= assignment operator 33, 263
== equality relational operator 34
> greater than relational operator 34
>= greater than or equal relational operator 34
>> right shift operator 41, 255
>>= extended assignment operator 43
[ ] array reference operator 47
^ bitwise exclusive or operator 39

A

\a alert or bell escape 22
abort library function 65, 175
abs library function 169
abs macro macro 363
abstract declarator 371
access modifiers 27
access UNIX function 324
acos library function 167
activation record 257
adb UNIX symbolic debugger 275
address arithmetic 113-114, 174
add_two.c program 5
aliasing 87
alignment problems 262
allocation of memory *see* dynamic memory allocation
anonymous union 75
a.out UNIX executable 4
ar UNIX utility 207-208
archives (UNIX libraries) 206
argc parameter to main 197, 213
arge parameter to main 220
arguments to functions 95
argv parameter to main 197, 213
arithmetic operators 7, 31-32
array references out of bounds 286
arrays 24-25
arrays, multi-dimensional 25
ASCII character set 314
asctime library function 177

Index

`asin` library function 167
`assert` macro 282, 367
`<assert.h>` header file 163, 282
assignment operator 33
assignment statement 7
associativity of operators 49-50
`atan, atan2` 167
`atexit` library function 175, 286
`atof` library function 169
`atoi` library function 169
`atol` library function 169
`auto` storage class specifier 101
`awk` UNIX utility 199, 318

B

`\b` backspace escape 22
binary files 135
binary search 173
binary trees 111, 222, 223, 249
bit shift operators 41-43
bit-fields 75-76, 269, 314
bitwise operators 39-43
blocks of statements 56
boolean type 304
boolean type (lack of) 34
Bourne shell 318
braces 9, 56, 298
`break` statement 62, 65, 358
`bsearch` library function 173-175, 229
buffering of files 129, 142, 279
BUFSIZ 142

C

C++ 200
call-by-reference 110
call-by-value 16, 99, 257, 266, 360
`calloc` library function 111-113, 170, 285
`case` clause 64
case-sensitivity 3
`cb` UNIX utility 296, 317
`cc -c` (separate compilation) 188
`cc -g` (debugger) 275
`cc -I` (header file inclusion) 205
`cc -O` (optimizer) 243
`cc -p` (profiler) 244
`cc` UNIX C compiler 4, 166, 188
`cd` UNIX shell command 318
`cdecl` UNIX utility 317, 372
`ceil` library function 166
`cexpl` UNIX utility 317
CFLAGS in `make` 203
`char` type 19, 269
character constants 22

character input/output 127
`CHAR_MAX, CHAR_MIN` constants 180
`check_address` debugging function 286
`check_pointer` debugging function 286
child process 325
`chmod` UNIX function 324
`chown` UNIX function 324
`clearerr` library function 135
clearing bits 40
`clock` library function 178, 245
`CLOCKS_PER_SEC` constant 178, 245
`close` UNIX function 320
code motion (out of loops) 250
comma operator 47, 60, 152, 366
command line arguments 212-218
comments 6, 296
common sub-expressions 254
compilation under UNIX 4
complicated declarations 370-372
concatenation of string constants 153
conditional compilation 154-158
`const` function parameters 100
`const` qualifier 27, 316
constants 21
`continue` statement 62
control statements 56-69
`core` file under UNIX 276
`cos` library function 167
`cosh` library function 167
`count_down.c` program 11
`count_to_10.c` program 10, 13, 14
`cpp` UNIX preprocessor 145
`creat` UNIX function 320
`crypt` UNIX function 324
`ctime` library function 177
`<ctrl-c>` keyboard interrupt 291
`<ctrl-\>` keyboard interrupt 292
`<ctrl-z>` keyboard interrupt 292
`<ctype.h>` header file 163-164, 247

D

dangling `else` ambiguity 58
dangling references 286, 361
data structure augmentation 245
data structures 268
date functions 176
`__DATE__` preprocessor special name 160
`DBL_DIG` constant 180
`DBL_EPSILON` constant 180
`DBL_MIN, DBL_MAX` constants 180
`dbx` UNIX symbolic debugger 275
De Morgan's laws 352
debugging 275-295
declarator 371

Index

decrement operator, -- 11, 36-38
`default` clause 64
`#define` preprocessor directive 13
`defined` preprocessor operator 156, 310
determinant of a matrix 231
`difftime` library function 176
direct access to files 136
directives to preprocessor 146
`div` library function 169
`do` loop 60-61
domain error 166
dot-dot-dot 225
`double` type 19
`dprintf` debugging function 277-279
`dup` UNIX function 321
`dup2` UNIX function 321
dynamic memory allocation 111-113, 170, 260, 271, 285

E

EBCDIC character set 314
EDOM error code (domain error) 166
efficiency 22, 33, 36, 37, 38, 63, 66, 83, 102, 114, 129, 132, 142, 149, 164, 165, 222, 223, 242-274
EINTR error code 292
`#elif` preprocessor directive 154, 310
ellipsis (... token) 225
`else` clause 57
`#else` preprocessor directive 154
empty loop 63, 297, 358
empty statement 63
empty string 88
end-of-file 130
`#endif` preprocessor directive 154
ENOENT error code 135
`enum` type 76-77
environment variables 323
`envp` parameter to `main` 220
EOF, end-of-file constant 130, 132
EPERM error code 135
ERANGE error code (range error) 166
`errno` library variable 135, 166, 292, 318
`<errno.h>` header file 134, 318
`#error` preprocessor directive 159
escapes (backslash characters) 22
`/etc/passwd` UNIX password file 324
exception handling 67
exclusive-or 39
`execve` UNIX function 326
`exit` library function 65, 175
`EXIT_SUCCESS, EXIT_FAILURE` 175, 220
`exp` library function 168
extended assignment operators 38, 39, 255

extended bitwise operators 39
extended shift operators 43

F

`\f` formfeed escape 22
`fabs` library function 166
`factorial` function 221
falling through in `switch` 65, 358
`fclose` library function 131
`feof` library function 134
`ferror` library function 134
`fflush` library function 142, 280
`fgetc` library function 134
`fgetpos` library function 138
`fgets` library function 133
field width in `printf` 120
file descriptors 319
`FILE*` pointer 130
`__FILE__` preprocessor special name 159, 283
files 129-144
filter program 214
`float` type 19
`<float.h>` header file 180-181
floating point constants 21
`floor` library function 166
flow of control *see* control statements
`FLT_DIG` constant 180
`FLT_EPSILON` constant 180
`FLT_MIN, FLT_MAX` constants 180
`fmod` library function 166
`fopen` library function 131
`FOPEN_MAX` constant 132
`for` loop 10-12, 59-60
`fork` UNIX function 325
format string 117
formatted input (`scanf`) 122
formatted output (`printf`) 117
forward declarations 189
forward declarations of functions 371
`fpos_t` type 138
`fprintf` library function 133
`fputc` library function 134
`fputs` library function 133
`fread` library function 135
`free` library function 111-113, 170, 285, 361
`free_node` function 261
`freopen` library function 143
`frexp` library function 168
`fscanf` library function 133
`fseek` library function 137
`fsetpos` library function 138
`ftell` library function 138
function call operator 48
function prototypes 189

Index   393

functions 14-16, 93-228
`fwrite` library function 135

G

garbage (unfreed memory) 285, 361
generic pointer *see* `void` pointers
generic pointers 111
`getc` library function 134
`getchar` library function 127
`getenv` library function 175, 176, 323
`getopt` UNIX function 218
`getpass` UNIX function 324
`getpid` UNIX function 324
`getppid` UNIX function 324
`getpwent, getpwuid, getpwnam` 324
`gets` library function 126
`getuid` UNIX function 324
gid (group-id) 324
global variables 98, 304
`gmtime` library function 177
`goto` statement 66, 303
`gprof` UNIX utility 243
`grep` UNIX utility 196, 318
`guess.c` program 16

H

header files 147, 163, 191, 205
heap *see* dynamic memory allocation
hello world program 3
hexadecimal constants 21, 40
hidden functions 223
HOME UNIX shell variable 323
HUGE_VAL constant 166

I

I/O 117-128
identifiers 6
`#if` preprocessor directive 154
`if` statement 9-10, 57-58
if-if-else ambiguity 58
`#ifdef` preprocessor directive 154
`#ifndef` preprocessor directive 154
implicit type conversions 28
`#include` preprocessor directive 146-147
increment operator, ++ 11, 36-38
incremental algorithms 248
`indent` UNIX utility 296, 317
indentation style 11, 297
independent compilation 187-188, 356
induction variables 252
infinite loops 62
initialization 23, 61, 103-106

inorder tree traversal 222
input (`scanf`) 122
`int` type 19
interface functions 223
international programs *see* `<locale.h>`
INT_MAX, INT_MIN constants 180
_IOFBF, _IOLBF, _IONBF 142
`isalnum` library function 163
`isalpha` library function 163
`iscntrl` library function 163
`isdigit` library function 163
`isgraph` library function 163
`islower` library function 163
`isprint` library function 163
`ispunct` library function 163
`isspace` library function 163
`isupper` library function 163, 246
`isvowel` function 94
`isxdigit` library function 163
iterative algorithms 222

J

`jmp_buf` type 67
jump table 230

L

l-values 34
labels for `goto` 66
`labs` library function 169
large programs 187-210
lazy evaluation 247
LC_ALL constant (and others) 181
`ldexp` library function 168
`ldiv` library function 169
left shift operator 41
`lex` UNIX utility 318
libraries 206
library functions 162-183
`<limits.h>` header file 180-181
line by line input/output 126
`#line` preprocessor directive 159
line splicing 150, 310
__LINE__ preprocessor special name 159, 283
linkage 190, 310
linked lists 60, 111, 262, 268, 286
`lint` UNIX utility 276-277, 357
local variables 61, 97-98
`localeconv` library function 182
`<locale.h>` header file 181
`localtime` library function 177
`log` library function 168
`log10` library function 168
logical operators 12, 35-36

394 Index

`long double` type 20
`long` type qualifier 20, 26
`longjmp` library function 67-68, 293
LONG_MAX, LONG_MIN constants 180
loop unrolling 251
`ls` UNIX command 205
`lseek` UNIX function 322

M

macros, preprocessor 148, 258
`main` function 65, 212-221
`make` UNIX utility 201
`malloc` library function 111-113, 170, 270, 285, 362
`<math.h>` header file 165-168
matrix routines 231
`memchr` library function 164
`memcmp` library function 164
`memcpy` library function 164, 264, 265
`memmove` library function 164
memory leak 285, 361
`memset` library function 164
`mktime` library function 177
modulus (remainder) 32
`mon.out` file, generated by `prof` 244
multi-dimensional arrays 25
multibyte characters 168, 182
multiple cases (`switch`) 64
mutually recursive structures 79
`my_malloc` function 286

N

`\n` newline escape 22
name spaces 72
NDEBUG macro name (`<assert.h>`) 163, 282
`new_node` function 261
non-ANSI compilers 308
non-prototyping 95-96, 189, 227, 279, 356, 357
NULL pointers 311
null statement 63
numerical constants 21

O

.o suffix for object files 188
object files 188
object oriented programming 200
O_CREAT, O_APPEND, O_TRUNC 320
octal constants 21, 40
`offsetof` library macro 180
one's complement 39
`open` UNIX function 320
operators 31-55

optimizer for C, `cc -O` 243
order of evaluation 50-54, 254
O_RDONLY, O_WRONLY, O_RDWR 320
output, `printf` 117
overflow in `<math.h>` 166
overflow in expressions 313
overlaying a process (`execve`) 326

P

parameterized macros 148
parameters 95
Pascal programming 64, 305, 339-349
pass-by-value 99
PATH UNIX shell variable 323
`pclose` UNIX function 330
`perror` library function 134, 319
pid (process id) 324
`pixie` UNIX utility 243
pointer to function 372
pointers 108-116
pointers to functions 48, 229-231
`popen` UNIX function 330
portability 172, 307-315
`pow` library function 168
`#pragma` preprocessor directive 159
precedence 42, 45, 48-49, 255
precision specification in `printf` 120
precomputation 246
preorder tree traversal 249
preprocessor 145-161
`print_block_list` debugging function 286
`printf` library function 117
`print_max.c` program 9
print_number 15
`print_tree` function 223
process id 324
`prof` UNIX utility 243
`ptr_diff_t` standard type 180
`putc` library function 134
`putchar` library function 127
`puts` library function 126

Q

`qsort` library function 171-173, 229

R

`\r` carriage return escape 22
r-values 34
`raise` library function 179, 293
`rand` library function 17, 171
RAND_MAX constant 171
random number generation 17, 171

range error 166
`ranlib` UNIX utility 207, 208
`read` UNIX function 292, 321
`realloc` library function 111-113, 170, 285
recalculation 268
records *see* `structs`
recursion 221-225, 249, 271
recursive macros 151
recursive structures 78
redirecting input/output 322
`register` storage class specifier 101, 256
relational operators 10, 34
remainder operator 32
`remove` library function 141, 321
`rename` library function 141
`repeat-until` (Pascal) 342
`return` statement 97
`rewind` library function 137
right shift operator 41

S

safe operators 52
`scanf` library function 7, 122
`sccs` UNIX utility 317
`SCHAR_MAX`, `SCHAR_MIN` constants 180
scope 27, 97, 98, 103, 190
`sdb` UNIX symbolic debugger 275
searching arrays 173-175, 248
`sed` UNIX utility 196, 318
segmentation fault 293, 361
self-referential structures 78
semicolons 56
sentinels 213, 248
separate compilation *see* independent compilation
sequence points 53-54
sequential search 248
set-user-id UNIX mode 324
`setbuf` library function 142, 280
`setenv` UNIX function 323
`setjmp` library function 67-68
`<setjmp.h>` header file 67-68
`setlocale` library function 181
setting bits 40
`setuid` UNIX function 324
`setup_heap` function 261
`setvbuf` library function 142
shared memory 28
shift operators 41-43
`short` type qualifier 20, 26, 269
short-circuiting 35-36, 52, 354
side effects 36, 53, 278, 354, 365
`SIGABRT` signal (abort) 66
`SIGBUF` signal 293
`SIG_DFL` to reset signals 179, 291

`SIG_ERR`, error code for `signal` 179
`SIGFPE` signal (floating point exception) 179, 293
`SIG_IGN` to ignore signals 179, 291
`SIGINT` keyboard interrupt signal 179, 292
sign extension 42, 255
`signal` library function 179, 291
`<signal.h>` header file 179-180
signals 66, 333-337
`signed` type qualifier 26
`SIGQUIT` signal 179, 292
`SIGSEGV` signal (segmentation fault) 179, 293
`SIGTRAP` signal 293
`SIGTSTP` signal 179, 292
`sin` library function 167
`sinh` library function 167
`sizeof` operator 45, 107
`size_t` type 170, 180
sorting arrays 171-173
`sprintf` library function 86
`sqrt` library function 166
`square` function 15
`srand` library function 17, 171
`sscanf` library function 86
standard library 162-183
statements 56
`static` (single file scope) 103, 190
`static` storage class specifier 102
`<stdarg.h>` header file 226, 279
`__STDC__` preprocessor special name 160
`<stddef.h>` header file 180
`stderr` 130, 319
`stdin` 130, 319
`<stdlib.h>` header file 168-176
`stdout` 130, 319
storage classes 101-103
`strcat` library function 82, 264
`strchr` library function 84
`strcmp` library function 83
`strcoll` library function 181
`strcpy` library function 82, 264
`strcspn` library function 84
`strdup` library function 112, 295
strength reduction 252
`strerror` library function 84
`strftime` library function 177
`<string.h>` header file 82-86, 164
stringize preprocessor operator 152, 283
strings 80-92
`strip` UNIX utility 268
`strlen` library function 82, 362
`strncat` library function 84
`strncmp` library function 84, 90
`strncpy` library function 84, 90
`strpbrk` library function 84
`strrchr` library function 84

396 Index

`strspn` library function 84
`strstr` library function 84
`strtok` library function 84
`strtol, strtoul, strtod` 169
struct operators 43
structures 70-79
style 64, 296-306
suffixes for constants 22
`switch` statement 63, 358
symbolic constants 13, 27, 77
symbolic constants with `#define` 148
symbolic debuggers 275, 281
`system` library function 175, 318

T

`\t` tab escape 22
table lookup 246
tag name (`struct`/`union`/`enum`) 70
tail recursion 223, 249
`tan` library function 167
`tanh` library function 167
templates 65
temporary files 141
ternary operator 46, 53
text files 130-135
throwing away values 353
`time` library function 17, 171, 176, 245
`__TIME__` preprocessor special name 160
`<time.h>` header file 176-179, 245
`tmpfile` library function 141
`tmpnam` library function 141
token pasting preprocessor operator, `##` 153
`tolower` library function 163
`touch` UNIX command 206
`toupper` library function 163
traditional C 95-96, 308
type casting 44, 371
type conversions (automatic) 28
type qualifiers 26
`typedef` declaration 25, 77-78, 372
types 8-9, 19-20

U

`UCHAR_MAX` constant 180
uid (user-id) 324
`UINT_MAX` constant 180
`ULONG_MAX` constant 180
`umask` UNIX function 324

unary minus operator 32
unary plus operator 32
`#undef` preprocessor directive 152
underflow in `<math.h>` 166
`ungetc` library function 141
unions 74-75, 268
UNIX 317-338
`unlink` UNIX function 321
unrolling loops 251
unsafe operators 52
`unsetenv` UNIX function 323
`unsigned` type qualifier 26
USER UNIX shell variable 323
`USHRT_MAX` constant 180

V

`\v` vertical tab escape 22
`va_arg` macro 226
`va_end` macro 226
`va_list` type 226
`<varargs.h>` header file 228
variable declarations 6, 20
variable initialization 23
variable-length argument lists 225-228
variant record 75
`va_start` macro 226
`vfork` UNIX function 328
`vfprintf` library function 227
`vgrind` UNIX utility 317
`void` functions 95
void pointers 111
`volatile` type qualifier 28, 30, 273, 316
`vprintf` library function 227
`vsprintf` library function 227

W

wayward pointers 286
`while` loop 12, 58-59
`write` UNIX function 292, 321

X

`\x` hexadecimal escapes 22
XOR (exclusive-or) 39

Y

`yacc` UNIX utility 159, 318